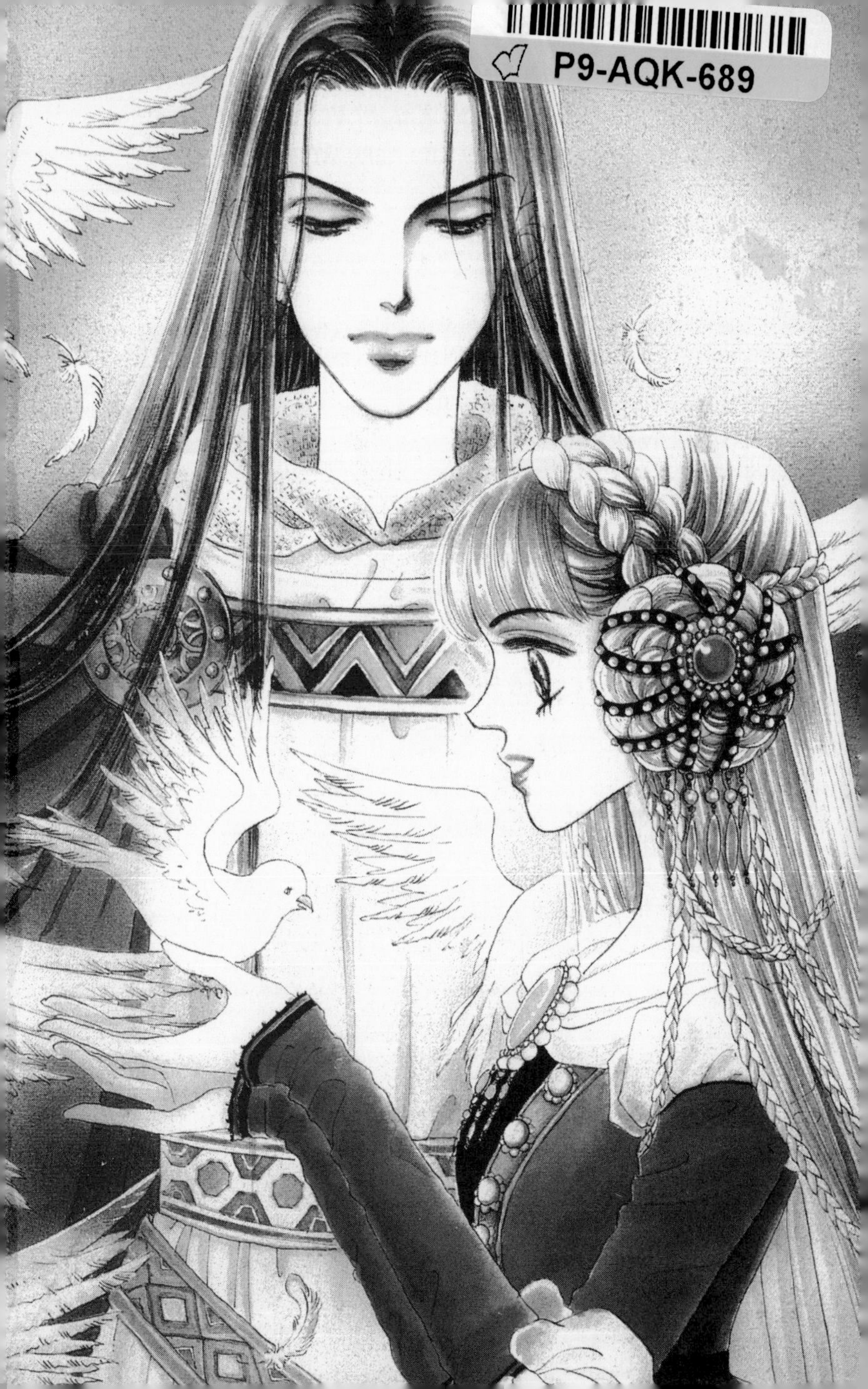

The Queen's Knight Vol. 1
Created by Kim Kang Won

Translation - Lauren Na
English Adaptation - Jeannie Anderson
Retouch and Lettering - Sophia Hong
Production Artist - Vicente Rivera, Jr.
Cover Design - Anna Kernbaum

Editor - Julie Taylor
Digital Imaging Manager - Chris Buford
Pre-Press Manager - Antonio DePietro
Production Managers - Jennifer Miller and Mutsumi Miyazaki
Art Director - Matt Alford
Managing Editor - Jill Freshney
VP of Production - Ron Klamert
President and C.O.O. - John Parker
Publisher and C.E.O. - Stuart Levy

A  Manga

TOKYOPOP Inc.
5900 Wilshire Blvd. Suite 2000
Los Angeles, CA 90036

E-mail: info@TOKYOPOP.com
Come visit us online at www.TOKYOPOP.com

ISBN: 1-59532-257-4

First TOKYOPOP printing: November 2004

10 9 8 7 6 5 4 3 2 1

Printed in the USA

THE QUEEN'S KNIGHT

VOLUME 1

BY KIM KANG WON

HAMBURG // LONDON // LOS ANGELES // TOKYO

THE QUEEN'S KNIGHT

VOLUME 1

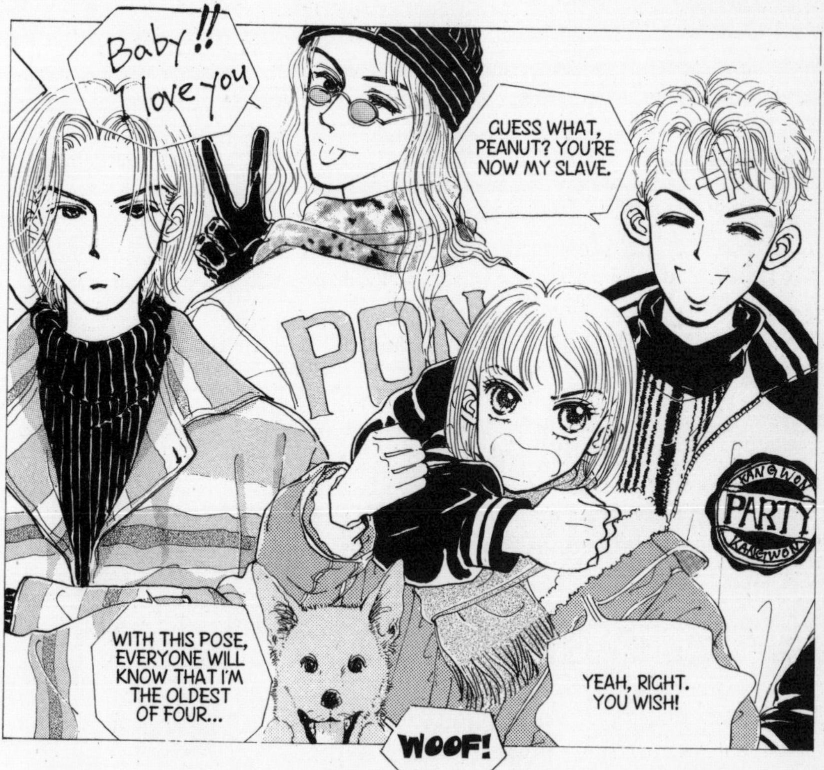
Baby!! I love you
GUESS WHAT, PEANUT? YOU'RE NOW MY SLAVE.
PON
KANG WON PARTY KANG WON
WITH THIS POSE, EVERYONE WILL KNOW THAT I'M THE OLDEST OF FOUR...
WOOF!
YEAH, RIGHT. YOU WISH!

KIM KANG WON

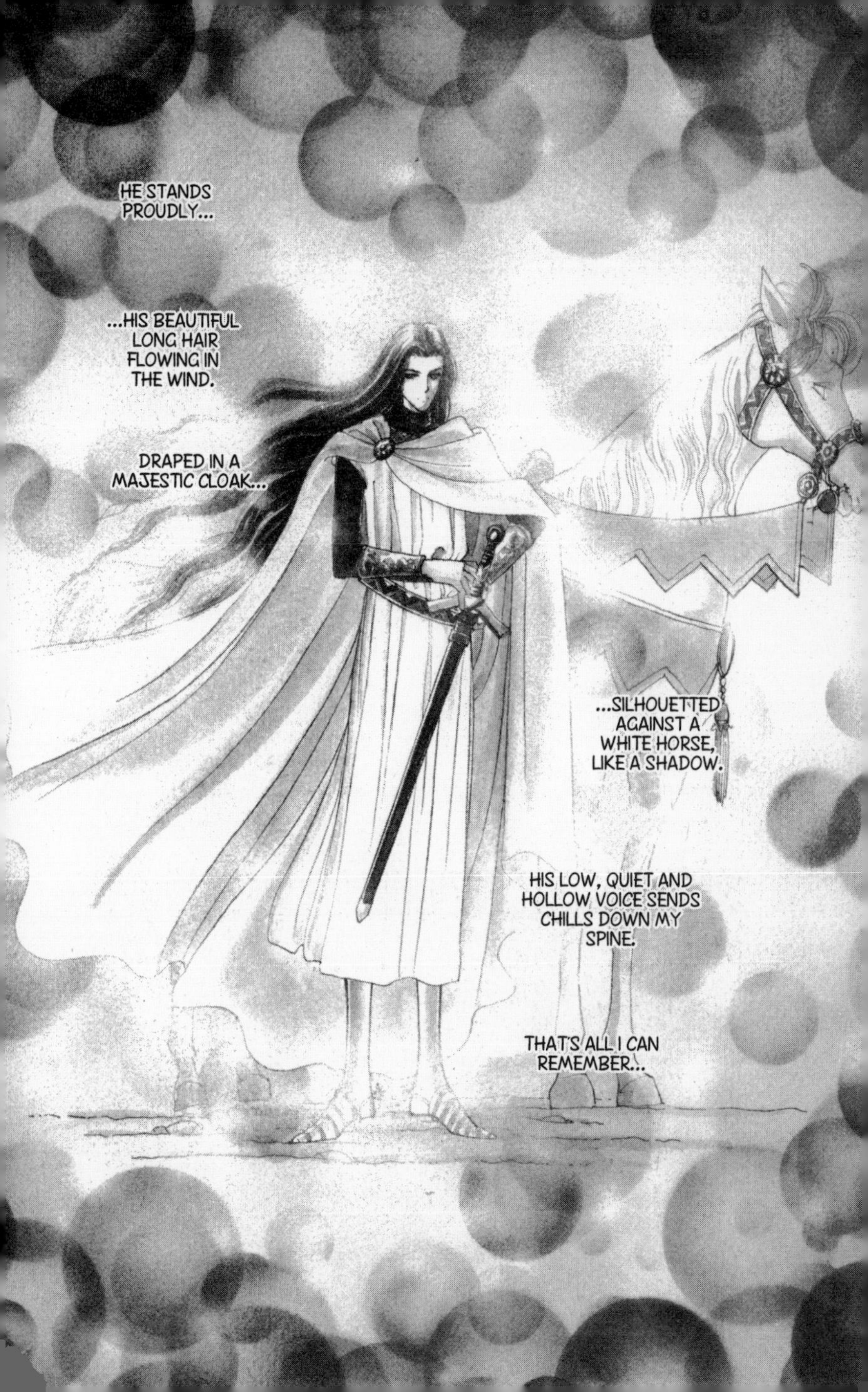
HE STANDS PROUDLY...
...HIS BEAUTIFUL LONG HAIR FLOWING IN THE WIND.
DRAPED IN A MAJESTIC CLOAK...
...SILHOUETTED AGAINST A WHITE HORSE, LIKE A SHADOW.
HIS LOW, QUIET AND HOLLOW VOICE SENDS CHILLS DOWN MY SPINE.
THAT'S ALL I CAN REMEMBER...

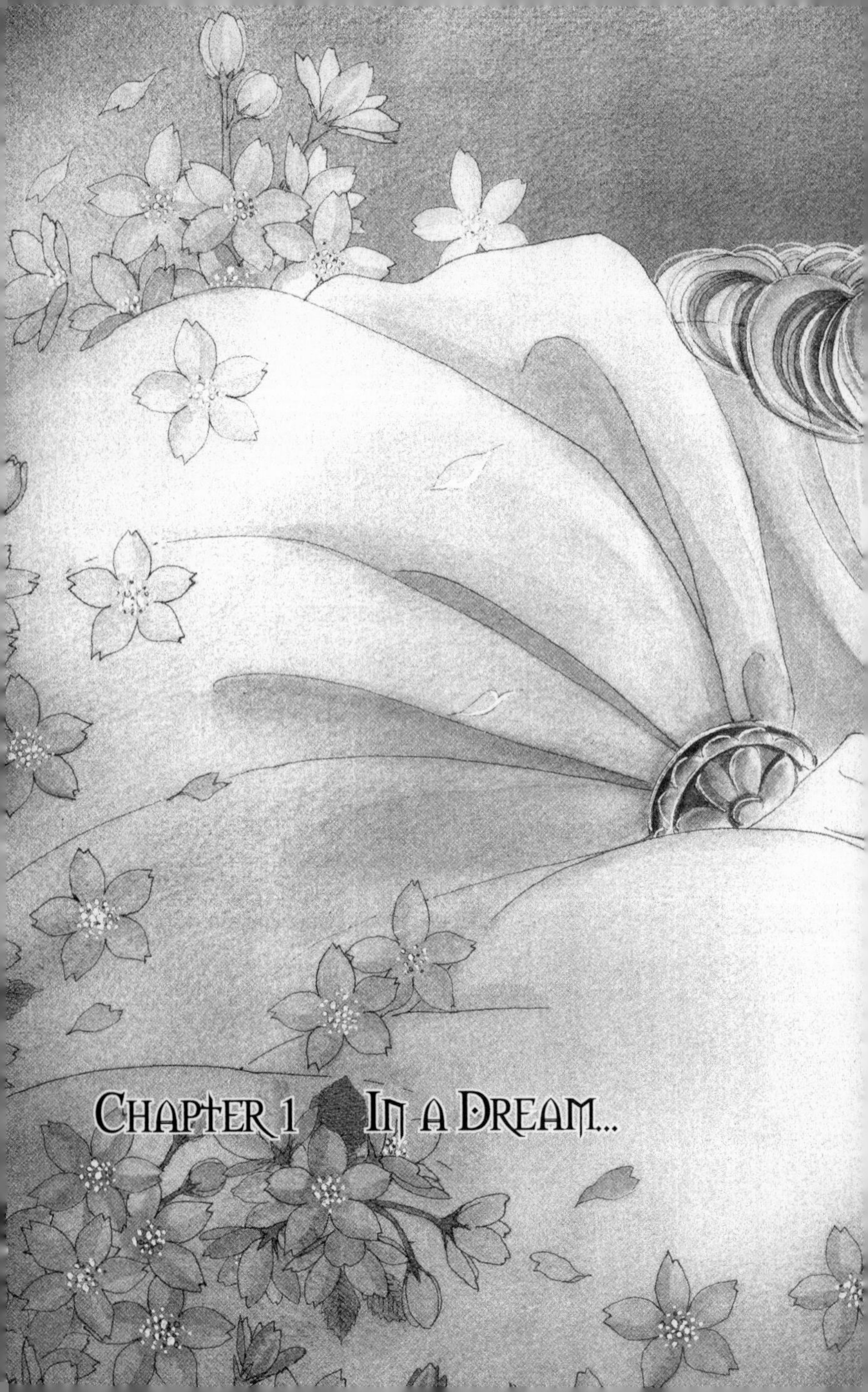

Chapter 1 In a Dream...

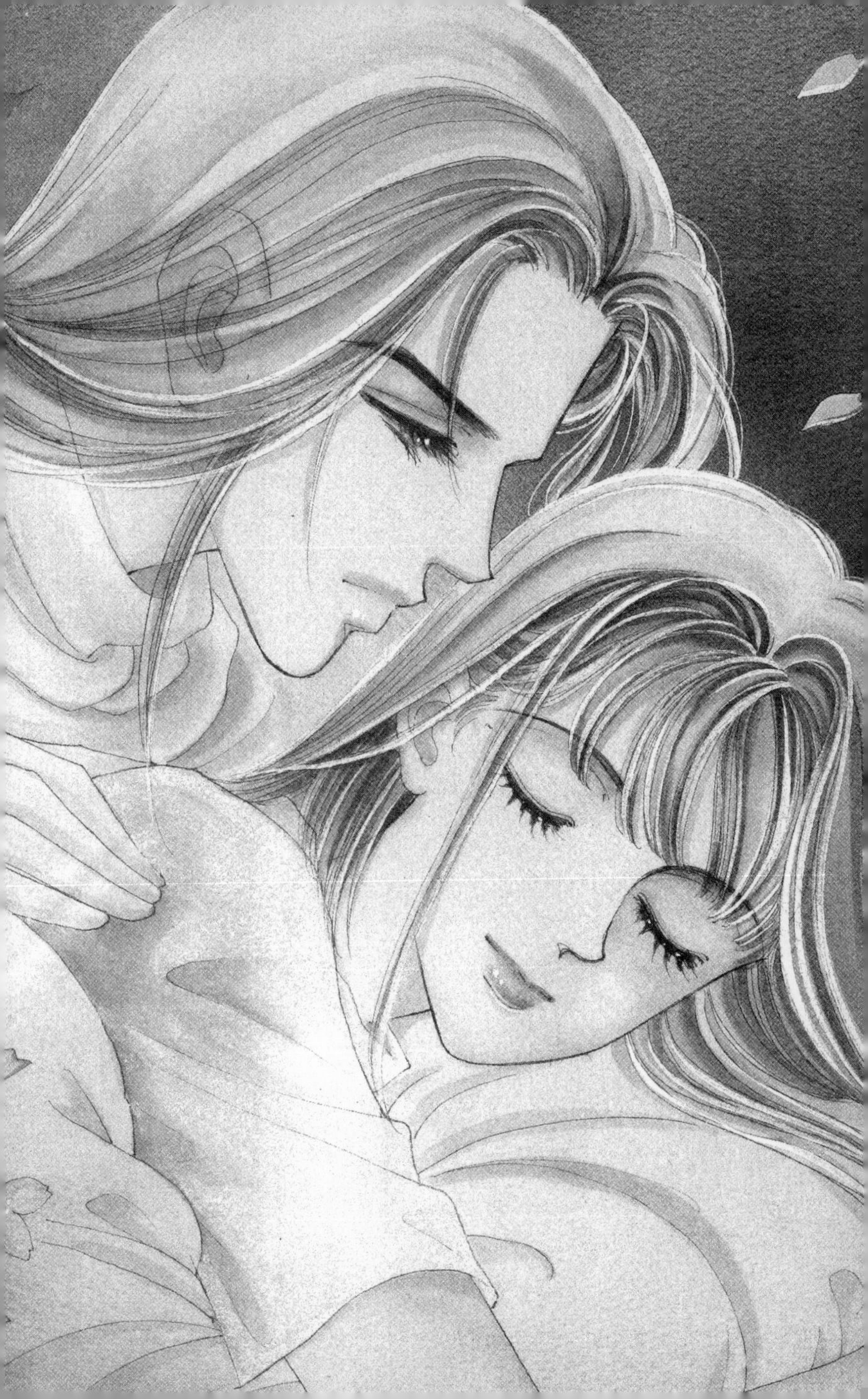

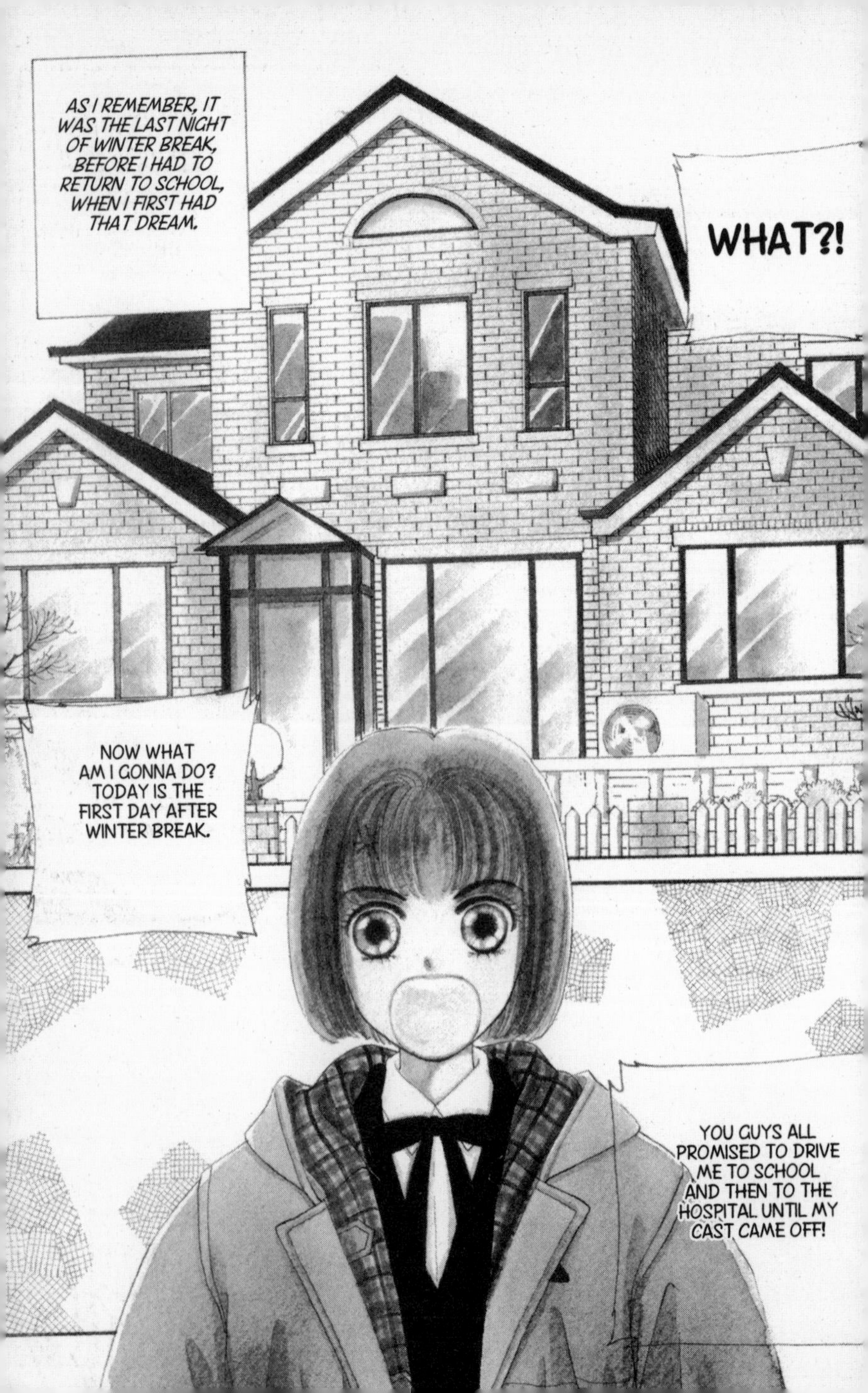
AS I REMEMBER, IT WAS THE LAST NIGHT OF WINTER BREAK, BEFORE I HAD TO RETURN TO SCHOOL, WHEN I FIRST HAD THAT DREAM.
WHAT?!
NOW WHAT AM I GONNA DO? TODAY IS THE FIRST DAY AFTER WINTER BREAK.
YOU GUYS ALL PROMISED TO DRIVE ME TO SCHOOL AND THEN TO THE HOSPITAL UNTIL MY CAST CAME OFF!

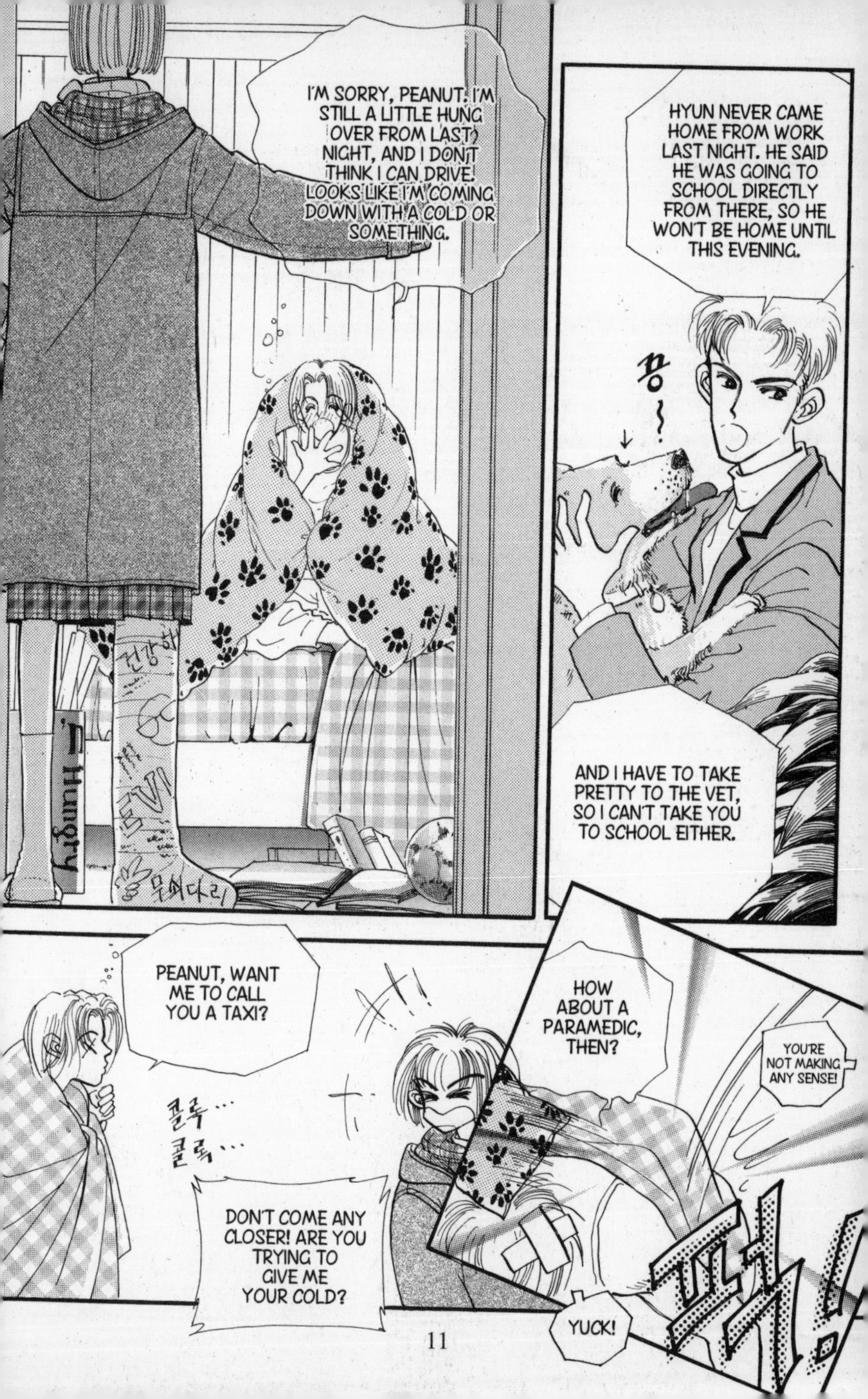
I'M SORRY, PEANUT. I'M STILL A LITTLE HUNG OVER FROM LAST NIGHT, AND I DON'T THINK I CAN DRIVE. LOOKS LIKE I'M COMING DOWN WITH A COLD OR SOMETHING.
Hungry
건강해
무쇠다리
HYUN NEVER CAME HOME FROM WORK LAST NIGHT. HE SAID HE WAS GOING TO SCHOOL DIRECTLY FROM THERE, SO HE WON'T BE HOME UNTIL THIS EVENING.
킁~?
AND I HAVE TO TAKE PRETTY TO THE VET, SO I CAN'T TAKE YOU TO SCHOOL EITHER.
PEANUT, WANT ME TO CALL YOU A TAXI?
콜록...
콜록...
DON'T COME ANY CLOSER! ARE YOU TRYING TO GIVE ME YOUR COLD?
HOW ABOUT A PARAMEDIC, THEN?
YOU'RE NOT MAKING ANY SENSE!
YUCK!

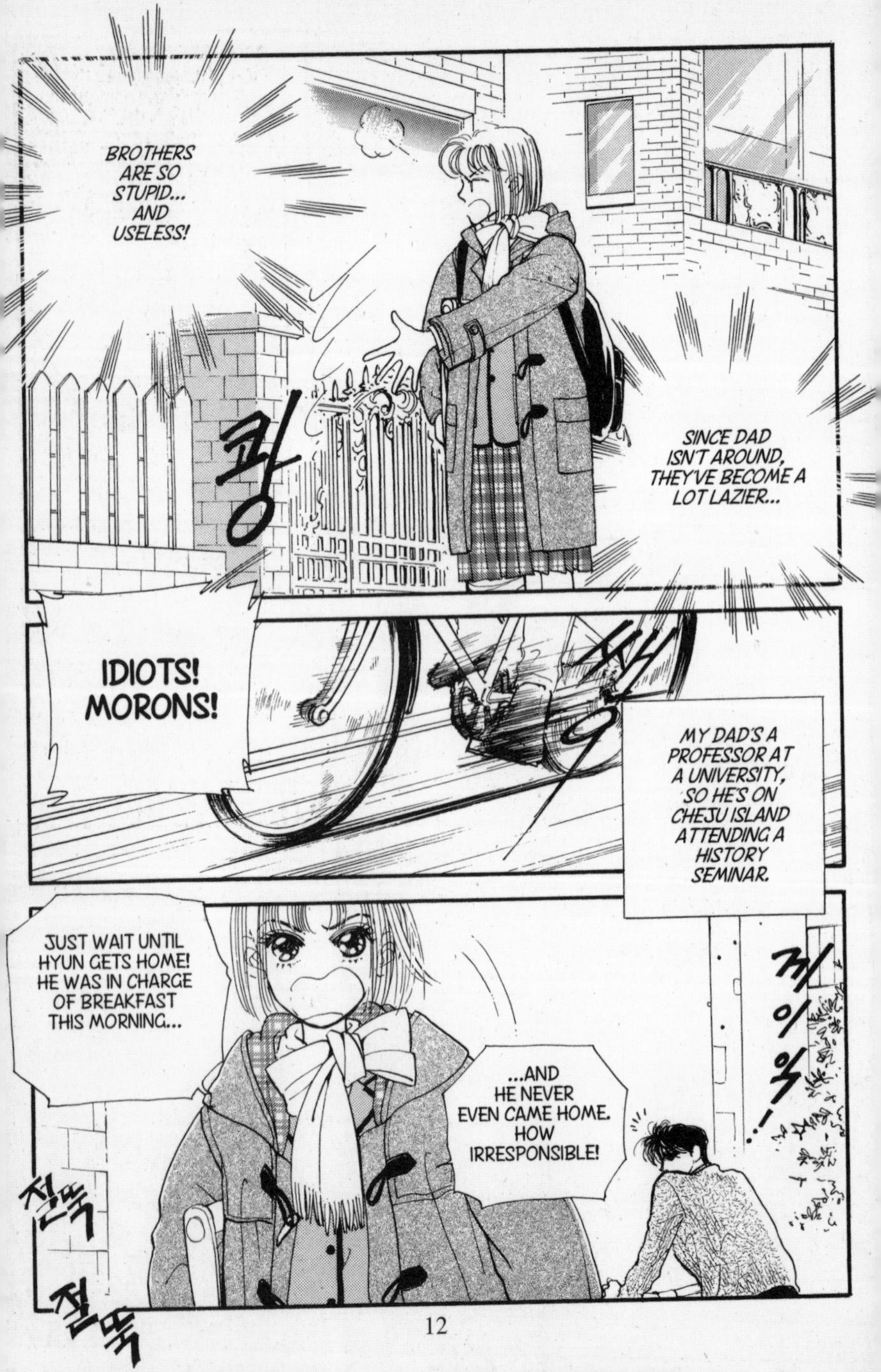
BROTHERS ARE SO STUPID... AND USELESS!
쾅
SINCE DAD ISN'T AROUND, THEY'VE BECOME A LOT LAZIER...
IDIOTS! MORONS!
MY DAD'S A PROFESSOR AT A UNIVERSITY, SO HE'S ON CHEJU ISLAND ATTENDING A HISTORY SEMINAR.
JUST WAIT UNTIL HYUN GETS HOME! HE WAS IN CHARGE OF BREAKFAST THIS MORNING...
...AND HE NEVER EVEN CAME HOME. HOW IRRESPONSIBLE!
절뚝
절뚝

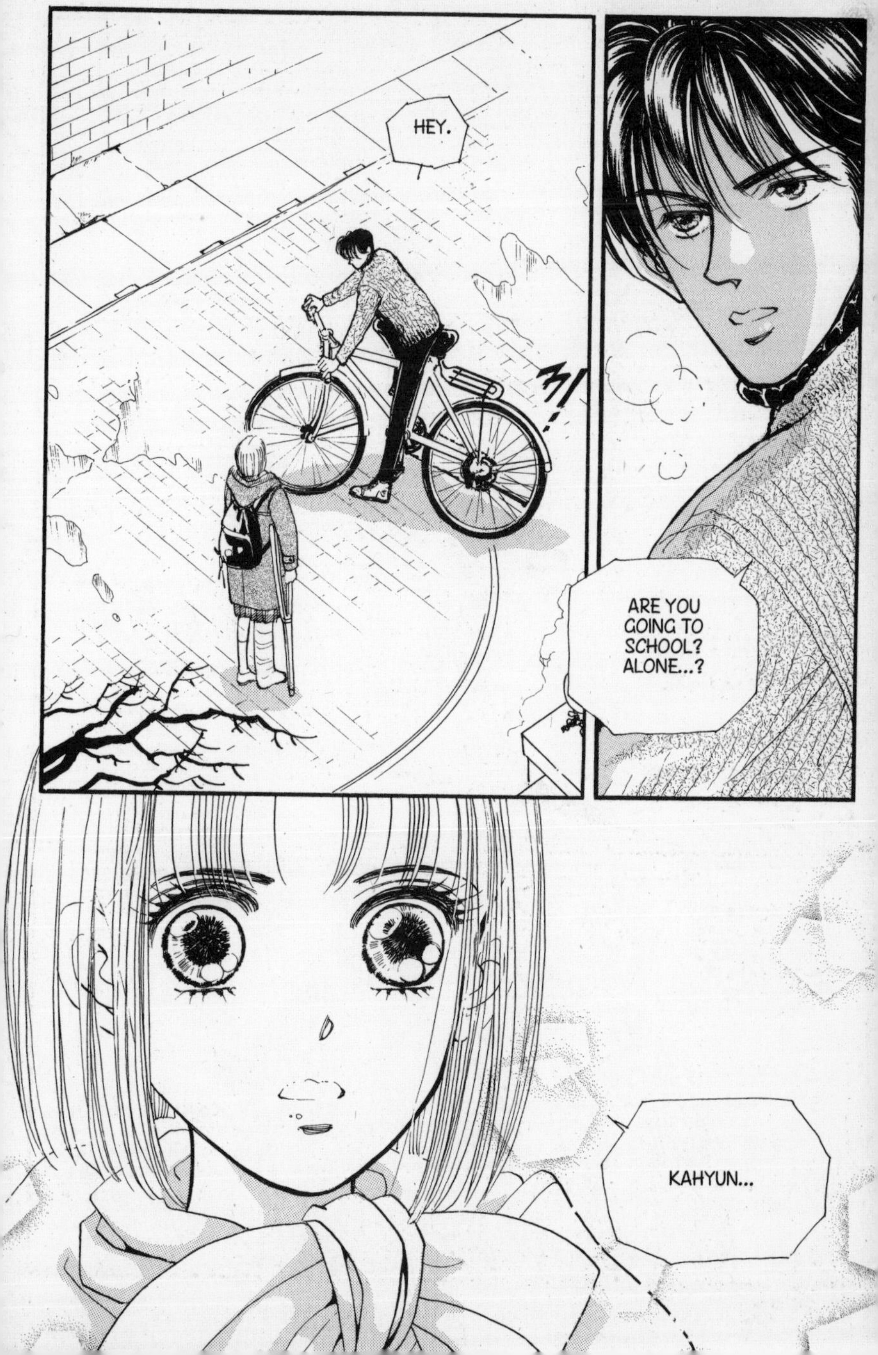
HEY.
ARE YOU GOING TO SCHOOL? ALONE...?
KAHYUN...

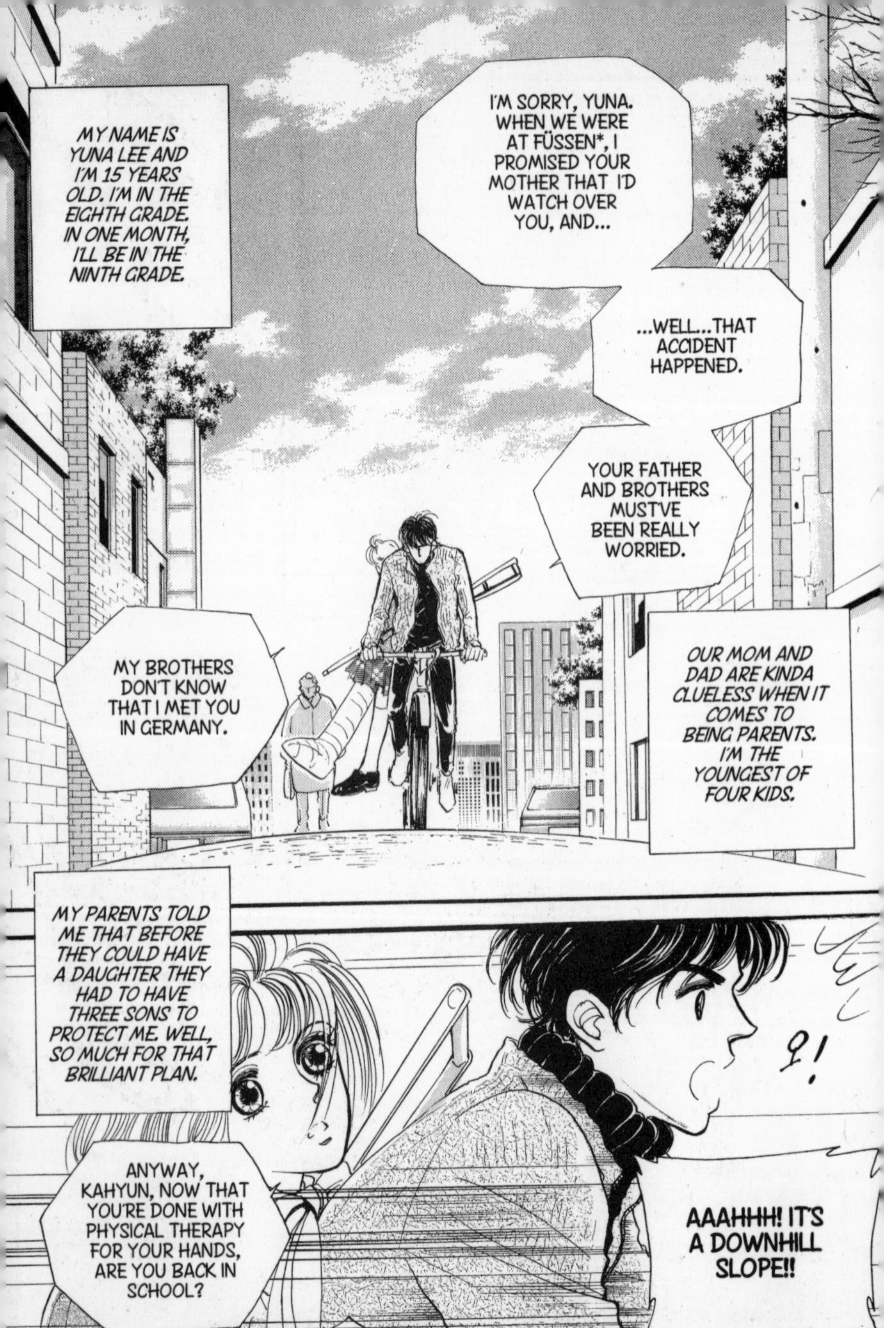
MY NAME IS YUNA LEE AND I'M 15 YEARS OLD. I'M IN THE EIGHTH GRADE. IN ONE MONTH, I'LL BE IN THE NINTH GRADE.
I'M SORRY, YUNA. WHEN WE WERE AT FÜSSEN*, I PROMISED YOUR MOTHER THAT I'D WATCH OVER YOU, AND...
...WELL...THAT ACCIDENT HAPPENED.
YOUR FATHER AND BROTHERS MUST'VE BEEN REALLY WORRIED.
MY BROTHERS DON'T KNOW THAT I MET YOU IN GERMANY.
OUR MOM AND DAD ARE KINDA CLUELESS WHEN IT COMES TO BEING PARENTS. I'M THE YOUNGEST OF FOUR KIDS.
MY PARENTS TOLD ME THAT BEFORE THEY COULD HAVE A DAUGHTER THEY HAD TO HAVE THREE SONS TO PROTECT ME. WELL, SO MUCH FOR THAT BRILLIANT PLAN.
?!
ANYWAY, KAHYUN, NOW THAT YOU'RE DONE WITH PHYSICAL THERAPY FOR YOUR HANDS, ARE YOU BACK IN SCHOOL?
AAAHHH! IT'S A DOWNHILL SLOPE!!

*AUTHOR'S NOTE: Füssen: A small village located in Southern Germany. The famous Neuschwanstein castle is located here. It's a two-hour train ride fr Munich. In Füssen, you can see the Alps and the Tyrol Mountain. Füssen is a beautiful area with many lakes.

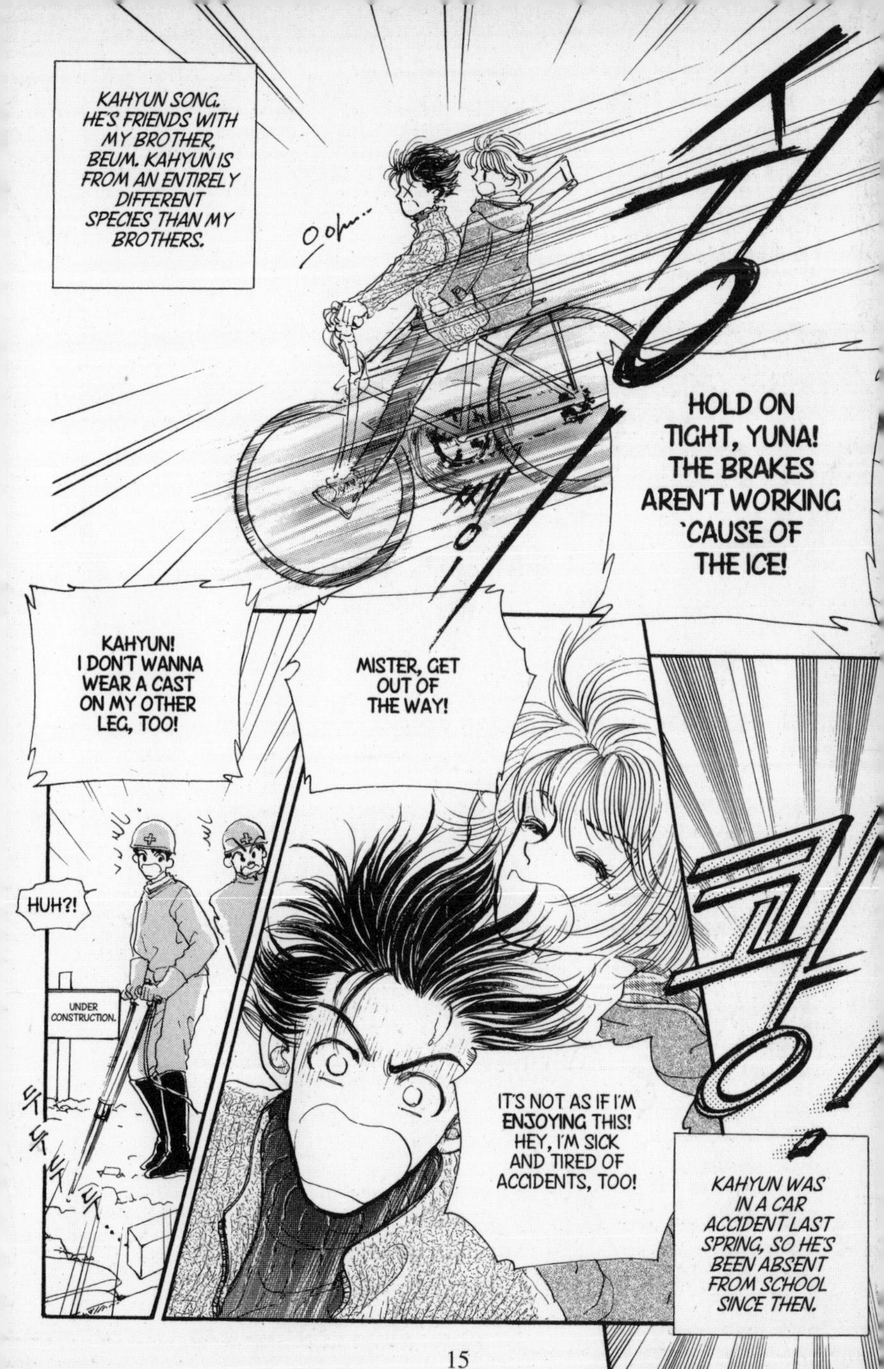
KAHYUN SONG. HE'S FRIENDS WITH MY BROTHER, BEUM. KAHYUN IS FROM AN ENTIRELY DIFFERENT SPECIES THAN MY BROTHERS.
HOLD ON TIGHT, YUNA! THE BRAKES AREN'T WORKING `CAUSE OF THE ICE!
KAHYUN! I DON'T WANNA WEAR A CAST ON MY OTHER LEG, TOO!
HUH?!
UNDER CONSTRUCTION.
MISTER, GET OUT OF THE WAY!
IT'S NOT AS IF I'M ENJOYING THIS! HEY, I'M SICK AND TIRED OF ACCIDENTS, TOO!
KAHYUN WAS IN A CAR ACCIDENT LAST SPRING, SO HE'S BEEN ABSENT FROM SCHOOL SINCE THEN.

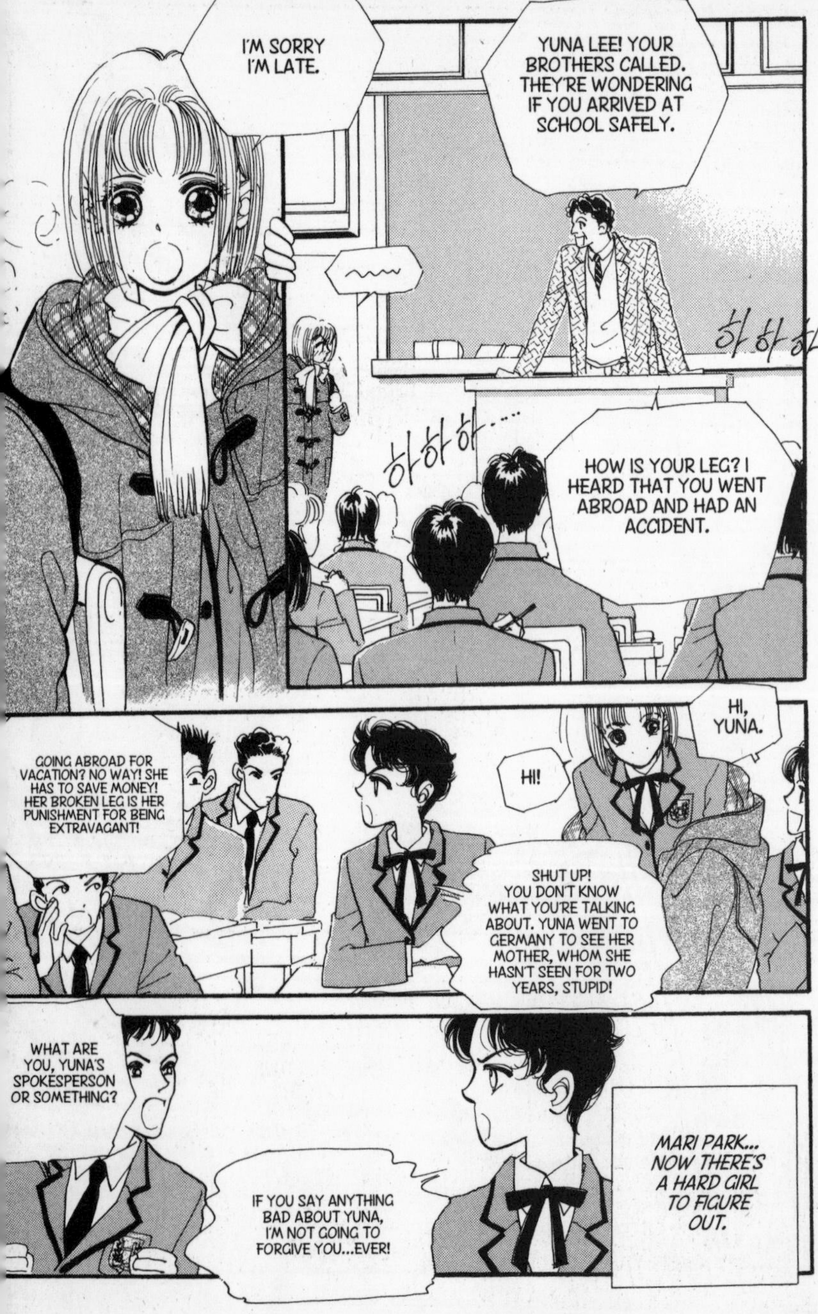
I'M SORRY I'M LATE.
YUNA LEE! YOUR BROTHERS CALLED. THEY'RE WONDERING IF YOU ARRIVED AT SCHOOL SAFELY.
하하하...
하하하...
HOW IS YOUR LEG? I HEARD THAT YOU WENT ABROAD AND HAD AN ACCIDENT.
GOING ABROAD FOR VACATION? NO WAY! SHE HAS TO SAVE MONEY! HER BROKEN LEG IS HER PUNISHMENT FOR BEING EXTRAVAGANT!
HI, YUNA.
HI!
SHUT UP! YOU DON'T KNOW WHAT YOU'RE TALKING ABOUT. YUNA WENT TO GERMANY TO SEE HER MOTHER, WHOM SHE HASN'T SEEN FOR TWO YEARS, STUPID!
WHAT ARE YOU, YUNA'S SPOKESPERSON OR SOMETHING?
IF YOU SAY ANYTHING BAD ABOUT YUNA, I'M NOT GOING TO FORGIVE YOU...EVER!
MARI PARK... NOW THERE'S A HARD GIRL TO FIGURE OUT.

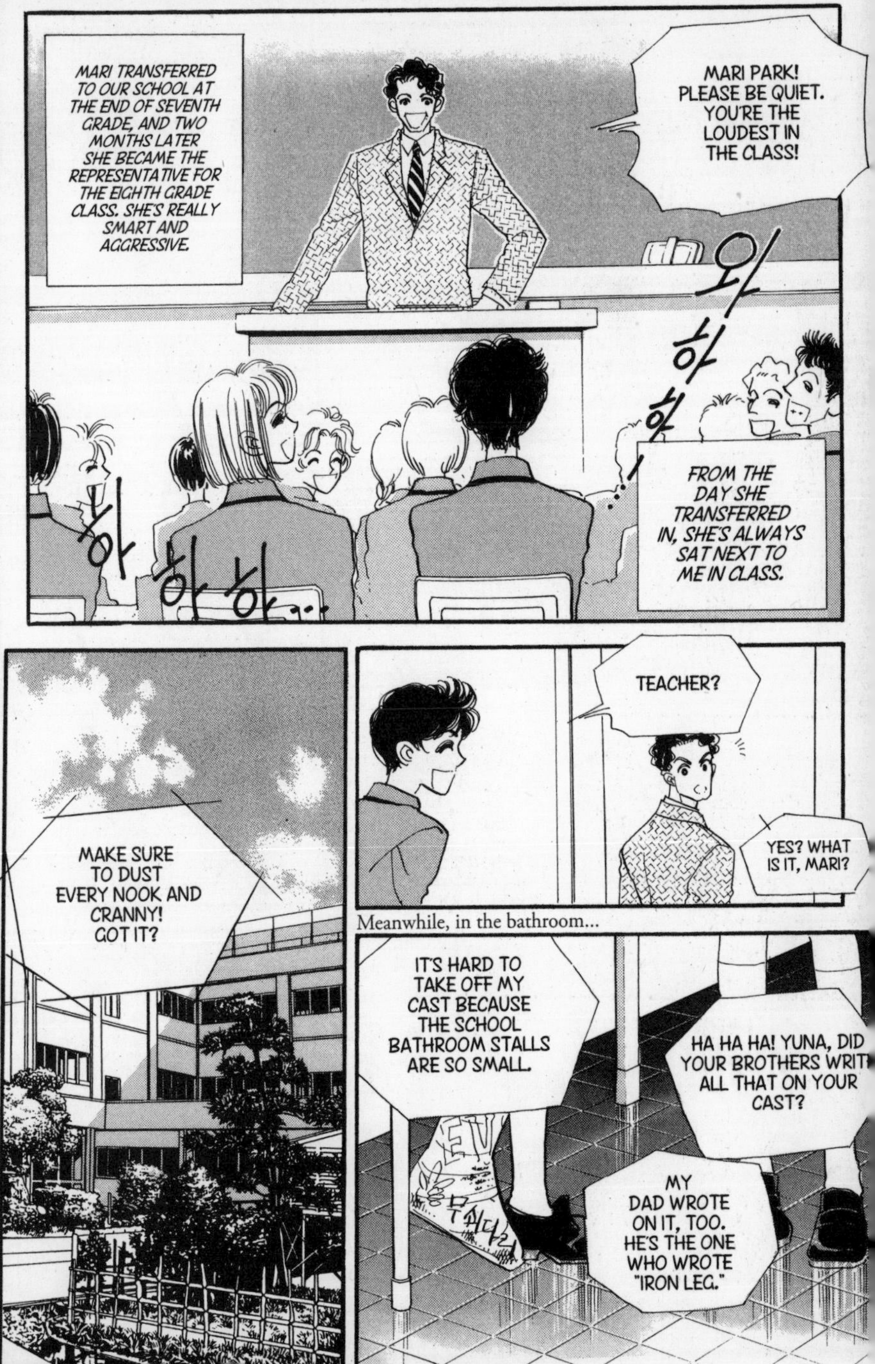
MARI TRANSFERRED TO OUR SCHOOL AT THE END OF SEVENTH GRADE, AND TWO MONTHS LATER SHE BECAME THE REPRESENTATIVE FOR THE EIGHTH GRADE CLASS. SHE'S REALLY SMART AND AGGRESSIVE.
MARI PARK! PLEASE BE QUIET. YOU'RE THE LOUDEST IN THE CLASS!
와하하...
하하하...
FROM THE DAY SHE TRANSFERRED IN, SHE'S ALWAYS SAT NEXT TO ME IN CLASS.
MAKE SURE TO DUST EVERY NOOK AND CRANNY! GOT IT?
TEACHER?
YES? WHAT IS IT, MARI?
Meanwhile, in the bathroom...
IT'S HARD TO TAKE OFF MY CAST BECAUSE THE SCHOOL BATHROOM STALLS ARE SO SMALL.
HA HA HA! YUNA, DID YOUR BROTHERS WRIT ALL THAT ON YOUR CAST?
MY DAD WROTE ON IT, TOO. HE'S THE ONE WHO WROTE "IRON LEG."

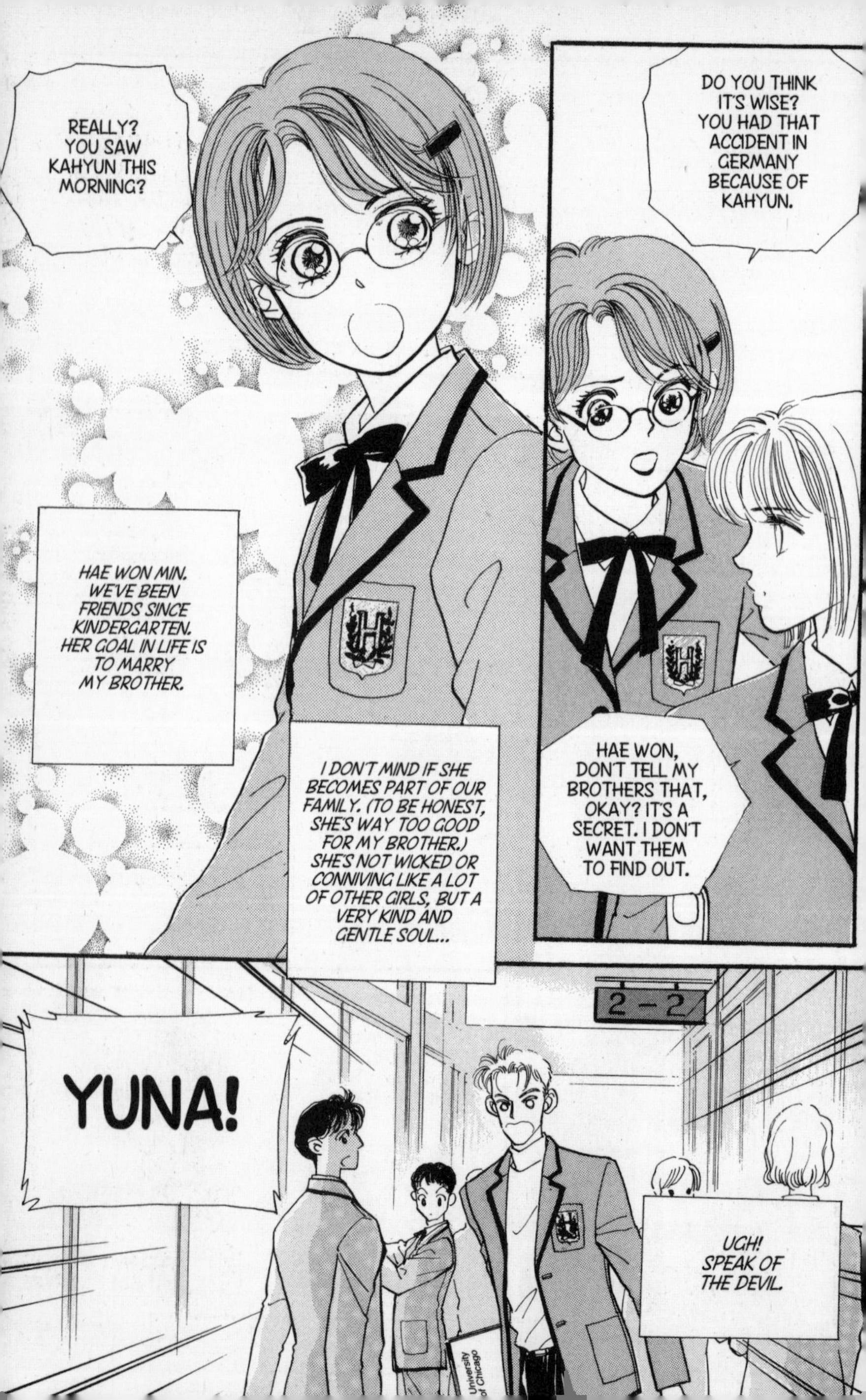

REALLY? YOU SAW KAHYUN THIS MORNING?
HAE WON MIN. WE'VE BEEN FRIENDS SINCE KINDERGARTEN. HER GOAL IN LIFE IS TO MARRY MY BROTHER.
I DON'T MIND IF SHE BECOMES PART OF OUR FAMILY. (TO BE HONEST, SHE'S WAY TOO GOOD FOR MY BROTHER.) SHE'S NOT WICKED OR CONNIVING LIKE A LOT OF OTHER GIRLS, BUT A VERY KIND AND GENTLE SOUL...
DO YOU THINK IT'S WISE? YOU HAD THAT ACCIDENT IN GERMANY BECAUSE OF KAHYUN.
HAE WON, DON'T TELL MY BROTHERS THAT, OKAY? IT'S A SECRET. I DON'T WANT THEM TO FIND OUT.
2-2
YUNA!
University of Chicago
UGH! SPEAK OF THE DEVIL.

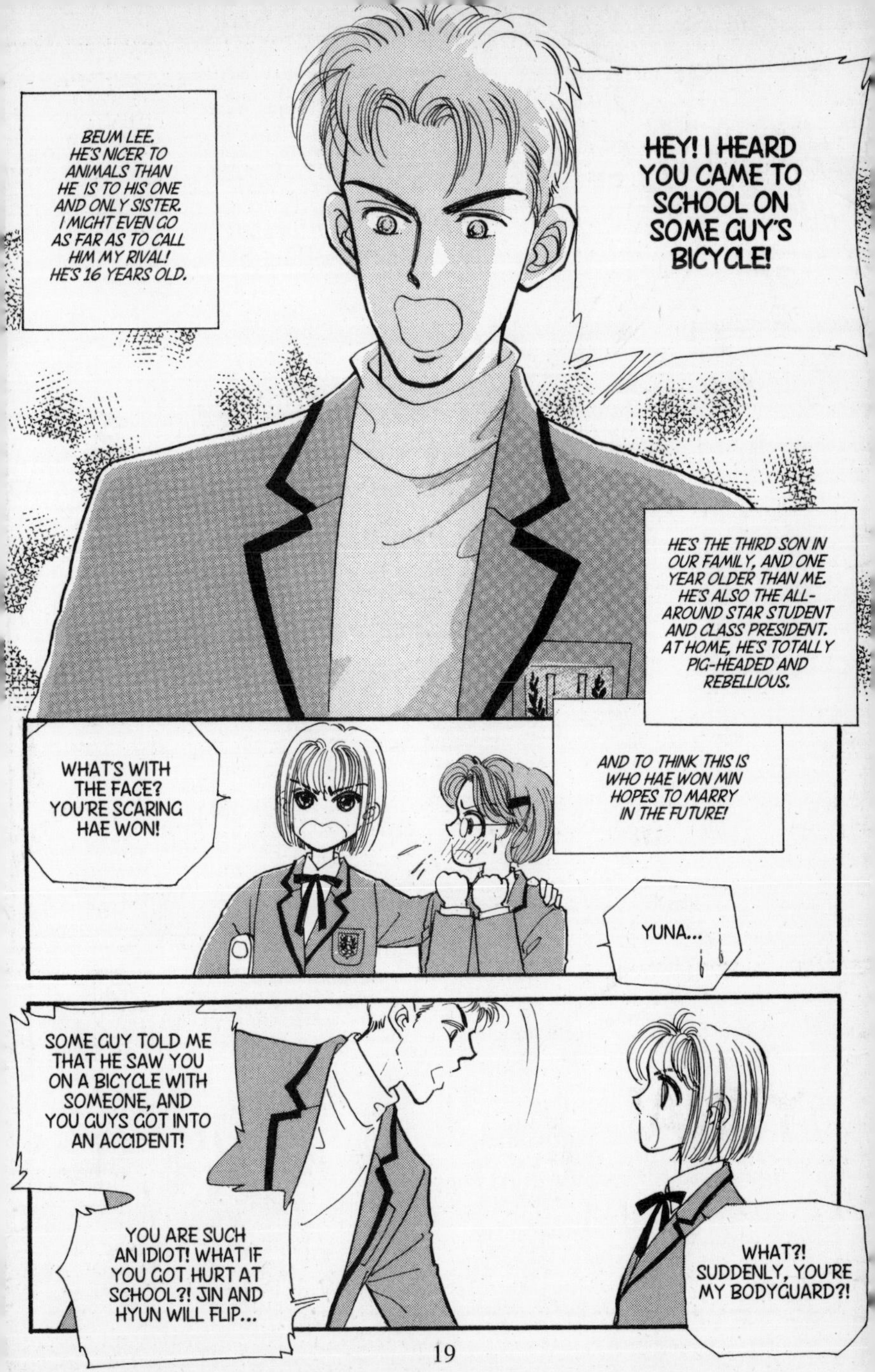

BEUM LEE. HE'S NICER TO ANIMALS THAN HE IS TO HIS ONE AND ONLY SISTER. I MIGHT EVEN GO AS FAR AS TO CALL HIM MY RIVAL! HE'S 16 YEARS OLD.
HEY! I HEARD YOU CAME TO SCHOOL ON SOME GUY'S BICYCLE!
HE'S THE THIRD SON IN OUR FAMILY, AND ONE YEAR OLDER THAN ME. HE'S ALSO THE ALL-AROUND STAR STUDENT AND CLASS PRESIDENT. AT HOME, HE'S TOTALLY PIG-HEADED AND REBELLIOUS.
WHAT'S WITH THE FACE? YOU'RE SCARING HAE WON!
AND TO THINK THIS IS WHO HAE WON MIN HOPES TO MARRY IN THE FUTURE!
YUNA...
SOME GUY TOLD ME THAT HE SAW YOU ON A BICYCLE WITH SOMEONE, AND YOU GUYS GOT INTO AN ACCIDENT!
YOU ARE SUCH AN IDIOT! WHAT IF YOU GOT HURT AT SCHOOL?! JIN AND HYUN WILL FLIP...
WHAT?! SUDDENLY, YOU'RE MY BODYGUARD?!

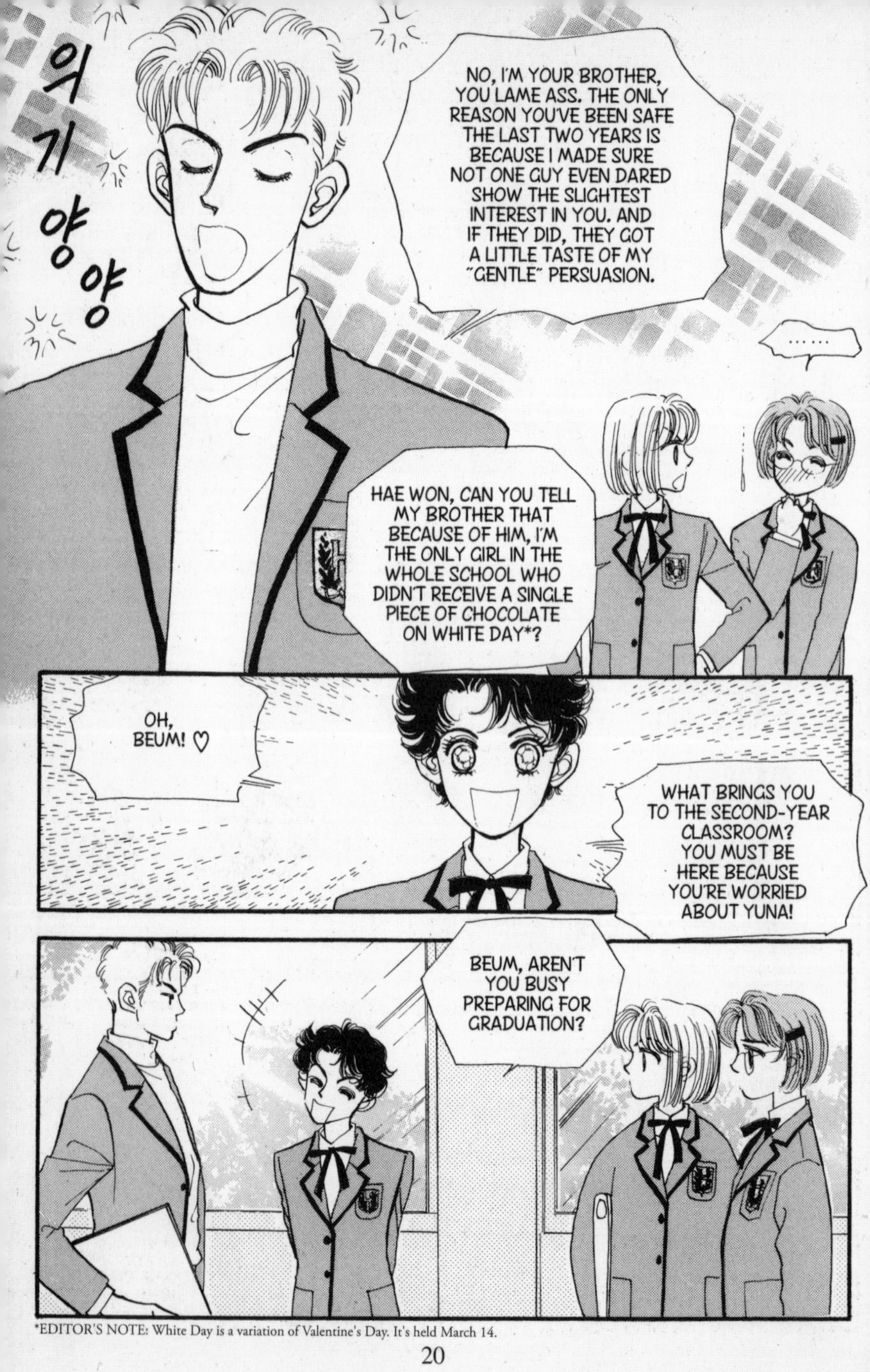
의기양양
NO, I'M YOUR BROTHER, YOU LAME ASS. THE ONLY REASON YOU'VE BEEN SAFE THE LAST TWO YEARS IS BECAUSE I MADE SURE NOT ONE GUY EVEN DARED SHOW THE SLIGHTEST INTEREST IN YOU. AND IF THEY DID, THEY GOT A LITTLE TASTE OF MY "GENTLE" PERSUASION.
......
HAE WON, CAN YOU TELL MY BROTHER THAT BECAUSE OF HIM, I'M THE ONLY GIRL IN THE WHOLE SCHOOL WHO DIDN'T RECEIVE A SINGLE PIECE OF CHOCOLATE ON WHITE DAY*?
OH, BEUM! ♡
WHAT BRINGS YOU TO THE SECOND-YEAR CLASSROOM? YOU MUST BE HERE BECAUSE YOU'RE WORRIED ABOUT YUNA!
BEUM, AREN'T YOU BUSY PREPARING FOR GRADUATION?

*EDITOR'S NOTE: White Day is a variation of Valentine's Day. It's held March 14.

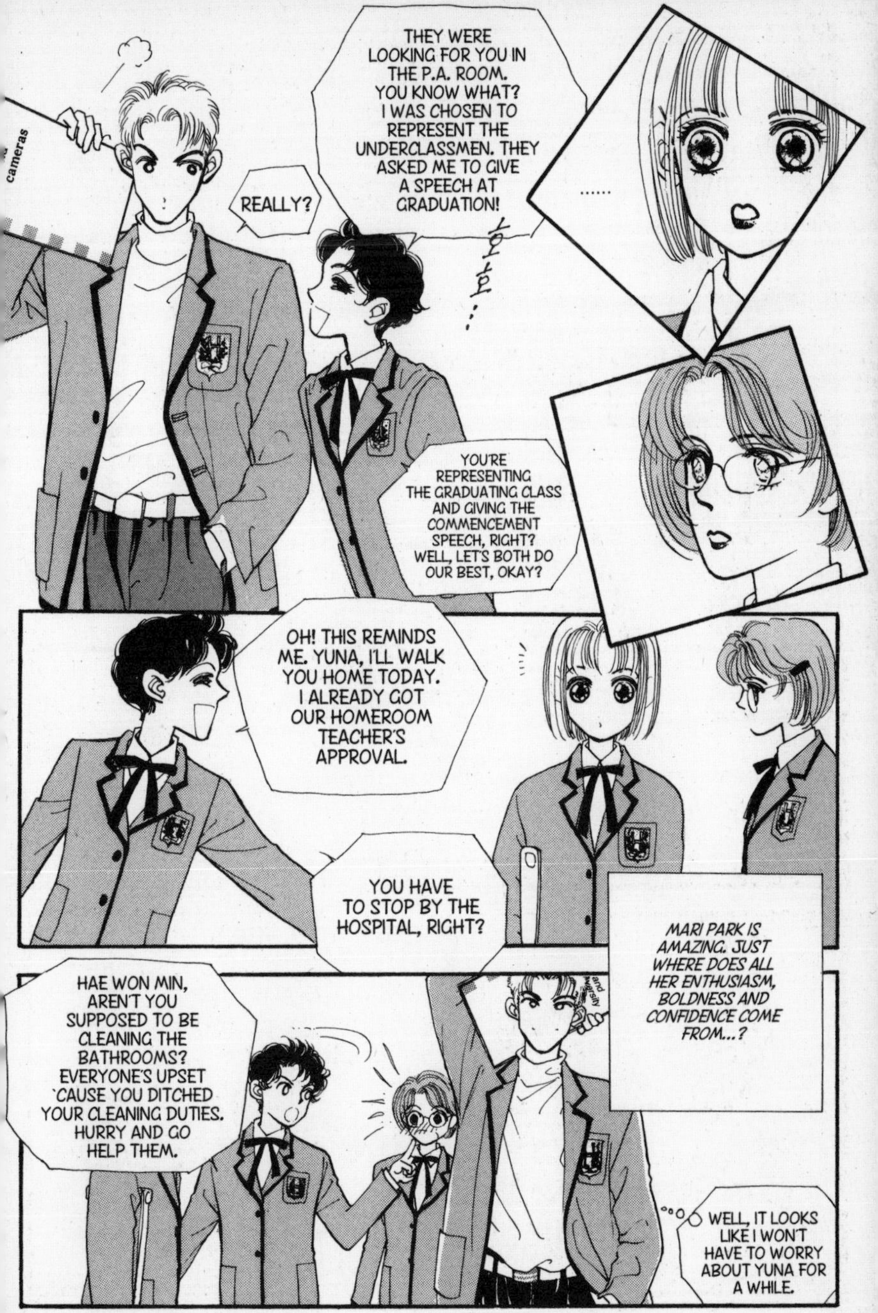
cameras
THEY WERE LOOKING FOR YOU IN THE P.A. ROOM. YOU KNOW WHAT? I WAS CHOSEN TO REPRESENT THE UNDERCLASSMEN. THEY ASKED ME TO GIVE A SPEECH AT GRADUATION!
REALLY?
호호...
......
YOU'RE REPRESENTING THE GRADUATING CLASS AND GIVING THE COMMENCEMENT SPEECH, RIGHT? WELL, LET'S BOTH DO OUR BEST, OKAY?
OH! THIS REMINDS ME. YUNA, I'LL WALK YOU HOME TODAY. I ALREADY GOT OUR HOMEROOM TEACHER'S APPROVAL.
YOU HAVE TO STOP BY THE HOSPITAL, RIGHT?
HAE WON MIN, AREN'T YOU SUPPOSED TO BE CLEANING THE BATHROOMS? EVERYONE'S UPSET 'CAUSE YOU DITCHED YOUR CLEANING DUTIES. HURRY AND GO HELP THEM.
MARI PARK IS AMAZING. JUST WHERE DOES ALL HER ENTHUSIASM, BOLDNESS AND CONFIDENCE COME FROM...?
WELL, IT LOOKS LIKE I WON'T HAVE TO WORRY ABOUT YUNA FOR A WHILE.

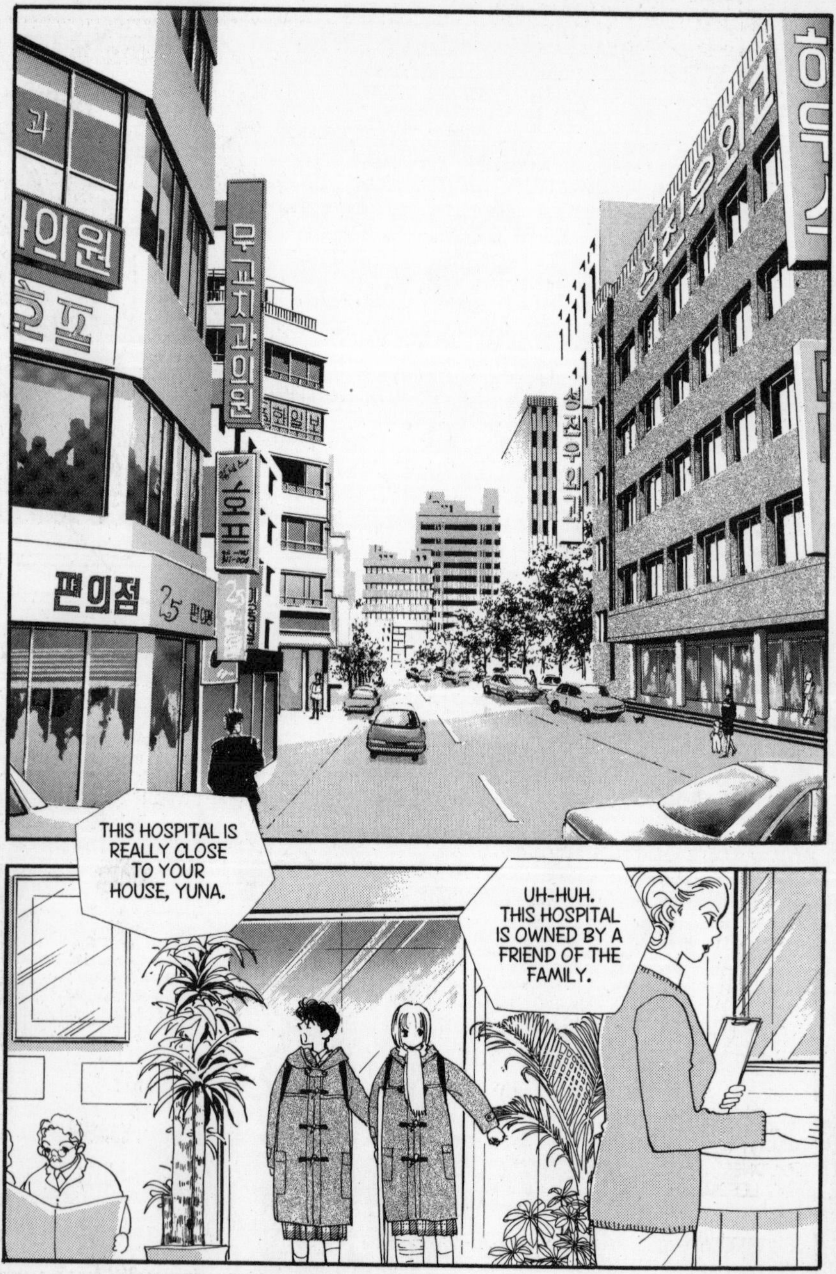
편의점
THIS HOSPITAL IS REALLY CLOSE TO YOUR HOUSE, YUNA.
UH-HUH. THIS HOSPITAL IS OWNED BY A FRIEND OF THE FAMILY.

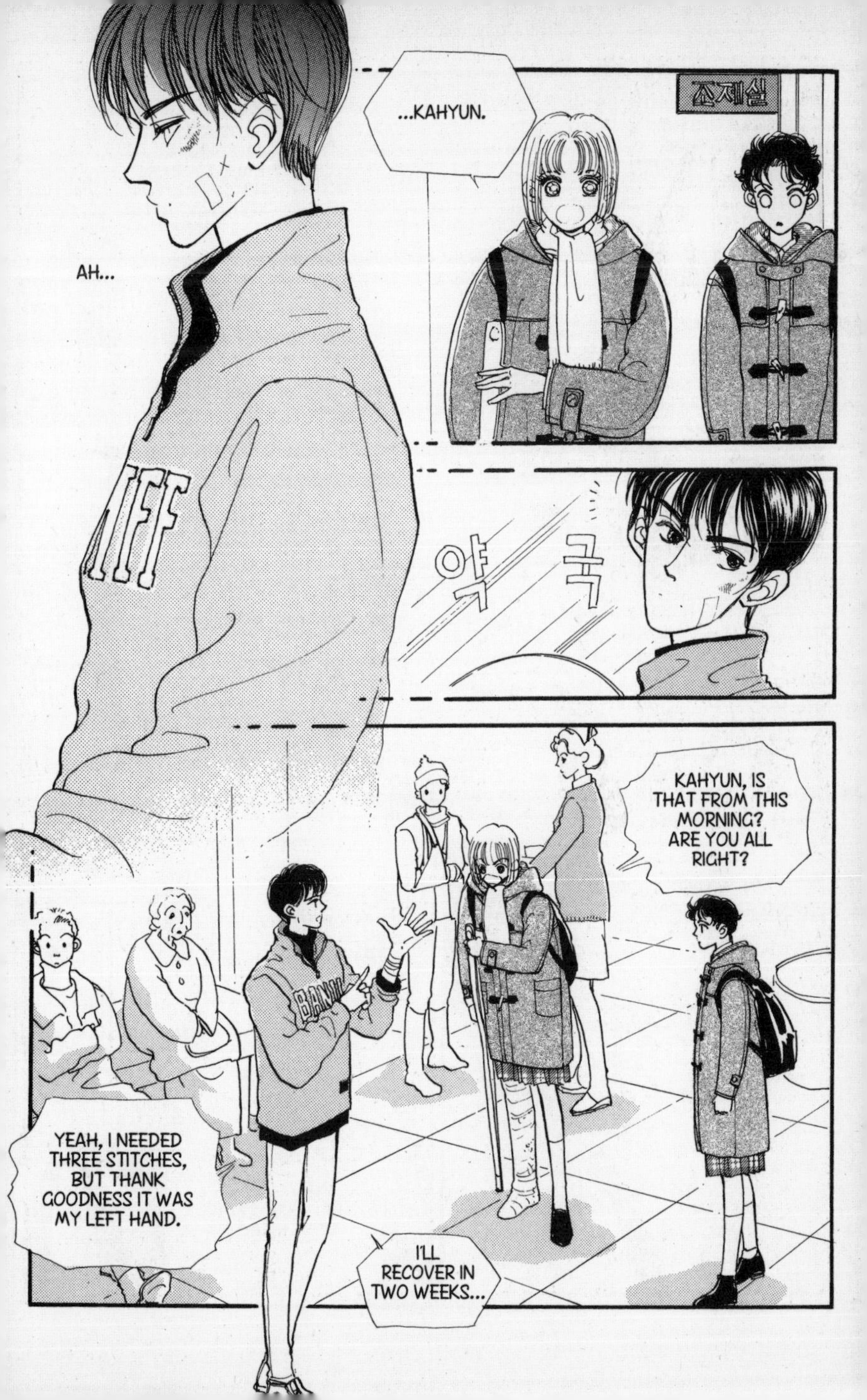

AH...
...KAHYUN.
조제실
약국
KAHYUN, IS THAT FROM THIS MORNING? ARE YOU ALL RIGHT?
YEAH, I NEEDED THREE STITCHES, BUT THANK GOODNESS IT WAS MY LEFT HAND.
I'LL RECOVER IN TWO WEEKS...

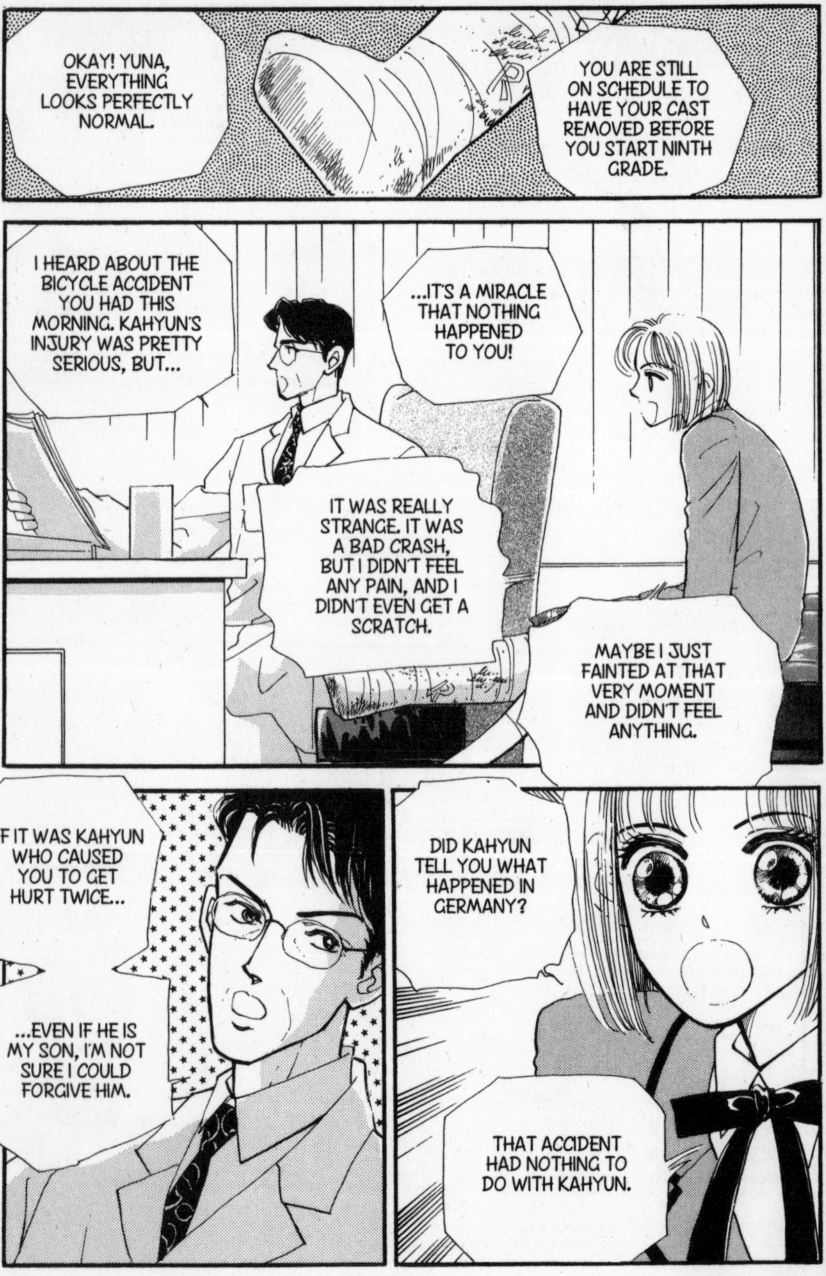
OKAY! YUNA, EVERYTHING LOOKS PERFECTLY NORMAL.
YOU ARE STILL ON SCHEDULE TO HAVE YOUR CAST REMOVED BEFORE YOU START NINTH GRADE.
I HEARD ABOUT THE BICYCLE ACCIDENT YOU HAD THIS MORNING. KAHYUN'S INJURY WAS PRETTY SERIOUS, BUT...
...IT'S A MIRACLE THAT NOTHING HAPPENED TO YOU!
IT WAS REALLY STRANGE. IT WAS A BAD CRASH, BUT I DIDN'T FEEL ANY PAIN, AND I DIDN'T EVEN GET A SCRATCH.
MAYBE I JUST FAINTED AT THAT VERY MOMENT AND DIDN'T FEEL ANYTHING.
IF IT WAS KAHYUN WHO CAUSED YOU TO GET HURT TWICE...
...EVEN IF HE IS MY SON, I'M NOT SURE I COULD FORGIVE HIM.
DID KAHYUN TELL YOU WHAT HAPPENED IN GERMANY?
THAT ACCIDENT HAD NOTHING TO DO WITH KAHYUN.

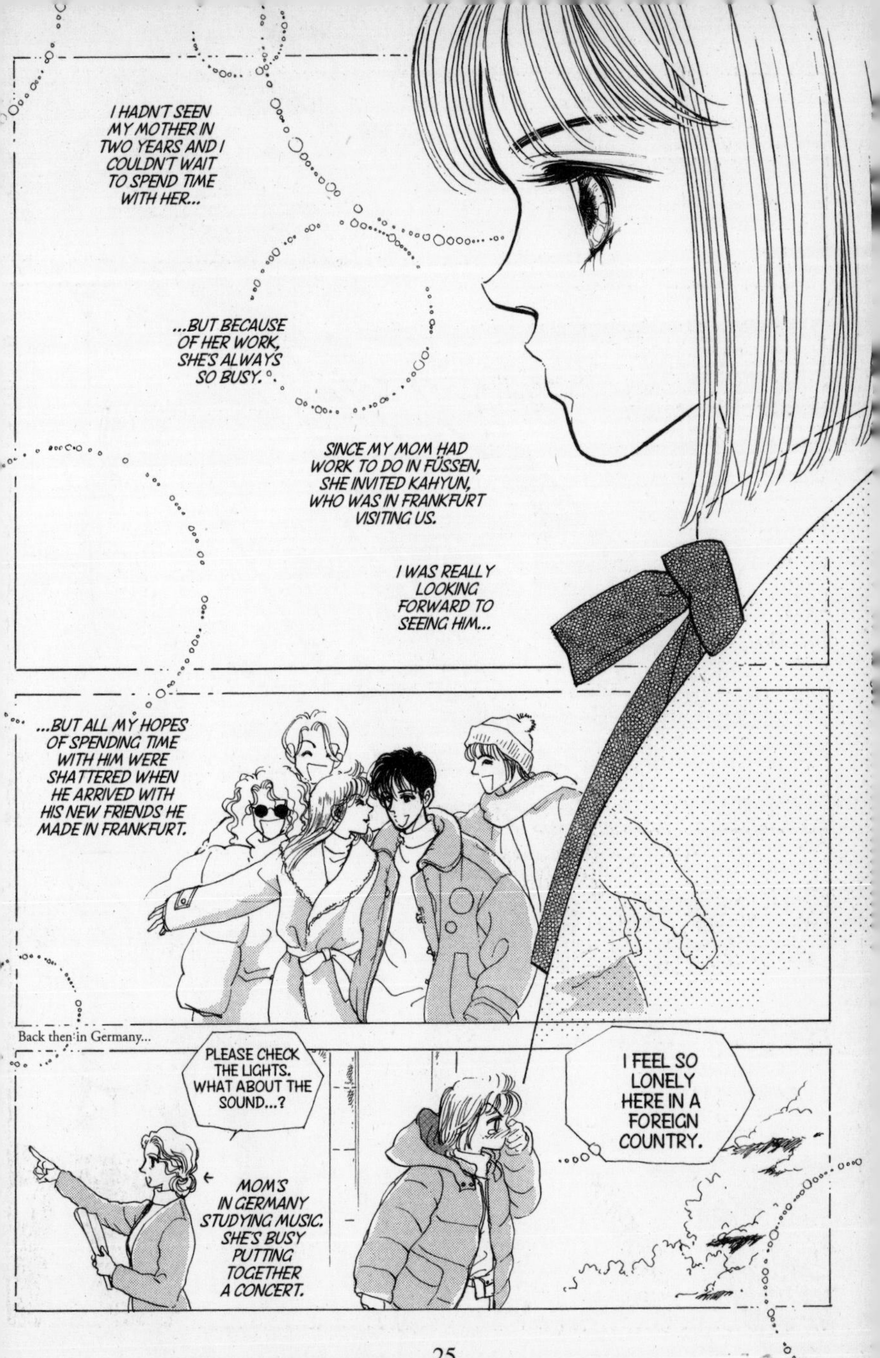
I HADN'T SEEN MY MOTHER IN TWO YEARS AND I COULDN'T WAIT TO SPEND TIME WITH HER...
...BUT BECAUSE OF HER WORK, SHE'S ALWAYS SO BUSY.
SINCE MY MOM HAD WORK TO DO IN FÜSSEN, SHE INVITED KAHYUN, WHO WAS IN FRANKFURT VISITING US.
I WAS REALLY LOOKING FORWARD TO SEEING HIM...
...BUT ALL MY HOPES OF SPENDING TIME WITH HIM WERE SHATTERED WHEN HE ARRIVED WITH HIS NEW FRIENDS HE MADE IN FRANKFURT.
Back then in Germany...
PLEASE CHECK THE LIGHTS. WHAT ABOUT THE SOUND...?
MOM'S IN GERMANY STUDYING MUSIC. SHE'S BUSY PUTTING TOGETHER A CONCERT.
I FEEL SO LONELY HERE IN A FOREIGN COUNTRY.

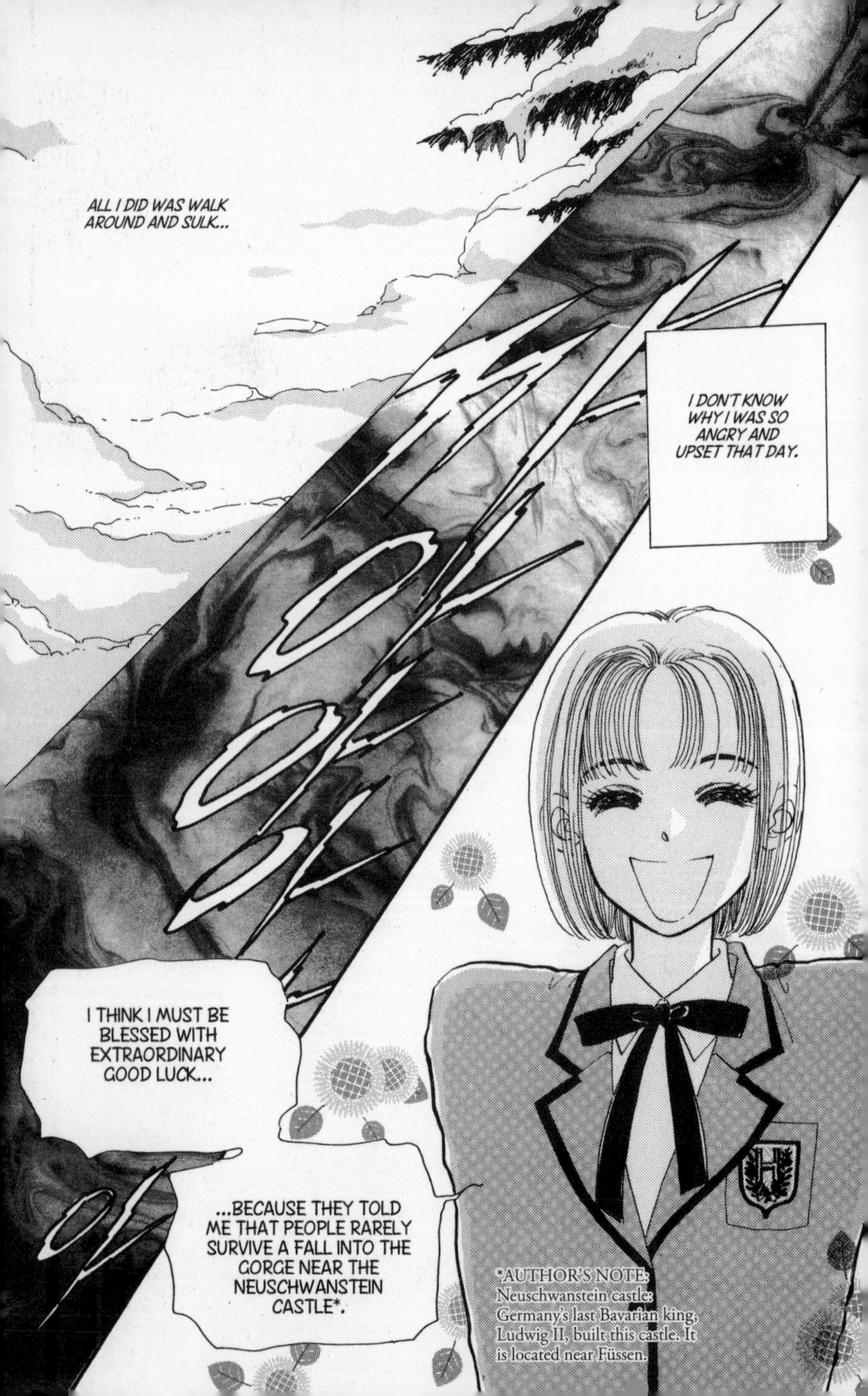

ALL I DID WAS WALK AROUND AND SULK...
I DON'T KNOW WHY I WAS SO ANGRY AND UPSET THAT DAY.
I THINK I MUST BE BLESSED WITH EXTRAORDINARY GOOD LUCK...
...BECAUSE THEY TOLD ME THAT PEOPLE RARELY SURVIVE A FALL INTO THE GORGE NEAR THE NEUSCHWANSTEIN CASTLE*.
*AUTHOR'S NOTE: Neuschwanstein castle: Germany's last Bavarian king, Ludwig II, built this castle. It is located near Füssen.

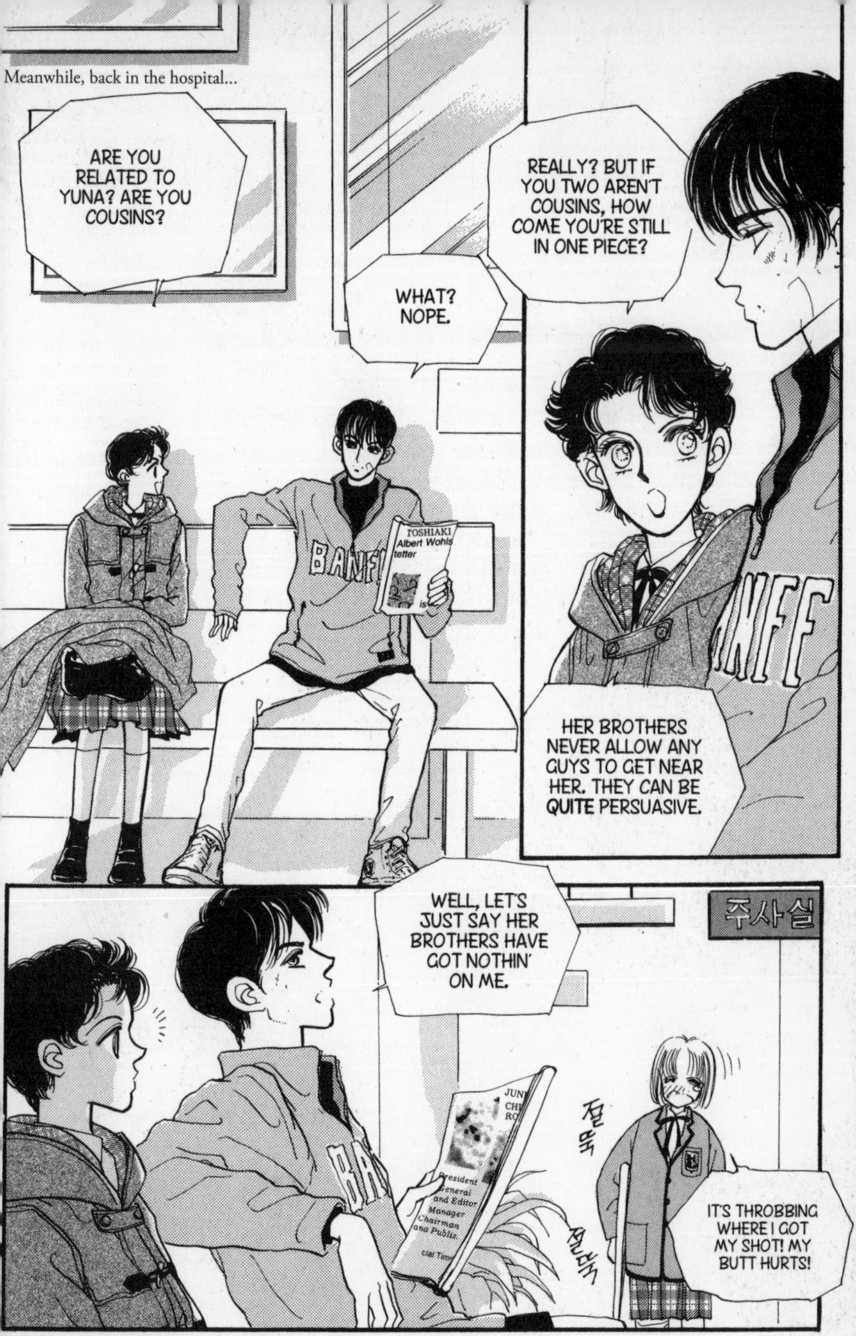
Meanwhile, back in the hospital...
ARE YOU RELATED TO YUNA? ARE YOU COUSINS?
WHAT? NOPE.
REALLY? BUT IF YOU TWO AREN'T COUSINS, HOW COME YOU'RE STILL IN ONE PIECE?
HER BROTHERS NEVER ALLOW ANY GUYS TO GET NEAR HER. THEY CAN BE QUITE PERSUASIVE.
WELL, LET'S JUST SAY HER BROTHERS HAVE GOT NOTHIN' ON ME.
주사실
절뚝
절뚝
IT'S THROBBING WHERE I GOT MY SHOT! MY BUTT HURTS!

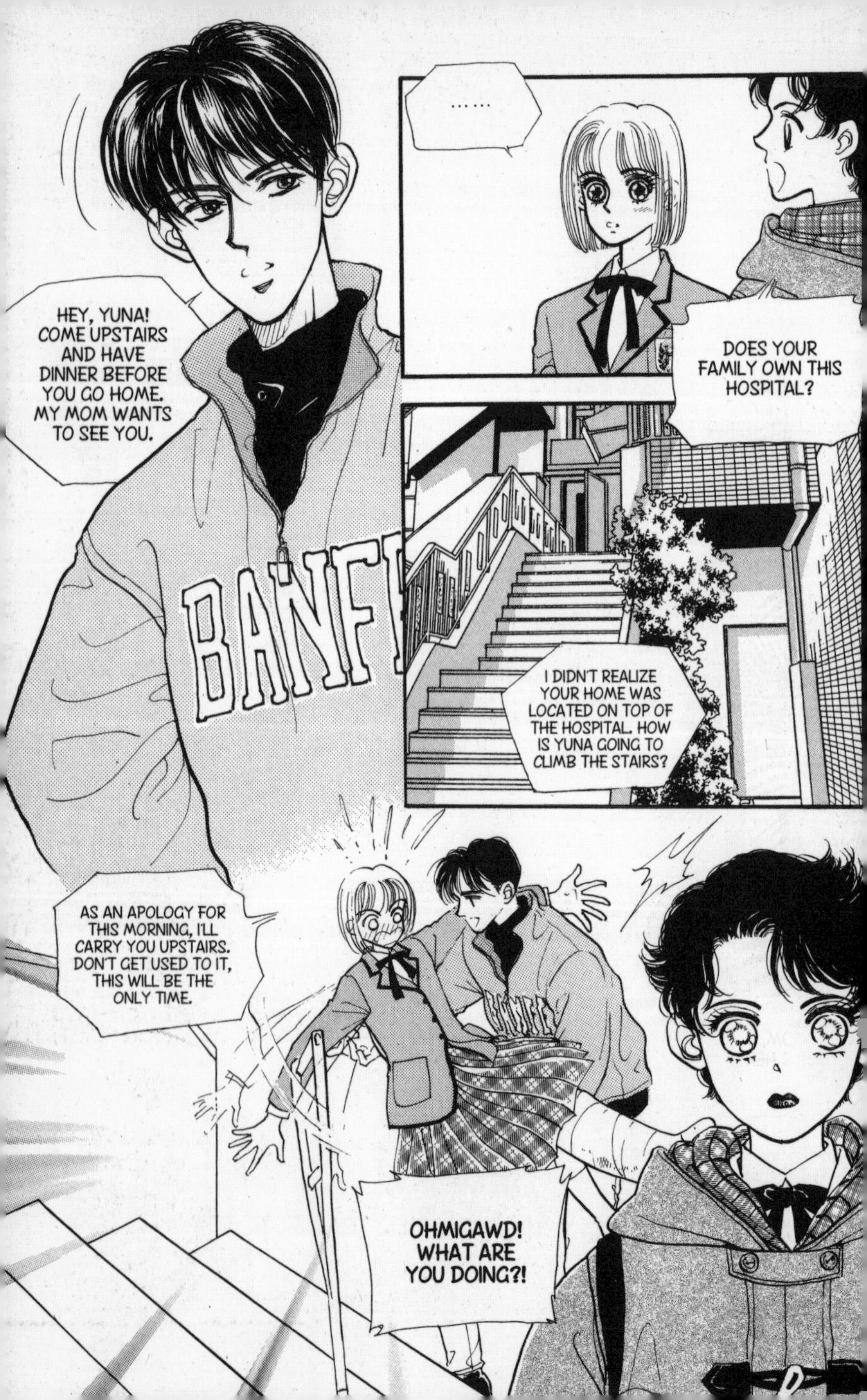
HEY, YUNA! COME UPSTAIRS AND HAVE DINNER BEFORE YOU GO HOME. MY MOM WANTS TO SEE YOU.
......
DOES YOUR FAMILY OWN THIS HOSPITAL?
I DIDN'T REALIZE YOUR HOME WAS LOCATED ON TOP OF THE HOSPITAL. HOW IS YUNA GOING TO CLIMB THE STAIRS?
AS AN APOLOGY FOR THIS MORNING, I'LL CARRY YOU UPSTAIRS. DON'T GET USED TO IT, THIS WILL BE THE ONLY TIME.
OHMIGAWD! WHAT ARE YOU DOING?!

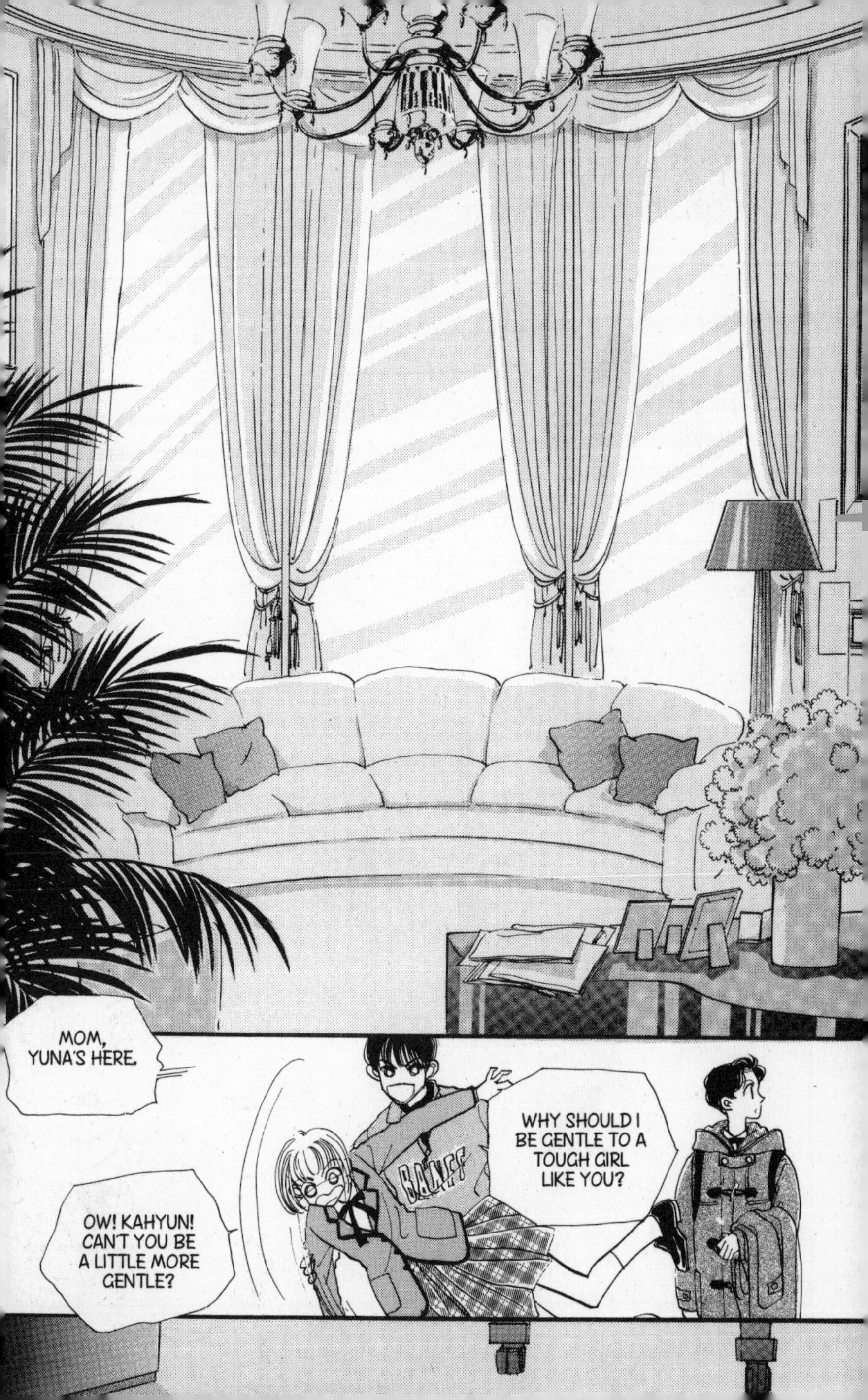
MOM, YUNA'S HERE.
OW! KAHYUN! CAN'T YOU BE A LITTLE MORE GENTLE?
WHY SHOULD I BE GENTLE TO A TOUGH GIRL LIKE YOU?

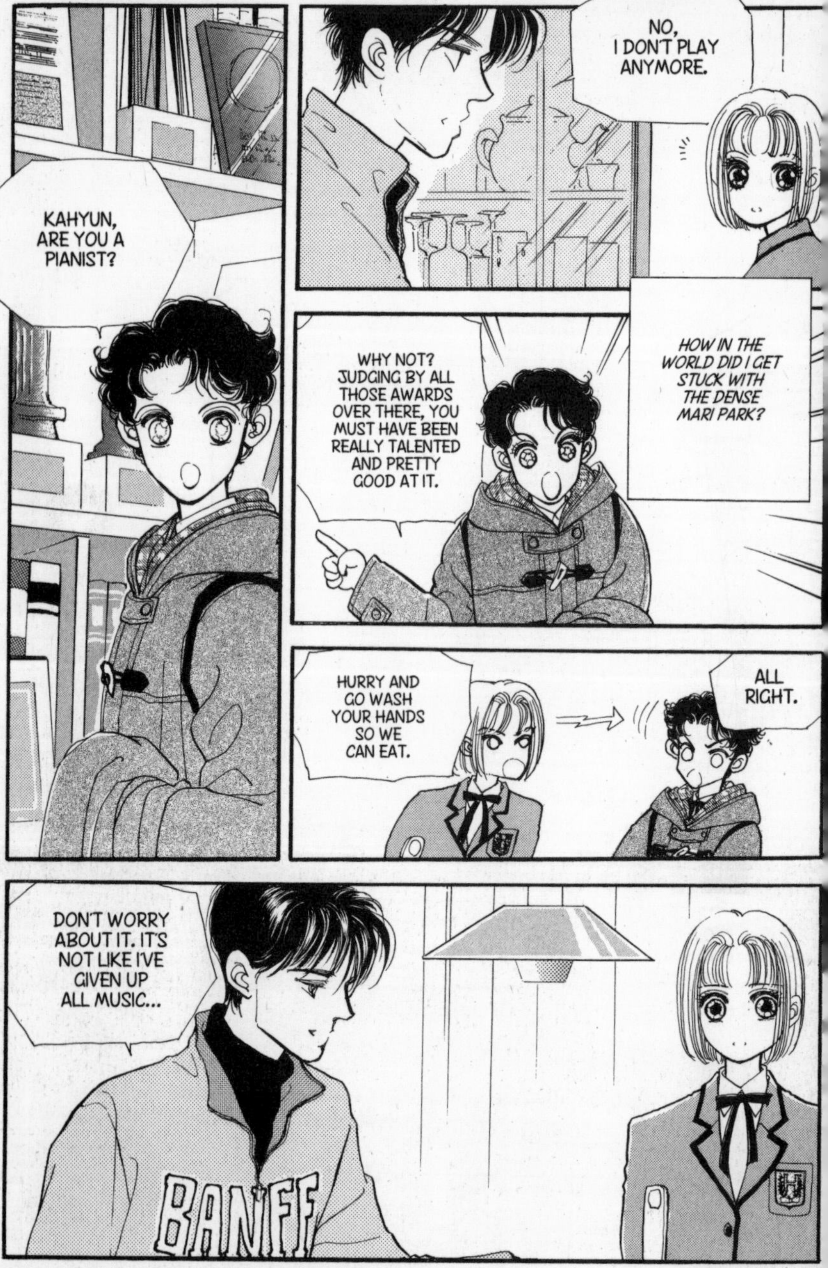
KAHYUN, ARE YOU A PIANIST?
NO, I DON'T PLAY ANYMORE.
WHY NOT? JUDGING BY ALL THOSE AWARDS OVER THERE, YOU MUST HAVE BEEN REALLY TALENTED AND PRETTY GOOD AT IT.
HOW IN THE WORLD DID I GET STUCK WITH THE DENSE MARI PARK?
HURRY AND GO WASH YOUR HANDS SO WE CAN EAT.
ALL RIGHT.
DON'T WORRY ABOUT IT. IT'S NOT LIKE I'VE GIVEN UP ALL MUSIC...
BANFF

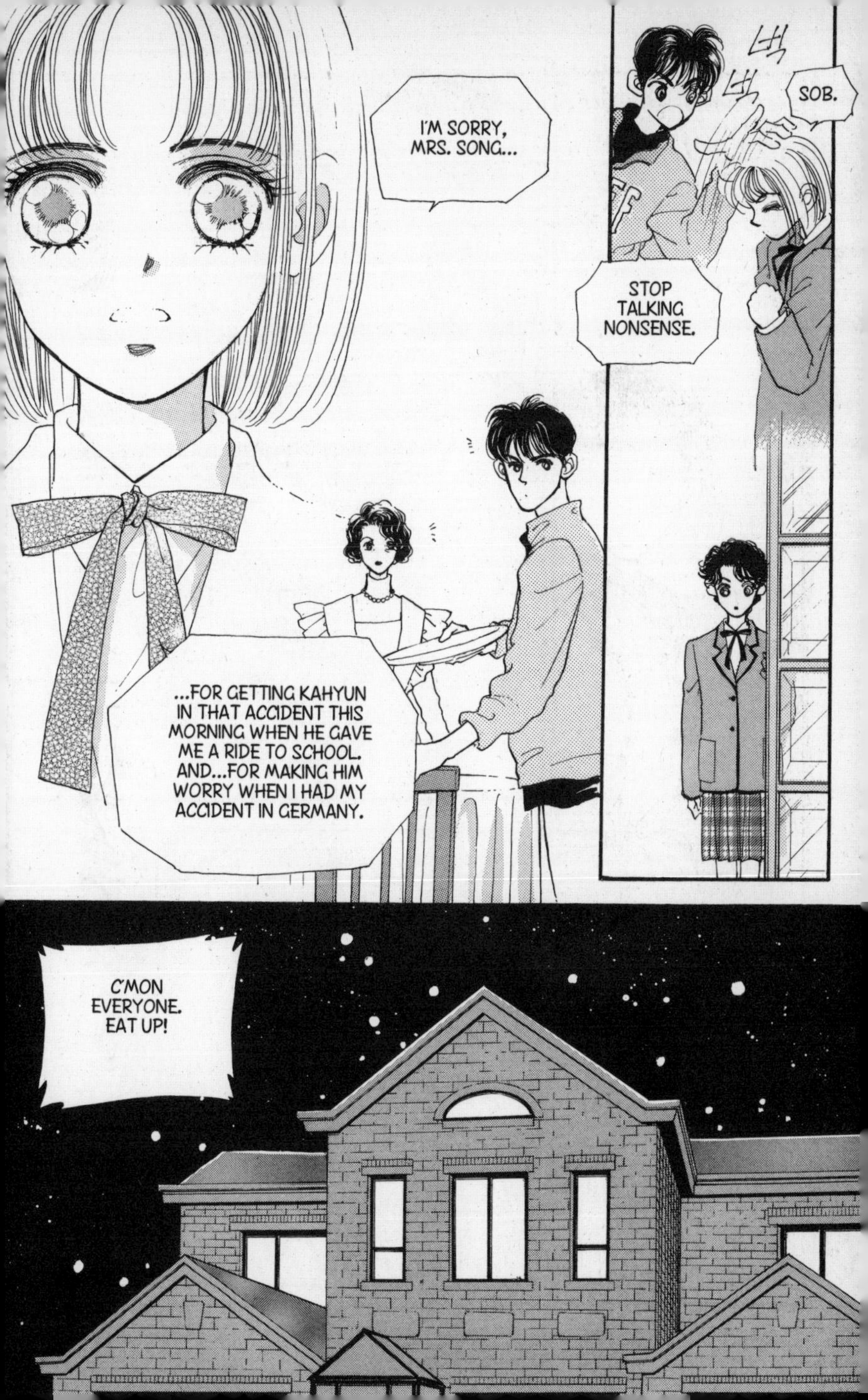
I'M SORRY, MRS. SONG...
...FOR GETTING KAHYUN IN THAT ACCIDENT THIS MORNING WHEN HE GAVE ME A RIDE TO SCHOOL. AND...FOR MAKING HIM WORRY WHEN I HAD MY ACCIDENT IN GERMANY.
SOB.
STOP TALKING NONSENSE.
C'MON EVERYONE. EAT UP!

The next day...

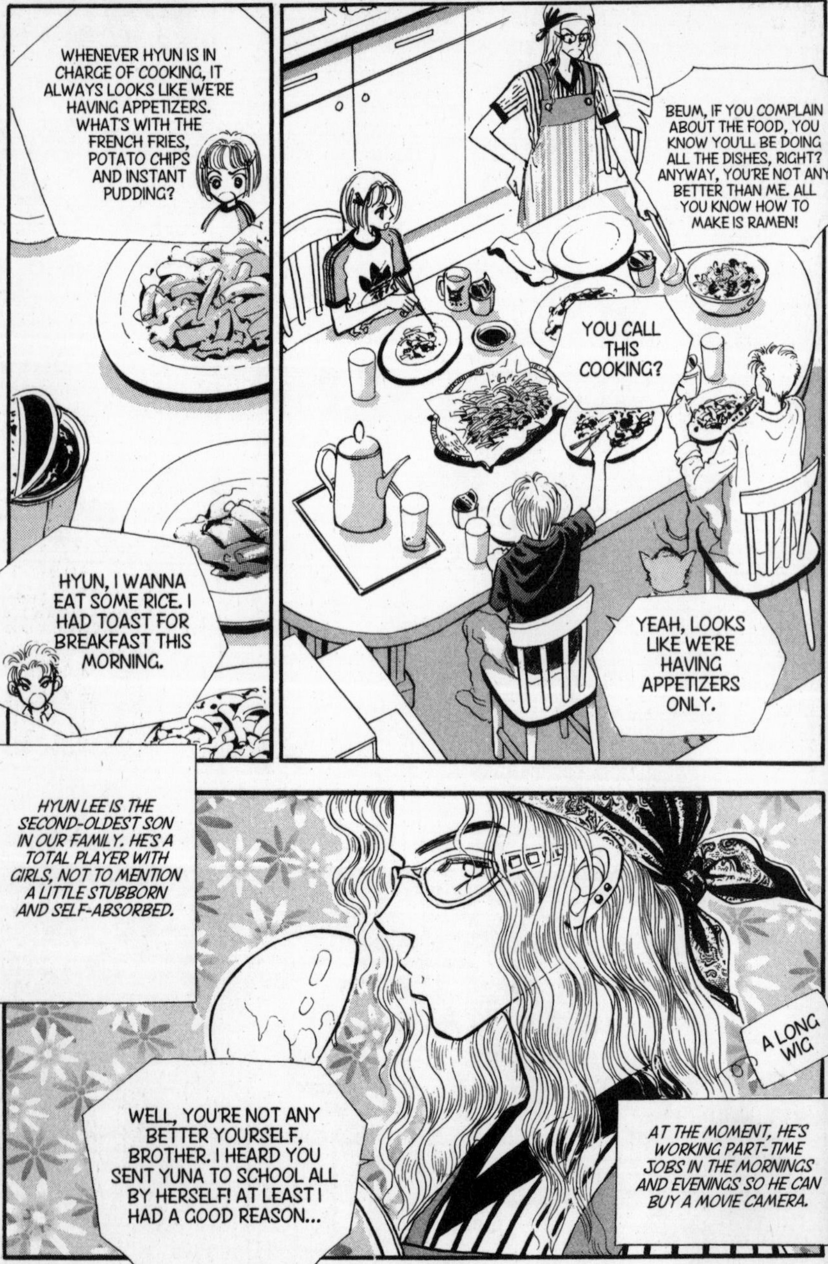
WHENEVER HYUN IS IN CHARGE OF COOKING, IT ALWAYS LOOKS LIKE WE'RE HAVING APPETIZERS. WHAT'S WITH THE FRENCH FRIES, POTATO CHIPS AND INSTANT PUDDING?
HYUN, I WANNA EAT SOME RICE. I HAD TOAST FOR BREAKFAST THIS MORNING.
BEUM, IF YOU COMPLAIN ABOUT THE FOOD, YOU KNOW YOU'LL BE DOING ALL THE DISHES, RIGHT? ANYWAY, YOU'RE NOT ANY BETTER THAN ME. ALL YOU KNOW HOW TO MAKE IS RAMEN!
YOU CALL THIS COOKING?
YEAH, LOOKS LIKE WE'RE HAVING APPETIZERS ONLY.
HYUN LEE IS THE SECOND-OLDEST SON IN OUR FAMILY. HE'S A TOTAL PLAYER WITH GIRLS, NOT TO MENTION A LITTLE STUBBORN AND SELF-ABSORBED.
A LONG WIG
WELL, YOU'RE NOT ANY BETTER YOURSELF, BROTHER. I HEARD YOU SENT YUNA TO SCHOOL ALL BY HERSELF! AT LEAST I HAD A GOOD REASON...
AT THE MOMENT, HE'S WORKING PART-TIME JOBS IN THE MORNINGS AND EVENINGS SO HE CAN BUY A MOVIE CAMERA.

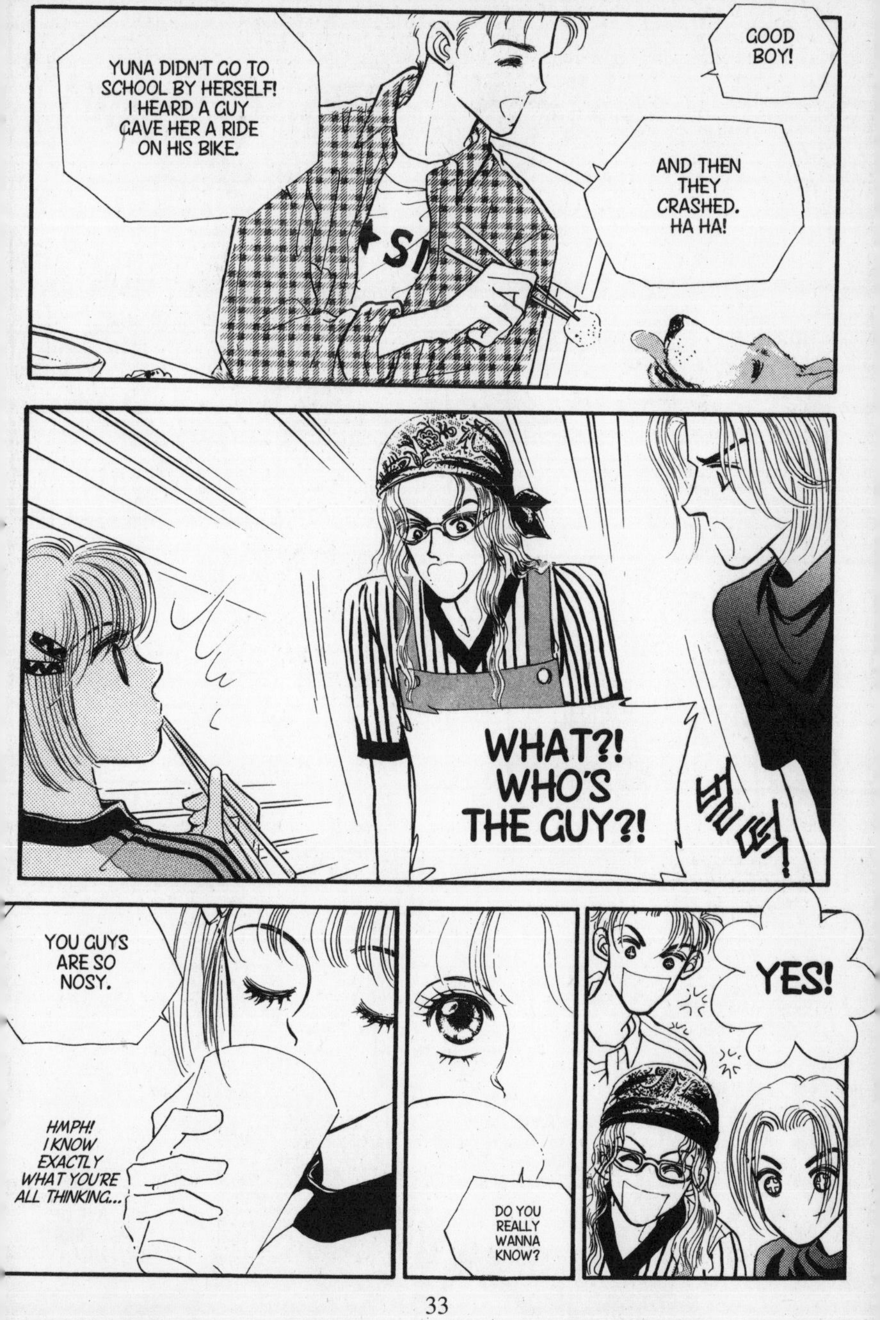
YUNA DIDN'T GO TO SCHOOL BY HERSELF! I HEARD A GUY GAVE HER A RIDE ON HIS BIKE.
GOOD BOY!
AND THEN THEY CRASHED. HA HA!
WHAT?! WHO'S THE GUY?!
YOU GUYS ARE SO NOSY.
HMPH! I KNOW EXACTLY WHAT YOU'RE ALL THINKING...
DO YOU REALLY WANNA KNOW?
YES!

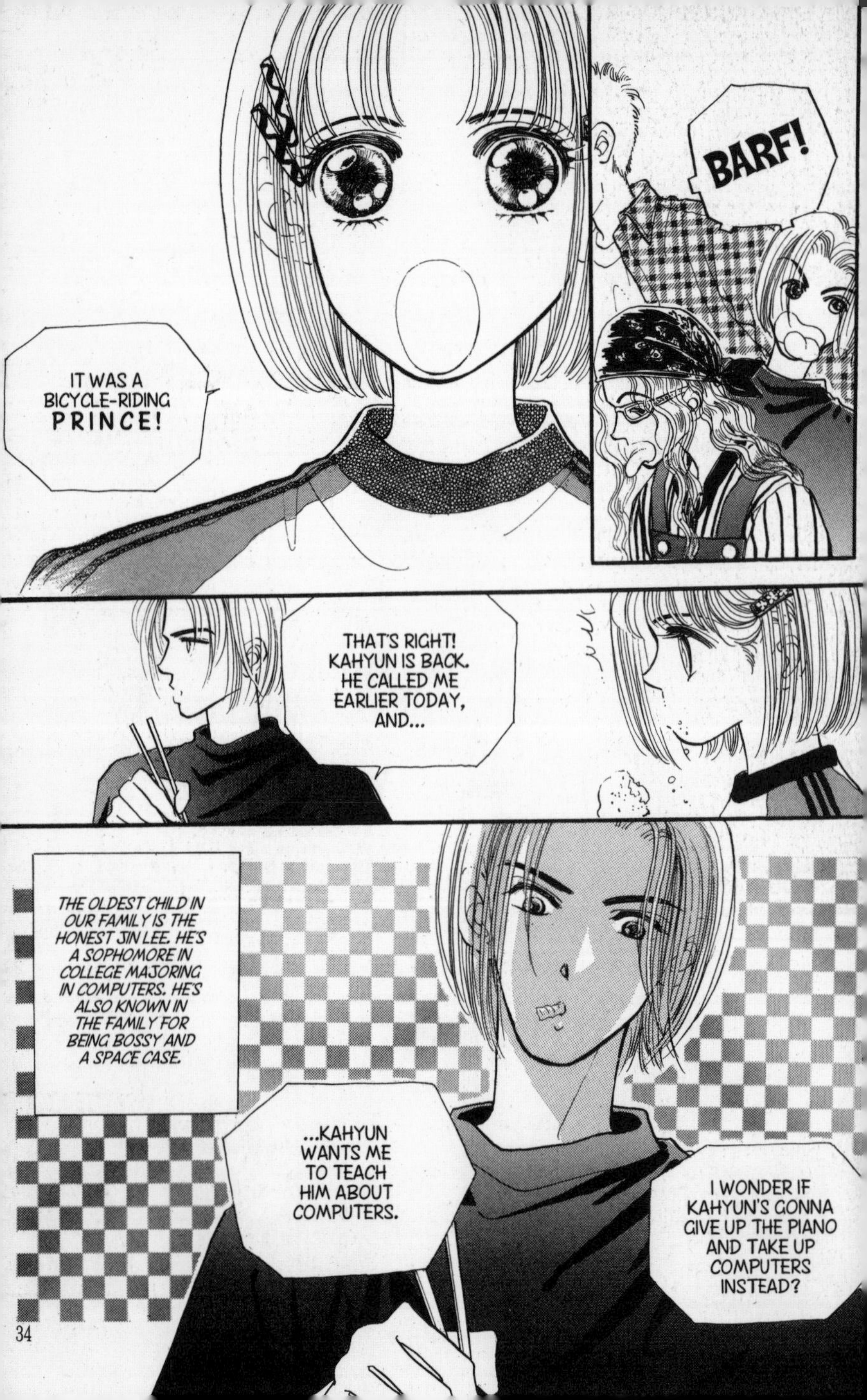

IT WAS A BICYCLE-RIDING PRINCE!
BARF!
THAT'S RIGHT! KAHYUN IS BACK. HE CALLED ME EARLIER TODAY, AND...
THE OLDEST CHILD IN OUR FAMILY IS THE HONEST JIN LEE. HE'S A SOPHOMORE IN COLLEGE MAJORING IN COMPUTERS. HE'S ALSO KNOWN IN THE FAMILY FOR BEING BOSSY AND A SPACE CASE.
...KAHYUN WANTS ME TO TEACH HIM ABOUT COMPUTERS.
I WONDER IF KAHYUN'S GONNA GIVE UP THE PIANO AND TAKE UP COMPUTERS INSTEAD?

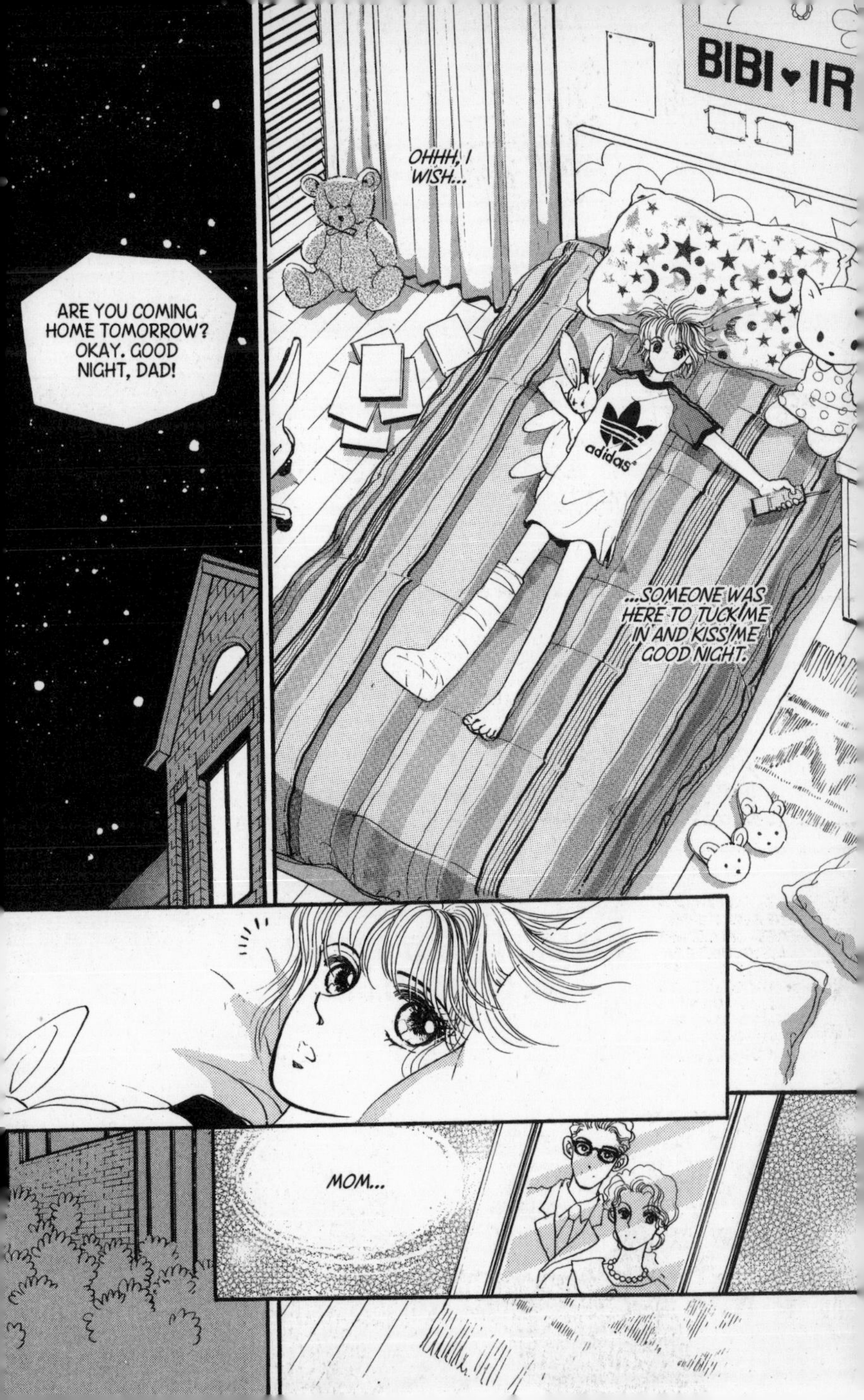
ARE YOU COMING HOME TOMORROW? OKAY. GOOD NIGHT, DAD!
BIBI♥IR
OHHH, I WISH...
...SOMEONE WAS HERE TO TUCK ME IN AND KISS ME GOOD NIGHT.
adidas
MOM...

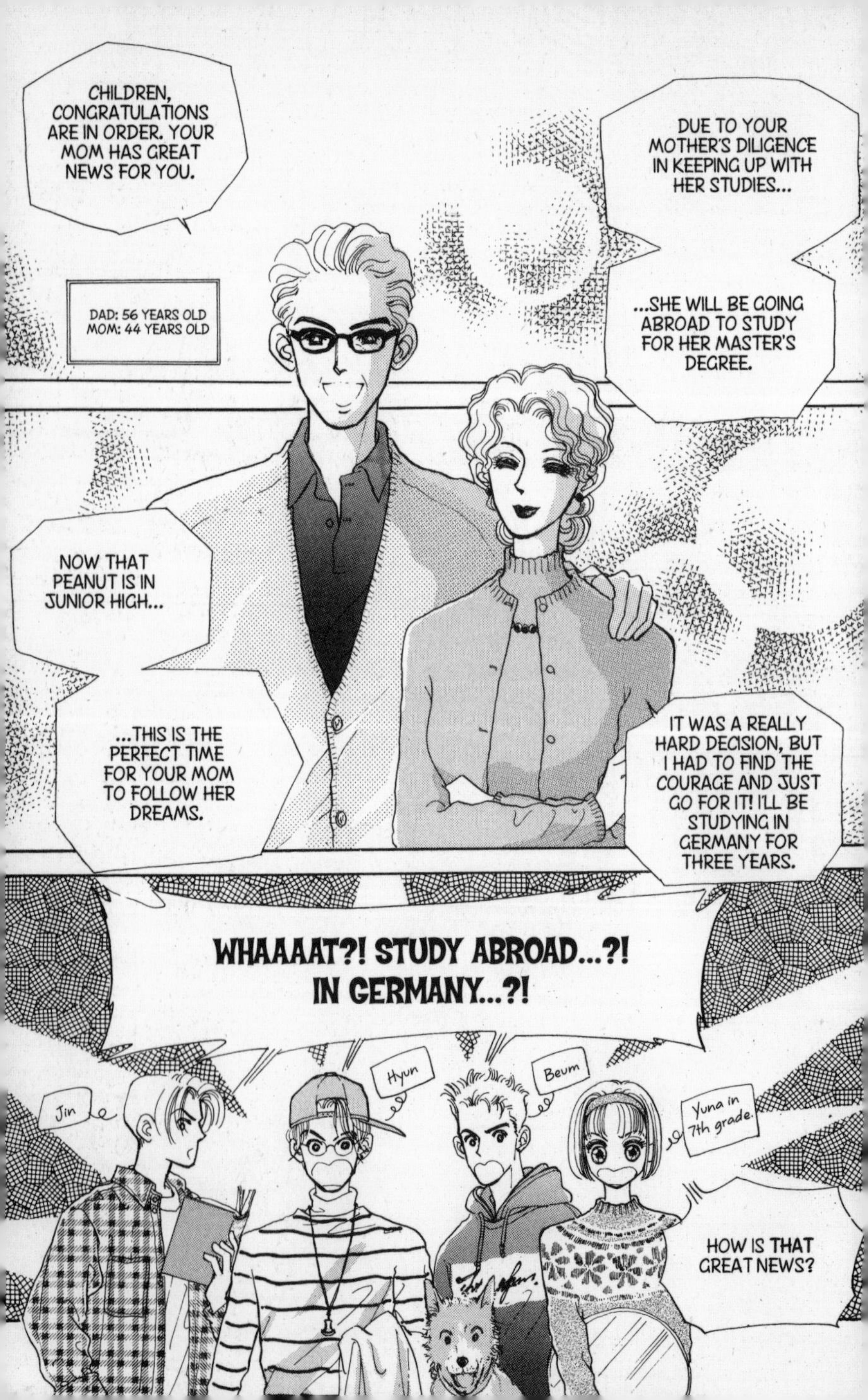

CHILDREN, CONGRATULATIONS ARE IN ORDER. YOUR MOM HAS GREAT NEWS FOR YOU.
DAD: 56 YEARS OLD
MOM: 44 YEARS OLD
DUE TO YOUR MOTHER'S DILIGENCE IN KEEPING UP WITH HER STUDIES...
...SHE WILL BE GOING ABROAD TO STUDY FOR HER MASTER'S DEGREE.
NOW THAT PEANUT IS IN JUNIOR HIGH...
...THIS IS THE PERFECT TIME FOR YOUR MOM TO FOLLOW HER DREAMS.
IT WAS A REALLY HARD DECISION, BUT I HAD TO FIND THE COURAGE AND JUST GO FOR IT! I'LL BE STUDYING IN GERMANY FOR THREE YEARS.
WHAAAAT?! STUDY ABROAD...?! IN GERMANY...?!
Jin
Hyun
Beum
Yuna in 7th grade.
HOW IS THAT GREAT NEWS?

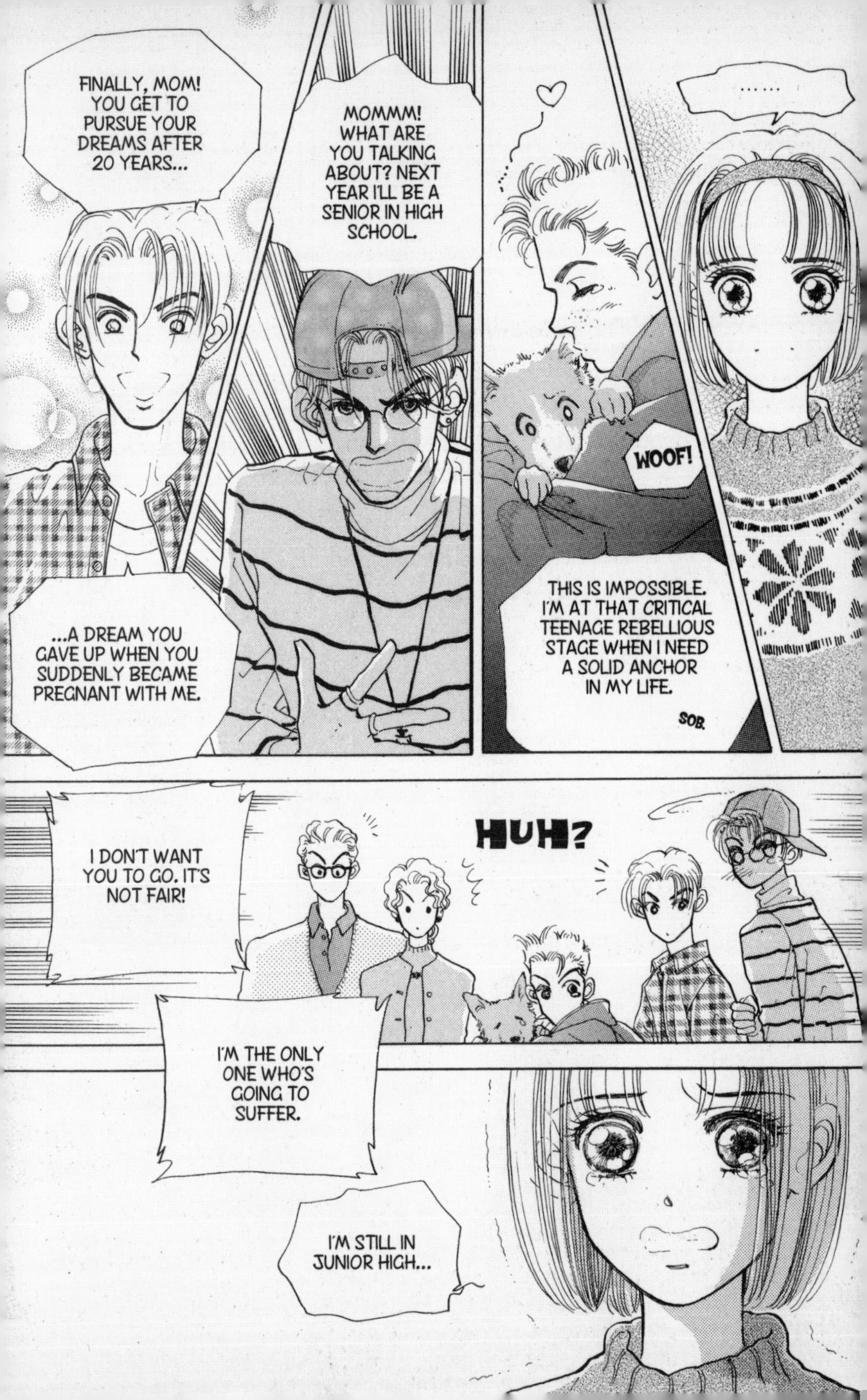
FINALLY, MOM! YOU GET TO PURSUE YOUR DREAMS AFTER 20 YEARS...
...A DREAM YOU GAVE UP WHEN YOU SUDDENLY BECAME PREGNANT WITH ME.
MOMMM! WHAT ARE YOU TALKING ABOUT? NEXT YEAR I'LL BE A SENIOR IN HIGH SCHOOL.
WOOF!
THIS IS IMPOSSIBLE. I'M AT THAT CRITICAL TEENAGE REBELLIOUS STAGE WHEN I NEED A SOLID ANCHOR IN MY LIFE.
SOB.
......
I DON'T WANT YOU TO GO. IT'S NOT FAIR!
HUH?
I'M THE ONLY ONE WHO'S GOING TO SUFFER.
I'M STILL IN JUNIOR HIGH...

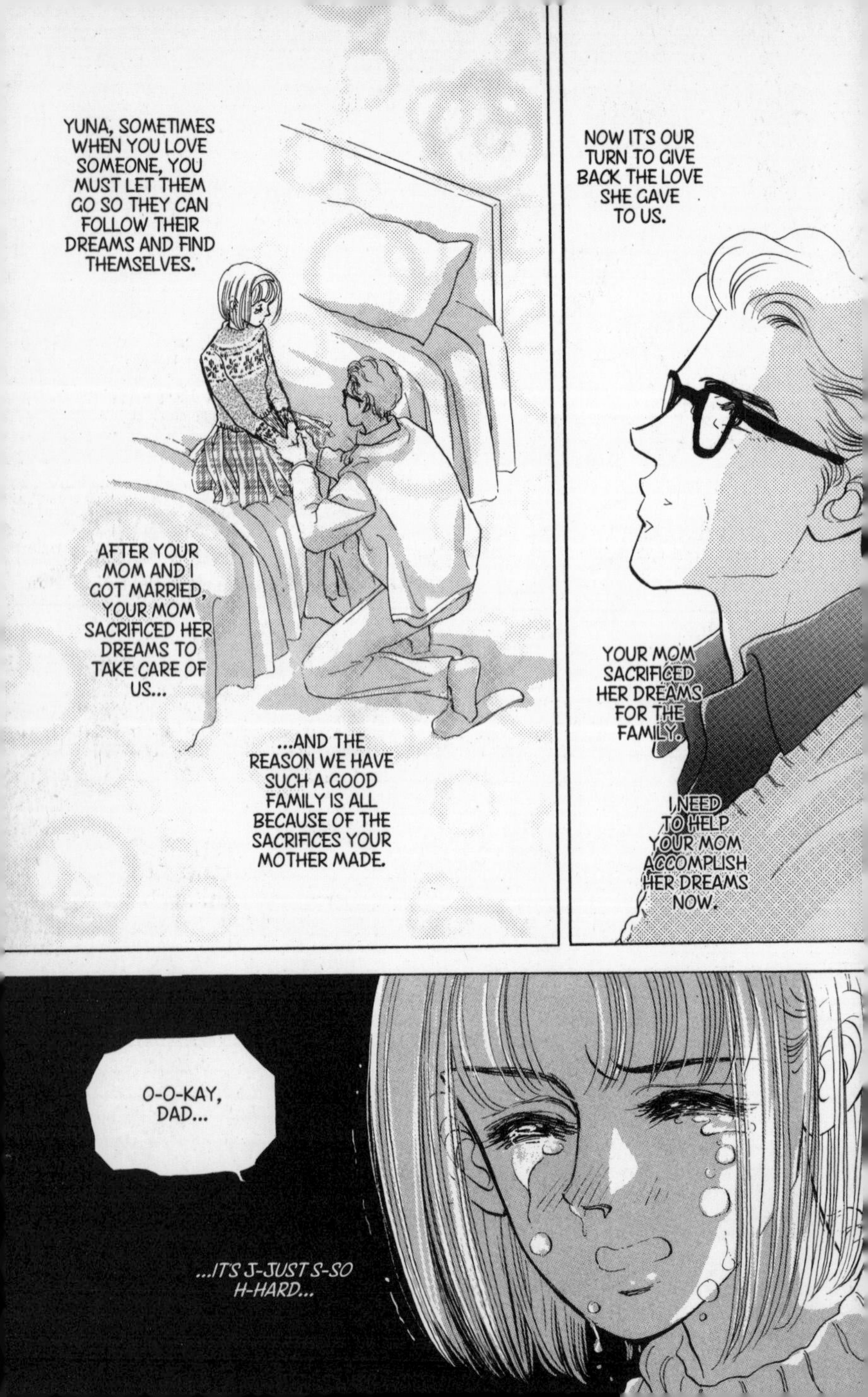
YUNA, SOMETIMES WHEN YOU LOVE SOMEONE, YOU MUST LET THEM GO SO THEY CAN FOLLOW THEIR DREAMS AND FIND THEMSELVES.
AFTER YOUR MOM AND I GOT MARRIED, YOUR MOM SACRIFICED HER DREAMS TO TAKE CARE OF US...
...AND THE REASON WE HAVE SUCH A GOOD FAMILY IS ALL BECAUSE OF THE SACRIFICES YOUR MOTHER MADE.
NOW IT'S OUR TURN TO GIVE BACK THE LOVE SHE GAVE TO US.
YOUR MOM SACRIFICED HER DREAMS FOR THE FAMILY.
I NEED TO HELP YOUR MOM ACCOMPLISH HER DREAMS NOW.
O-O-KAY, DAD...
...IT'S J-JUST S-SO H-HARD...

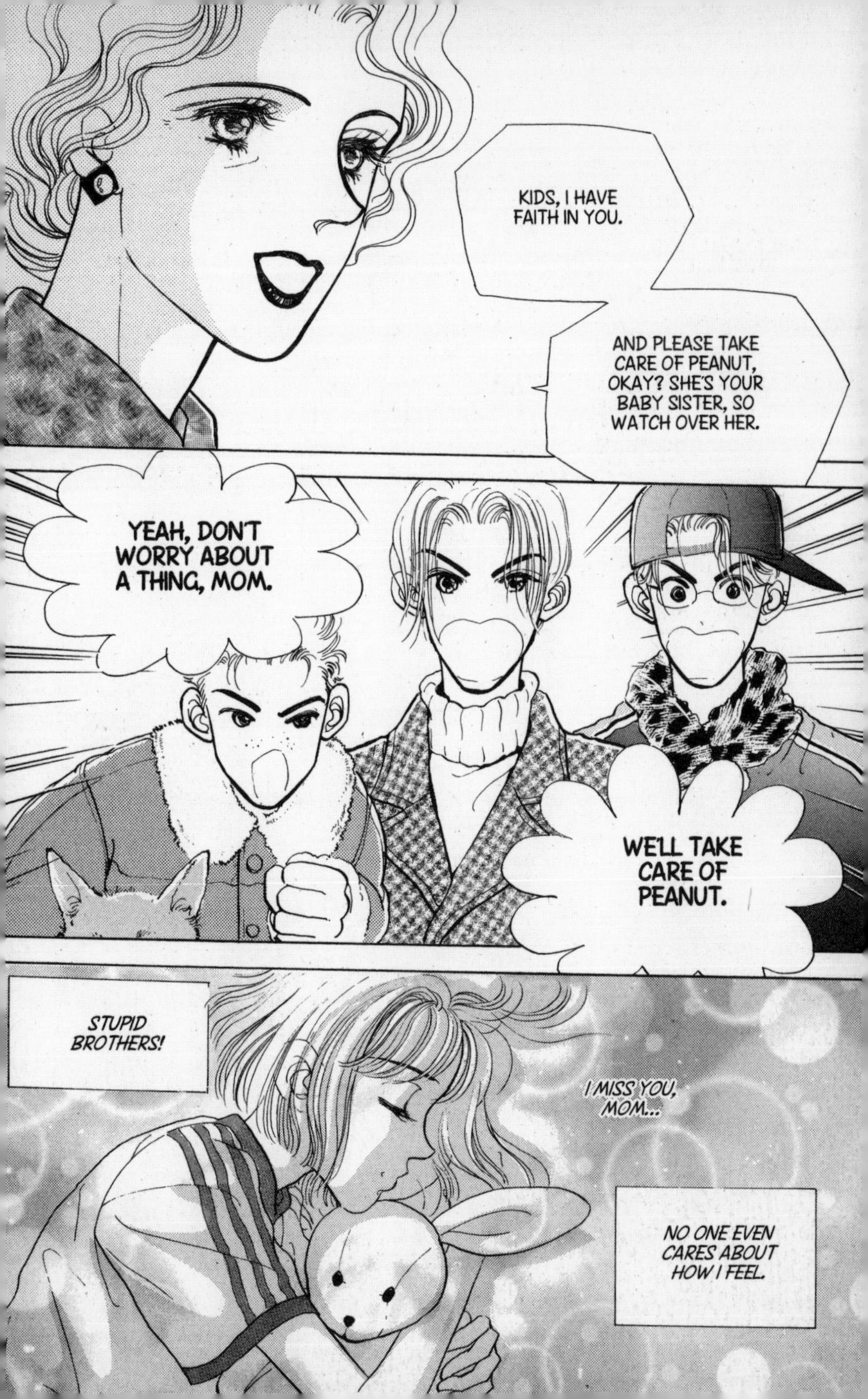
KIDS, I HAVE FAITH IN YOU.
AND PLEASE TAKE CARE OF PEANUT, OKAY? SHE'S YOUR BABY SISTER, SO WATCH OVER HER.
YEAH, DON'T WORRY ABOUT A THING, MOM.
WE'LL TAKE CARE OF PEANUT.
STUPID BROTHERS!
I MISS YOU, MOM...
NO ONE EVEN CARES ABOUT HOW I FEEL.

Back in Germany...

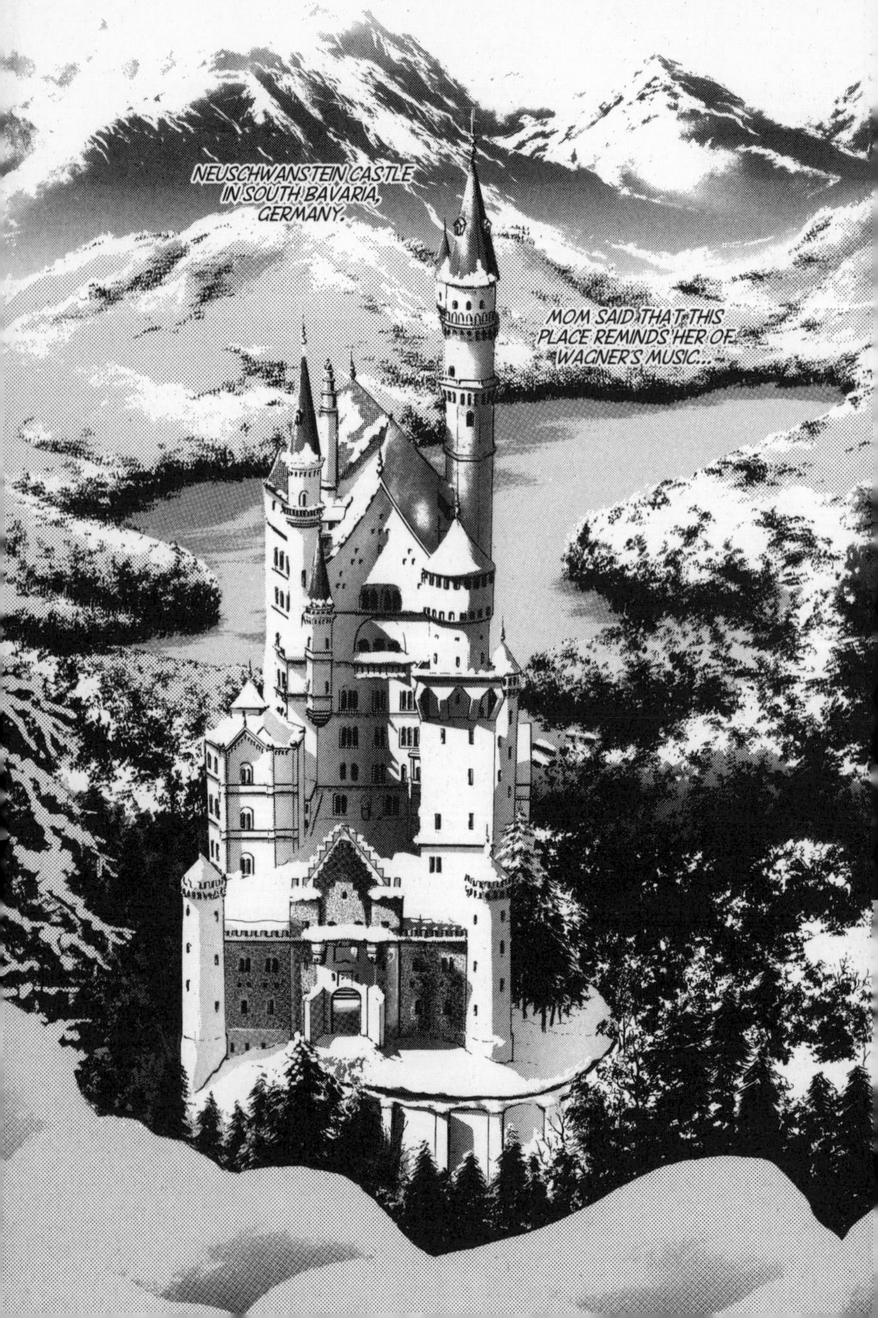
NEUSCHWANSTEIN CASTLE IN SOUTH BAVARIA, GERMANY.
MOM SAID THAT THIS PLACE REMINDS HER OF WAGNER'S MUSIC...

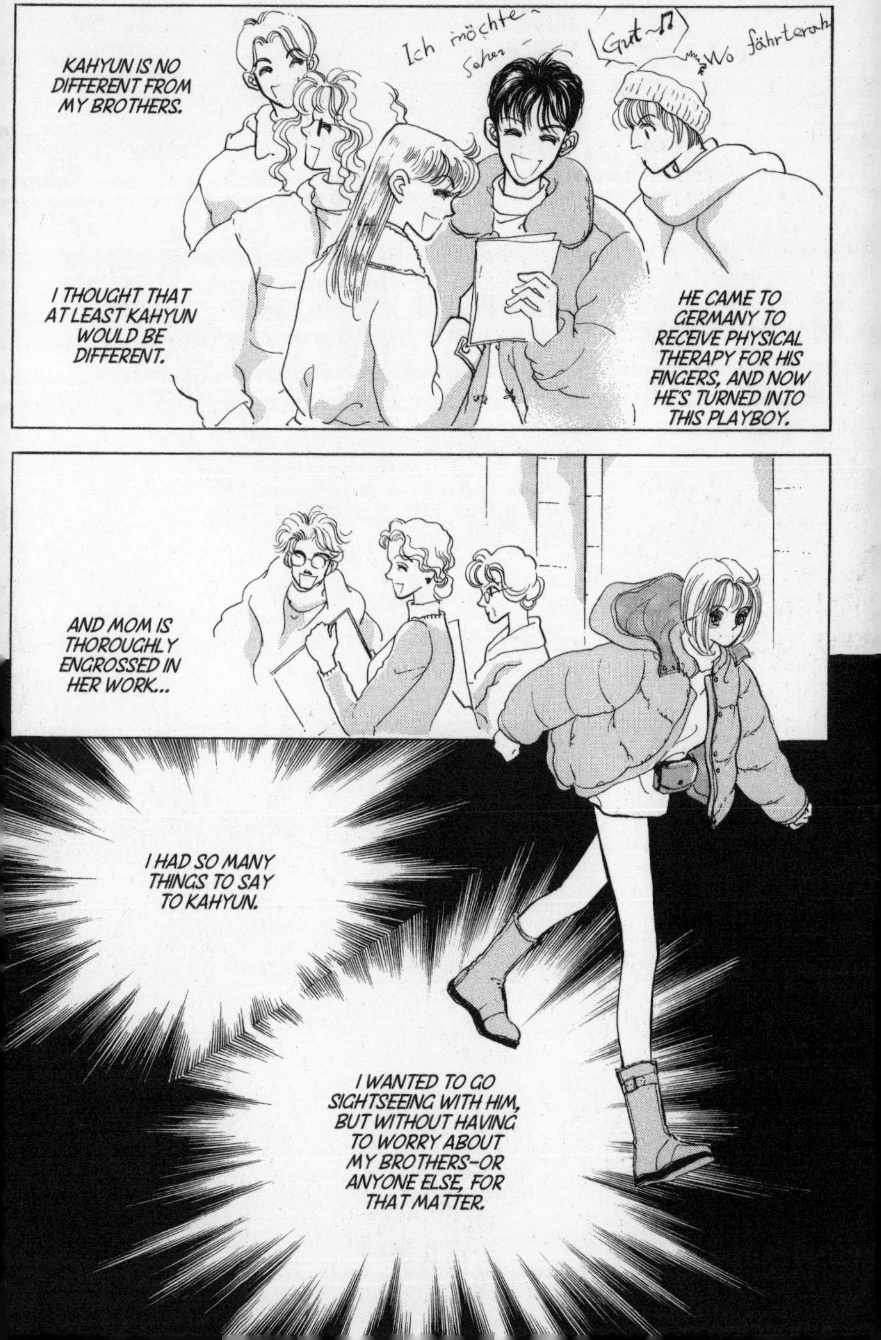

KAHYUN IS NO DIFFERENT FROM MY BROTHERS.
Ich möchte~ sehen~
Gut~♫
Wo fährter ab
I THOUGHT THAT AT LEAST KAHYUN WOULD BE DIFFERENT.
HE CAME TO GERMANY TO RECEIVE PHYSICAL THERAPY FOR HIS FINGERS, AND NOW HE'S TURNED INTO THIS PLAYBOY.
AND MOM IS THOROUGHLY ENGROSSED IN HER WORK...
I HAD SO MANY THINGS TO SAY TO KAHYUN.
I WANTED TO GO SIGHTSEEING WITH HIM, BUT WITHOUT HAVING TO WORRY ABOUT MY BROTHERS-OR ANYONE ELSE, FOR THAT MATTER.

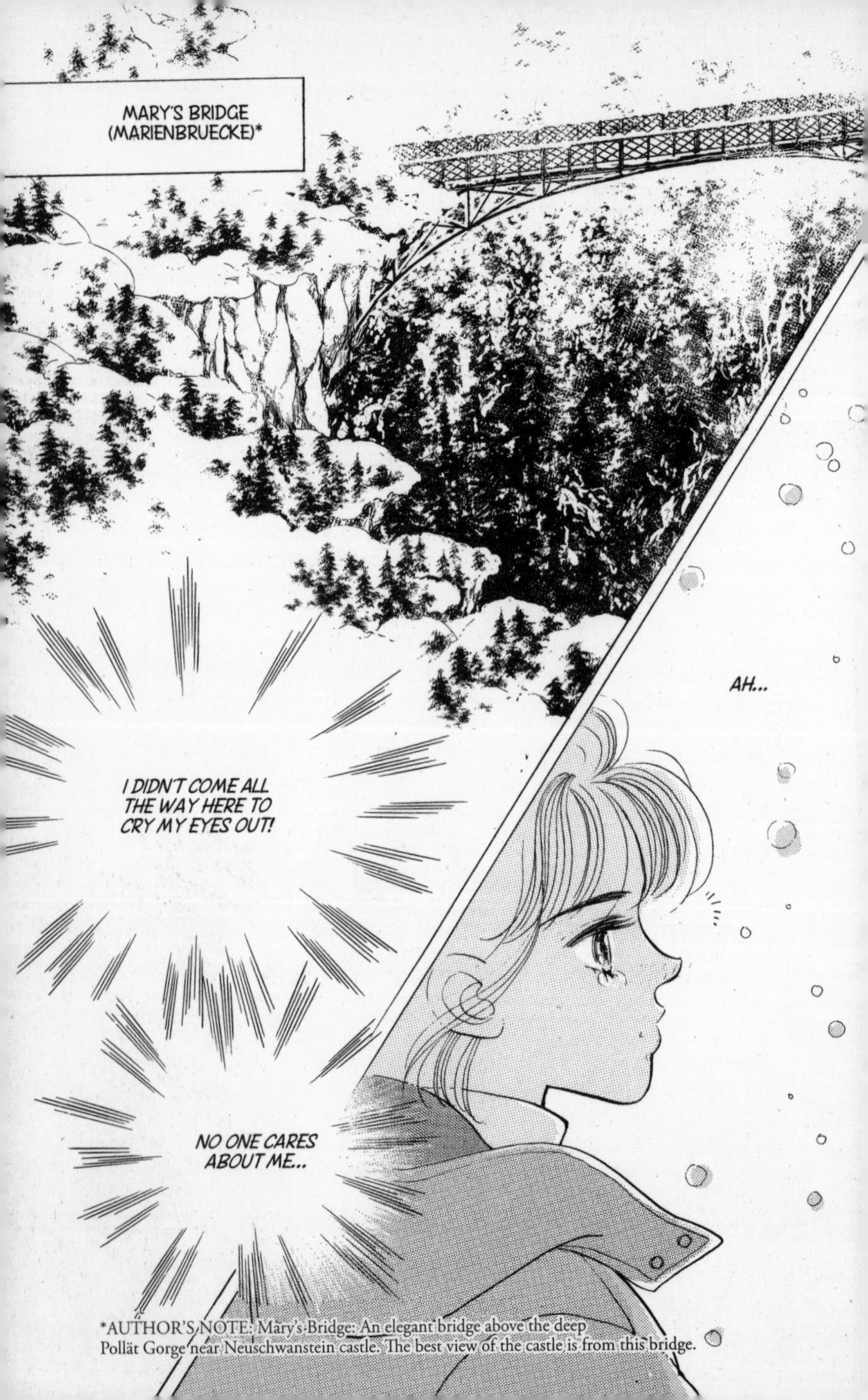
MARY'S BRIDGE (MARIENBRUECKE)*
I DIDN'T COME ALL THE WAY HERE TO CRY MY EYES OUT!
AH...
NO ONE CARES ABOUT ME...

*AUTHOR'S NOTE: Mary's Bridge: An elegant bridge above the deep Pollät Gorge near Neuschwanstein castle. The best view of the castle is from this bridge.

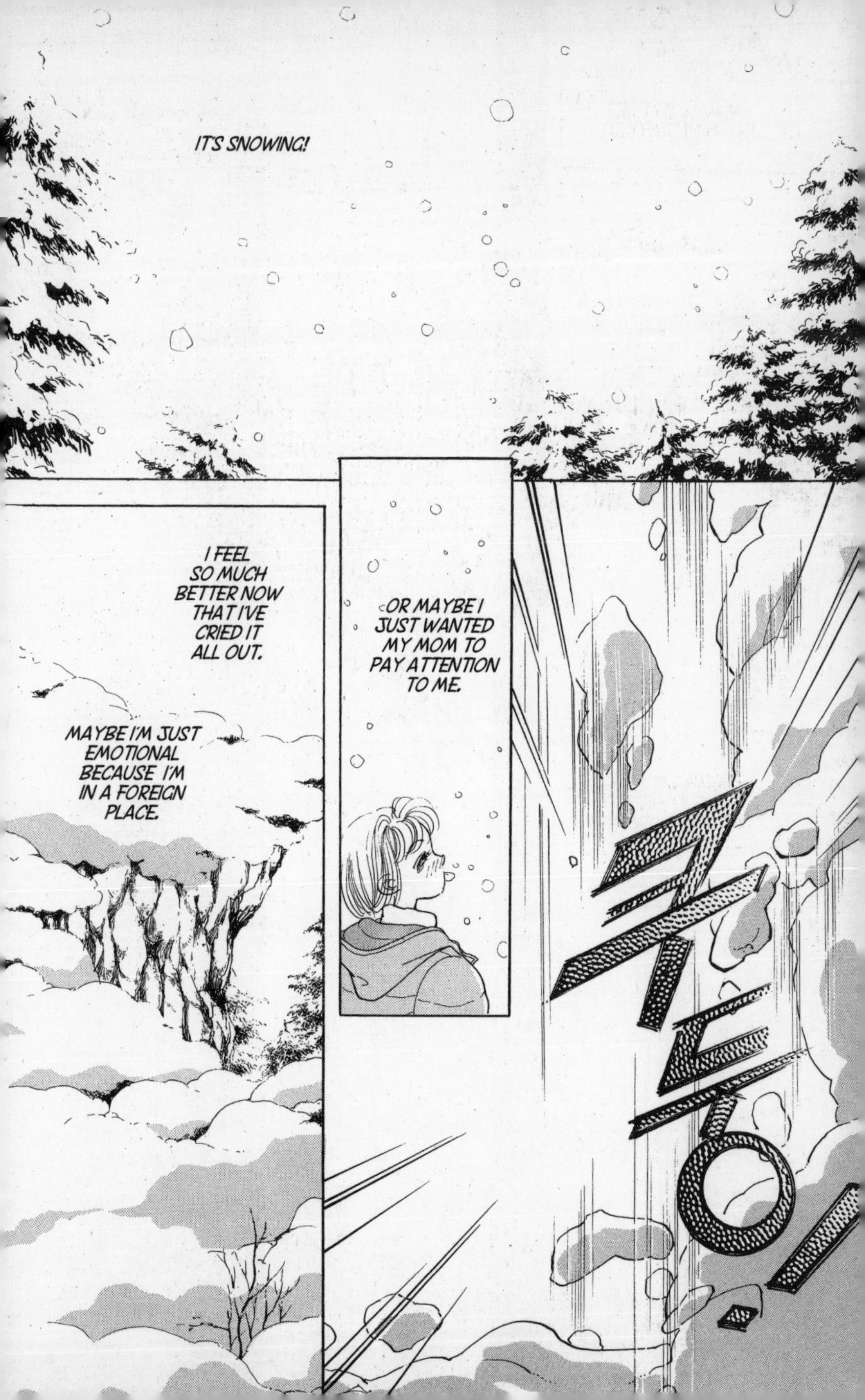
IT'S SNOWING!
I FEEL SO MUCH BETTER NOW THAT I'VE CRIED IT ALL OUT.
MAYBE I'M JUST EMOTIONAL BECAUSE I'M IN A FOREIGN PLACE.
OR MAYBE I JUST WANTED MY MOM TO PAY ATTENTION TO ME.

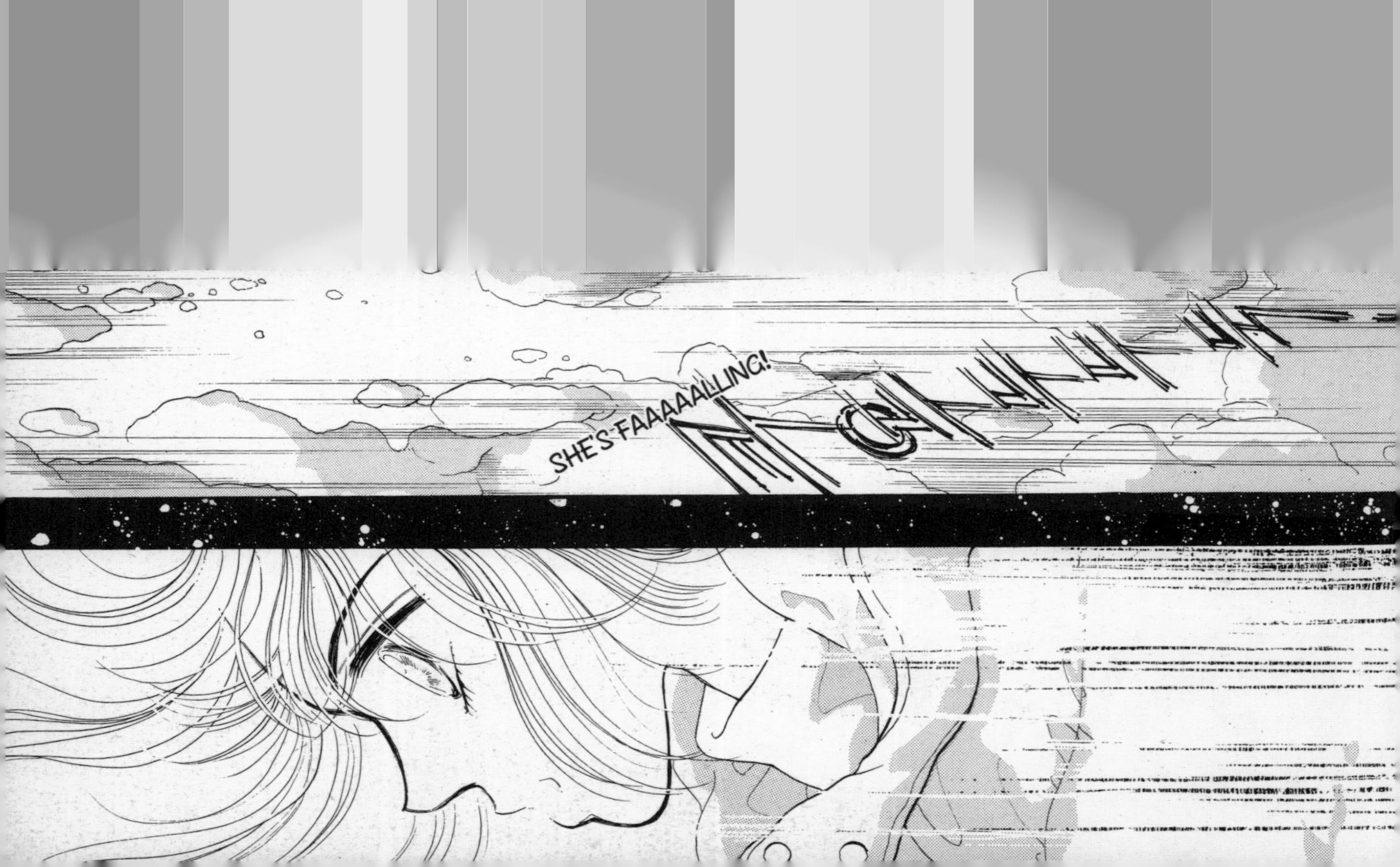
SHE'S FAAAAALLING!

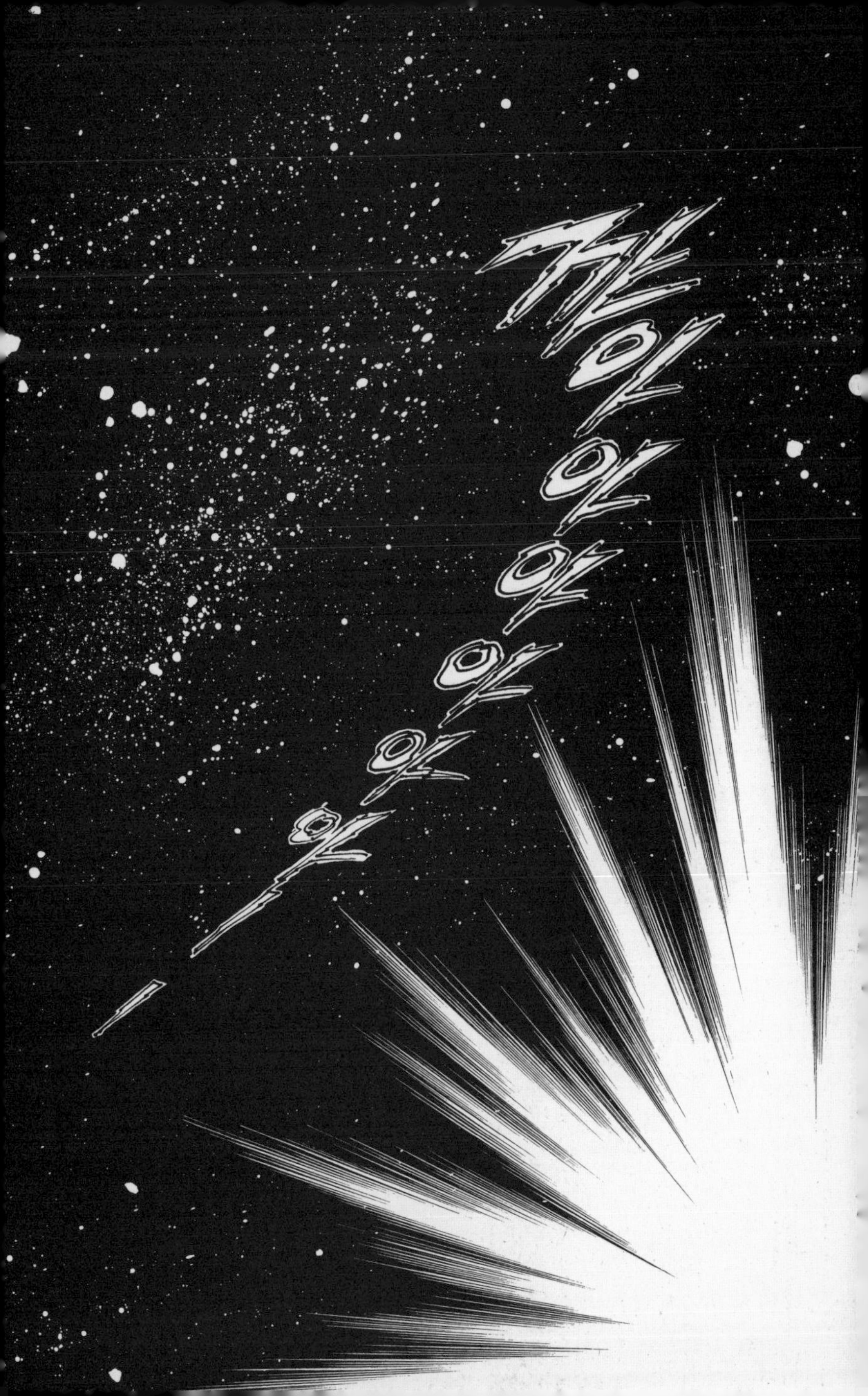
갸아아아아아아—

MY BODY FEELS SO
HEAVY...

AH...

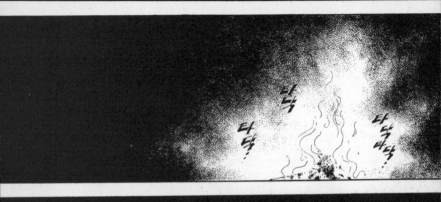

WHAT HAPPENED?

I THINK...
I SLIPPED
AND FELL DOWN...

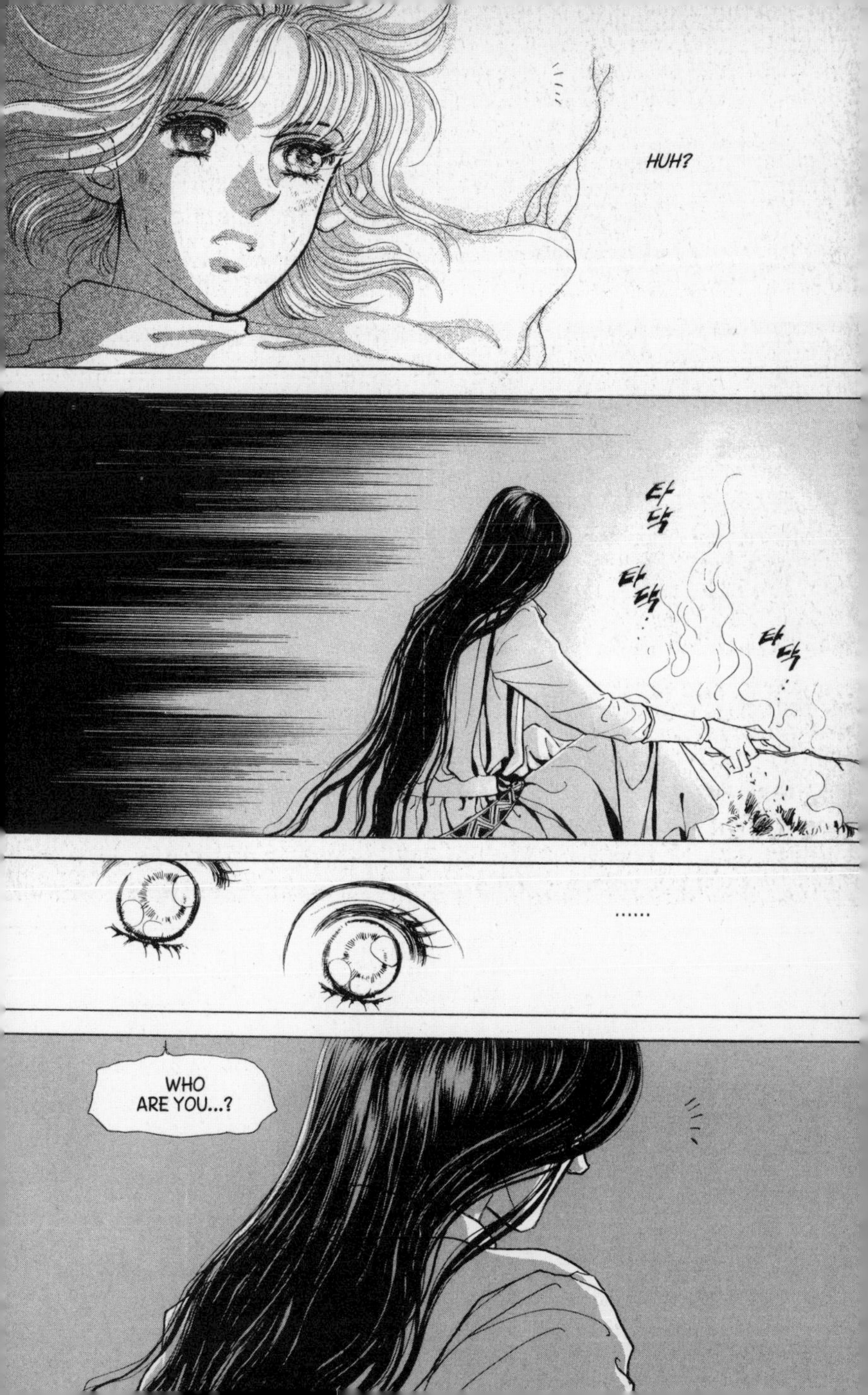
HUH?
타닥
타닥
타닥
......
WHO ARE YOU...?

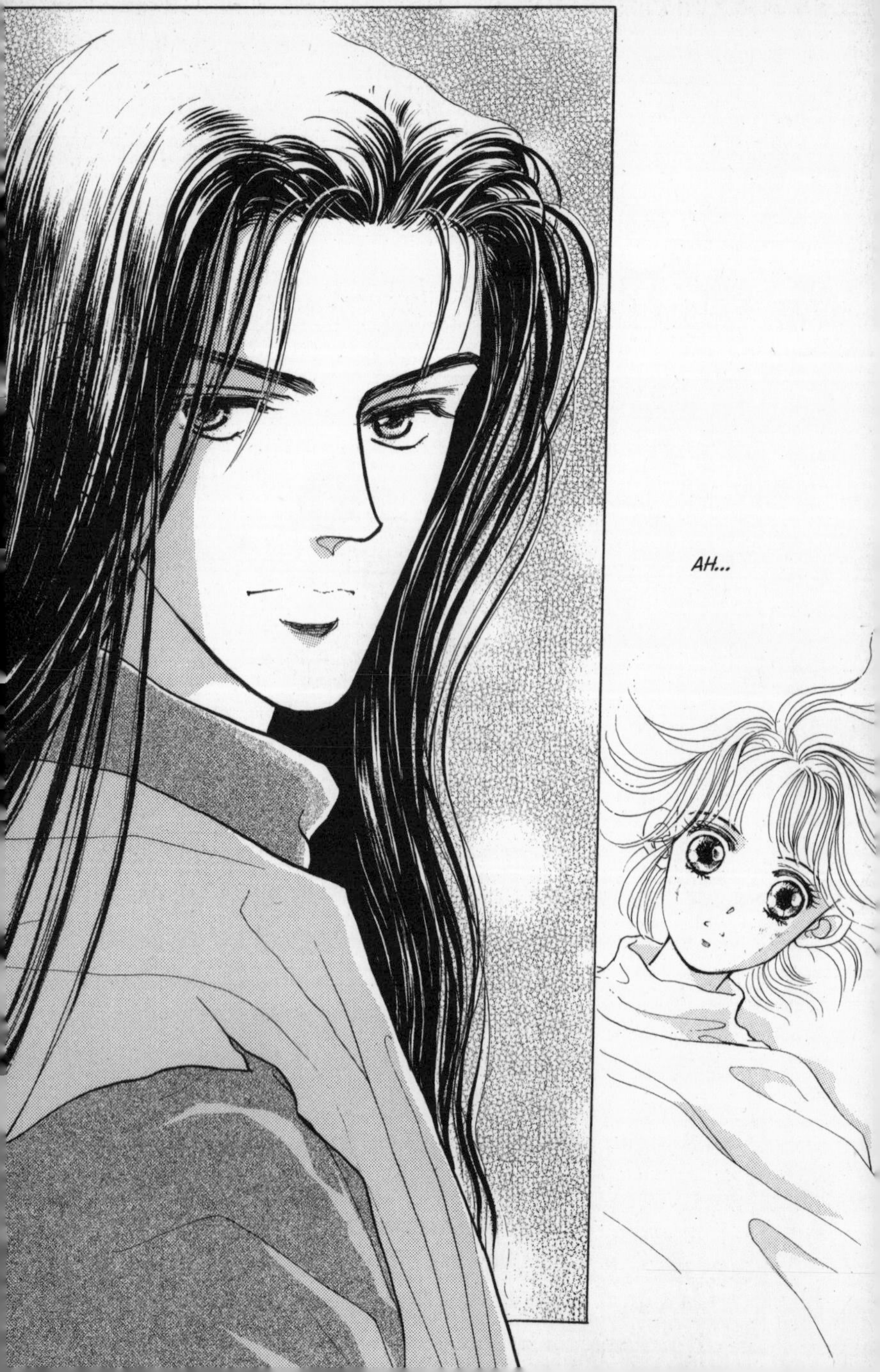
AH...

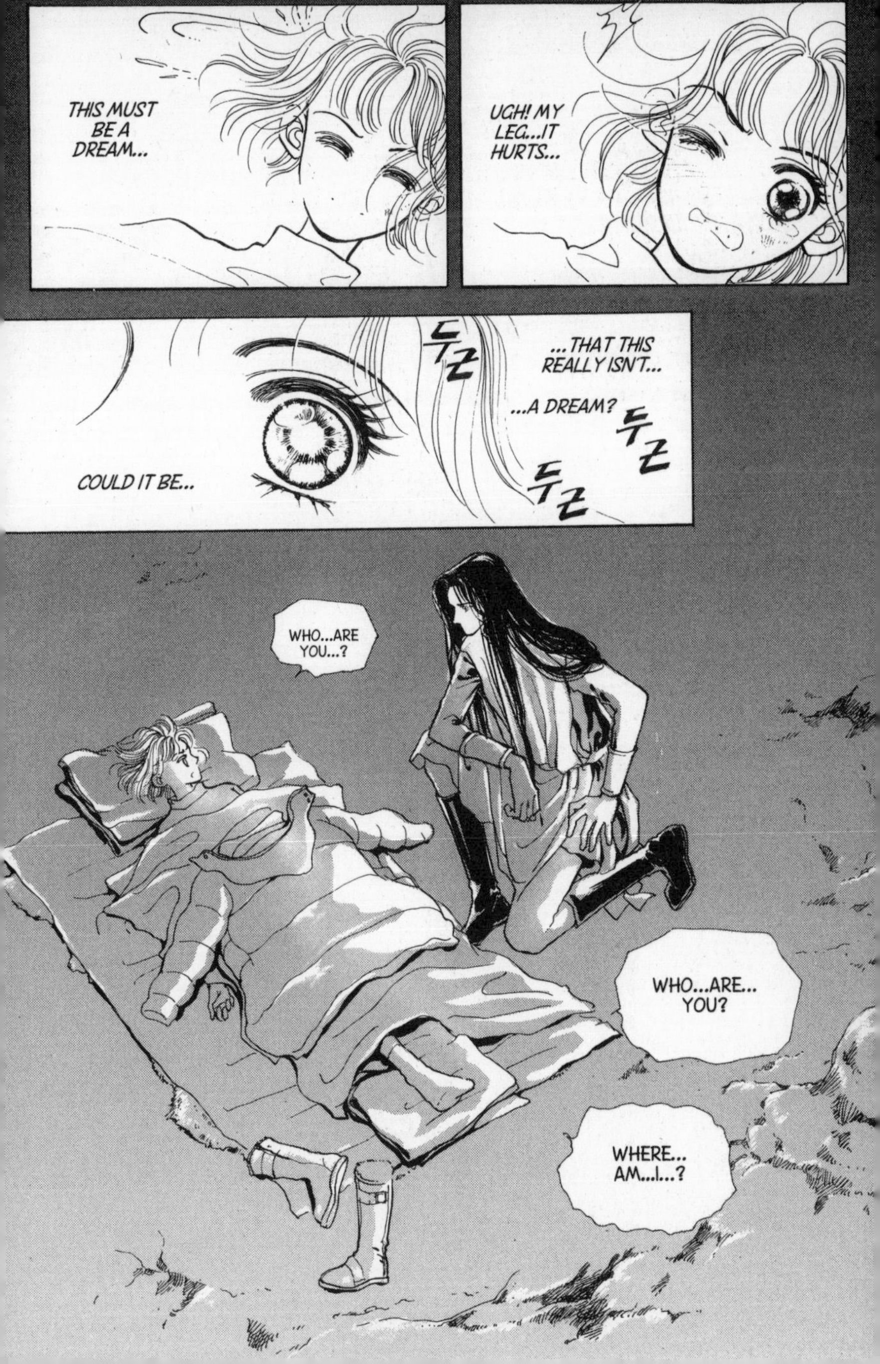
THIS MUST BE A DREAM...
UGH! MY LEG...IT HURTS...
COULD IT BE...
...THAT THIS REALLY ISN'T...
...A DREAM?
두근
두근
두근
WHO...ARE YOU...?
WHO...ARE... YOU?
WHERE... AM...I...?

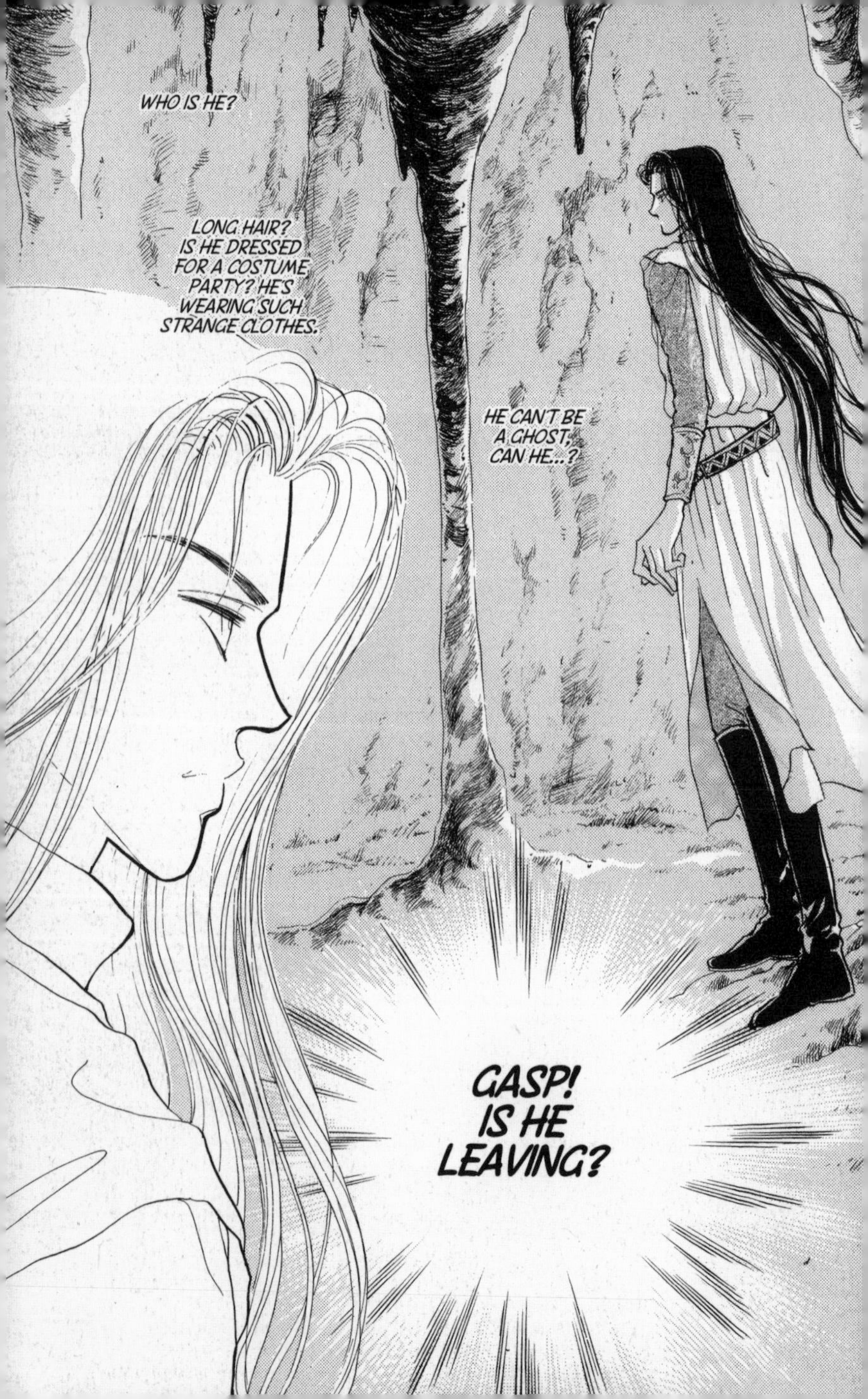
WHO IS HE?
LONG HAIR? IS HE DRESSED FOR A COSTUME PARTY? HE'S WEARING SUCH STRANGE CLOTHES.
HE CAN'T BE A GHOST, CAN HE...?
GASP! IS HE LEAVING?

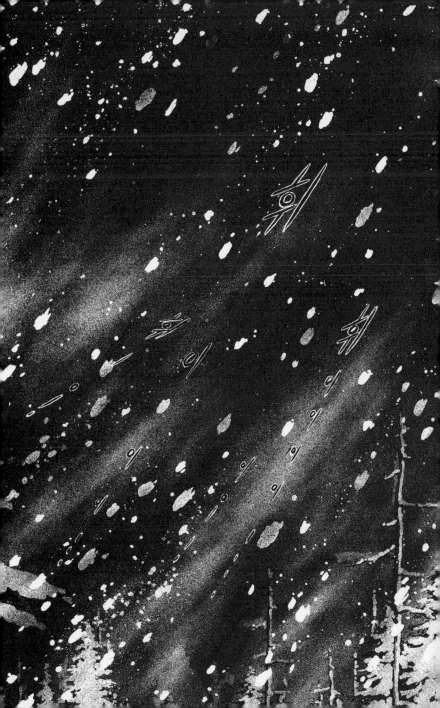

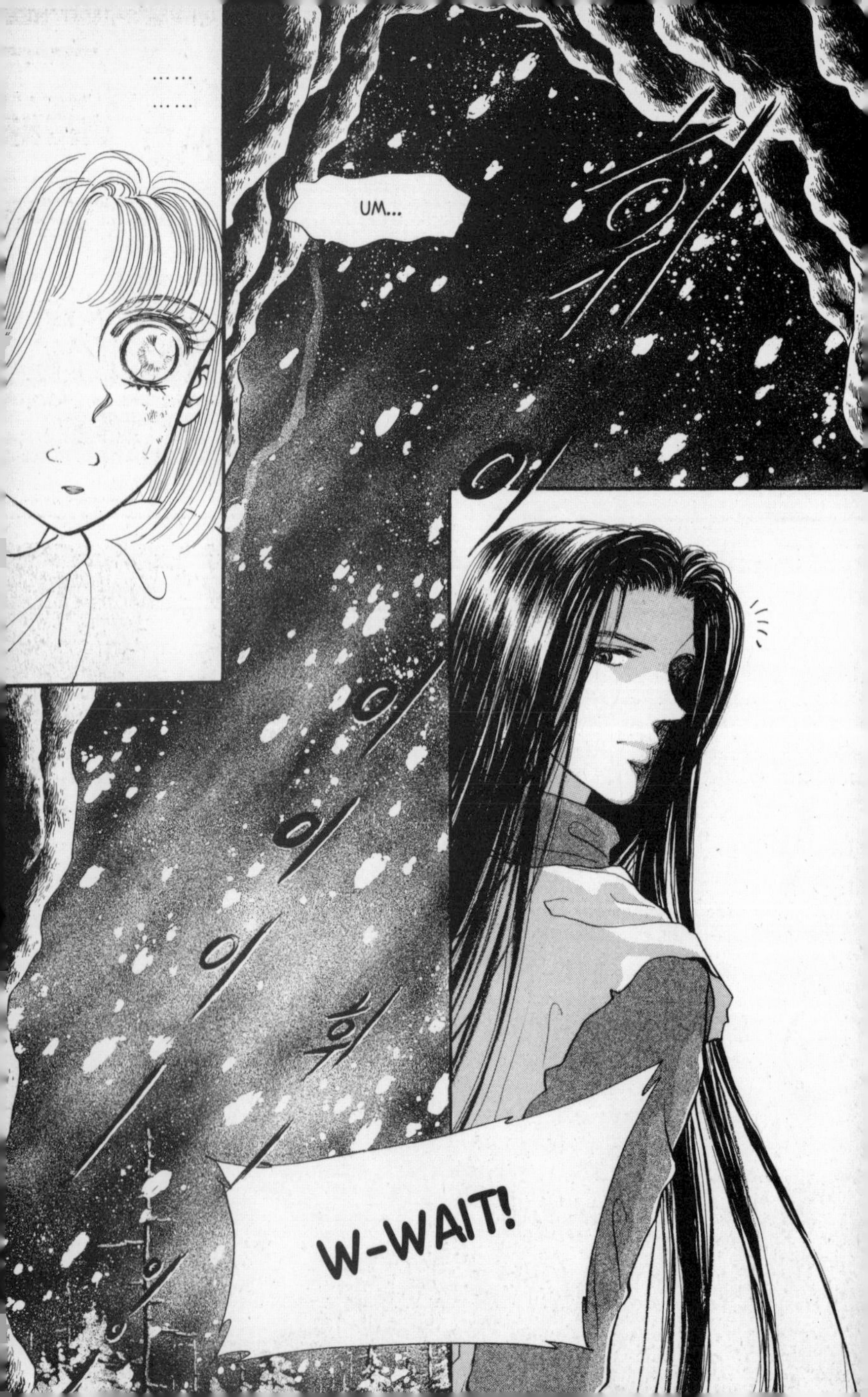
......
......
UM...
W-WAIT!

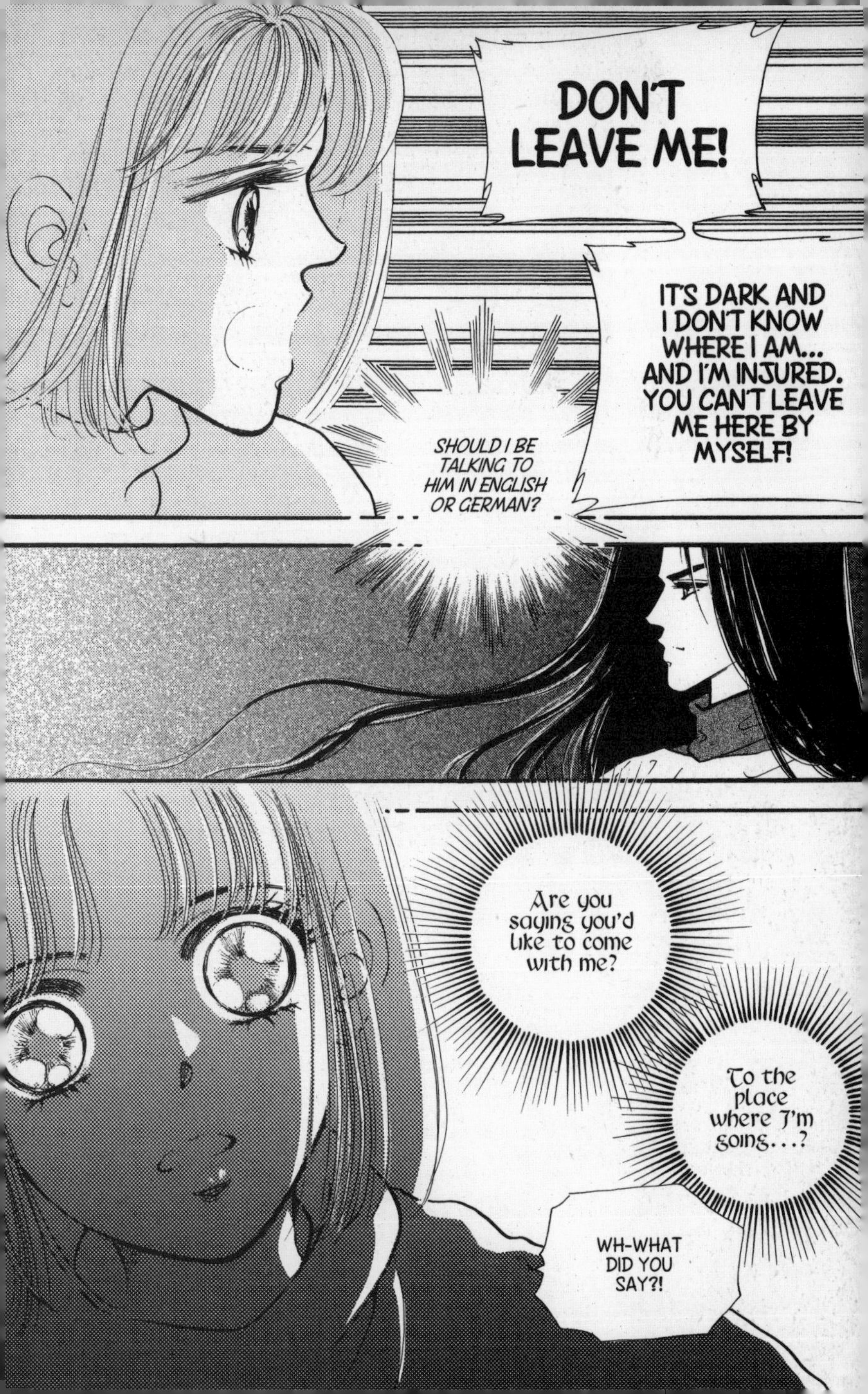
DON'T LEAVE ME!
IT'S DARK AND I DON'T KNOW WHERE I AM... AND I'M INJURED. YOU CAN'T LEAVE ME HERE BY MYSELF!
SHOULD I BE TALKING TO HIM IN ENGLISH OR GERMAN?
Are you saying you'd like to come with me?
To the place where I'm going...?
WH-WHAT DID YOU SAY?!

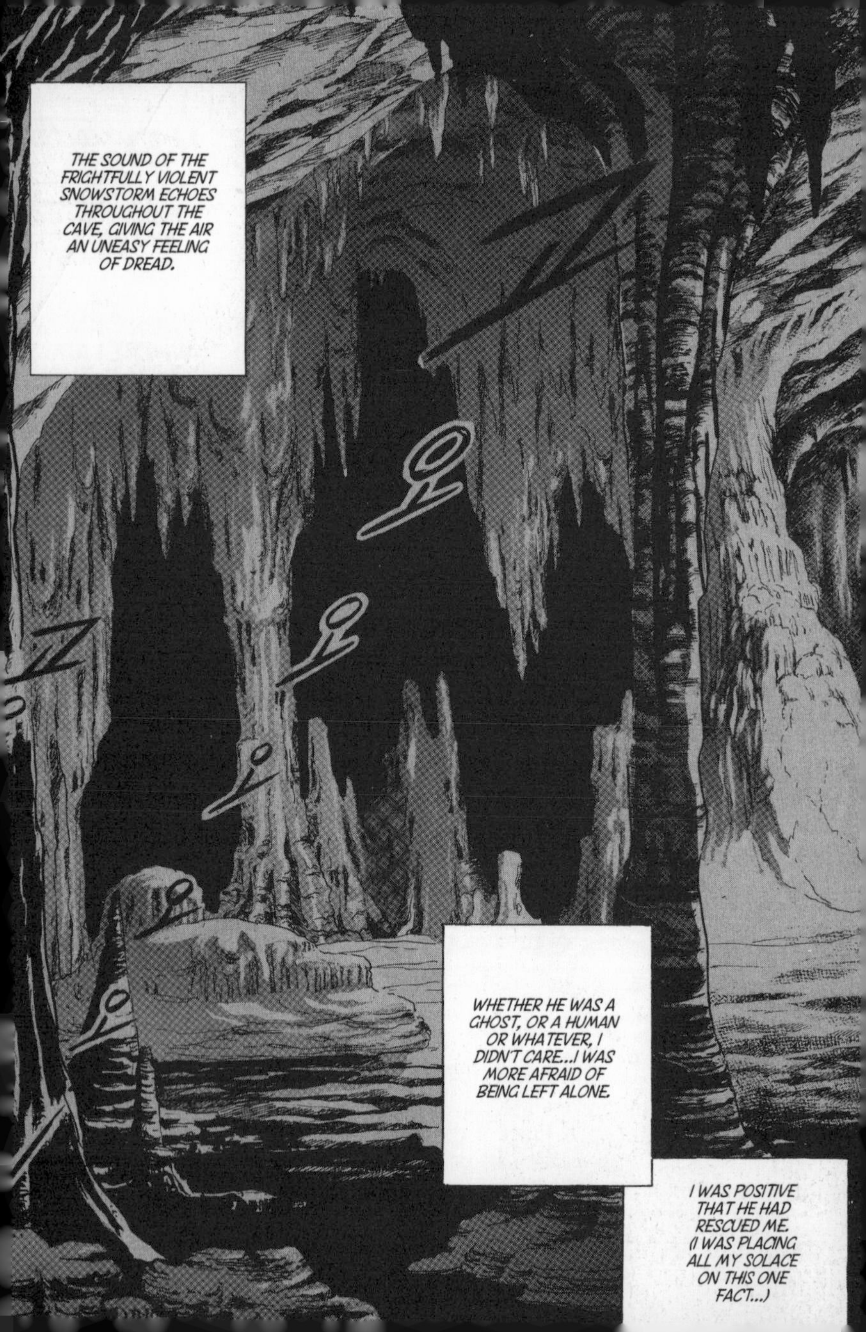
THE SOUND OF THE FRIGHTFULLY VIOLENT SNOWSTORM ECHOES THROUGHOUT THE CAVE, GIVING THE AIR AN UNEASY FEELING OF DREAD.
WHETHER HE WAS A GHOST, OR A HUMAN OR WHATEVER, I DIDN'T CARE...I WAS MORE AFRAID OF BEING LEFT ALONE.
I WAS POSITIVE THAT HE HAD RESCUED ME. (I WAS PLACING ALL MY SOLACE ON THIS ONE FACT...)

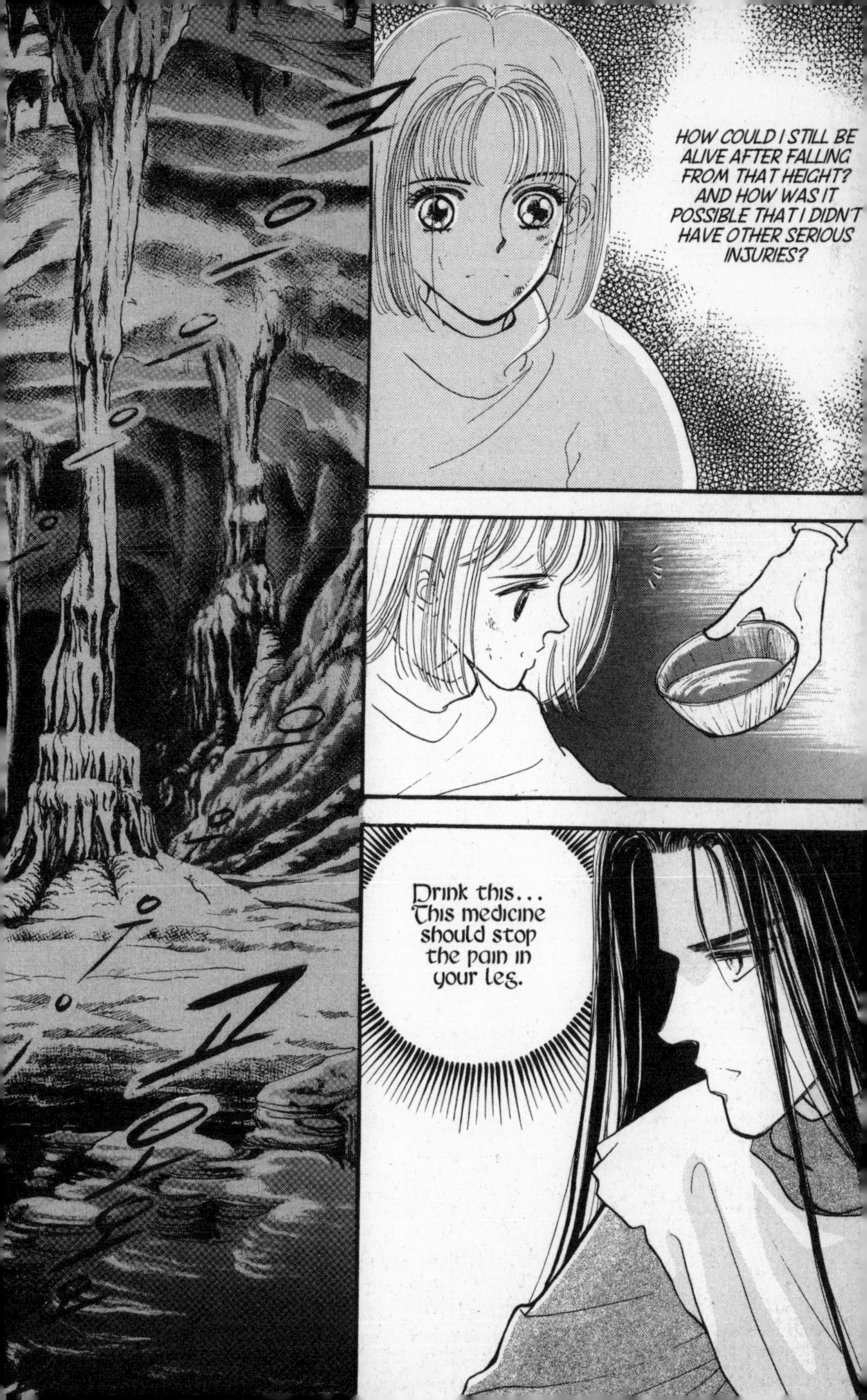
HOW COULD I STILL BE ALIVE AFTER FALLING FROM THAT HEIGHT? AND HOW WAS IT POSSIBLE THAT I DIDN'T HAVE OTHER SERIOUS INJURIES?
Drink this... This medicine should stop the pain in your leg.

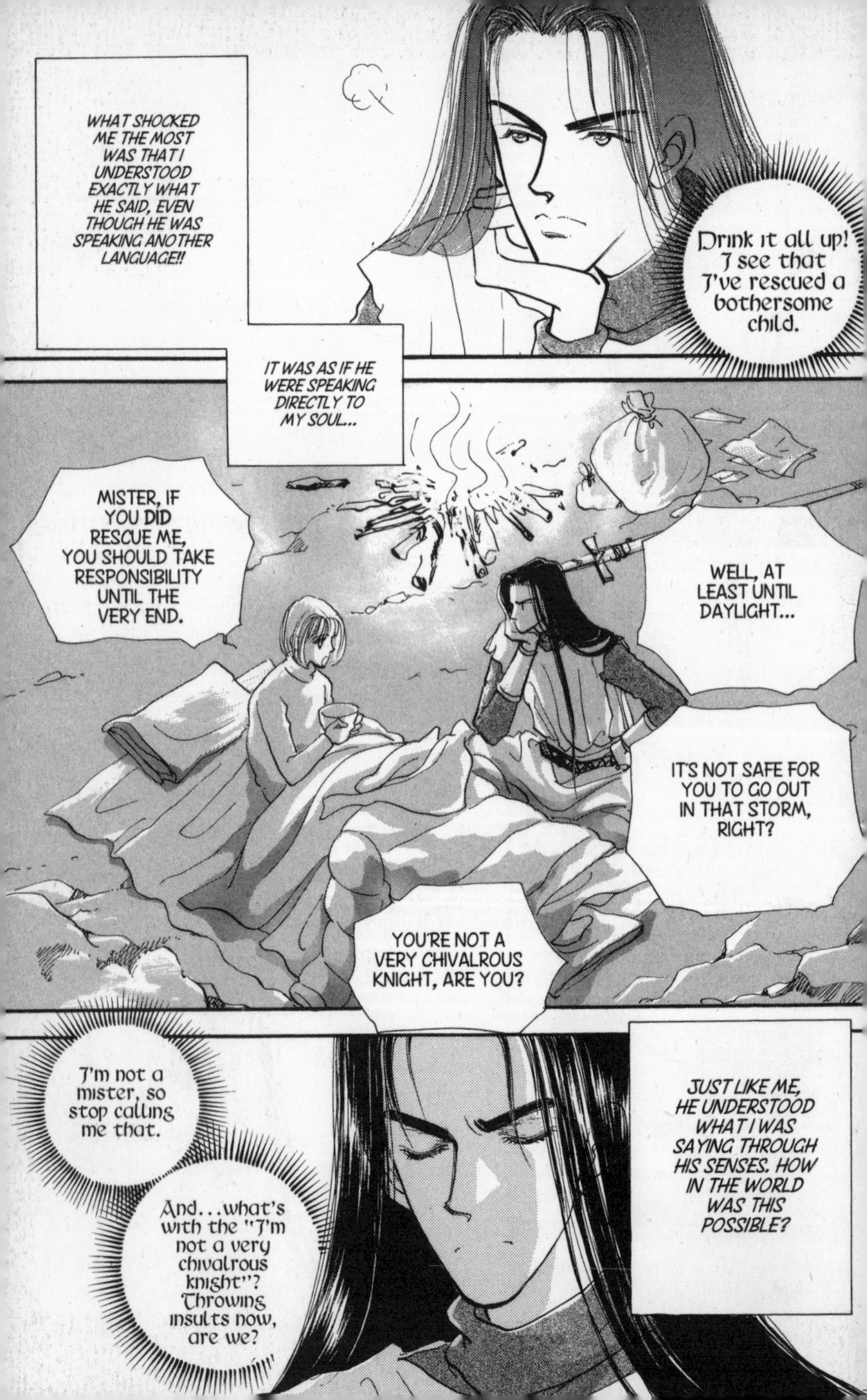
WHAT SHOCKED ME THE MOST WAS THAT I UNDERSTOOD EXACTLY WHAT HE SAID, EVEN THOUGH HE WAS SPEAKING ANOTHER LANGUAGE!!
Drink it all up! I see that I've rescued a bothersome child.
IT WAS AS IF HE WERE SPEAKING DIRECTLY TO MY SOUL...
MISTER, IF YOU **DID** RESCUE ME, YOU SHOULD TAKE RESPONSIBILITY UNTIL THE VERY END.
WELL, AT LEAST UNTIL DAYLIGHT...
IT'S NOT SAFE FOR YOU TO GO OUT IN THAT STORM, RIGHT?
YOU'RE NOT A VERY CHIVALROUS KNIGHT, ARE YOU?
I'm not a mister, so stop calling me that.
And...what's with the "I'm not a very chivalrous knight"? Throwing insults now, are we?
JUST LIKE ME, HE UNDERSTOOD WHAT I WAS SAYING THROUGH HIS SENSES. HOW IN THE WORLD WAS THIS POSSIBLE?

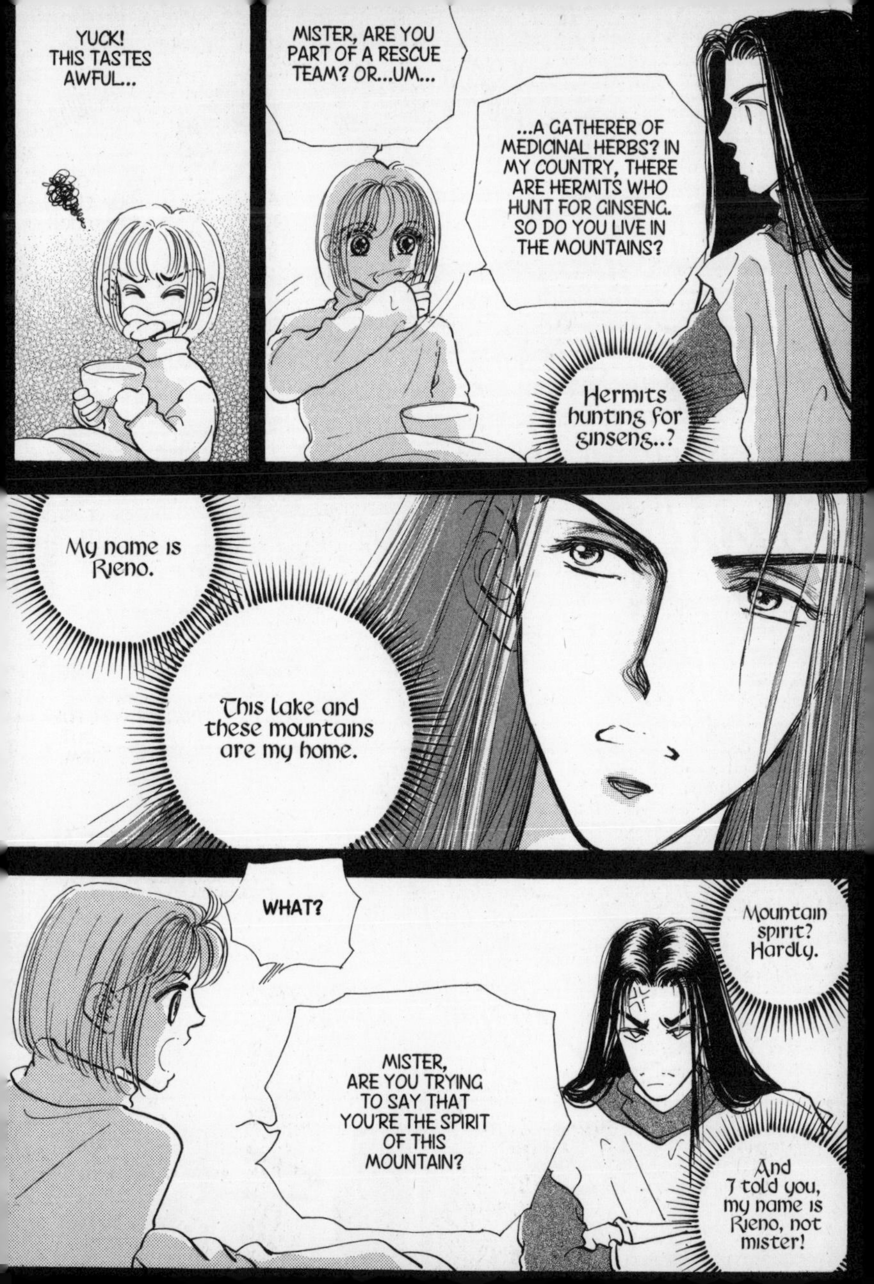
YUCK! THIS TASTES AWFUL...
MISTER, ARE YOU PART OF A RESCUE TEAM? OR...UM...
...A GATHERER OF MEDICINAL HERBS? IN MY COUNTRY, THERE ARE HERMITS WHO HUNT FOR GINSENG. SO DO YOU LIVE IN THE MOUNTAINS?
Hermits hunting for ginseng..?
My name is Rieno.
This lake and these mountains are my home.
WHAT?
MISTER, ARE YOU TRYING TO SAY THAT YOU'RE THE SPIRIT OF THIS MOUNTAIN?
Mountain spirit? Hardly.
And I told you, my name is Rieno, not mister!

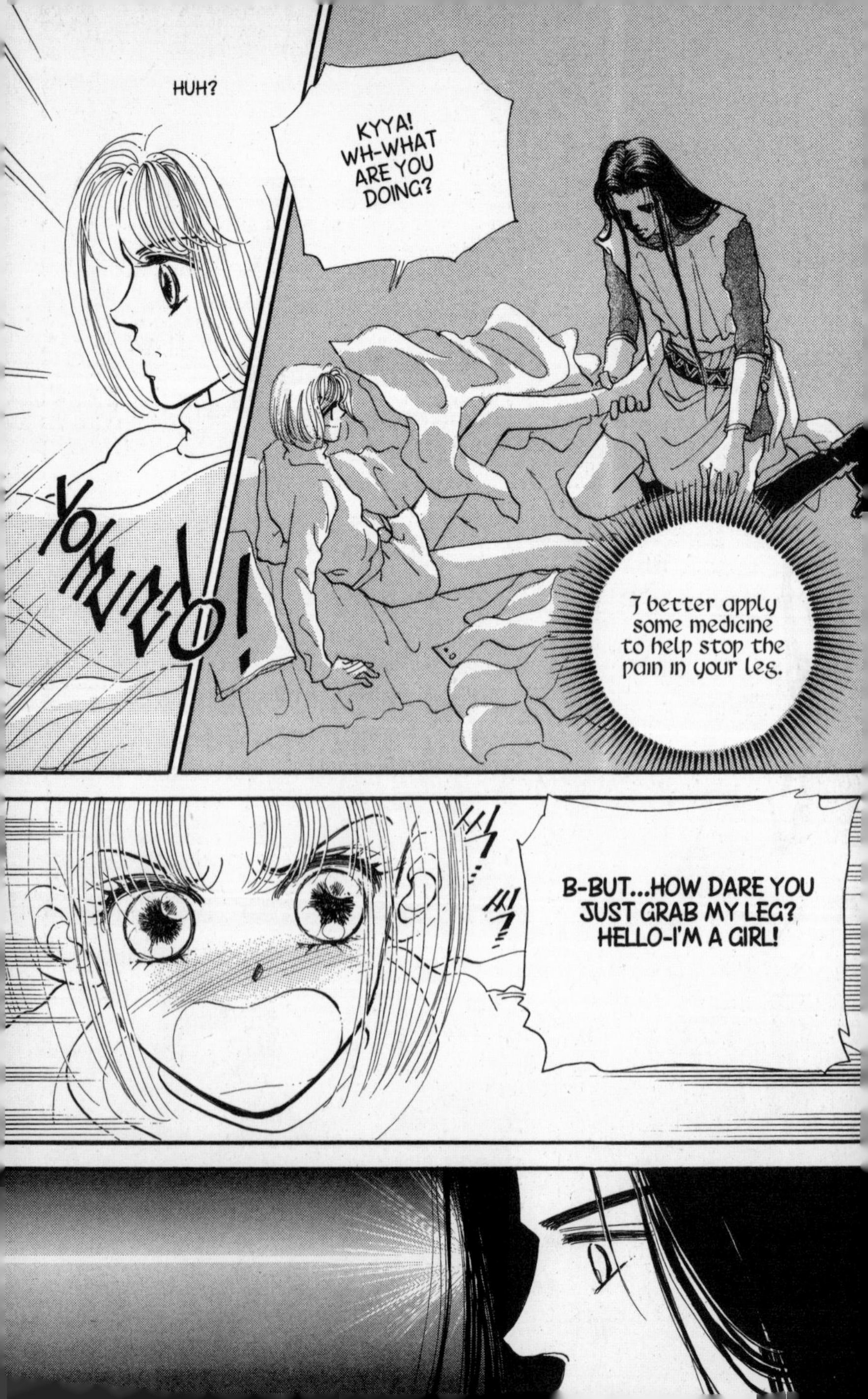
HUH?
YOHUEO!
KYYA! WH-WHAT ARE YOU DOING?
I better apply some medicine to help stop the pain in your leg.
씩...
씩...
B-BUT...HOW DARE YOU JUST GRAB MY LEG? HELLO-I'M A GIRL!

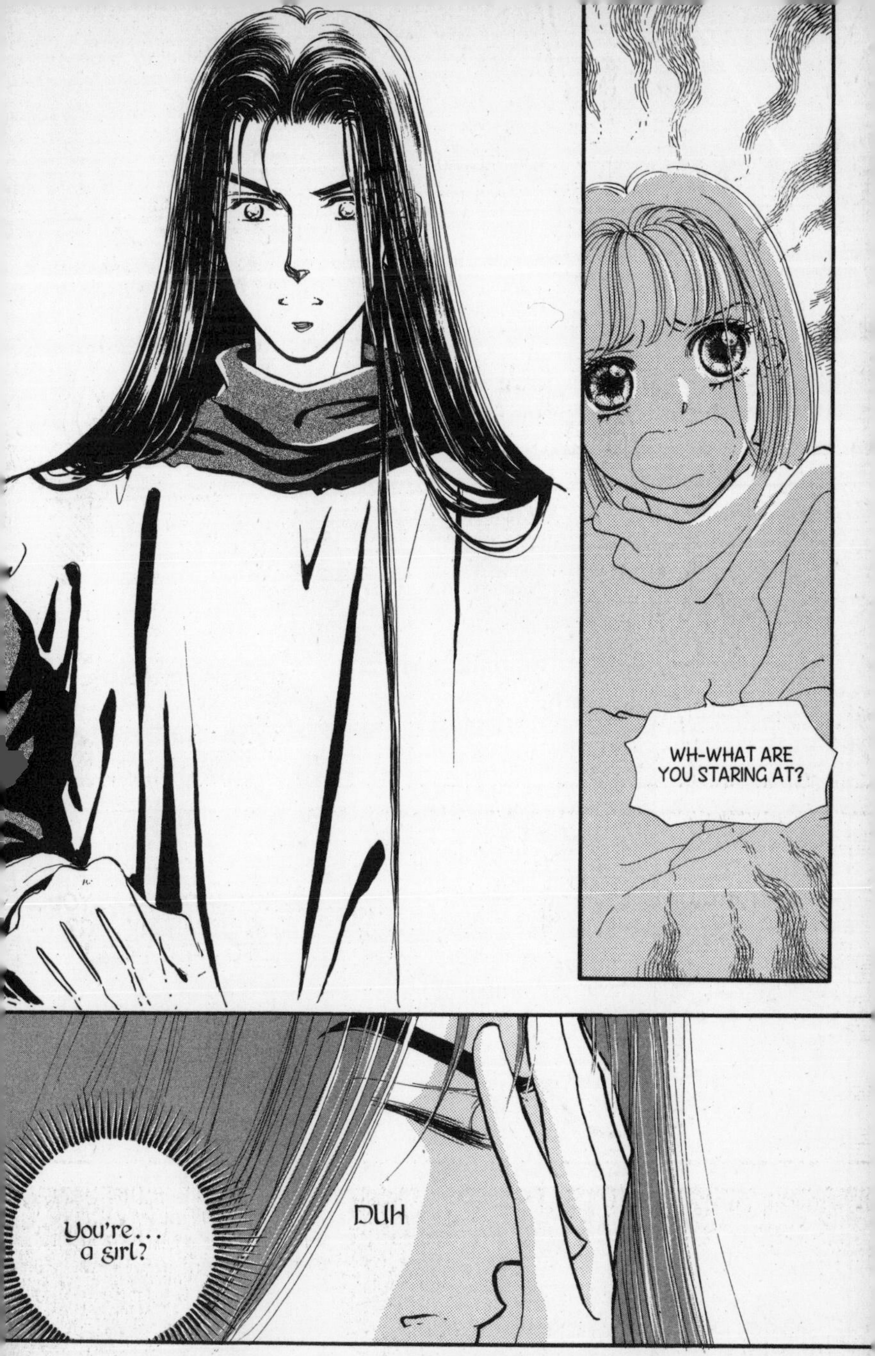
WH-WHAT ARE YOU STARING AT?
You're... a girl?
DUH

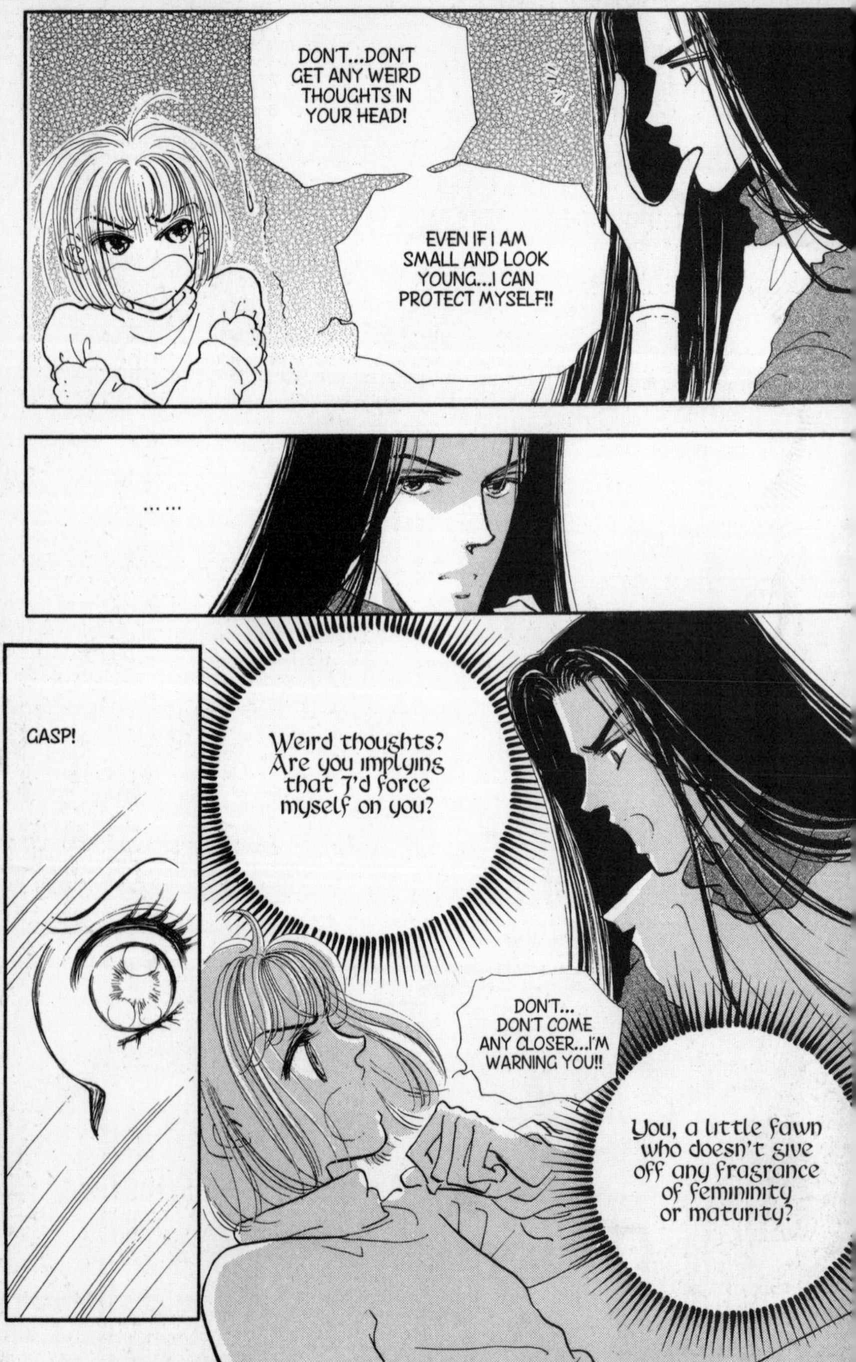
DON'T...DON'T GET ANY WEIRD THOUGHTS IN YOUR HEAD!
EVEN IF I AM SMALL AND LOOK YOUNG...I CAN PROTECT MYSELF!!
......
GASP!
Weird thoughts? Are you implying that I'd force myself on you?
DON'T... DON'T COME ANY CLOSER...I'M WARNING YOU!!
You, a little fawn who doesn't give off any fragrance of femininity or maturity?

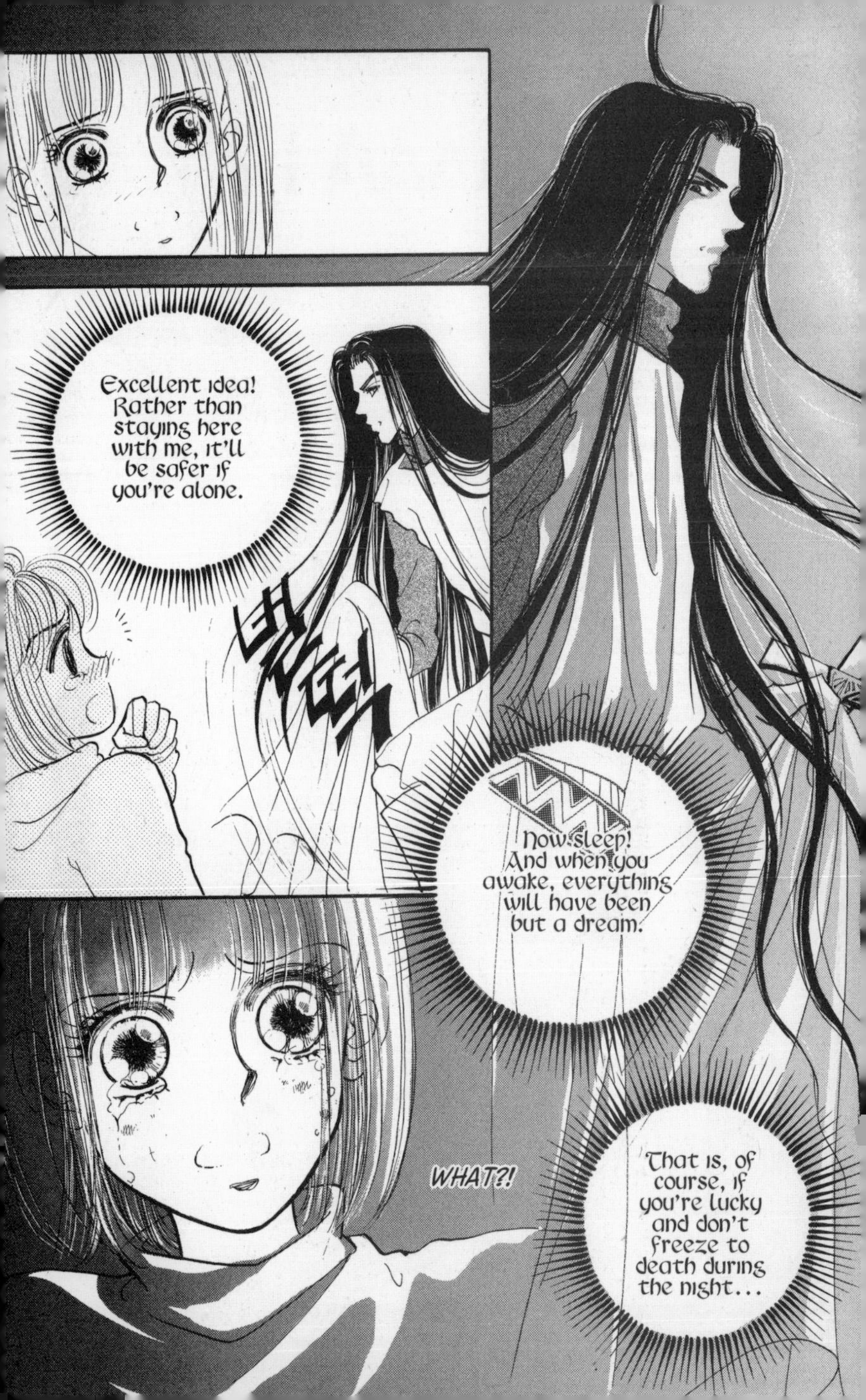
Excellent idea! Rather than staying here with me, it'll be safer if you're alone.
Now sleep! And when you awake, everything will have been but a dream.
WHAT?!
That is, of course, if you're lucky and don't freeze to death during the night...

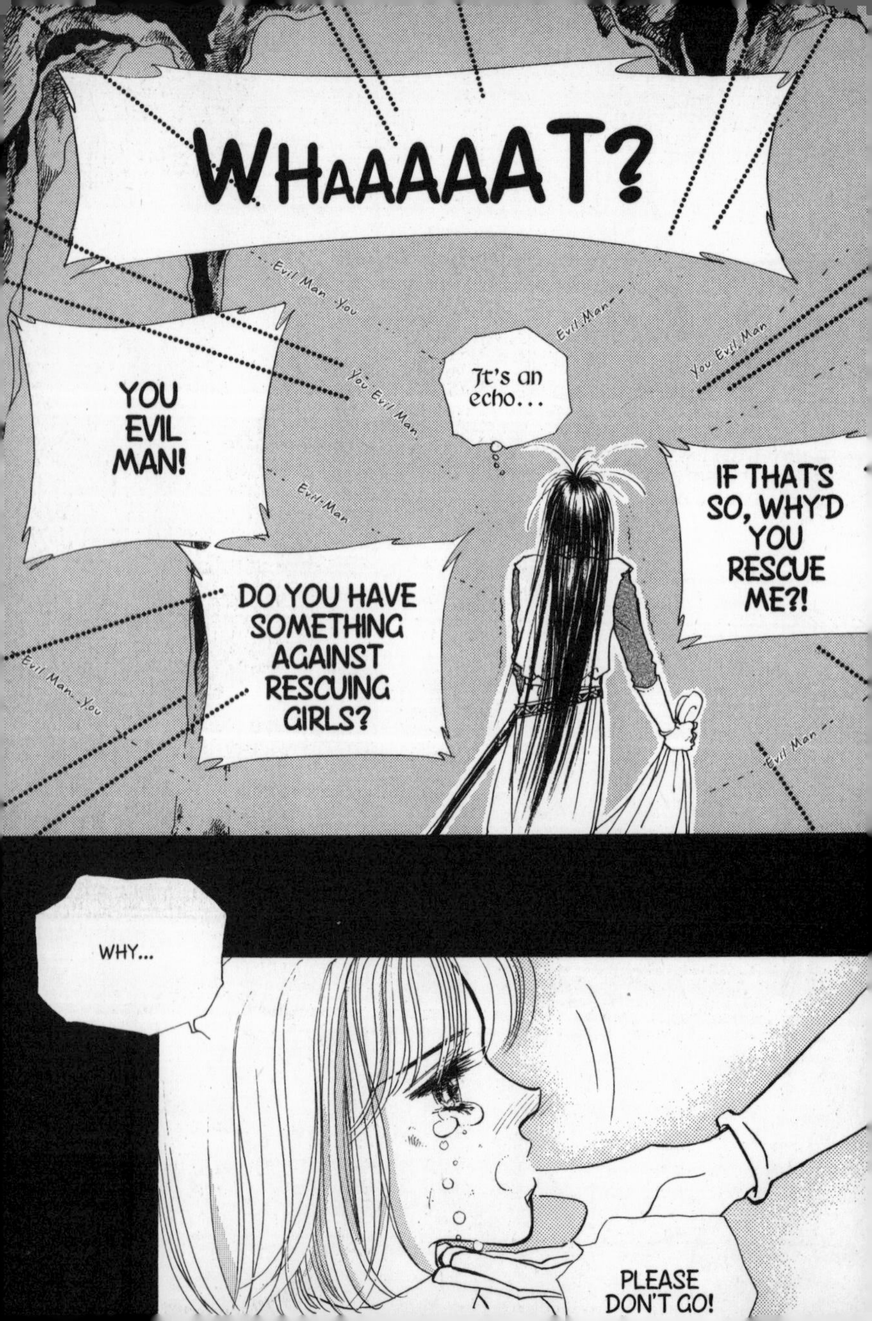
WHAAAAAT?
YOU EVIL MAN!
Evil Man -You
You Evil Man
Evil Man
Evil Man
You Evil Man
It's an echo...
IF THAT'S SO, WHY'D YOU RESCUE ME?!
DO YOU HAVE SOMETHING AGAINST RESCUING GIRLS?
Evil Man -You
Evil Man
WHY...
PLEASE DON'T GO!

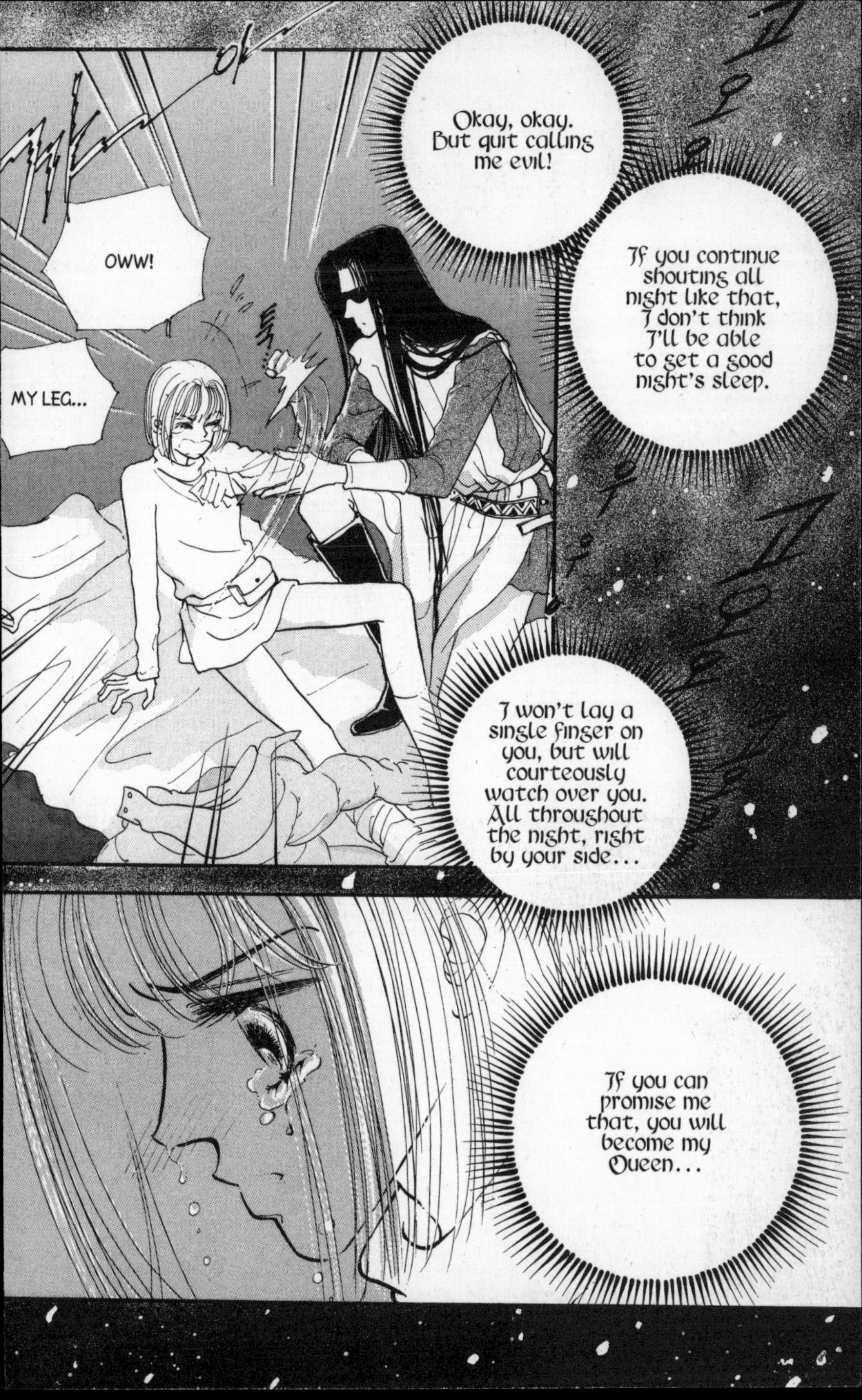
OWW!
MY LEG...
Okay, okay. But quit calling me evil!
If you continue shouting all night like that, I don't think I'll be able to get a good night's sleep.
I won't lay a single finger on you, but will courteously watch over you. All throughout the night, right by your side...
If you can promise me that, you will become my Queen...

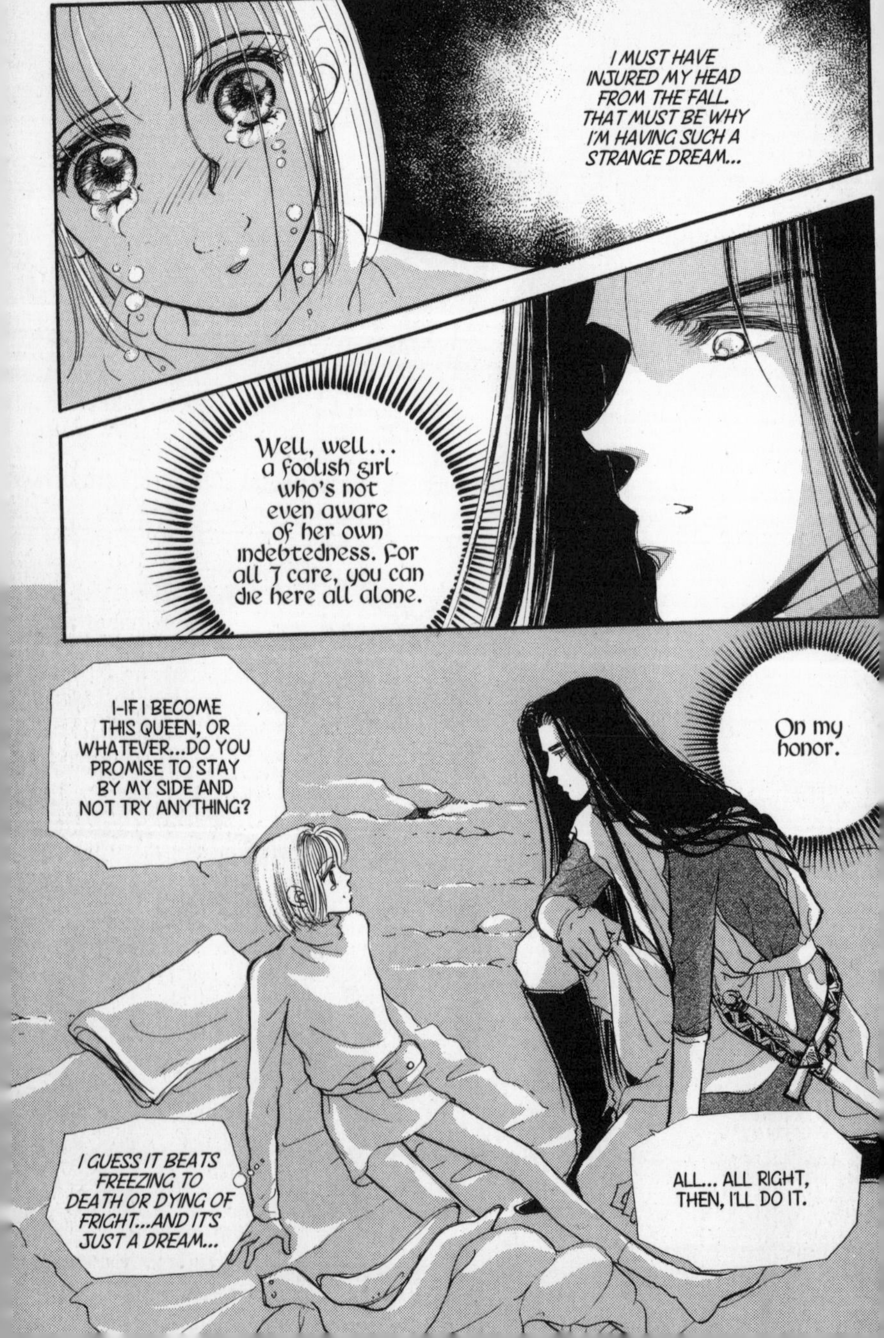
I MUST HAVE INJURED MY HEAD FROM THE FALL. THAT MUST BE WHY I'M HAVING SUCH A STRANGE DREAM...
Well, well... a foolish girl who's not even aware of her own indebtedness. For all I care, you can die here all alone.
I-IF I BECOME THIS QUEEN, OR WHATEVER...DO YOU PROMISE TO STAY BY MY SIDE AND NOT TRY ANYTHING?
On my honor.
I GUESS IT BEATS FREEZING TO DEATH OR DYING OF FRIGHT...AND ITS JUST A DREAM...
ALL... ALL RIGHT, THEN, I'LL DO IT.

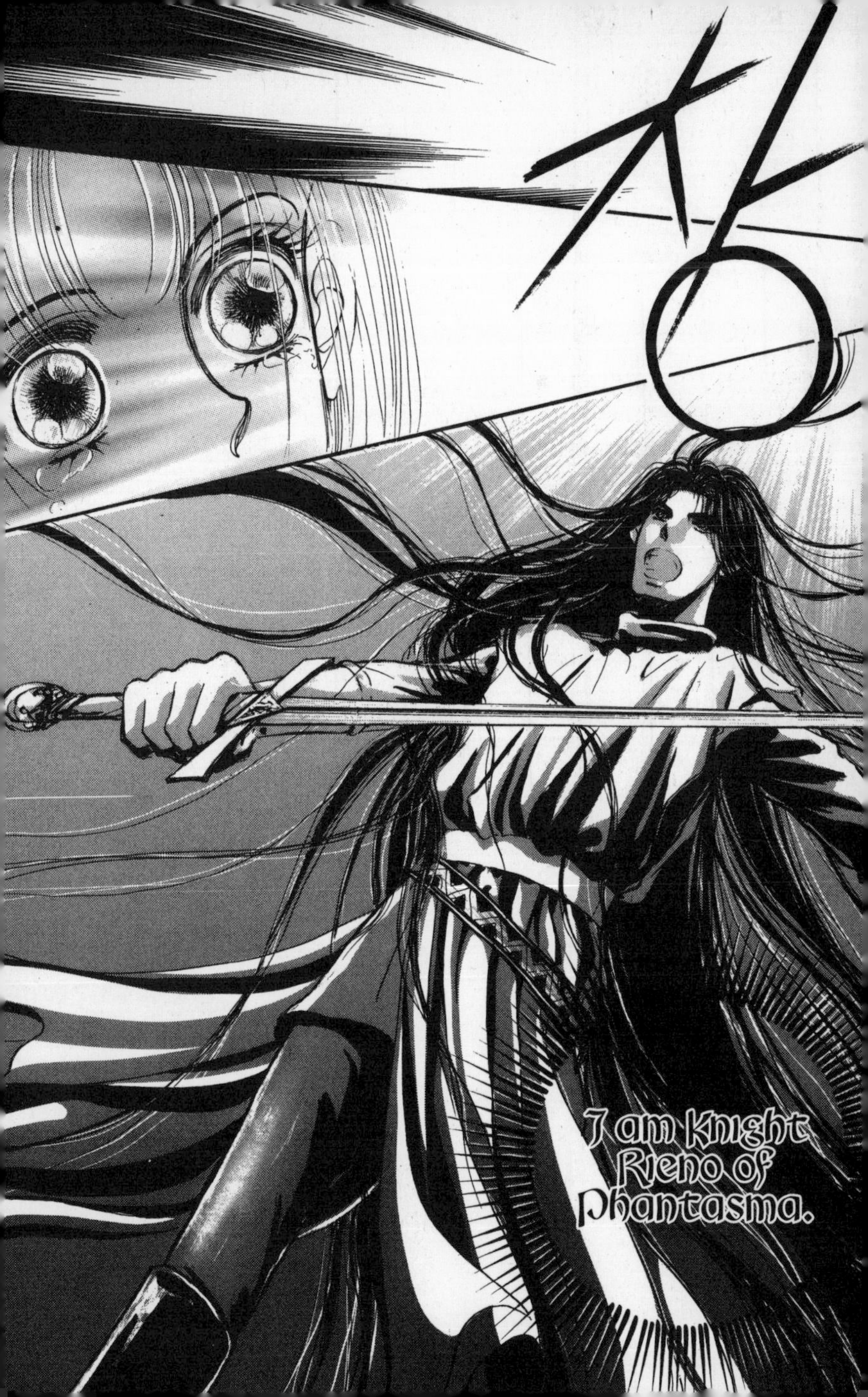
I am Knight Rieno of Phantasma.

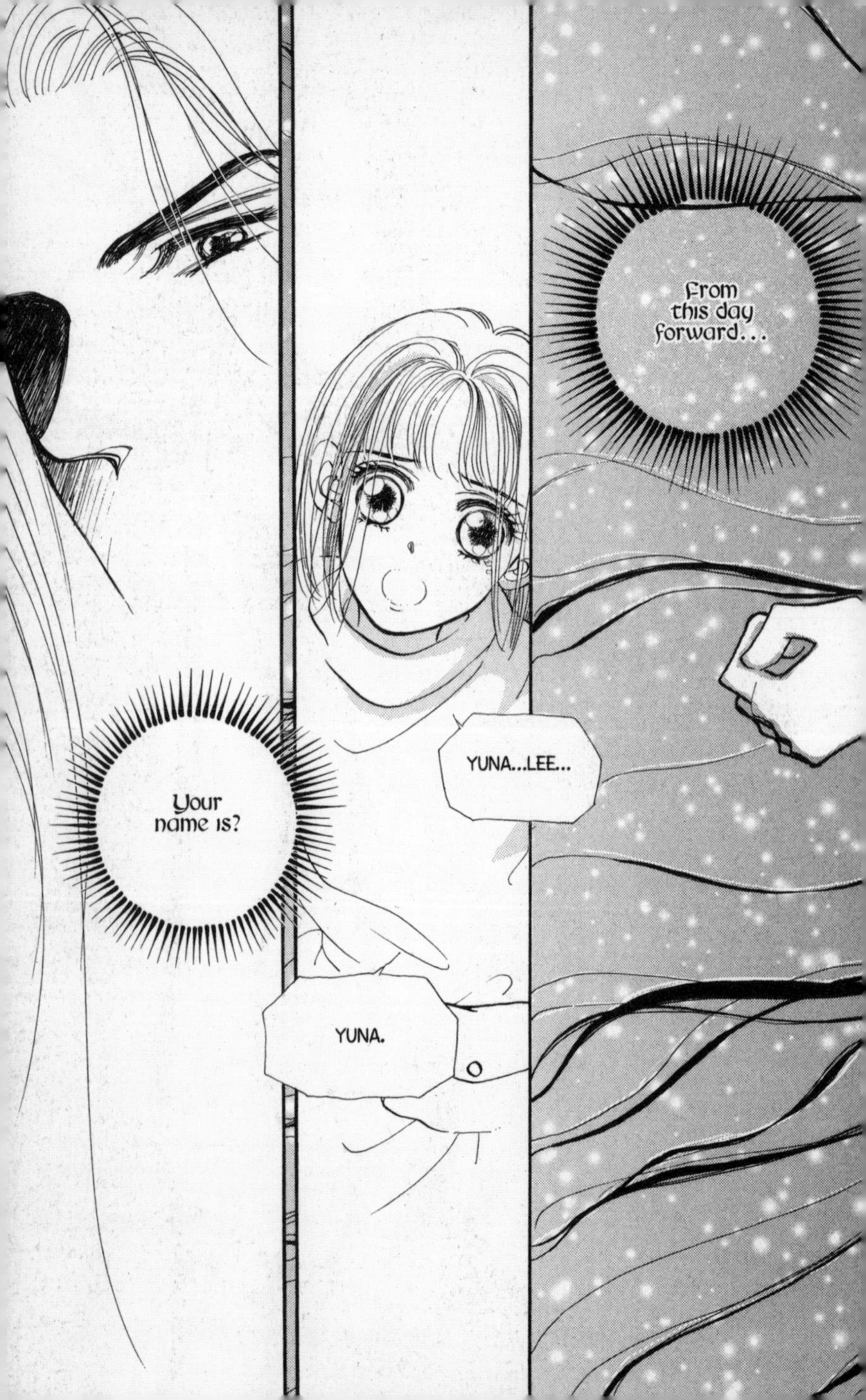
Your name is?
YUNA...LEE...
YUNA.
From this day forward...

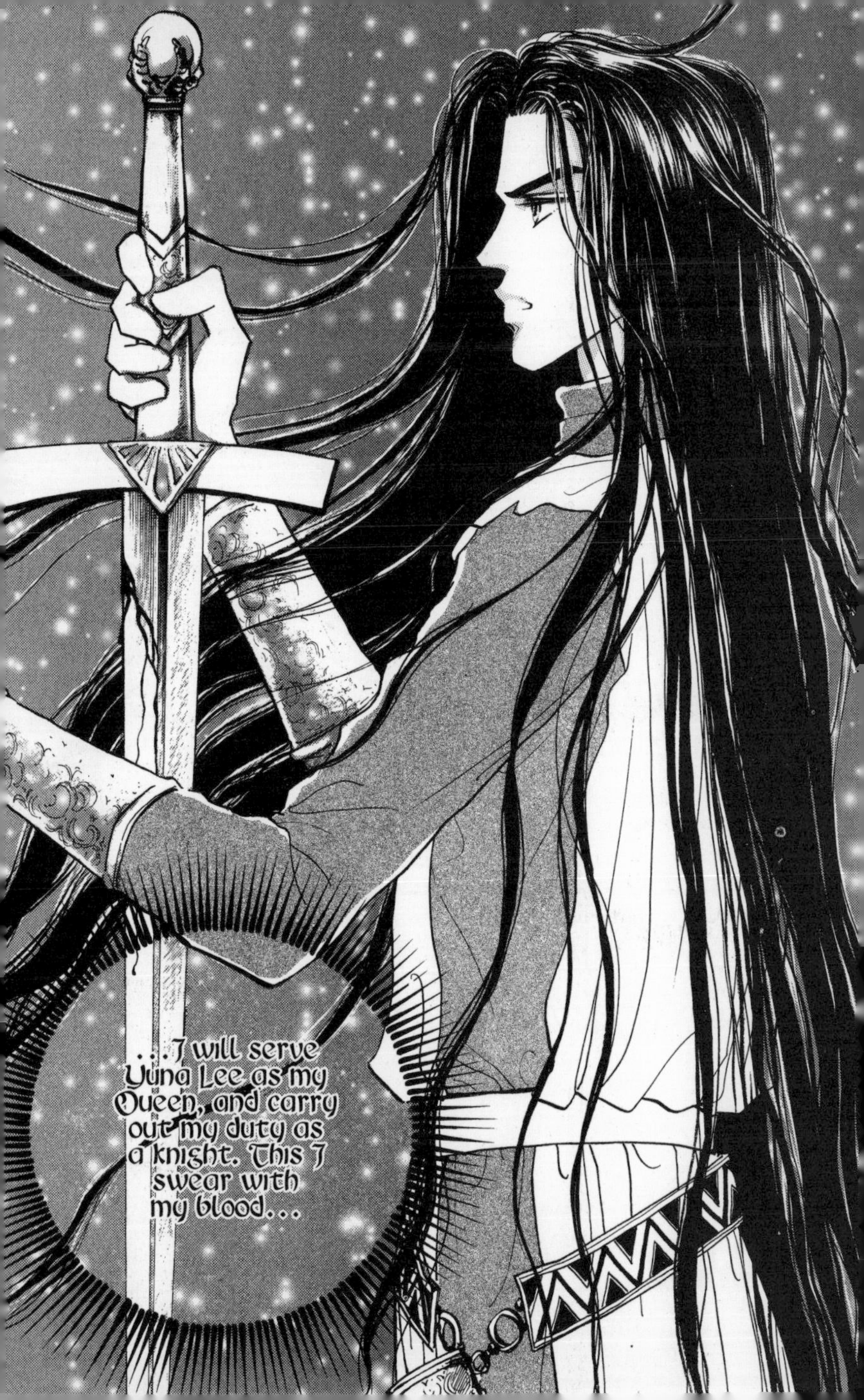
...I will serve Yuna Lee as my Queen, and carry out my duty as a knight. This I swear with my blood...

Back at home...

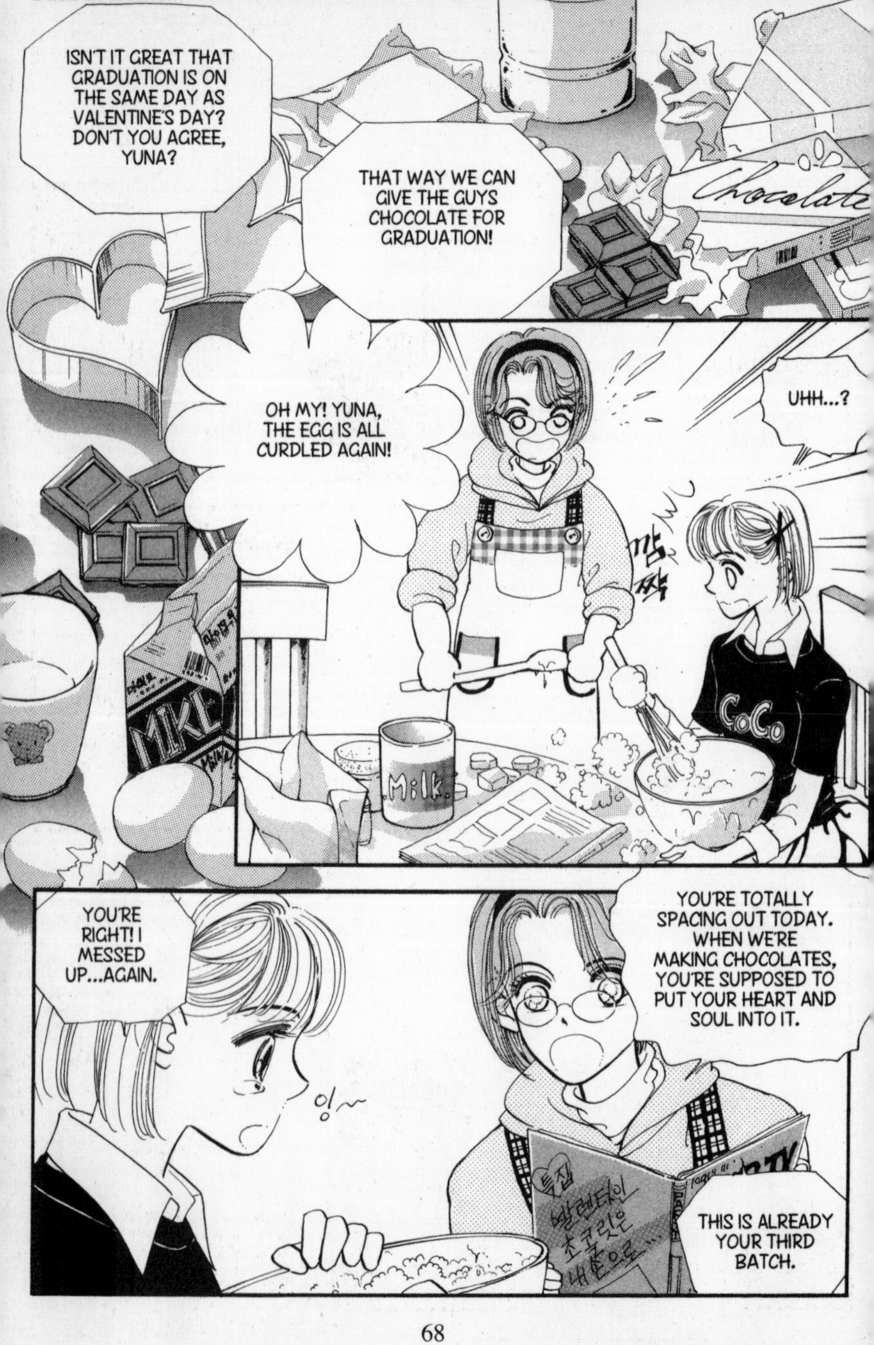

ISN'T IT GREAT THAT GRADUATION IS ON THE SAME DAY AS VALENTINE'S DAY? DON'T YOU AGREE, YUNA?
THAT WAY WE CAN GIVE THE GUYS CHOCOLATE FOR GRADUATION!
Chocolate
OH MY! YUNA, THE EGG IS ALL CURDLED AGAIN!
UHH...?
깜짝
Milk
CoCo
YOU'RE RIGHT! I MESSED UP...AGAIN.
YOU'RE TOTALLY SPACING OUT TODAY. WHEN WE'RE MAKING CHOCOLATES, YOU'RE SUPPOSED TO PUT YOUR HEART AND SOUL INTO IT.
THIS IS ALREADY YOUR THIRD BATCH.

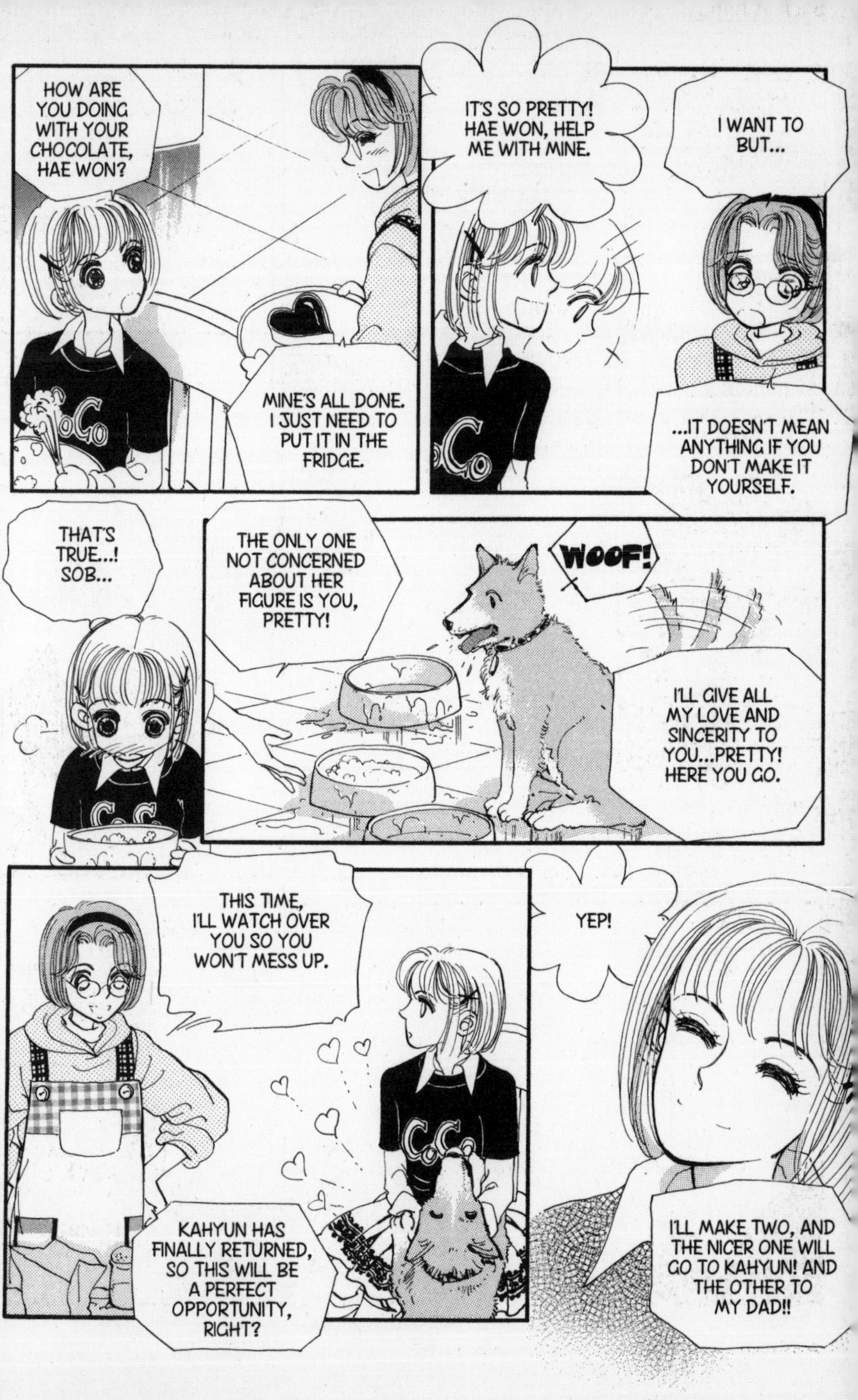
HOW ARE YOU DOING WITH YOUR CHOCOLATE, HAE WON?
MINE'S ALL DONE. I JUST NEED TO PUT IT IN THE FRIDGE.
IT'S SO PRETTY! HAE WON, HELP ME WITH MINE.
I WANT TO BUT...
...IT DOESN'T MEAN ANYTHING IF YOU DON'T MAKE IT YOURSELF.
THAT'S TRUE...! SOB...
THE ONLY ONE NOT CONCERNED ABOUT HER FIGURE IS YOU, PRETTY!
WOOF!
I'LL GIVE ALL MY LOVE AND SINCERITY TO YOU...PRETTY! HERE YOU GO.
THIS TIME, I'LL WATCH OVER YOU SO YOU WON'T MESS UP.
KAHYUN HAS FINALLY RETURNED, SO THIS WILL BE A PERFECT OPPORTUNITY, RIGHT?
YEP!
I'LL MAKE TWO, AND THE NICER ONE WILL GO TO KAHYUN! AND THE OTHER TO MY DAD!!

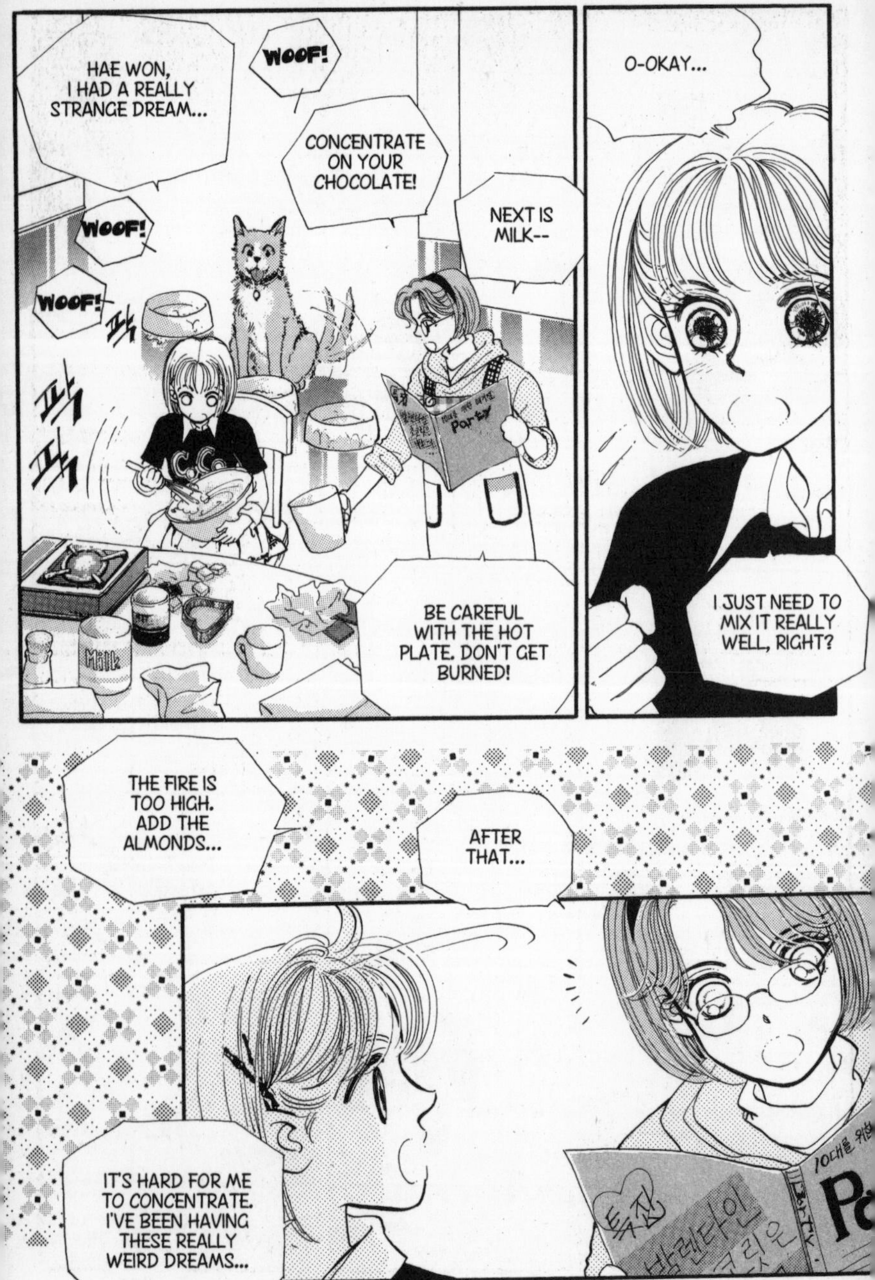
HAE WON, I HAD A REALLY STRANGE DREAM...
WOOF!
CONCENTRATE ON YOUR CHOCOLATE!
WOOF!
WOOF!
NEXT IS MILK--
Milk
BE CAREFUL WITH THE HOT PLATE. DON'T GET BURNED!
O-OKAY...
I JUST NEED TO MIX IT REALLY WELL, RIGHT?
THE FIRE IS TOO HIGH. ADD THE ALMONDS...
AFTER THAT...
IT'S HARD FOR ME TO CONCENTRATE. I'VE BEEN HAVING THESE REALLY WEIRD DREAMS...

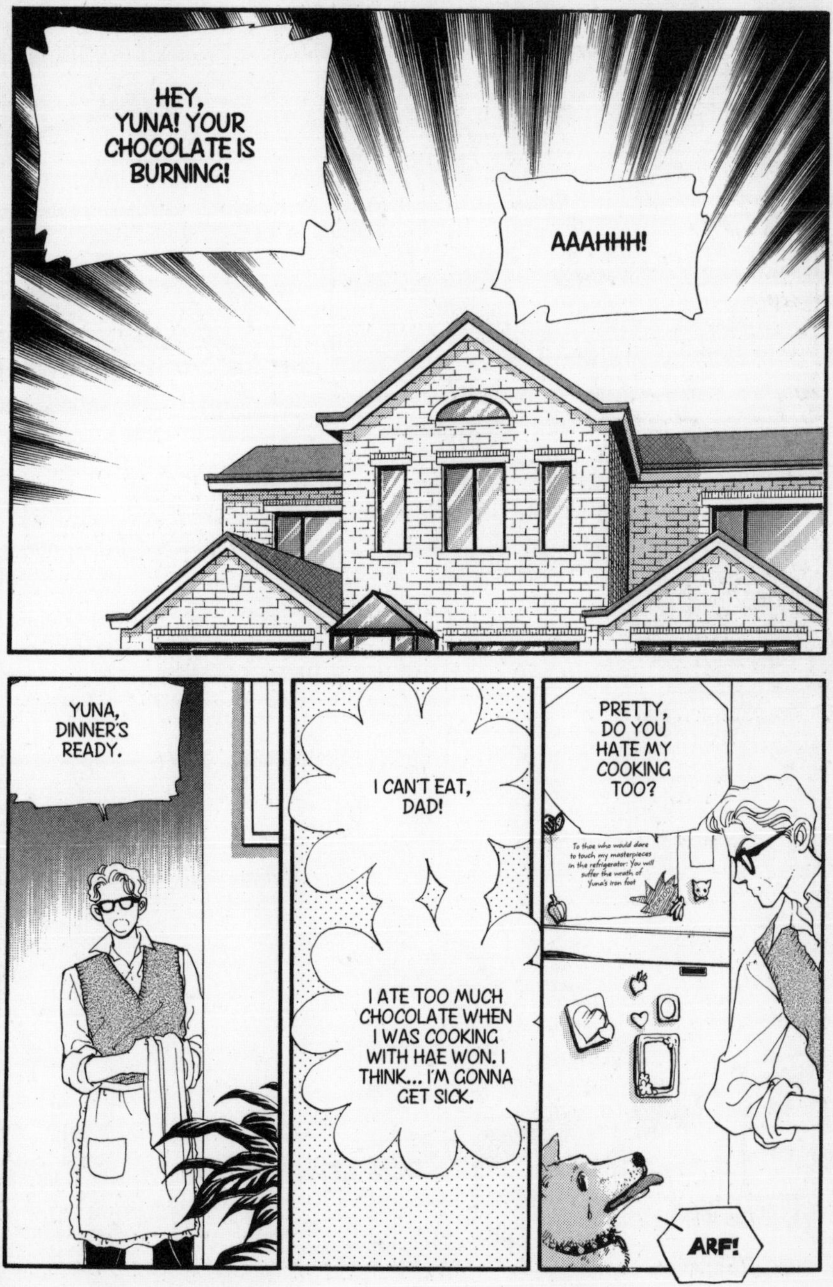
HEY, YUNA! YOUR CHOCOLATE IS BURNING!
AAAHHH!
YUNA, DINNER'S READY.
I CAN'T EAT, DAD!
I ATE TOO MUCH CHOCOLATE WHEN I WAS COOKING WITH HAE WON. I THINK... I'M GONNA GET SICK.
PRETTY, DO YOU HATE MY COOKING TOO?
To thoe who would dare to touch my masterpieces in the refrigerator: You will suffer the wrath of Yuna's iron foot
PERIOD!
ARF!

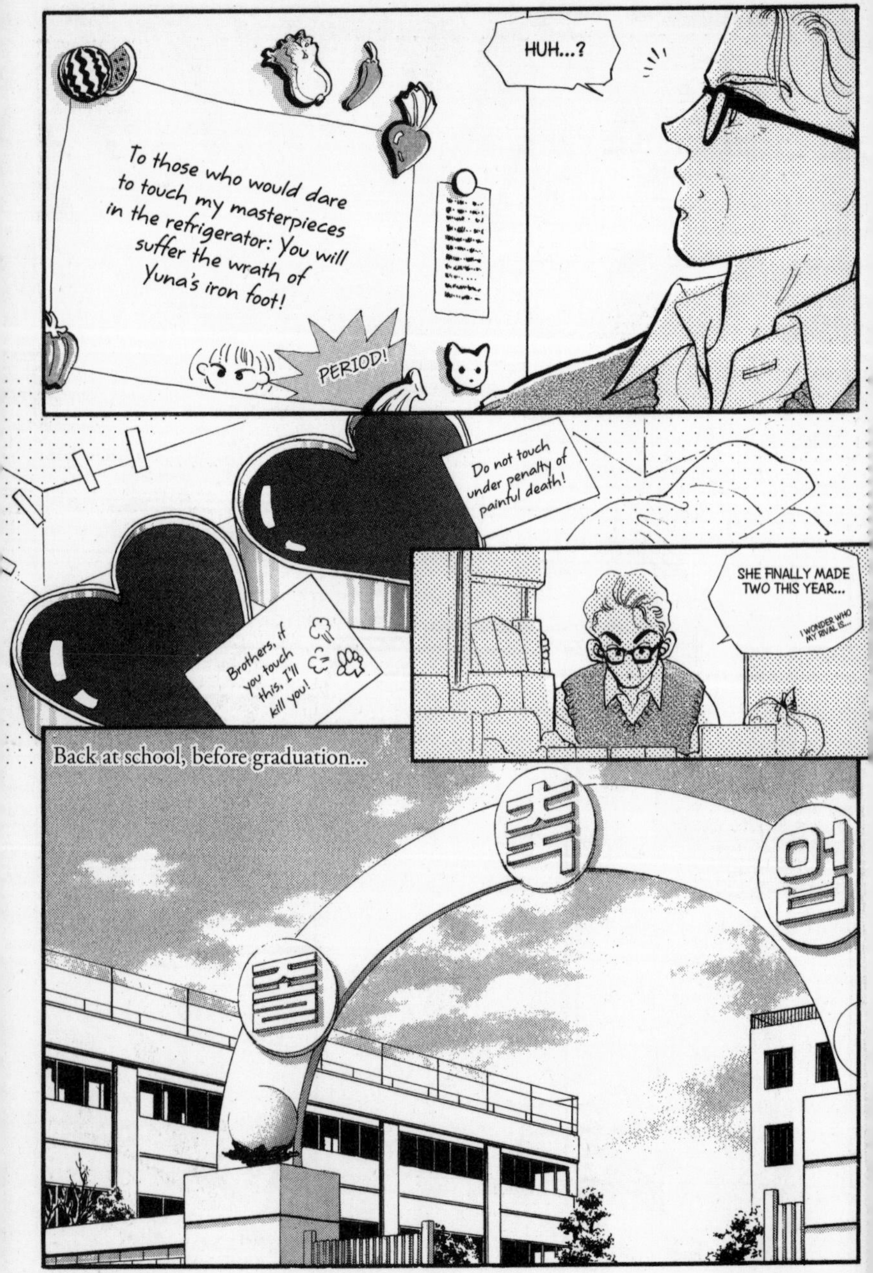
To those who would dare to touch my masterpieces in the refrigerator: You will suffer the wrath of Yuna's iron foot!
PERIOD!
HUH...?
Do not touch under penalty of painful death!
Brothers, if you touch this, I'll kill you!
SHE FINALLY MADE TWO THIS YEAR...
I WONDER WHO MY RIVAL IS...
Back at school, before graduation...
졸
축
업

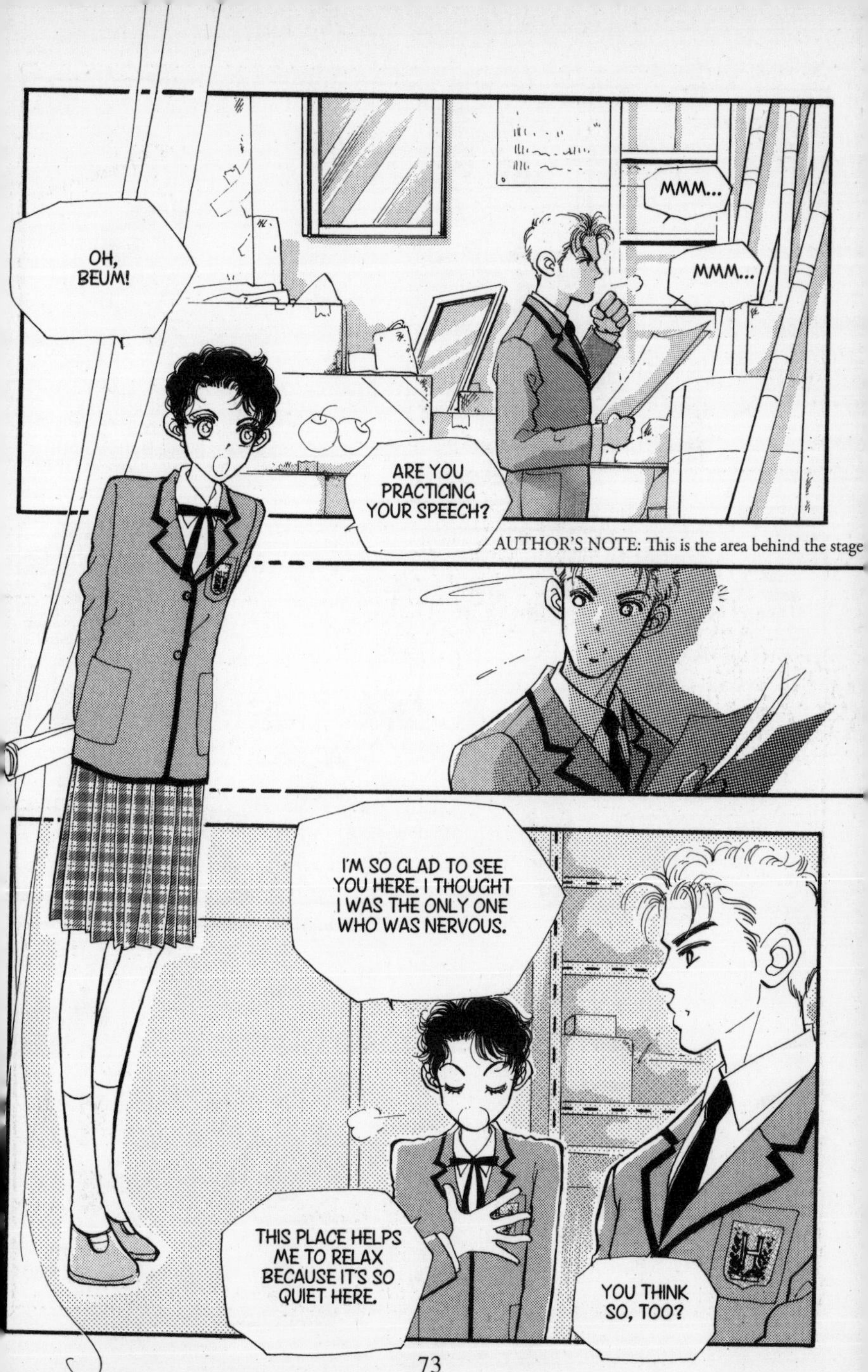

MMM...
MMM...
OH, BEUM!
ARE YOU PRACTICING YOUR SPEECH?
AUTHOR'S NOTE: This is the area behind the stage
I'M SO GLAD TO SEE YOU HERE. I THOUGHT I WAS THE ONLY ONE WHO WAS NERVOUS.
THIS PLACE HELPS ME TO RELAX BECAUSE IT'S SO QUIET HERE.
YOU THINK SO, TOO?

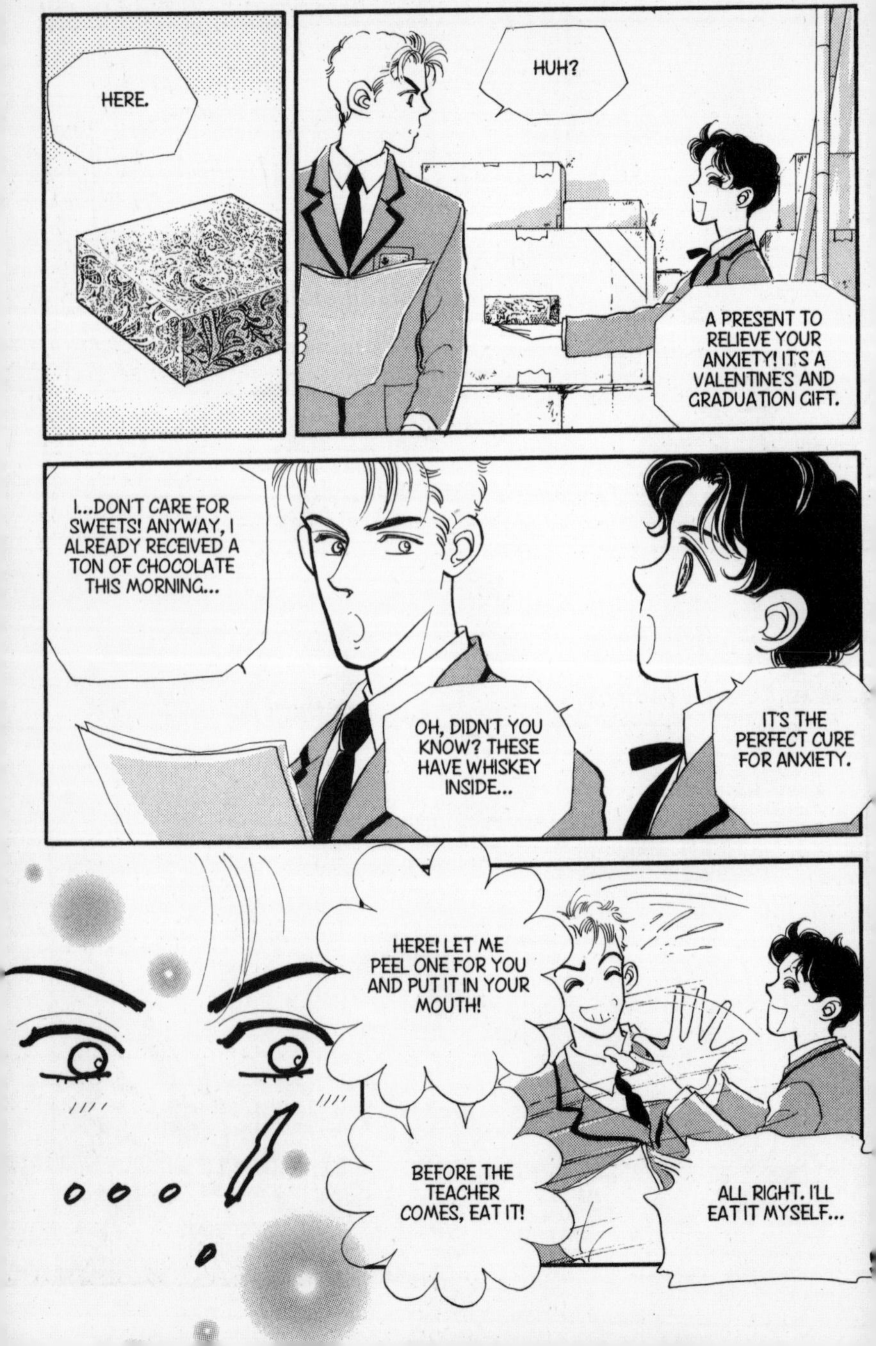
HERE.
HUH?
A PRESENT TO RELIEVE YOUR ANXIETY! IT'S A VALENTINE'S AND GRADUATION GIFT.
I...DON'T CARE FOR SWEETS! ANYWAY, I ALREADY RECEIVED A TON OF CHOCOLATE THIS MORNING...
OH, DIDN'T YOU KNOW? THESE HAVE WHISKEY INSIDE...
IT'S THE PERFECT CURE FOR ANXIETY.
HERE! LET ME PEEL ONE FOR YOU AND PUT IT IN YOUR MOUTH!
BEFORE THE TEACHER COMES, EAT IT!
ALL RIGHT. I'LL EAT IT MYSELF...

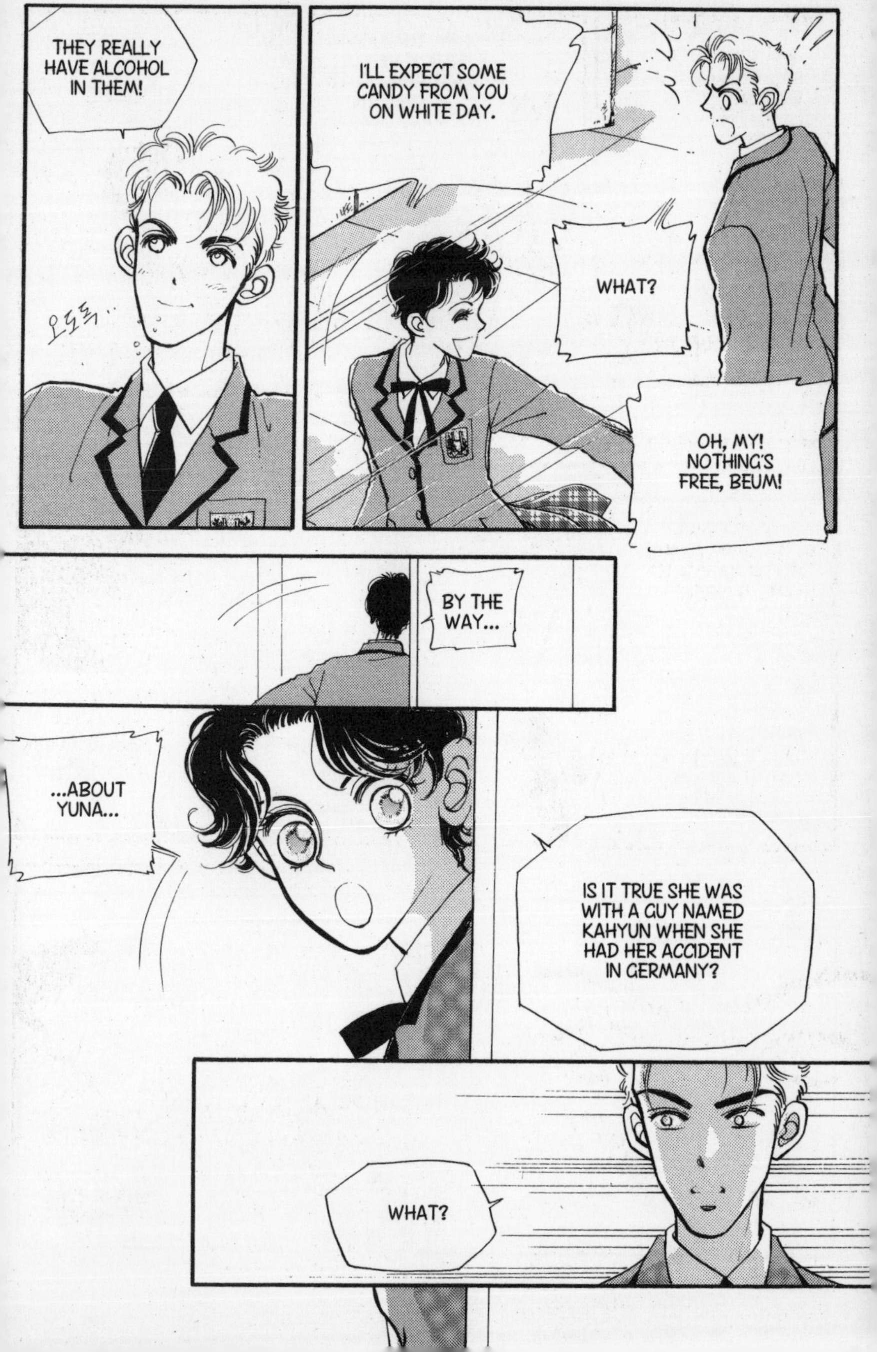
THEY REALLY HAVE ALCOHOL IN THEM!
오도득...
I'LL EXPECT SOME CANDY FROM YOU ON WHITE DAY.
WHAT?
OH, MY! NOTHING'S FREE, BEUM!
BY THE WAY...
...ABOUT YUNA...
IS IT TRUE SHE WAS WITH A GUY NAMED KAHYUN WHEN SHE HAD HER ACCIDENT IN GERMANY?
WHAT?

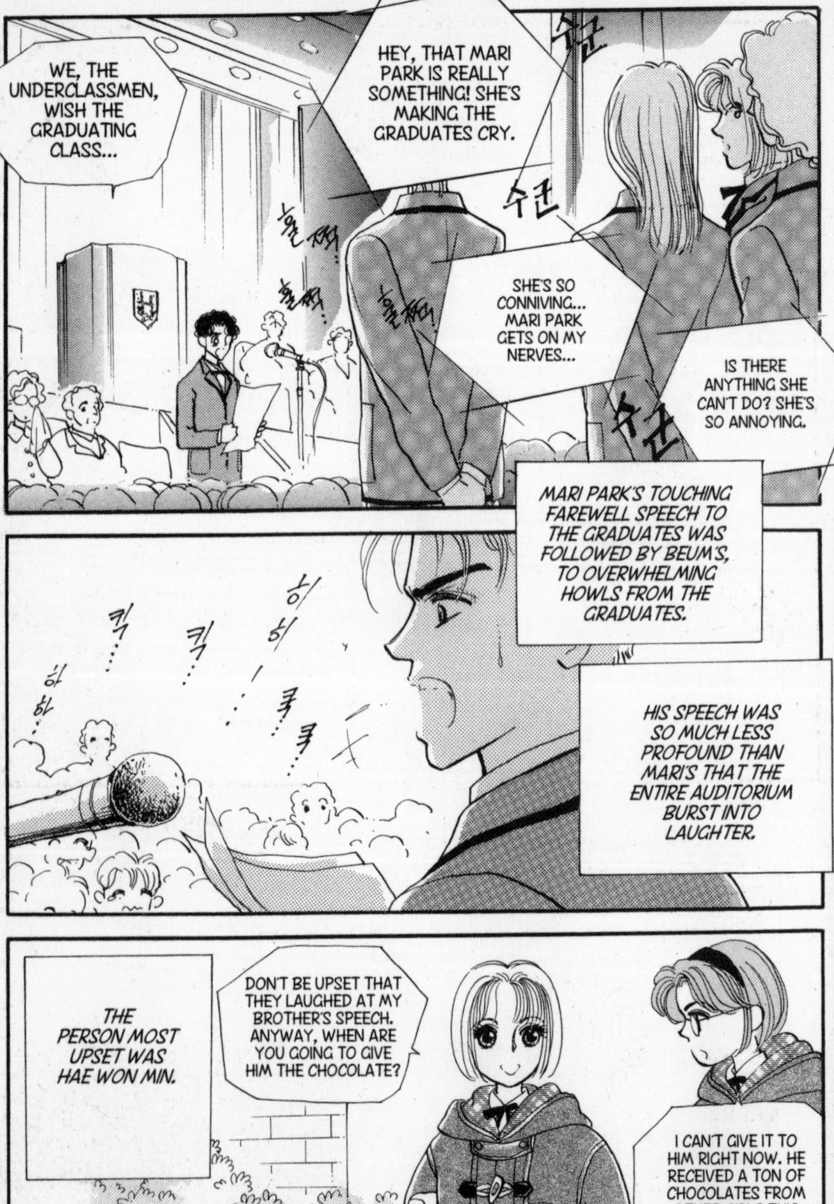
WE, THE UNDERCLASSMEN, WISH THE GRADUATING CLASS...
HEY, THAT MARI PARK IS REALLY SOMETHING! SHE'S MAKING THE GRADUATES CRY.
수군
훌쩍...
훌쩍...
훌쩍!
수군
SHE'S SO CONNIVING... MARI PARK GETS ON MY NERVES...
IS THERE ANYTHING SHE CAN'T DO? SHE'S SO ANNOYING.
수군
MARI PARK'S TOUCHING FAREWELL SPEECH TO THE GRADUATES WAS FOLLOWED BY BEUM'S, TO OVERWHELMING HOWLS FROM THE GRADUATES.
하하...
킥...
킥...
히히!...
쿡쿡
HIS SPEECH WAS SO MUCH LESS PROFOUND THAN MARI'S THAT THE ENTIRE AUDITORIUM BURST INTO LAUGHTER.
THE PERSON MOST UPSET WAS HAE WON MIN.
DON'T BE UPSET THAT THEY LAUGHED AT MY BROTHER'S SPEECH. ANYWAY, WHEN ARE YOU GOING TO GIVE HIM THE CHOCOLATE?
I CAN'T GIVE IT TO HIM RIGHT NOW. HE RECEIVED A TON OF CHOCOLATES FROM OTHER GIRLS THIS MORNING.

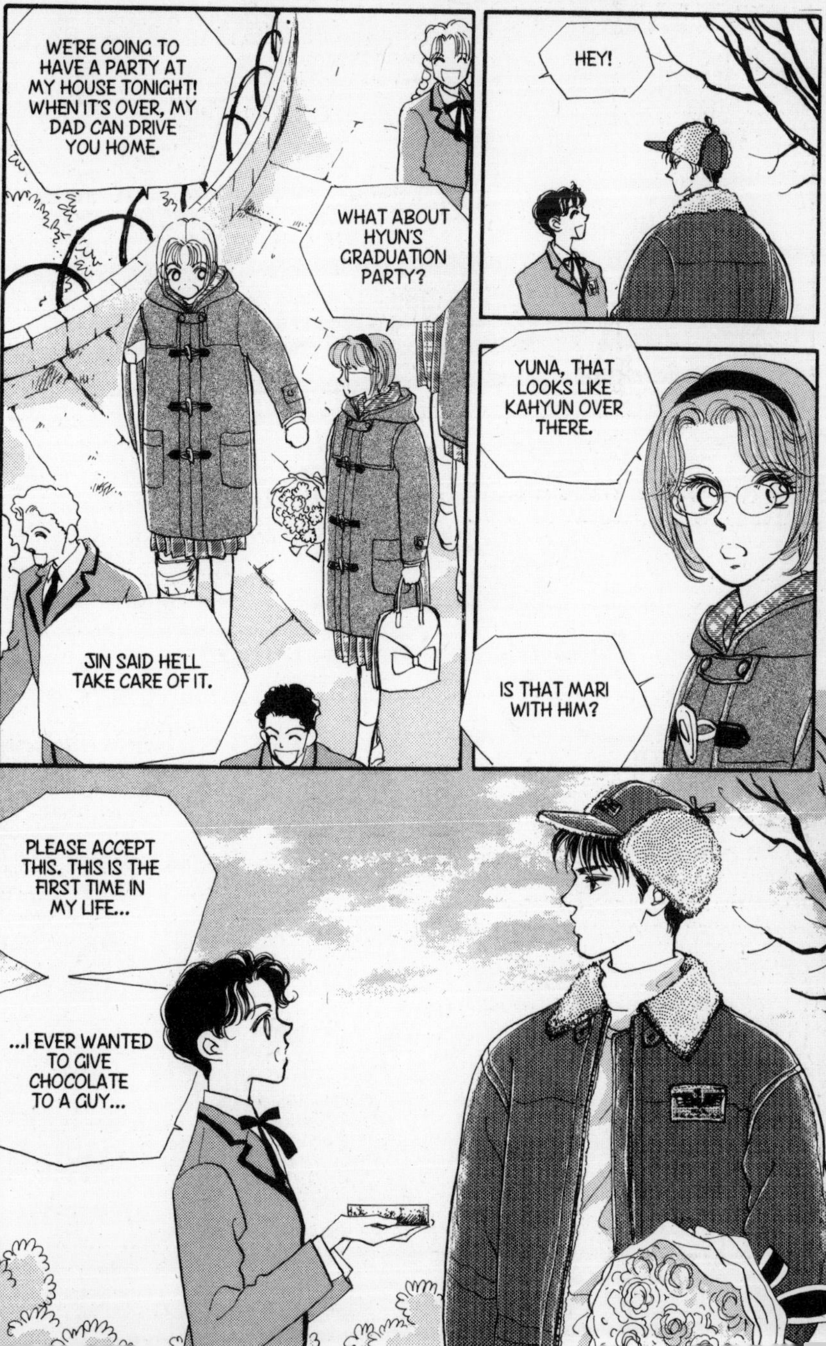
WE'RE GOING TO HAVE A PARTY AT MY HOUSE TONIGHT! WHEN IT'S OVER, MY DAD CAN DRIVE YOU HOME.
WHAT ABOUT HYUN'S GRADUATION PARTY?
JIN SAID HE'LL TAKE CARE OF IT.
HEY!
YUNA, THAT LOOKS LIKE KAHYUN OVER THERE.
IS THAT MARI WITH HIM?
PLEASE ACCEPT THIS. THIS IS THE FIRST TIME IN MY LIFE...
...I EVER WANTED TO GIVE CHOCOLATE TO A GUY...

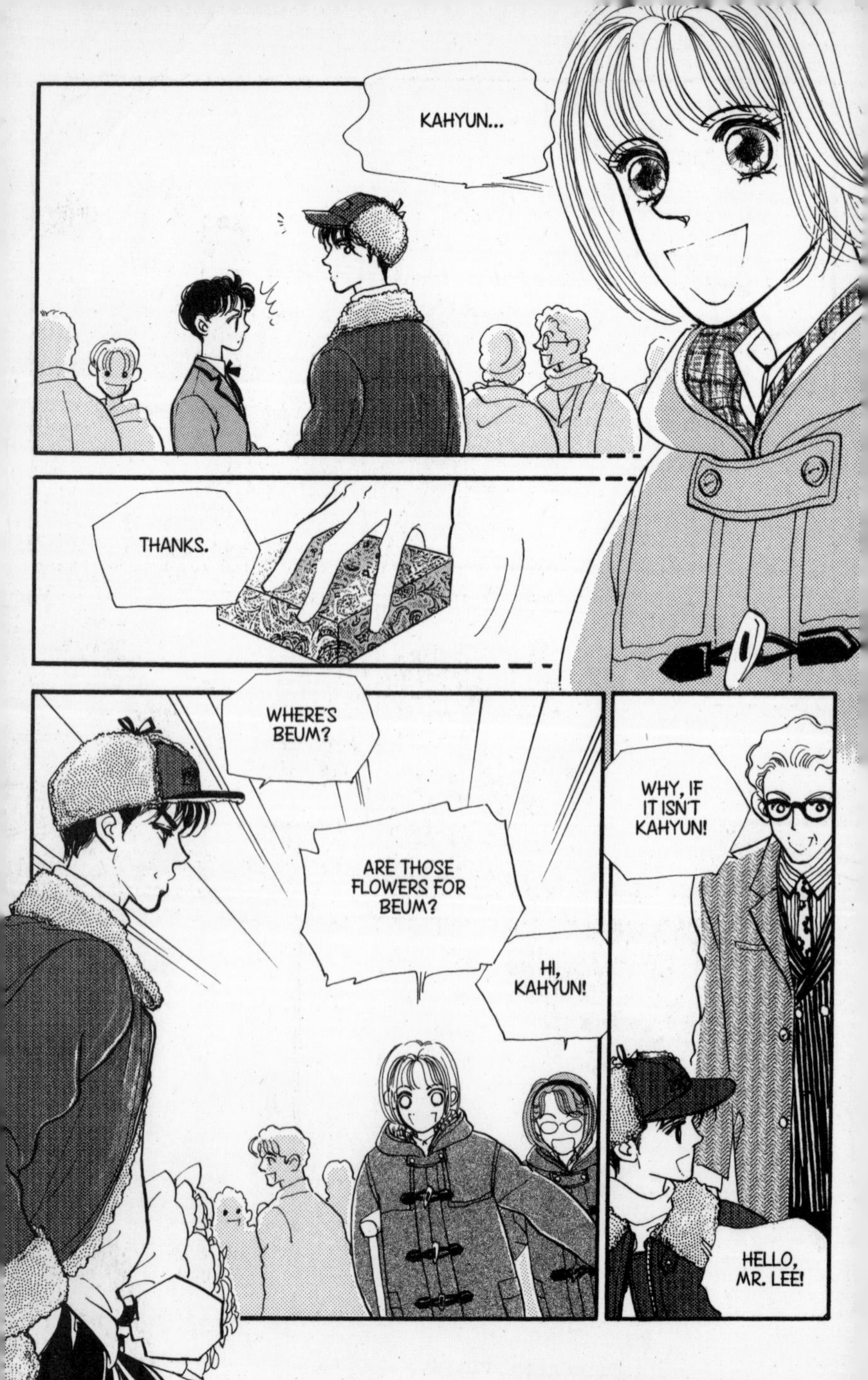
KAHYUN...
THANKS.
WHERE'S BEUM?
ARE THOSE FLOWERS FOR BEUM?
HI, KAHYUN!
WHY, IF IT ISN'T KAHYUN!
HELLO, MR. LEE!

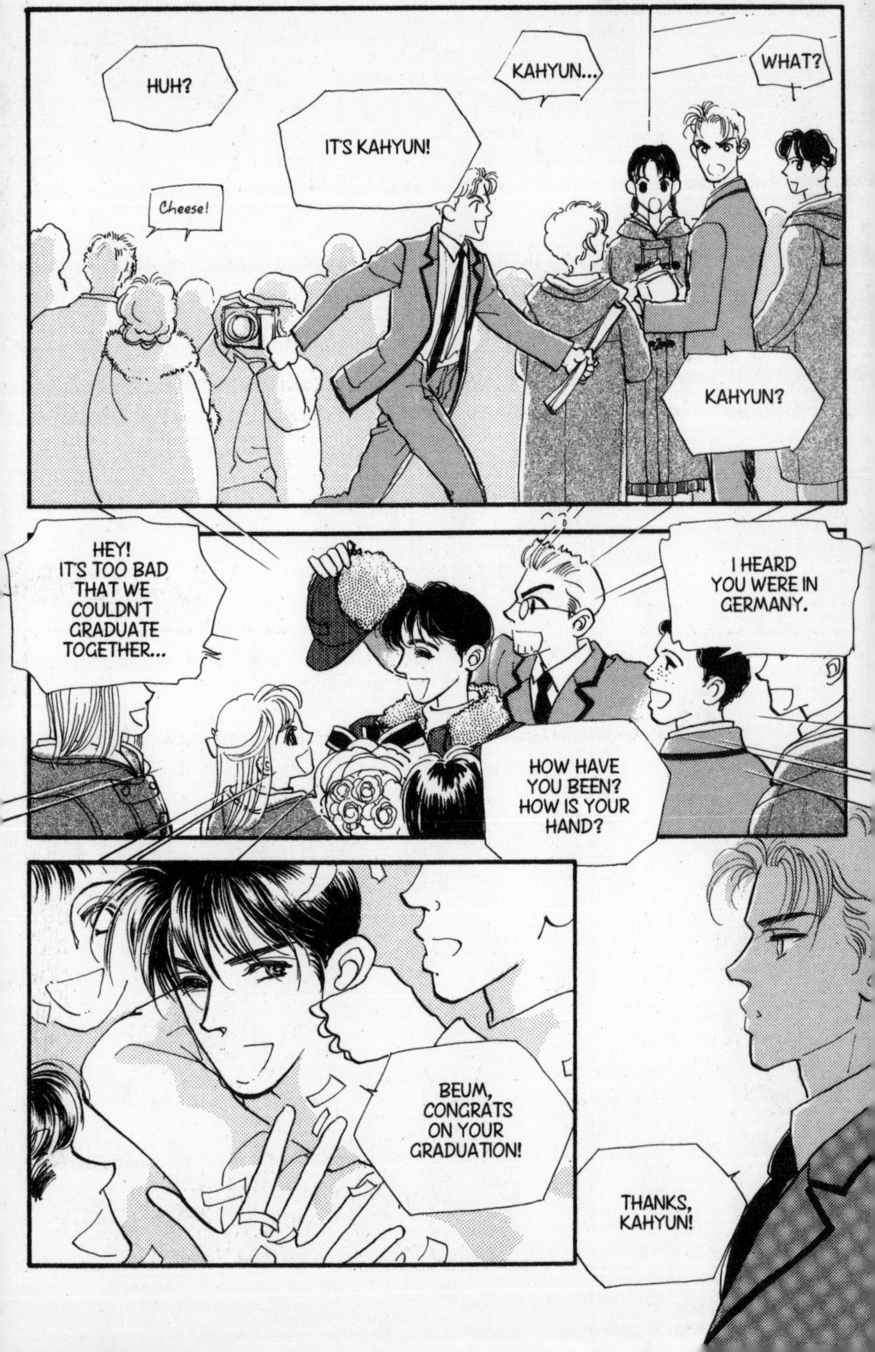
HUH?
Cheese!
IT'S KAHYUN!
KAHYUN...
WHAT?
KAHYUN?
HEY! IT'S TOO BAD THAT WE COULDN'T GRADUATE TOGETHER...
I HEARD YOU WERE IN GERMANY.
HOW HAVE YOU BEEN? HOW IS YOUR HAND?
BEUM, CONGRATS ON YOUR GRADUATION!
THANKS, KAHYUN!

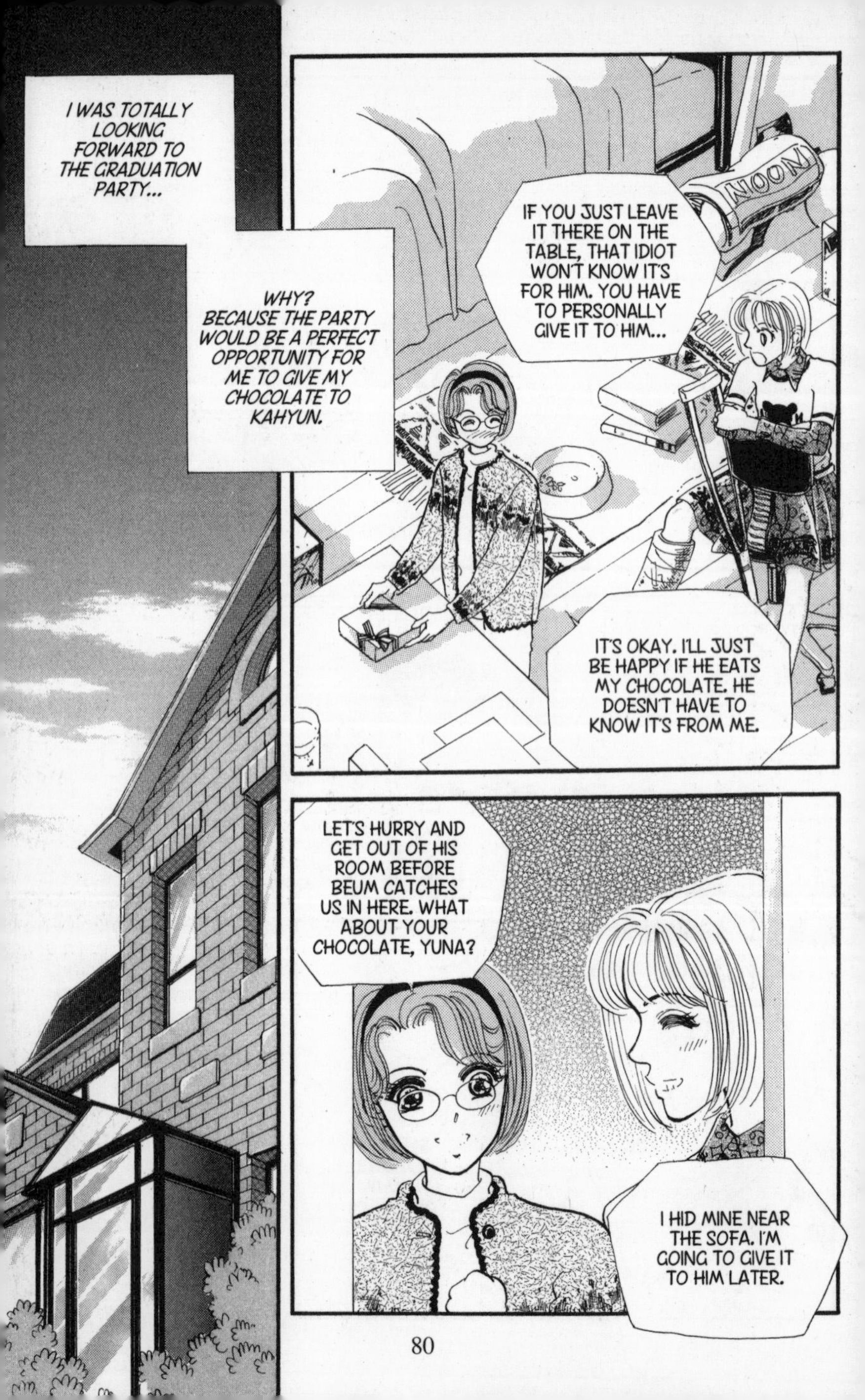
I WAS TOTALLY LOOKING FORWARD TO THE GRADUATION PARTY...
WHY? BECAUSE THE PARTY WOULD BE A PERFECT OPPORTUNITY FOR ME TO GIVE MY CHOCOLATE TO KAHYUN.
IF YOU JUST LEAVE IT THERE ON THE TABLE, THAT IDIOT WON'T KNOW IT'S FOR HIM. YOU HAVE TO PERSONALLY GIVE IT TO HIM...
IT'S OKAY. I'LL JUST BE HAPPY IF HE EATS MY CHOCOLATE. HE DOESN'T HAVE TO KNOW IT'S FROM ME.
LET'S HURRY AND GET OUT OF HIS ROOM BEFORE BEUM CATCHES US IN HERE. WHAT ABOUT YOUR CHOCOLATE, YUNA?
I HID MINE NEAR THE SOFA. I'M GOING TO GIVE IT TO HIM LATER.

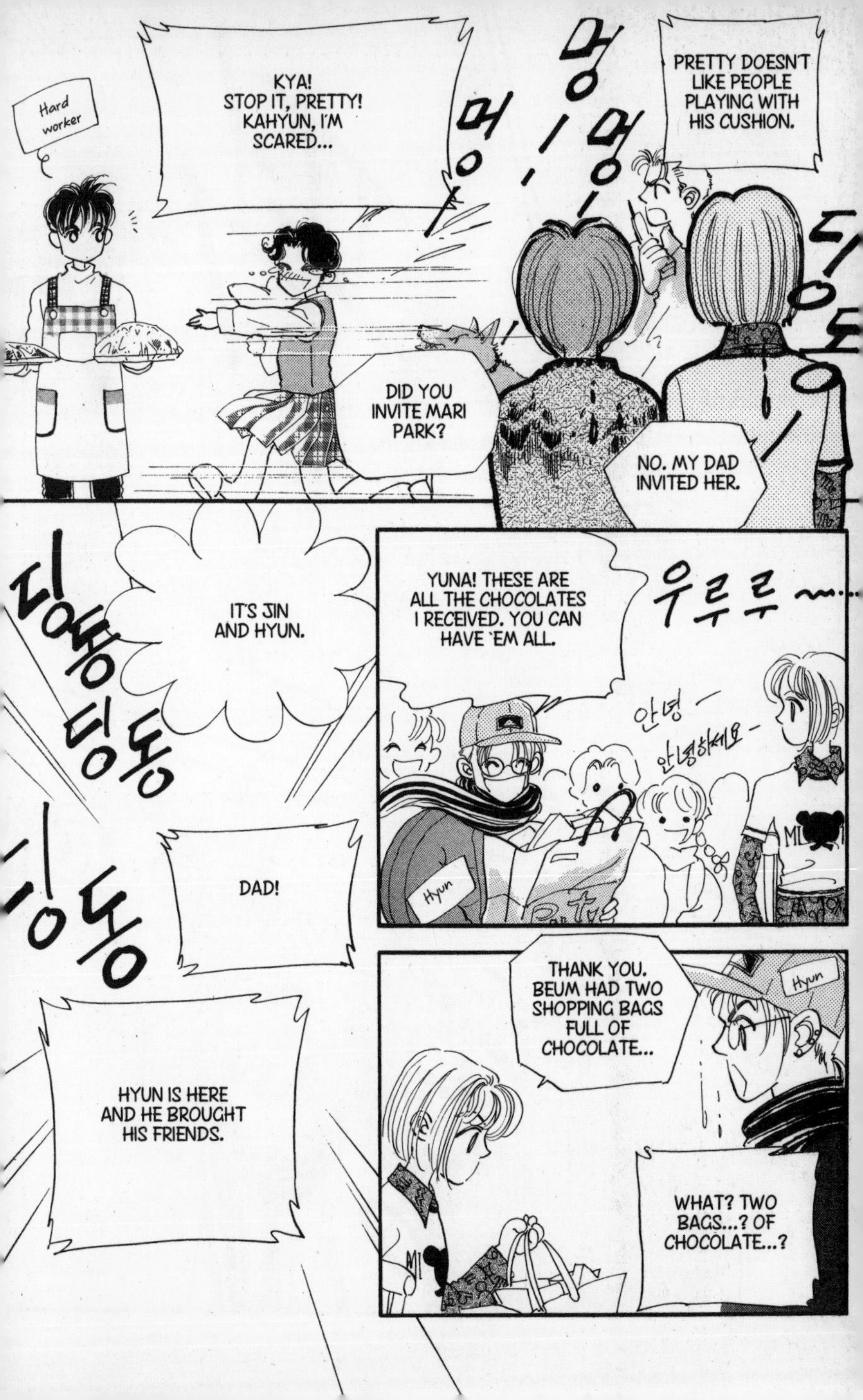
Hard worker
KYA! STOP IT, PRETTY! KAHYUN, I'M SCARED...
멍!
멍! 멍!
PRETTY DOESN'T LIKE PEOPLE PLAYING WITH HIS CUSHION.
딩동!
DID YOU INVITE MARI PARK?
NO. MY DAD INVITED HER.
딩동
IT'S JIN AND HYUN.
딩동
딩동
DAD!
HYUN IS HERE AND HE BROUGHT HIS FRIENDS.
YUNA! THESE ARE ALL THE CHOCOLATES I RECEIVED. YOU CAN HAVE 'EM ALL.
우루루~~...
안녕—
안녕하세요—
Hyun
THANK YOU. BEUM HAD TWO SHOPPING BAGS FULL OF CHOCOLATE...
Hyun
WHAT? TWO BAGS...? OF CHOCOLATE...?

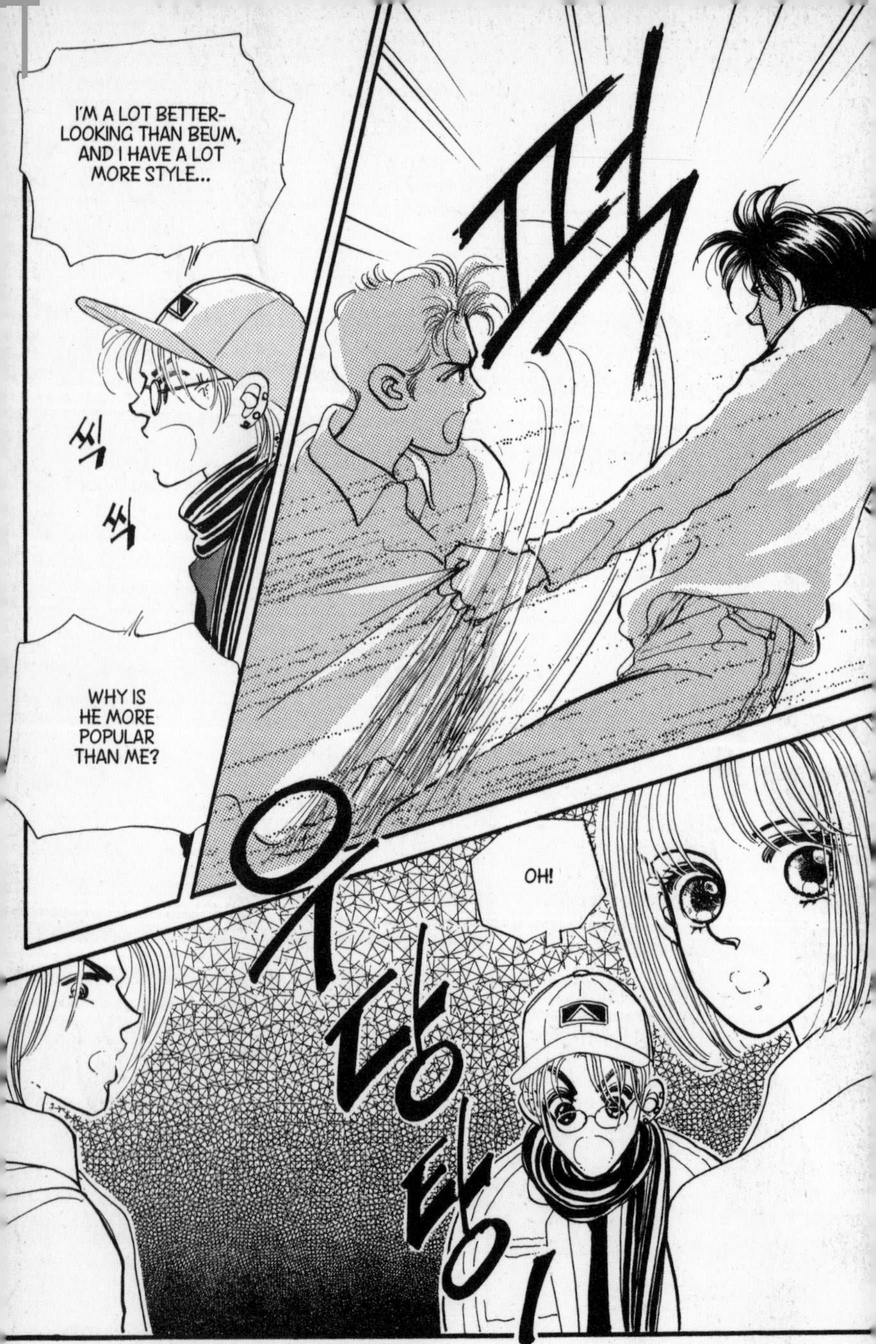
I'M A LOT BETTER-LOOKING THAN BEUM, AND I HAVE A LOT MORE STYLE...
WHY IS HE MORE POPULAR THAN ME?
OH!
우당탕!

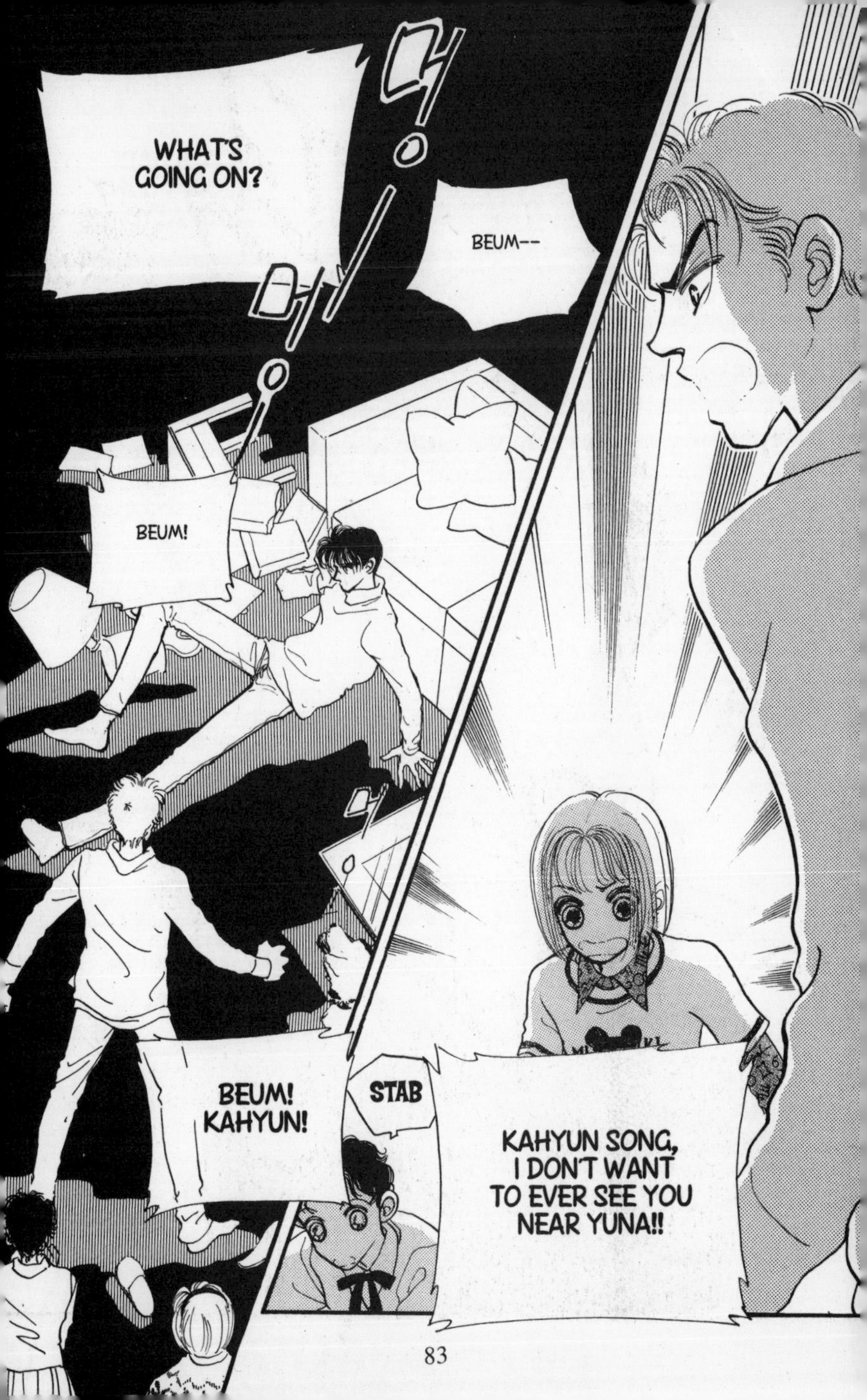
KAHYUN SONG, I DON'T WANT TO EVER SEE YOU NEAR YUNA!!
STAB
BEUM--
WHAT'S GOING ON?
BEUM!
BEUM! KAHYUN!

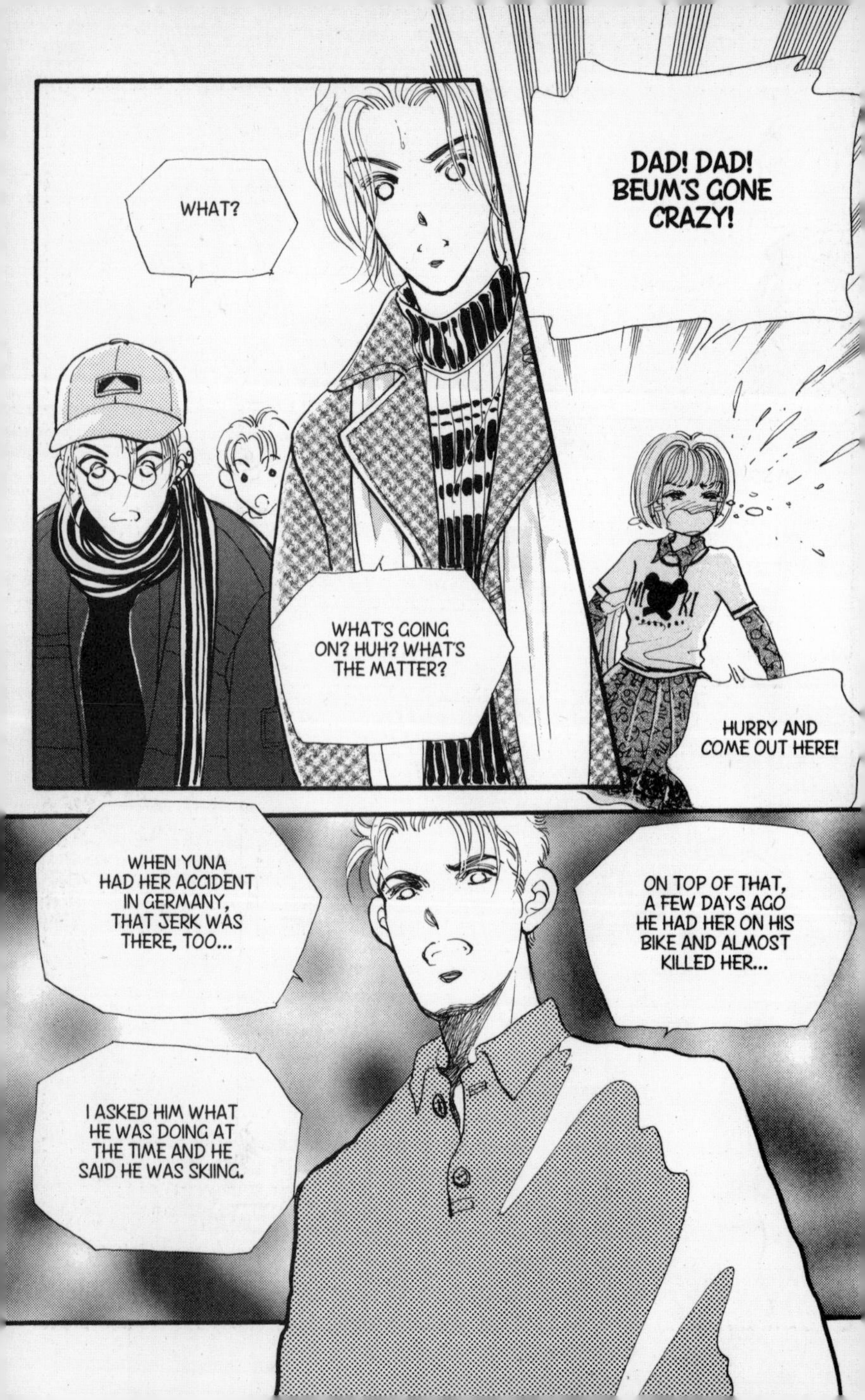
WHAT?
DAD! DAD! BEUM'S GONE CRAZY!
WHAT'S GOING ON? HUH? WHAT'S THE MATTER?
HURRY AND COME OUT HERE!
WHEN YUNA HAD HER ACCIDENT IN GERMANY, THAT JERK WAS THERE, TOO...
ON TOP OF THAT, A FEW DAYS AGO HE HAD HER ON HIS BIKE AND ALMOST KILLED HER...
I ASKED HIM WHAT HE WAS DOING AT THE TIME AND HE SAID HE WAS SKIING.

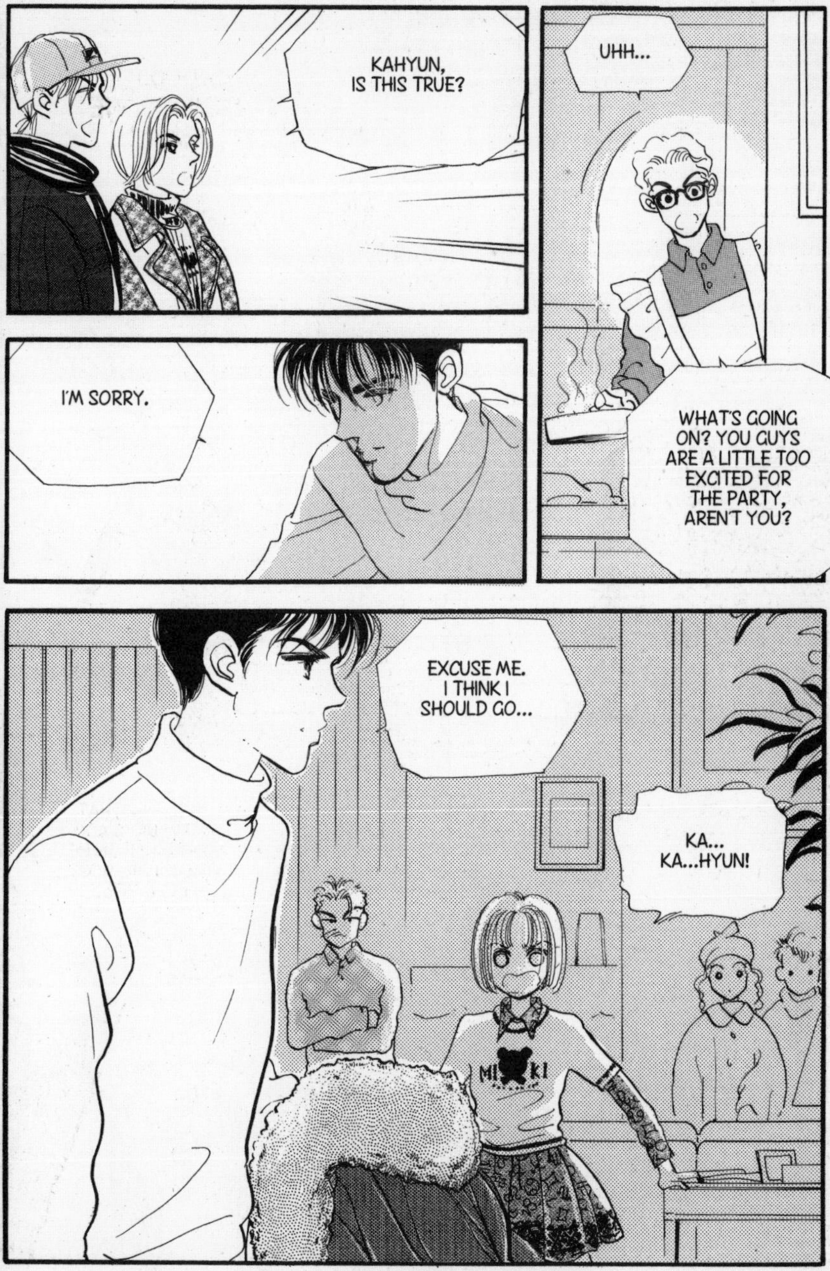
KAHYUN, IS THIS TRUE?
I'M SORRY.
UHH...
WHAT'S GOING ON? YOU GUYS ARE A LITTLE TOO EXCITED FOR THE PARTY, AREN'T YOU?
EXCUSE ME. I THINK I SHOULD GO...
KA... KA...HYUN!

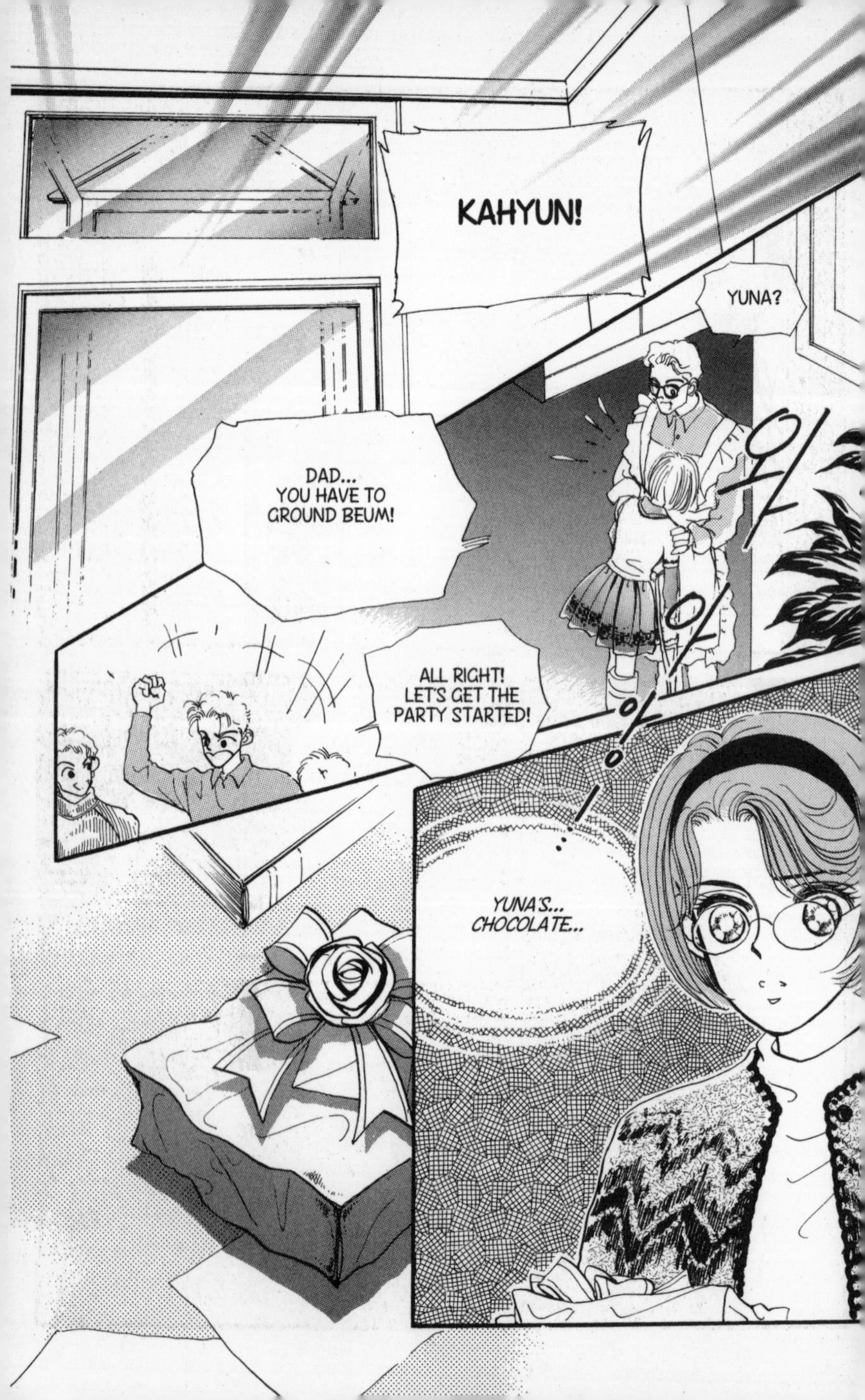
KAHYUN!
YUNA?
DAD...
YOU HAVE TO
GROUND BEUM!
ALL RIGHT!
LET'S GET THE
PARTY STARTED!
YUNA'S...
CHOCOLATE...

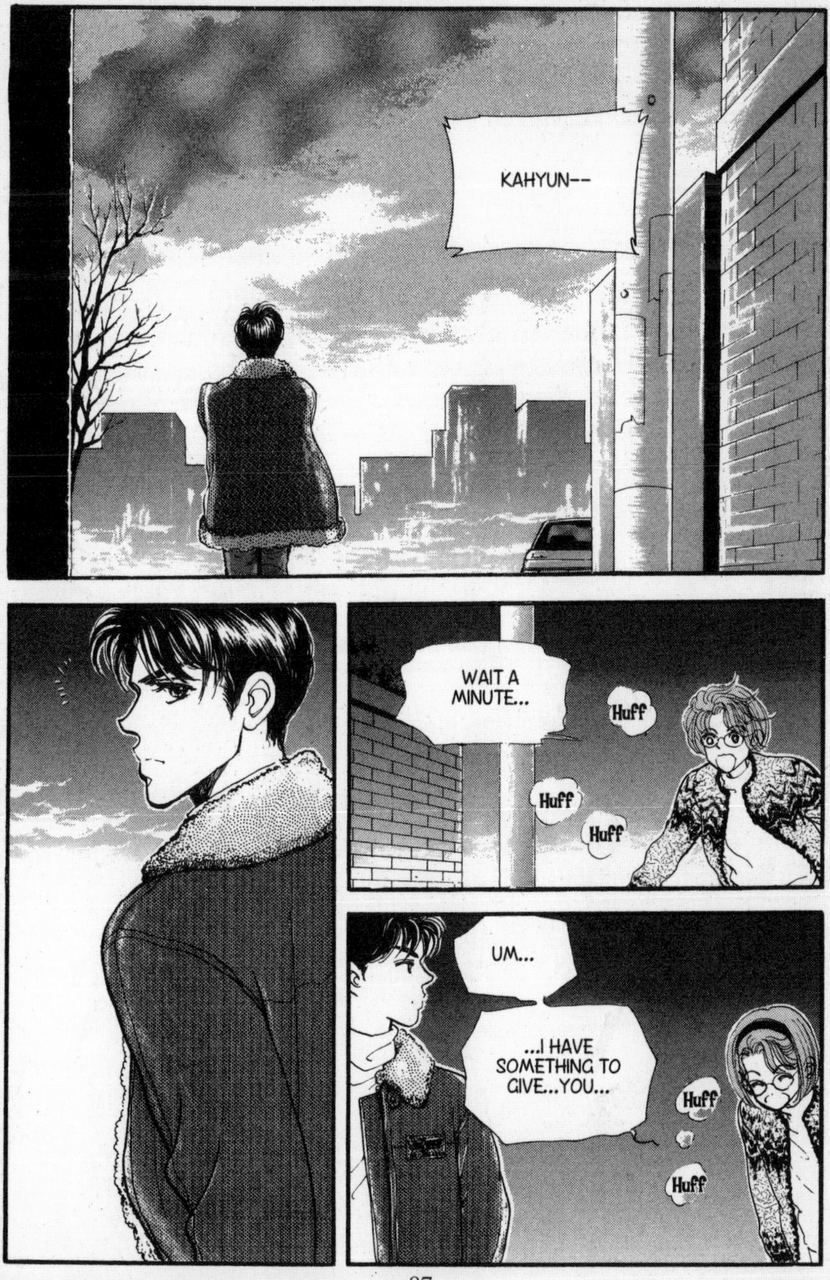
KAHYUN--
WAIT A MINUTE...
Huff
Huff
Huff
UM...
...I HAVE SOMETHING TO GIVE...YOU...
Huff
Huff

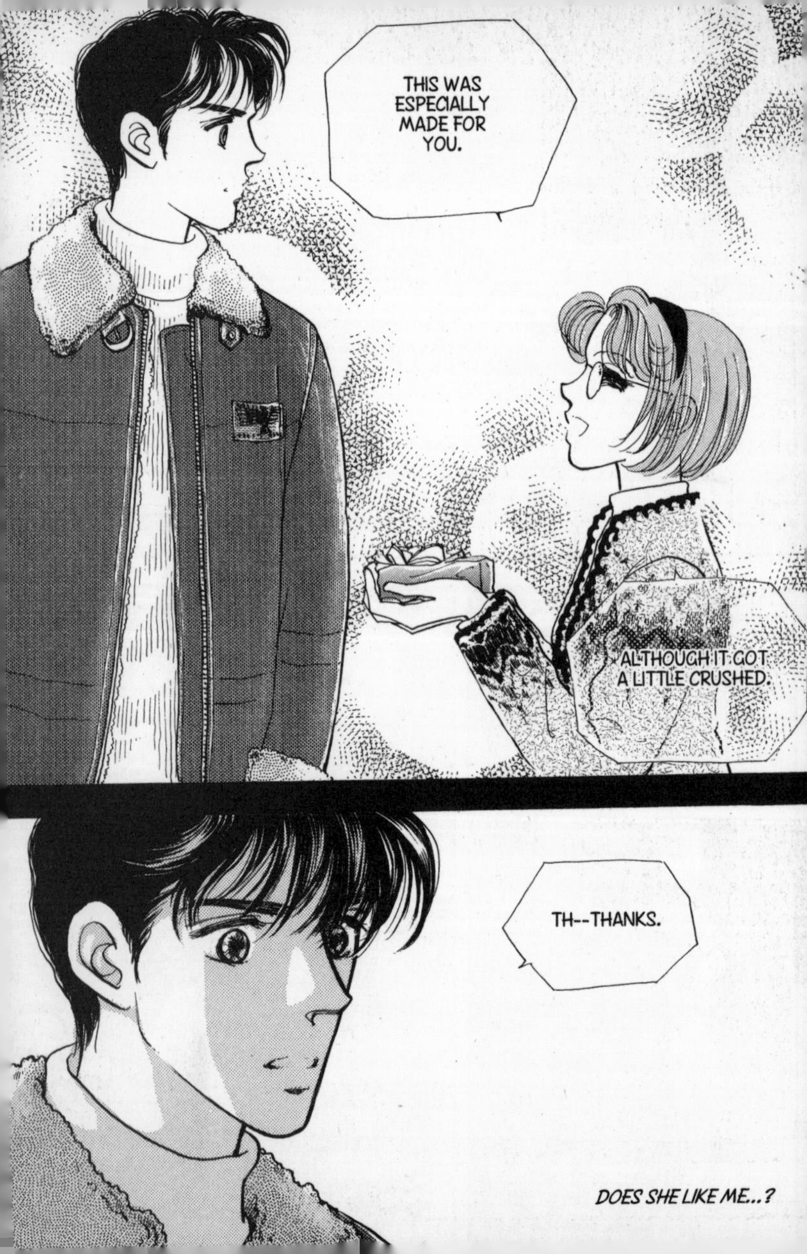
THIS WAS ESPECIALLY MADE FOR YOU.
ALTHOUGH IT GOT A LITTLE CRUSHED.
TH--THANKS.
DOES SHE LIKE ME...?

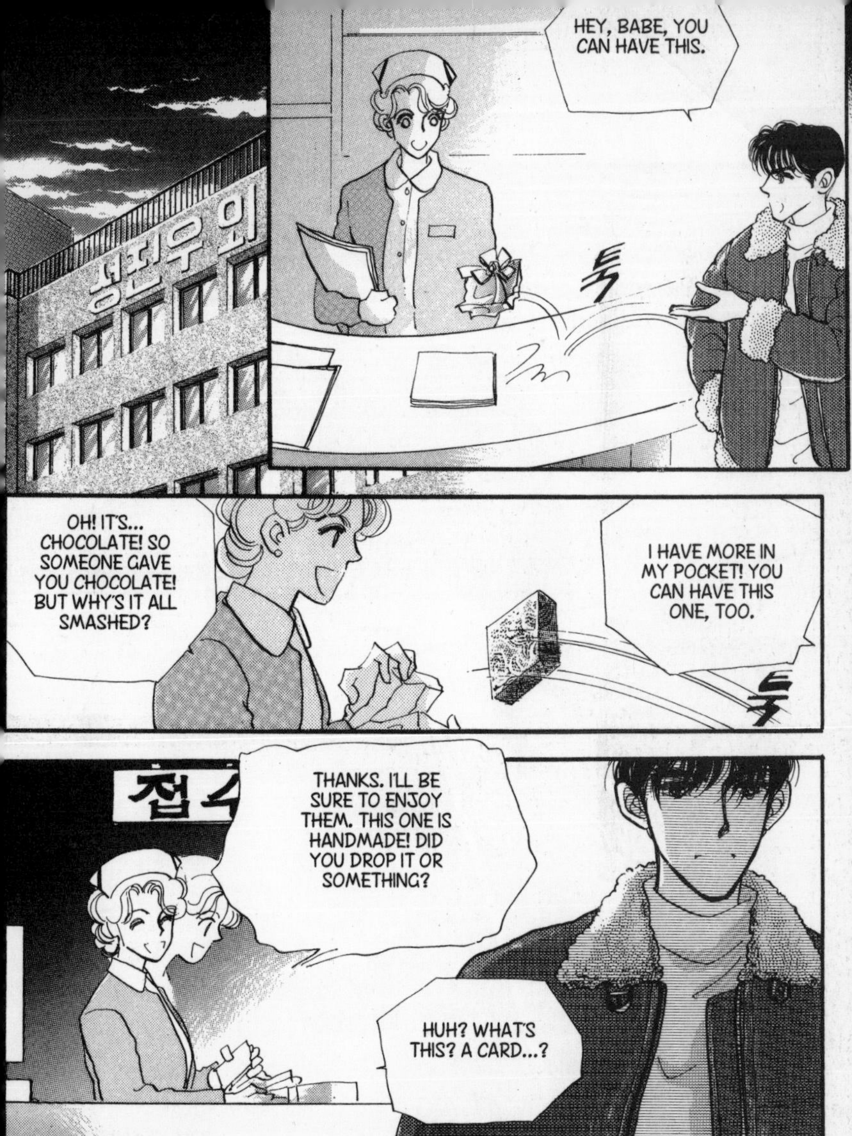
HEY, BABE, YOU CAN HAVE THIS.
툭
OH! IT'S... CHOCOLATE! SO SOMEONE GAVE YOU CHOCOLATE! BUT WHY'S IT ALL SMASHED?
I HAVE MORE IN MY POCKET! YOU CAN HAVE THIS ONE, TOO.
툭
접
THANKS. I'LL BE SURE TO ENJOY THEM. THIS ONE IS HANDMADE! DID YOU DROP IT OR SOMETHING?
HUH? WHAT'S THIS? A CARD...?

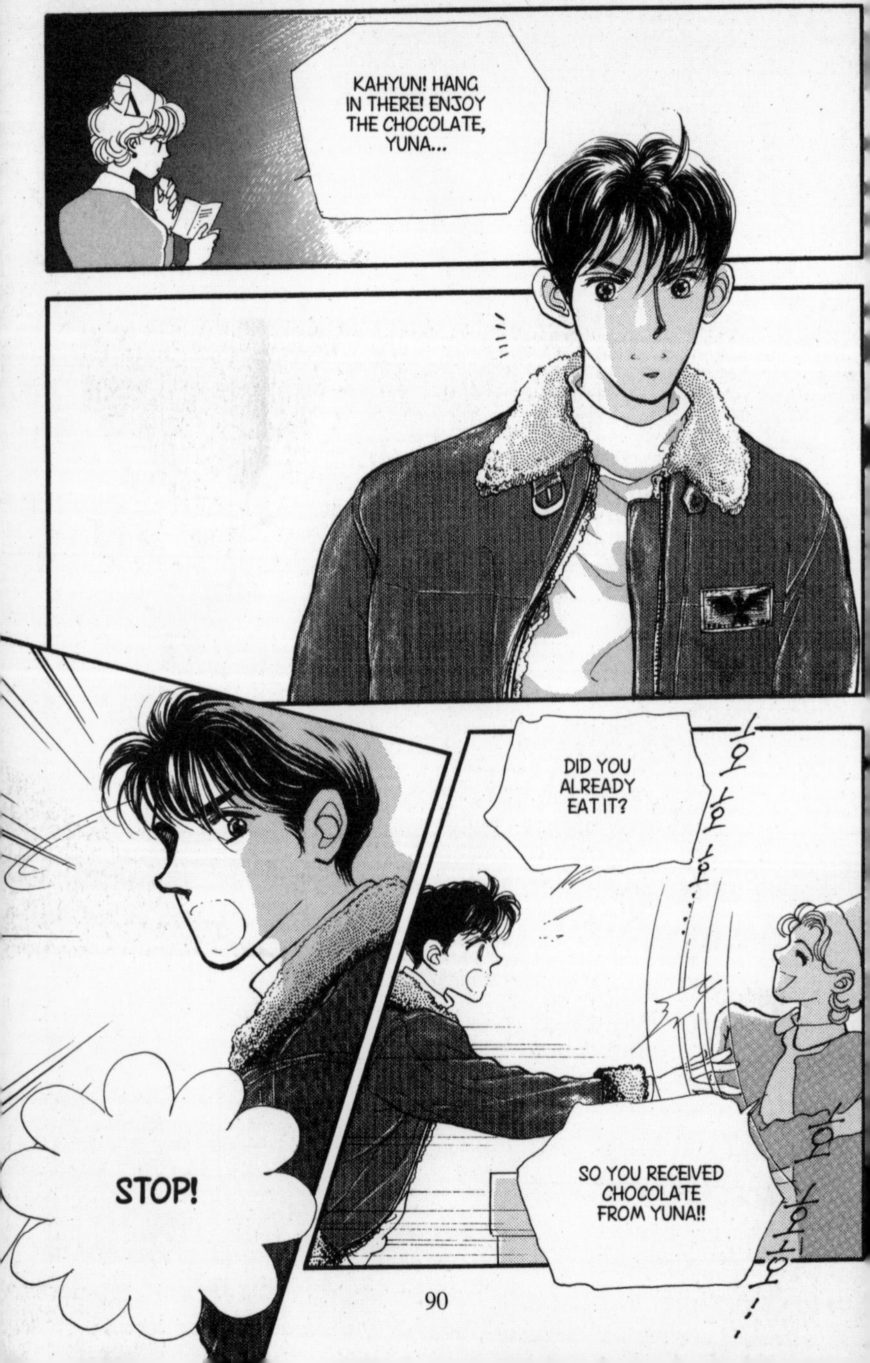
KAHYUN! HANG IN THERE! ENJOY THE CHOCOLATE, YUNA...
STOP!
DID YOU ALREADY EAT IT?
SO YOU RECEIVED CHOCOLATE FROM YUNA!!

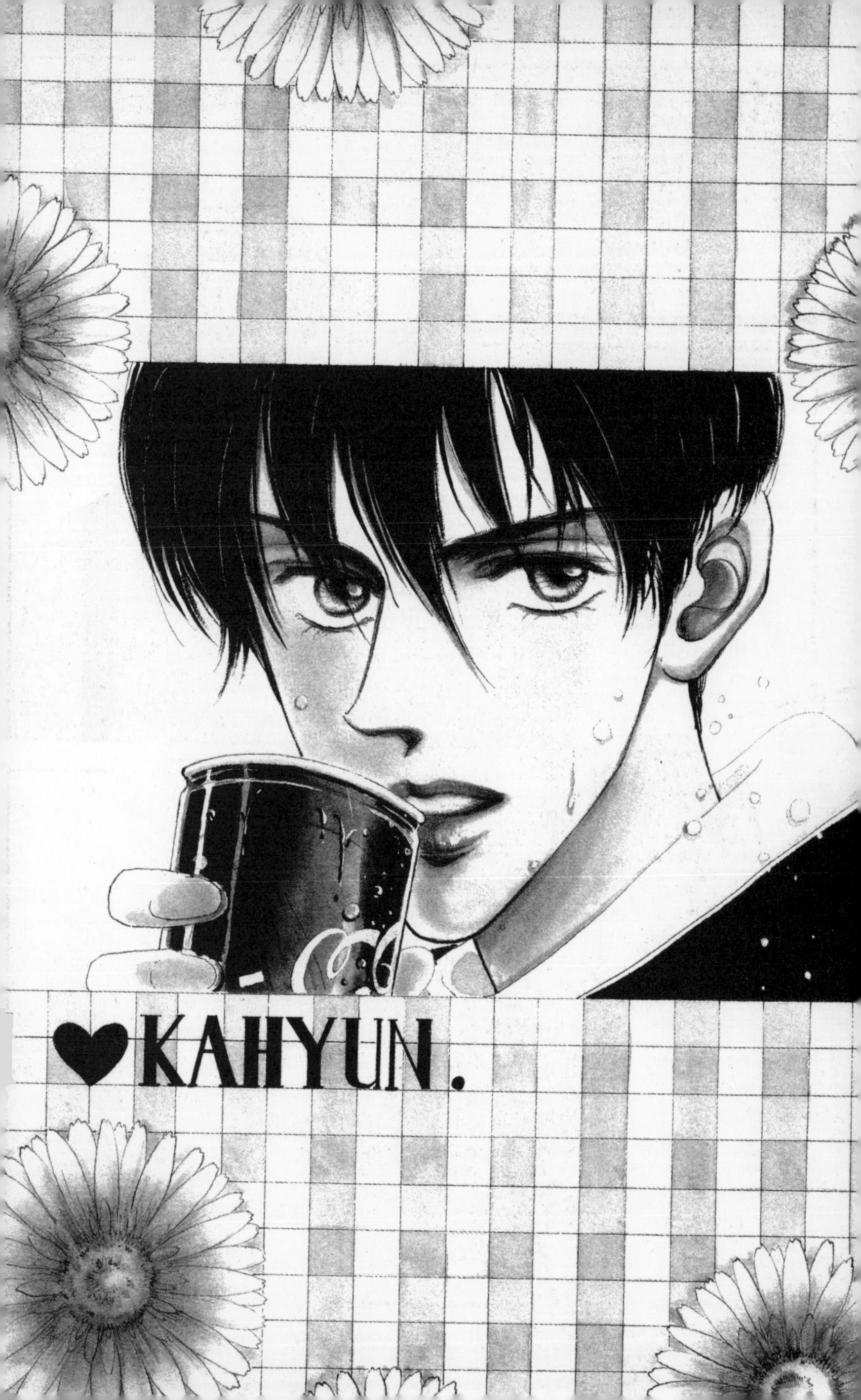
♥KAHYUN.

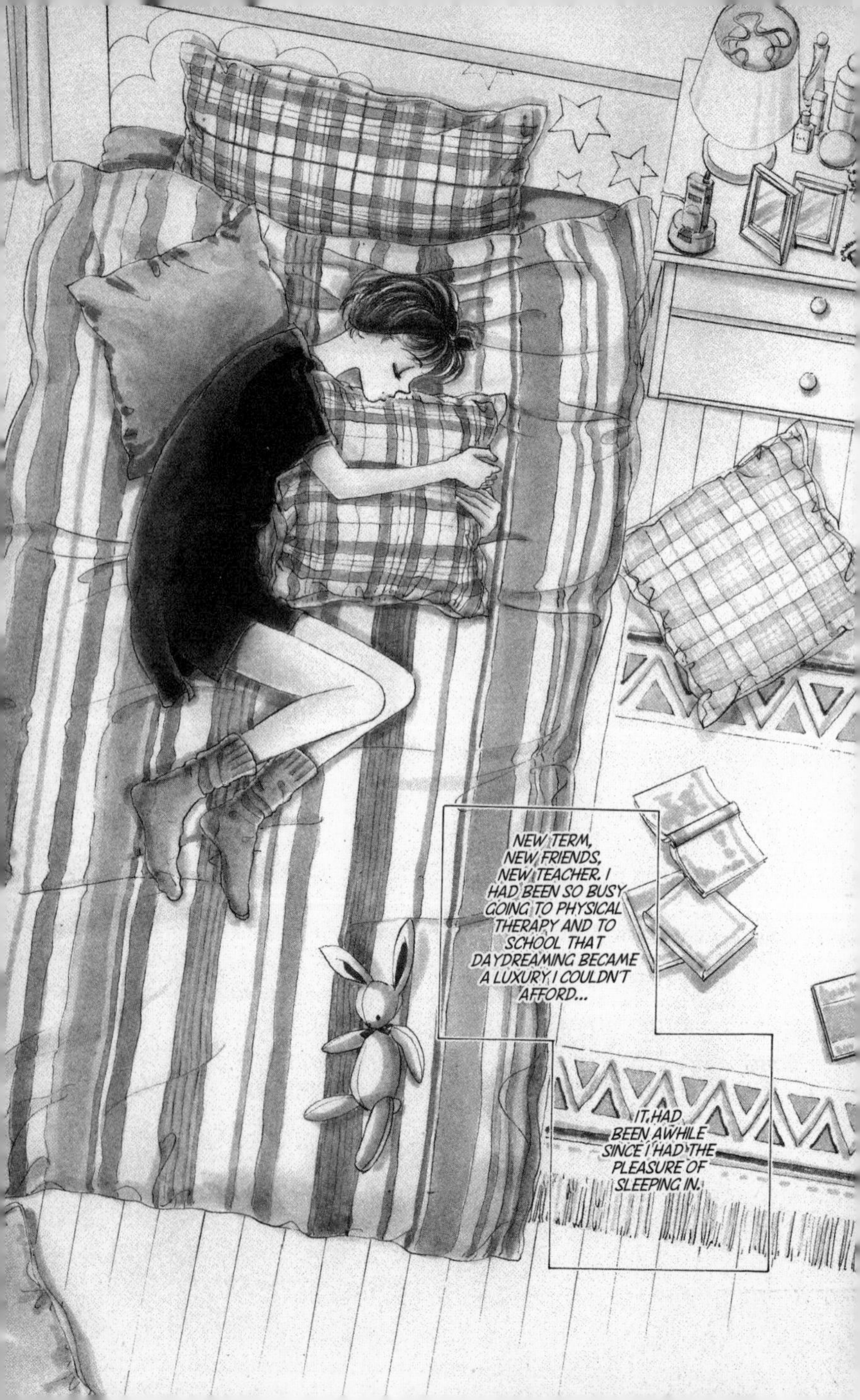
NEW TERM, NEW FRIENDS, NEW TEACHER. I HAD BEEN SO BUSY GOING TO PHYSICAL THERAPY AND TO SCHOOL THAT DAYDREAMING BECAME A LUXURY I COULDN'T AFFORD...
IT HAD BEEN AWHILE SINCE I HAD THE PLEASURE OF SLEEPING IN.

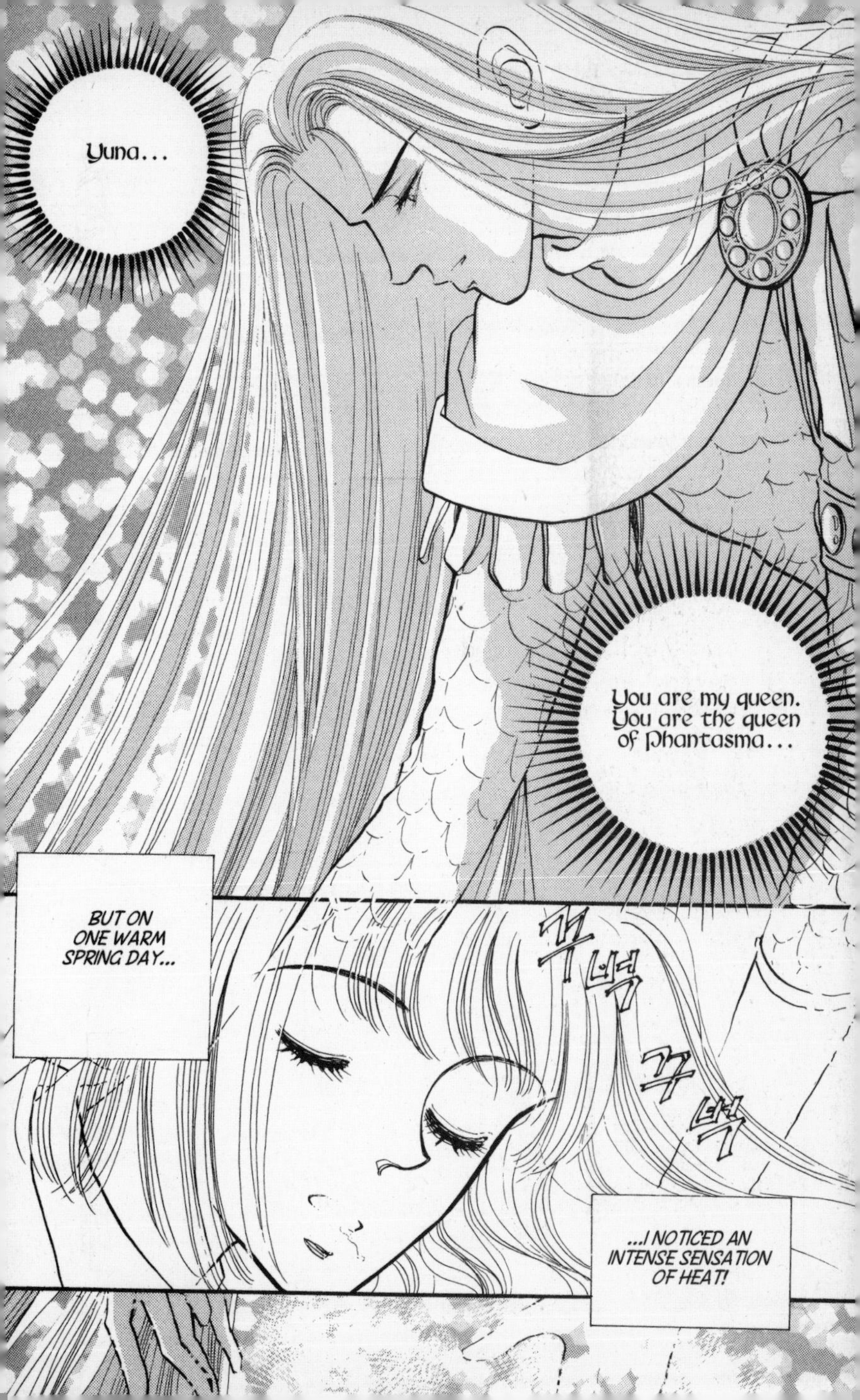
Yuna...
You are my queen. You are the queen of Phantasma...
BUT ON ONE WARM SPRING DAY...
꾸벅
꾸벅
...I NOTICED AN INTENSE SENSATION OF HEAT!

One day in March...

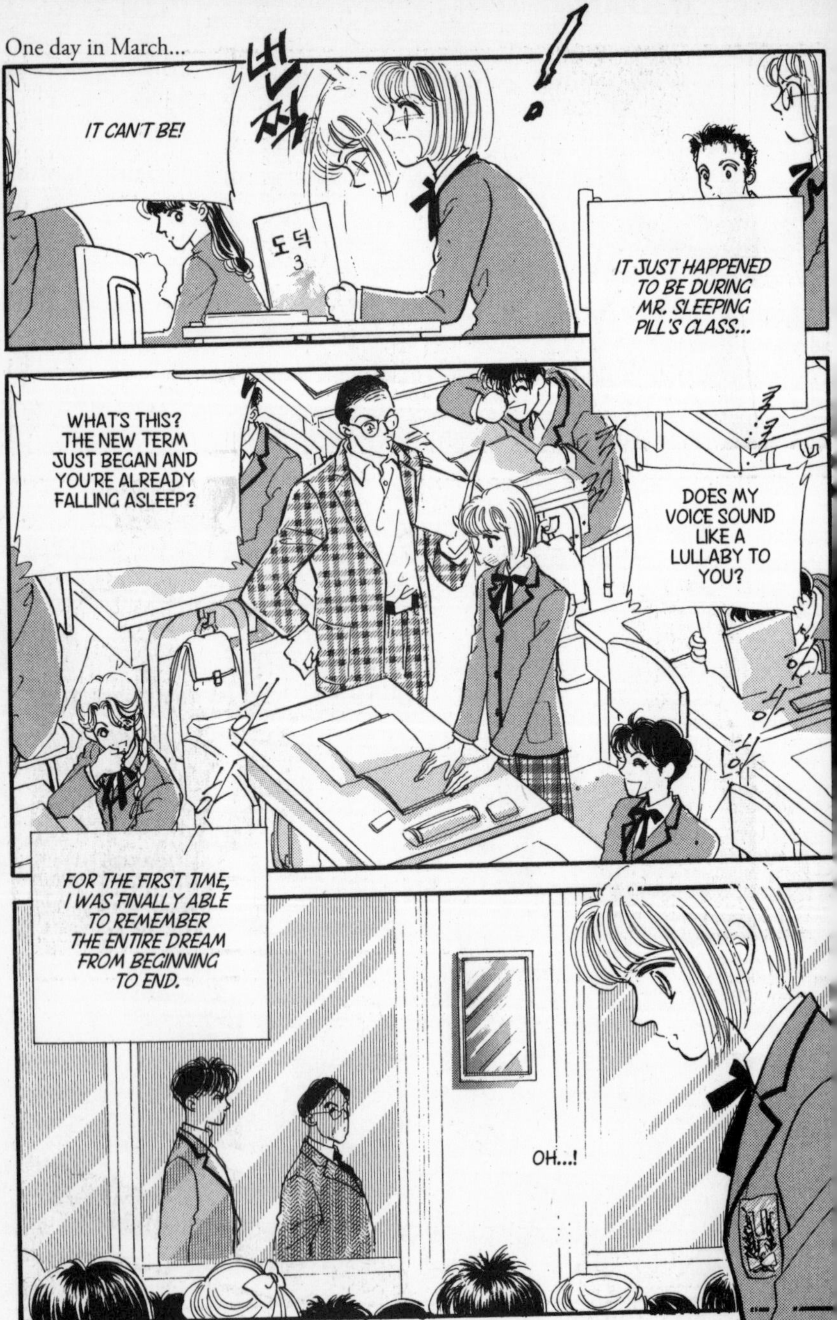

번쩍
IT CAN'T BE!
!
도덕
3
IT JUST HAPPENED TO BE DURING MR. SLEEPING PILL'S CLASS...
WHAT'S THIS? THE NEW TERM JUST BEGAN AND YOU'RE ALREADY FALLING ASLEEP?
DOES MY VOICE SOUND LIKE A LULLABY TO YOU?
FOR THE FIRST TIME, I WAS FINALLY ABLE TO REMEMBER THE ENTIRE DREAM FROM BEGINNING TO END.
OH...!

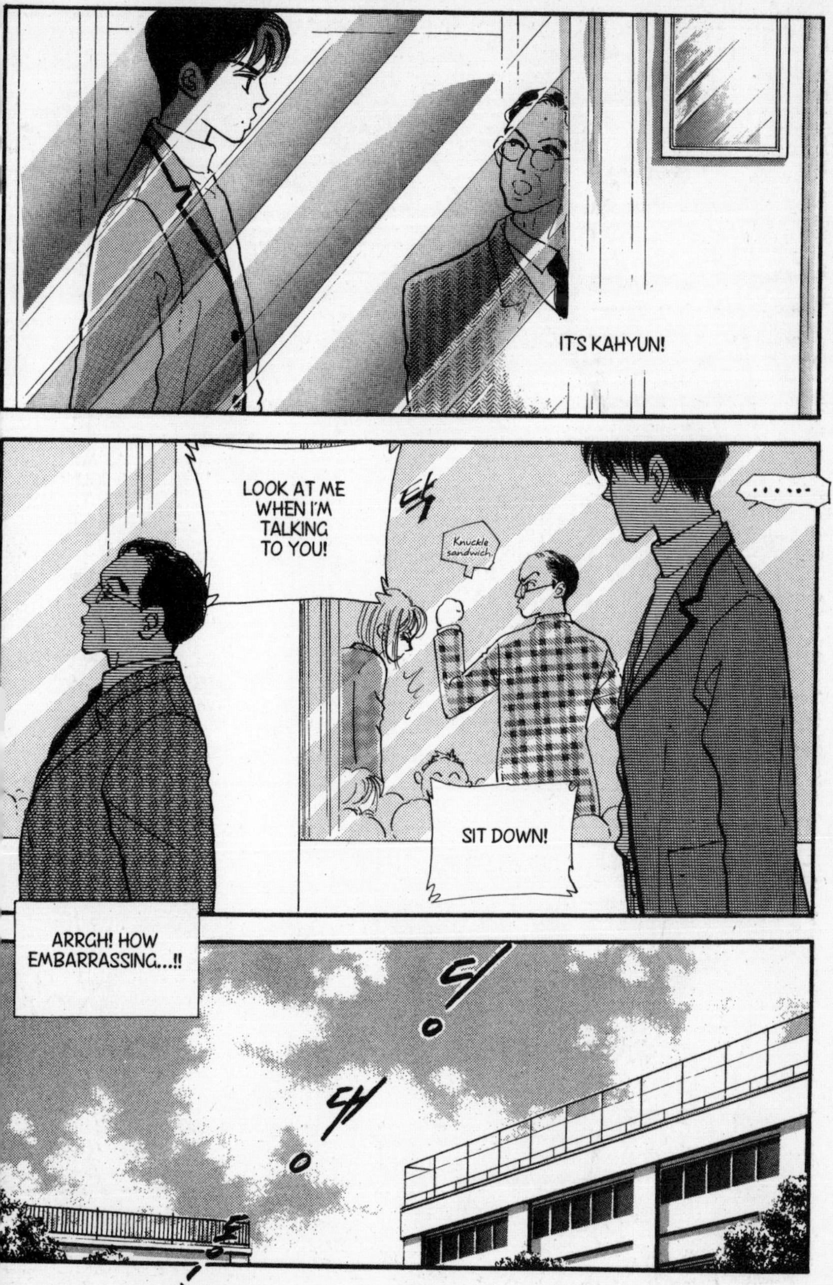
IT'S KAHYUN!
LOOK AT ME WHEN I'M TALKING TO YOU!
Knuckle sandwich.
.....
SIT DOWN!
ARRGH! HOW EMBARRASSING...!!

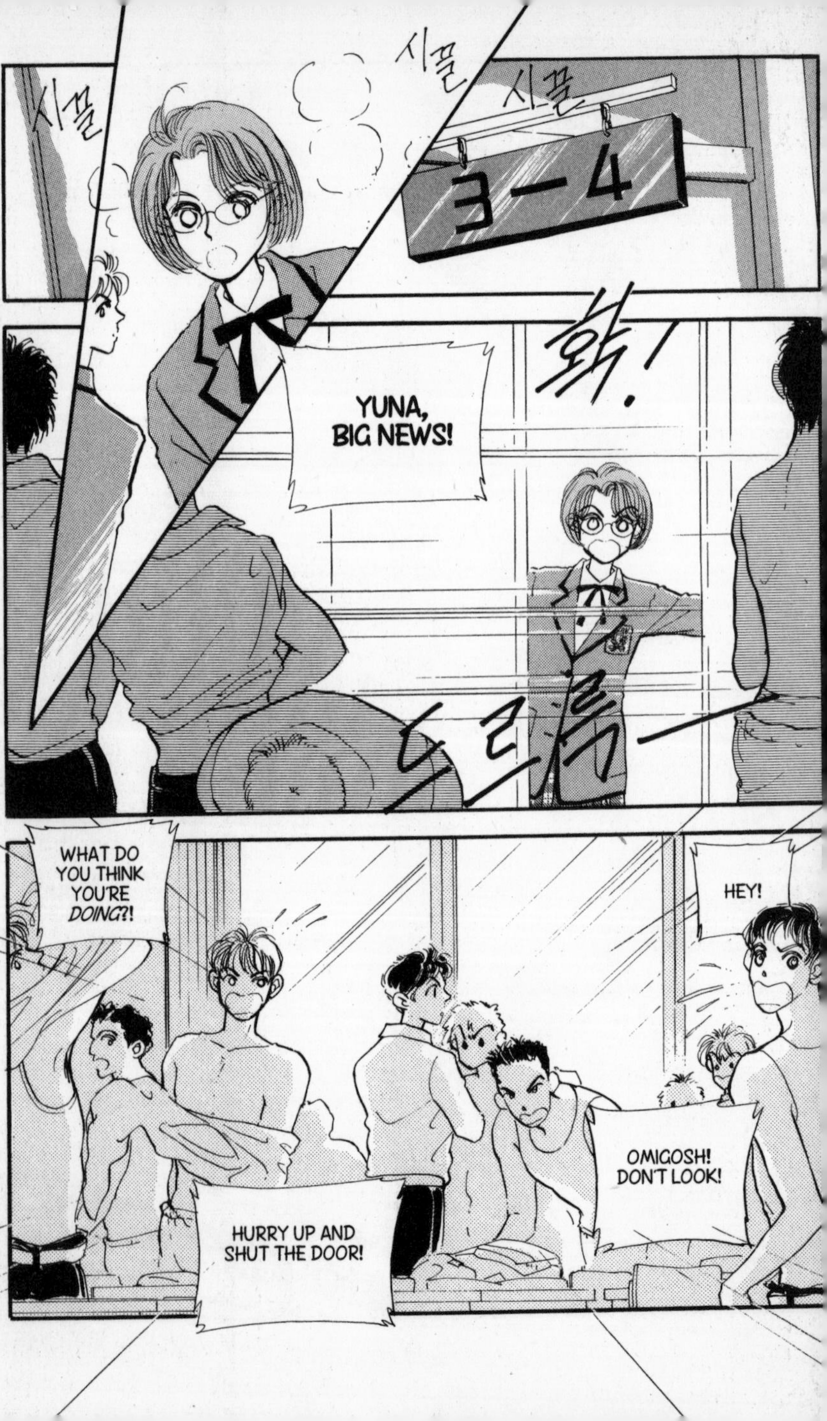
시끌
시끌
시끌
3-4
YUNA, BIG NEWS!
확!
드르륵
WHAT DO YOU THINK YOU'RE *DOING*?!
HEY!
OMIGOSH! DON'T LOOK!
HURRY UP AND SHUT THE DOOR!

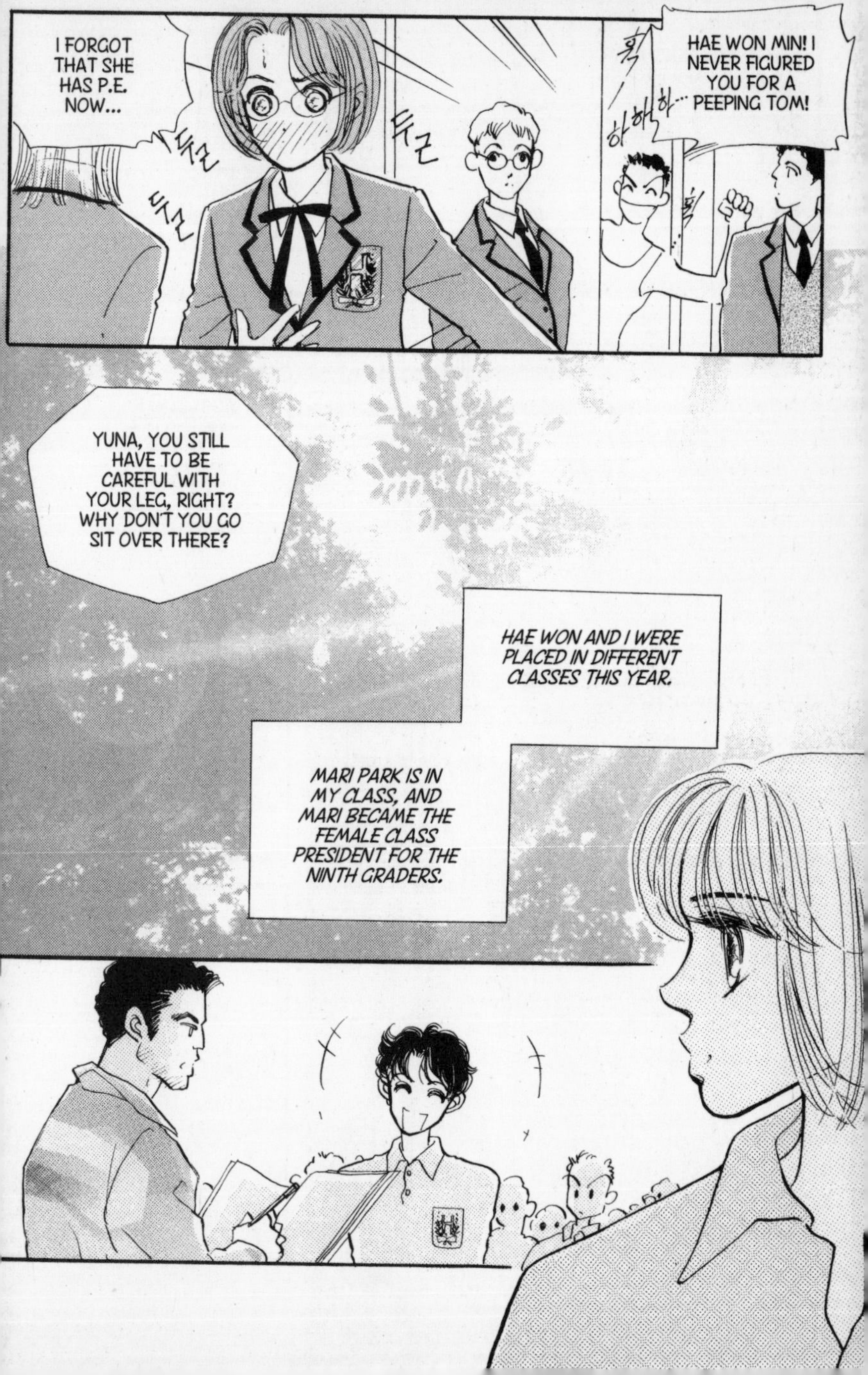
I FORGOT THAT SHE HAS P.E. NOW...
두근
두근
두근
HAE WON MIN! I NEVER FIGURED YOU FOR A PEEPING TOM!
YUNA, YOU STILL HAVE TO BE CAREFUL WITH YOUR LEG, RIGHT? WHY DON'T YOU GO SIT OVER THERE?
HAE WON AND I WERE PLACED IN DIFFERENT CLASSES THIS YEAR.
MARI PARK IS IN MY CLASS, AND MARI BECAME THE FEMALE CLASS PRESIDENT FOR THE NINTH GRADERS.

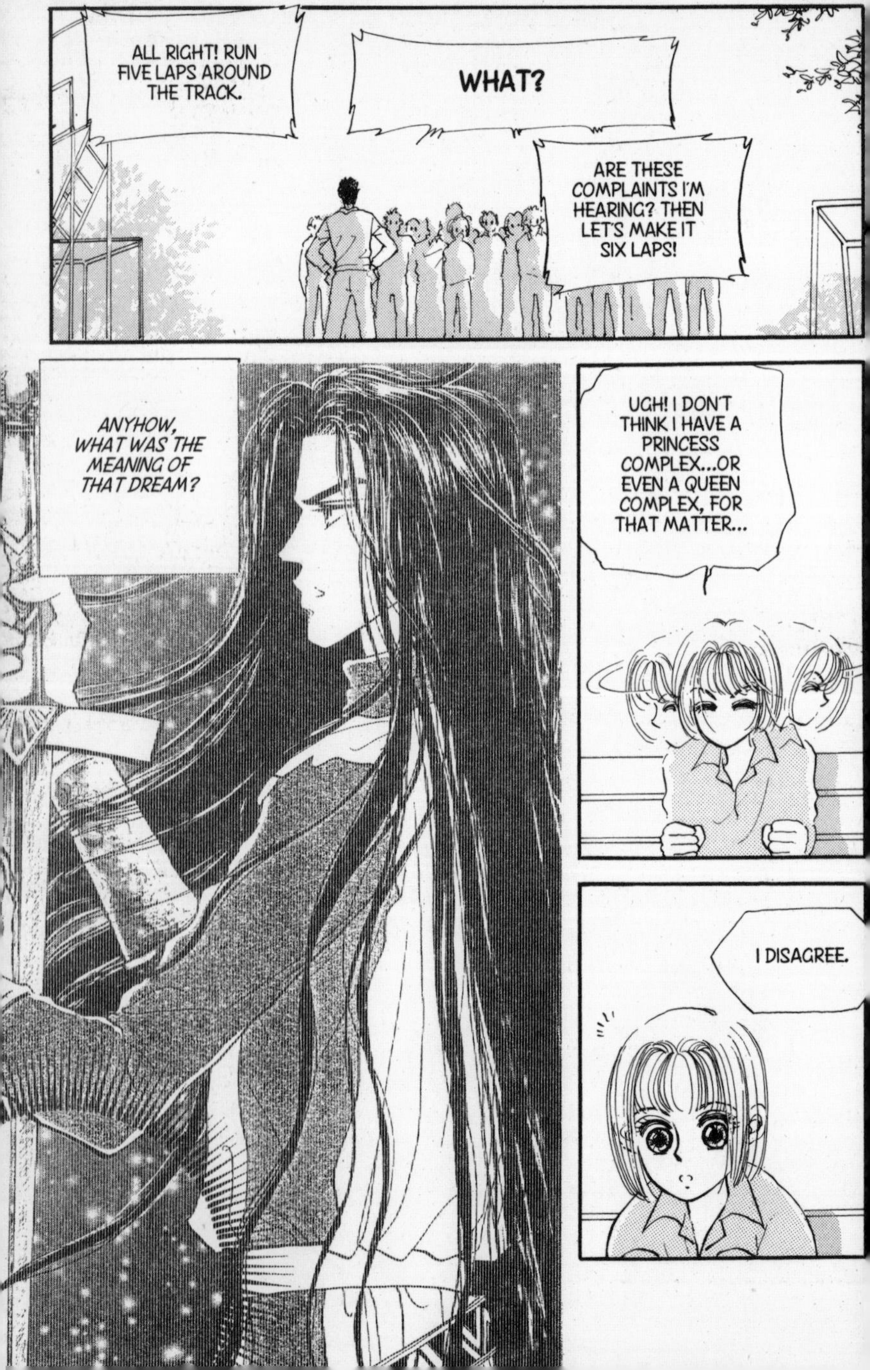
ALL RIGHT! RUN FIVE LAPS AROUND THE TRACK.
WHAT?
ARE THESE COMPLAINTS I'M HEARING? THEN LET'S MAKE IT SIX LAPS!
ANYHOW, WHAT WAS THE MEANING OF THAT DREAM?
UGH! I DON'T THINK I HAVE A PRINCESS COMPLEX...OR EVEN A QUEEN COMPLEX, FOR THAT MATTER...
I DISAGREE.

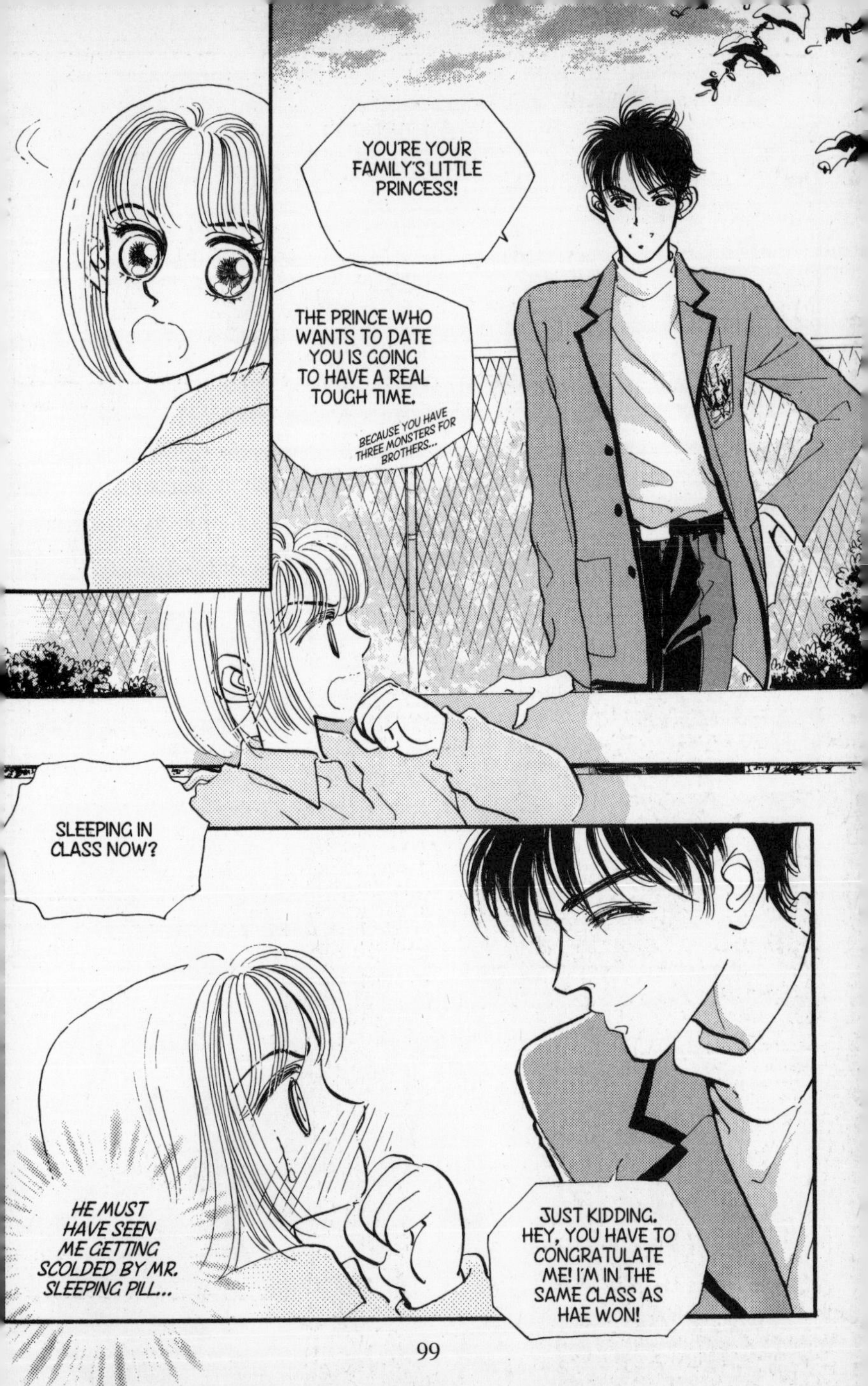
YOU'RE YOUR FAMILY'S LITTLE PRINCESS!
THE PRINCE WHO WANTS TO DATE YOU IS GOING TO HAVE A REAL TOUGH TIME.
BECAUSE YOU HAVE THREE MONSTERS FOR BROTHERS...
SLEEPING IN CLASS NOW?
HE MUST HAVE SEEN ME GETTING SCOLDED BY MR. SLEEPING PILL...
JUST KIDDING. HEY, YOU HAVE TO CONGRATULATE ME! I'M IN THE SAME CLASS AS HAE WON!

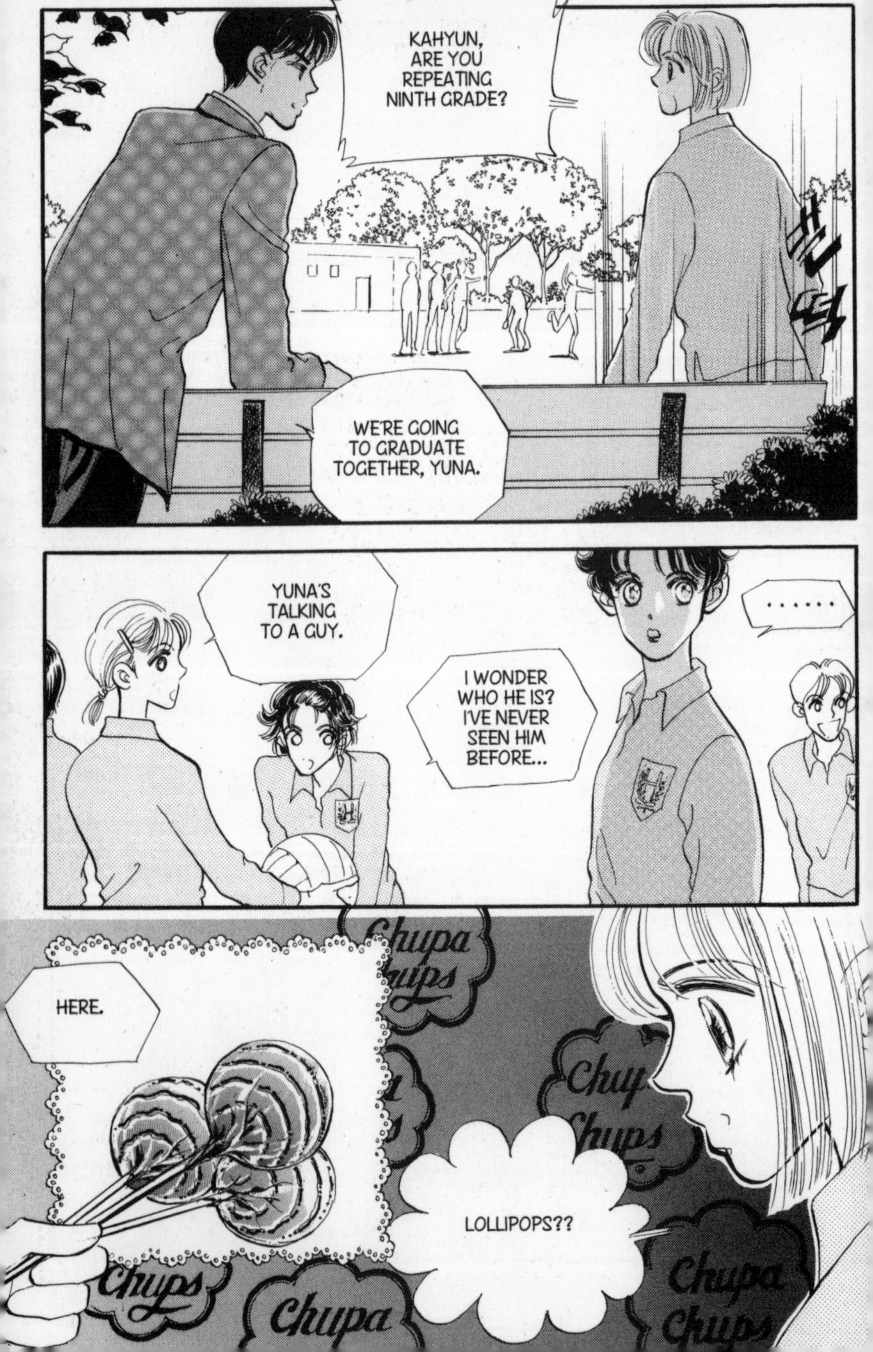
KAHYUN, ARE YOU REPEATING NINTH GRADE?
WE'RE GOING TO GRADUATE TOGETHER, YUNA.
YUNA'S TALKING TO A GUY.
I WONDER WHO HE IS? I'VE NEVER SEEN HIM BEFORE...
......
HERE.
Chupa Chups
LOLLIPOPS??

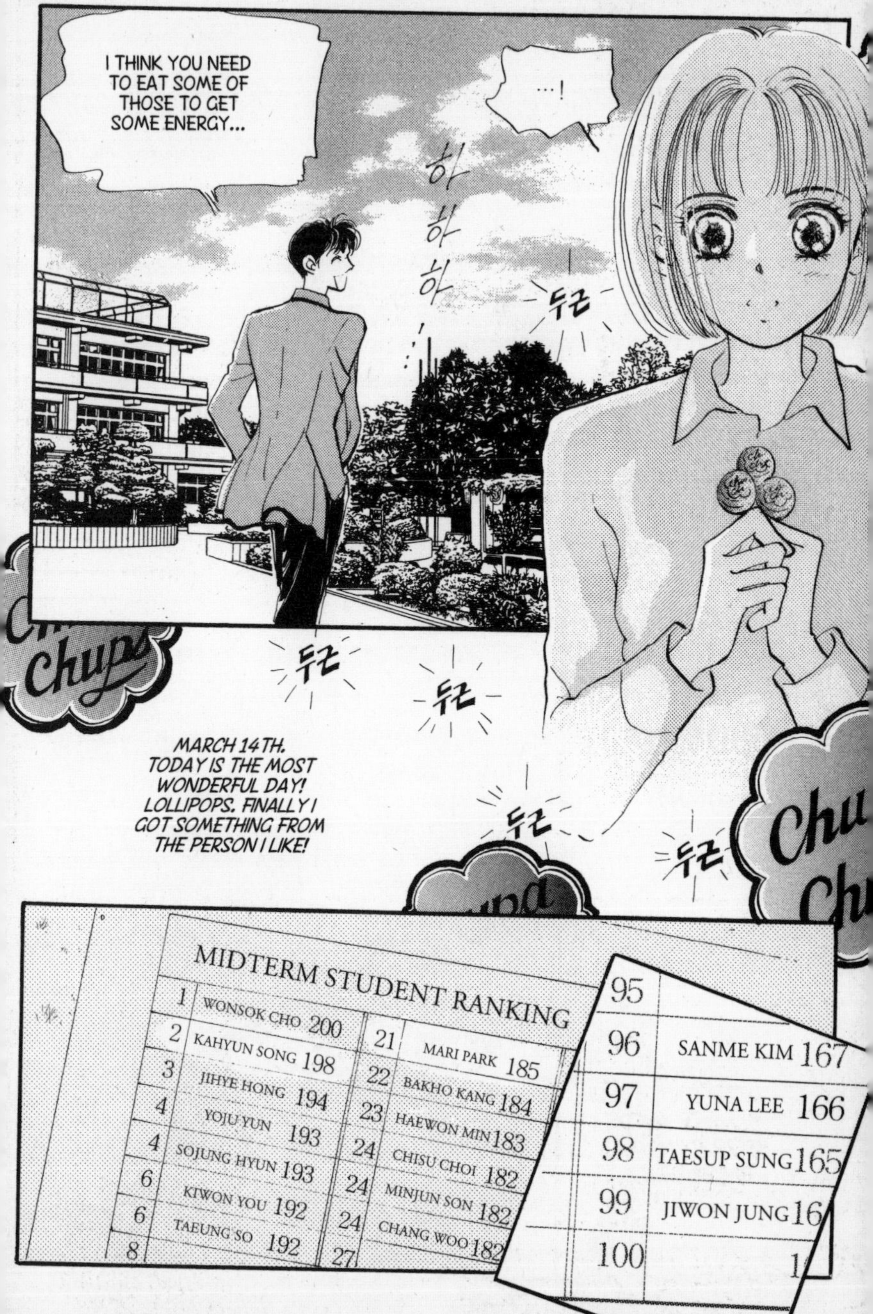
I THINK YOU NEED TO EAT SOME OF THOSE TO GET SOME ENERGY...
...!
하하하
두근
두근
두근
MARCH 14TH. TODAY IS THE MOST WONDERFUL DAY! LOLLIPOPS. FINALLY I GOT SOMETHING FROM THE PERSON I LIKE!
두근
두근
MIDTERM STUDENT RANKING
1 WONSOK CHO 200
2 KAHYUN SONG 198
3 JIHYE HONG 194
4 YOJU YUN 193
4 SOJUNG HYUN 193
6 KIWON YOU 192
6 TAEUNG SO 192
8
21 MARI PARK 185
22 BAKHO KANG 184
23 HAEWON MIN 183
24 CHISU CHOI 182
24 MINJUN SON 182
24 CHANG WOO 182
27
95
96 SANME KIM 167
97 YUNA LEE 166
98 TAESUP SUNG 165
99 JIWON JUNG
100

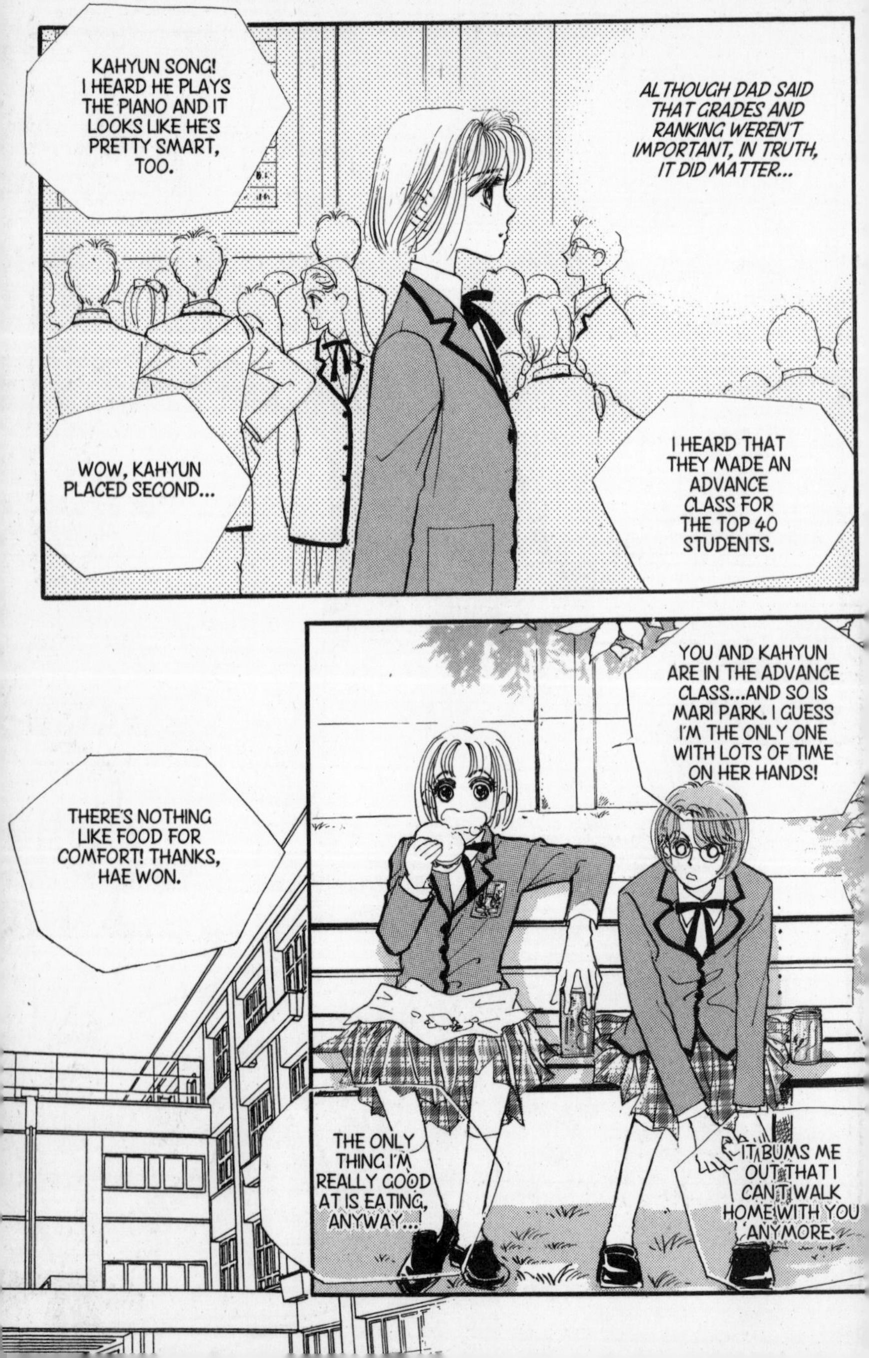
KAHYUN SONG! I HEARD HE PLAYS THE PIANO AND IT LOOKS LIKE HE'S PRETTY SMART, TOO.
ALTHOUGH DAD SAID THAT GRADES AND RANKING WEREN'T IMPORTANT, IN TRUTH, IT DID MATTER...
WOW, KAHYUN PLACED SECOND...
I HEARD THAT THEY MADE AN ADVANCE CLASS FOR THE TOP 40 STUDENTS.
YOU AND KAHYUN ARE IN THE ADVANCE CLASS...AND SO IS MARI PARK. I GUESS I'M THE ONLY ONE WITH LOTS OF TIME ON HER HANDS!
THERE'S NOTHING LIKE FOOD FOR COMFORT! THANKS, HAE WON.
THE ONLY THING I'M REALLY GOOD AT IS EATING, ANYWAY...
IT BUMS ME OUT THAT I CAN'T WALK HOME WITH YOU ANYMORE.

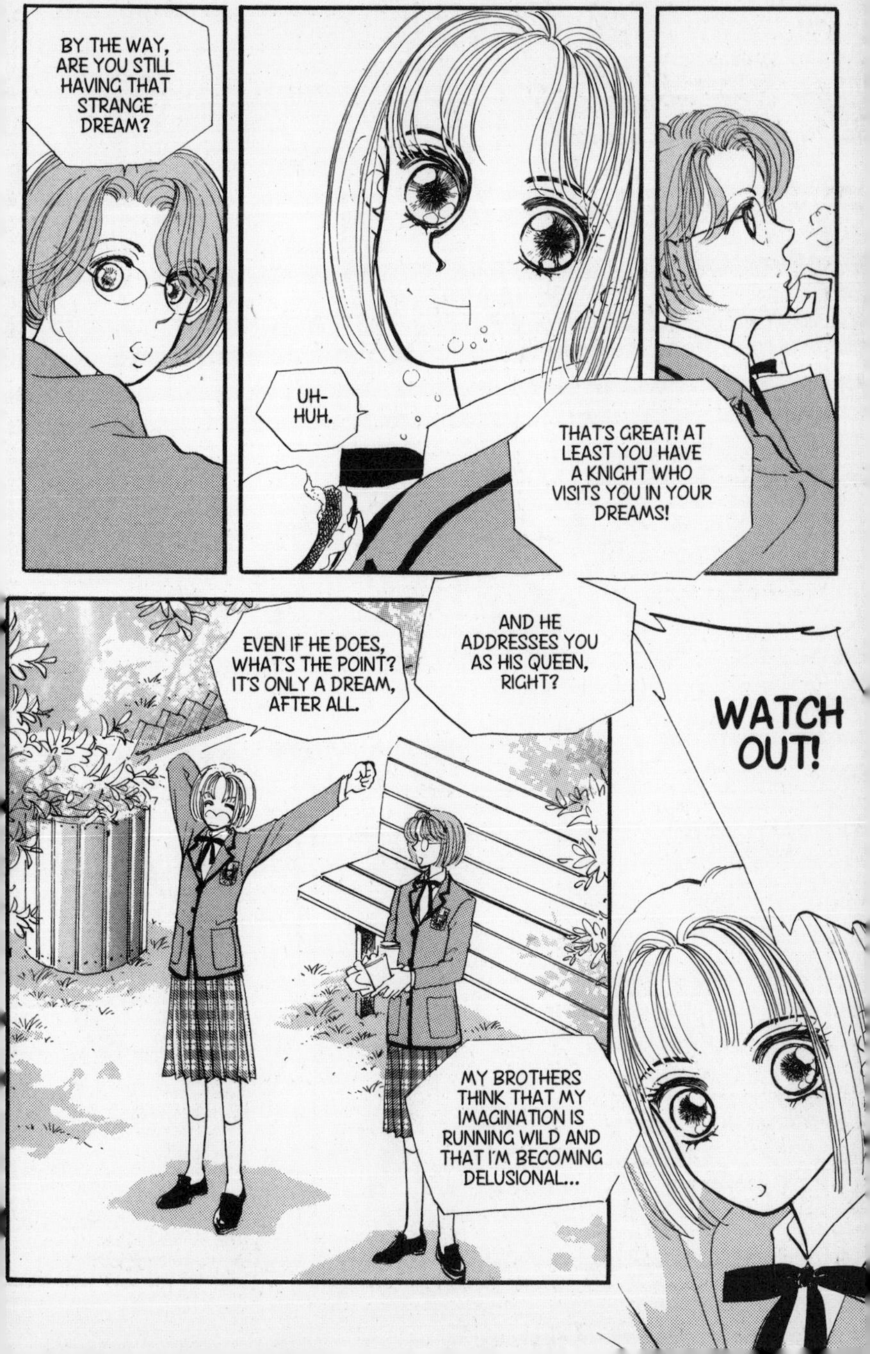
BY THE WAY, ARE YOU STILL HAVING THAT STRANGE DREAM?
UH-HUH.
THAT'S GREAT! AT LEAST YOU HAVE A KNIGHT WHO VISITS YOU IN YOUR DREAMS!
EVEN IF HE DOES, WHAT'S THE POINT? IT'S ONLY A DREAM, AFTER ALL.
AND HE ADDRESSES YOU AS HIS QUEEN, RIGHT?
MY BROTHERS THINK THAT MY IMAGINATION IS RUNNING WILD AND THAT I'M BECOMING DELUSIONAL...
WATCH OUT!

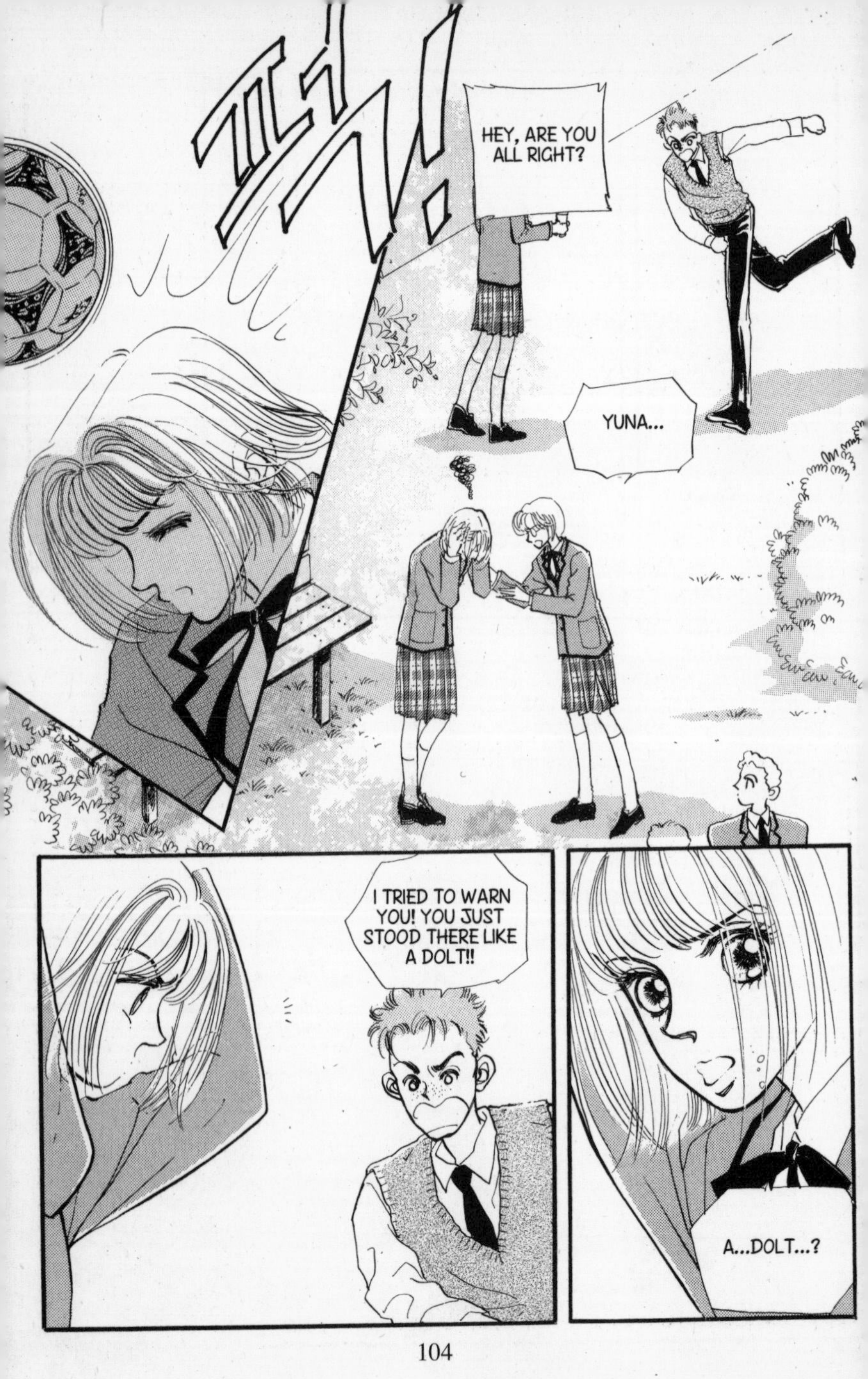
HEY, ARE YOU ALL RIGHT?
YUNA...
I TRIED TO WARN YOU! YOU JUST STOOD THERE LIKE A DOLT!!
A...DOLT...?

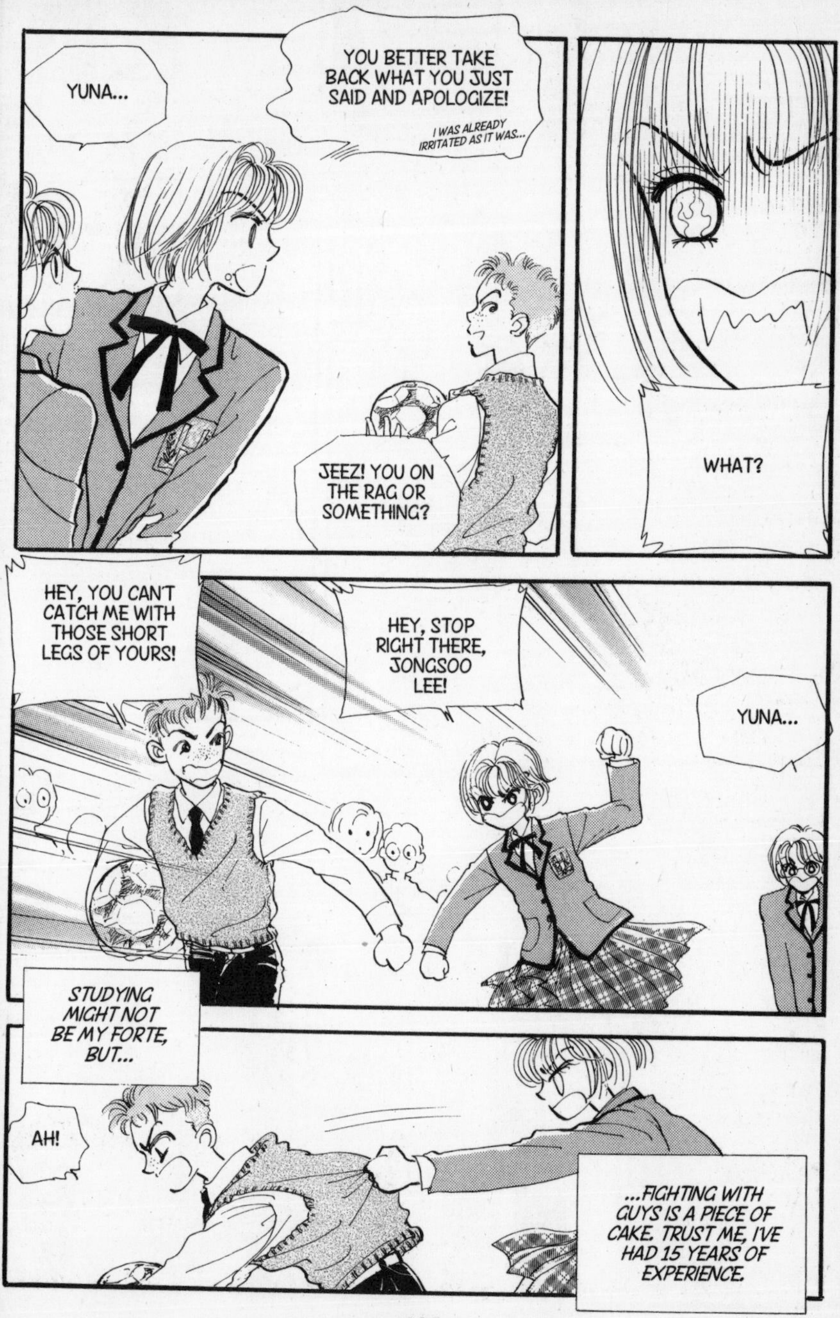

YUNA...
YOU BETTER TAKE BACK WHAT YOU JUST SAID AND APOLOGIZE!
I WAS ALREADY IRRITATED AS IT WAS...
JEEZ! YOU ON THE RAG OR SOMETHING?
WHAT?
HEY, YOU CAN'T CATCH ME WITH THOSE SHORT LEGS OF YOURS!
HEY, STOP RIGHT THERE, JONGSOO LEE!
YUNA...
STUDYING MIGHT NOT BE MY FORTE, BUT...
AH!
...FIGHTING WITH GUYS IS A PIECE OF CAKE. TRUST ME, I'VE HAD 15 YEARS OF EXPERIENCE.

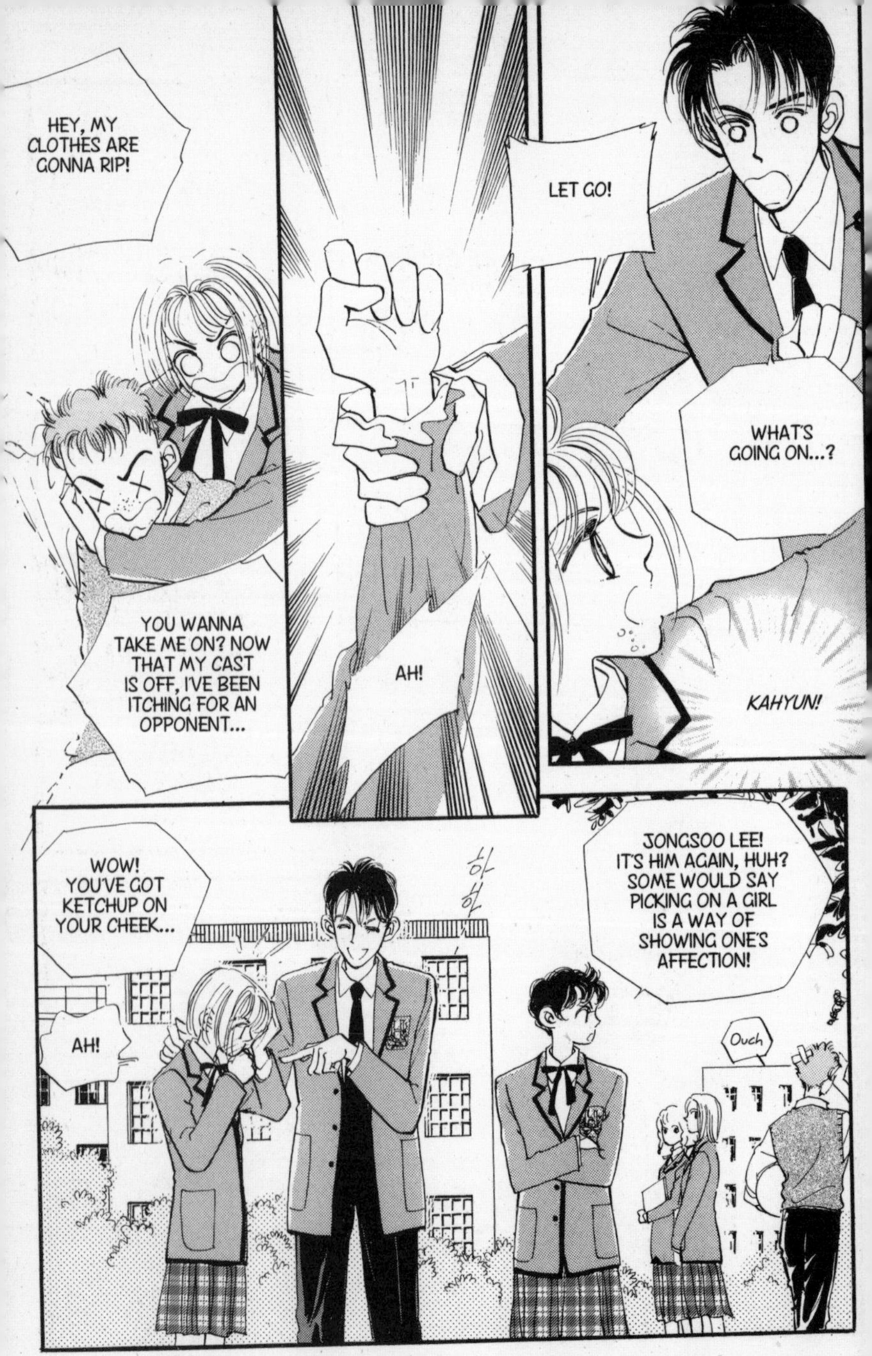
HEY, MY CLOTHES ARE GONNA RIP!
YOU WANNA TAKE ME ON? NOW THAT MY CAST IS OFF, I'VE BEEN ITCHING FOR AN OPPONENT...
AH!
LET GO!
WHAT'S GOING ON...?
KAHYUN!
WOW! YOU'VE GOT KETCHUP ON YOUR CHEEK...
AH!
하하
JONGSOO LEE! IT'S HIM AGAIN, HUH? SOME WOULD SAY PICKING ON A GIRL IS A WAY OF SHOWING ONE'S AFFECTION!
Ouch

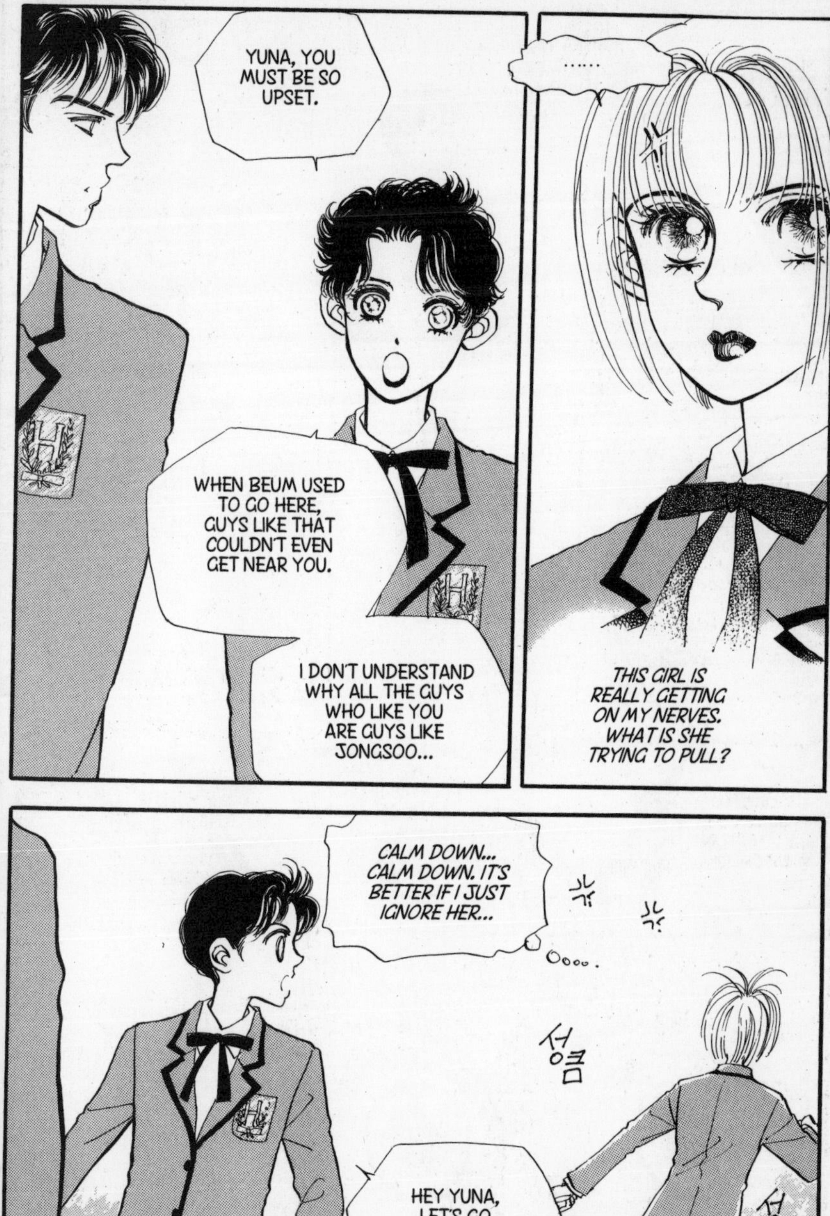
YUNA, YOU MUST BE SO UPSET.
WHEN BEUM USED TO GO HERE, GUYS LIKE THAT COULDN'T EVEN GET NEAR YOU.
I DON'T UNDERSTAND WHY ALL THE GUYS WHO LIKE YOU ARE GUYS LIKE JONGSOO...
......
THIS GIRL IS REALLY GETTING ON MY NERVES. WHAT IS SHE TRYING TO PULL?
CALM DOWN... CALM DOWN. IT'S BETTER IF I JUST IGNORE HER...
Oooo.
성큼
HEY YUNA, LET'S GO TOGETHER...
성큼

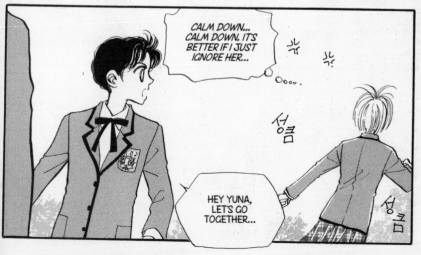

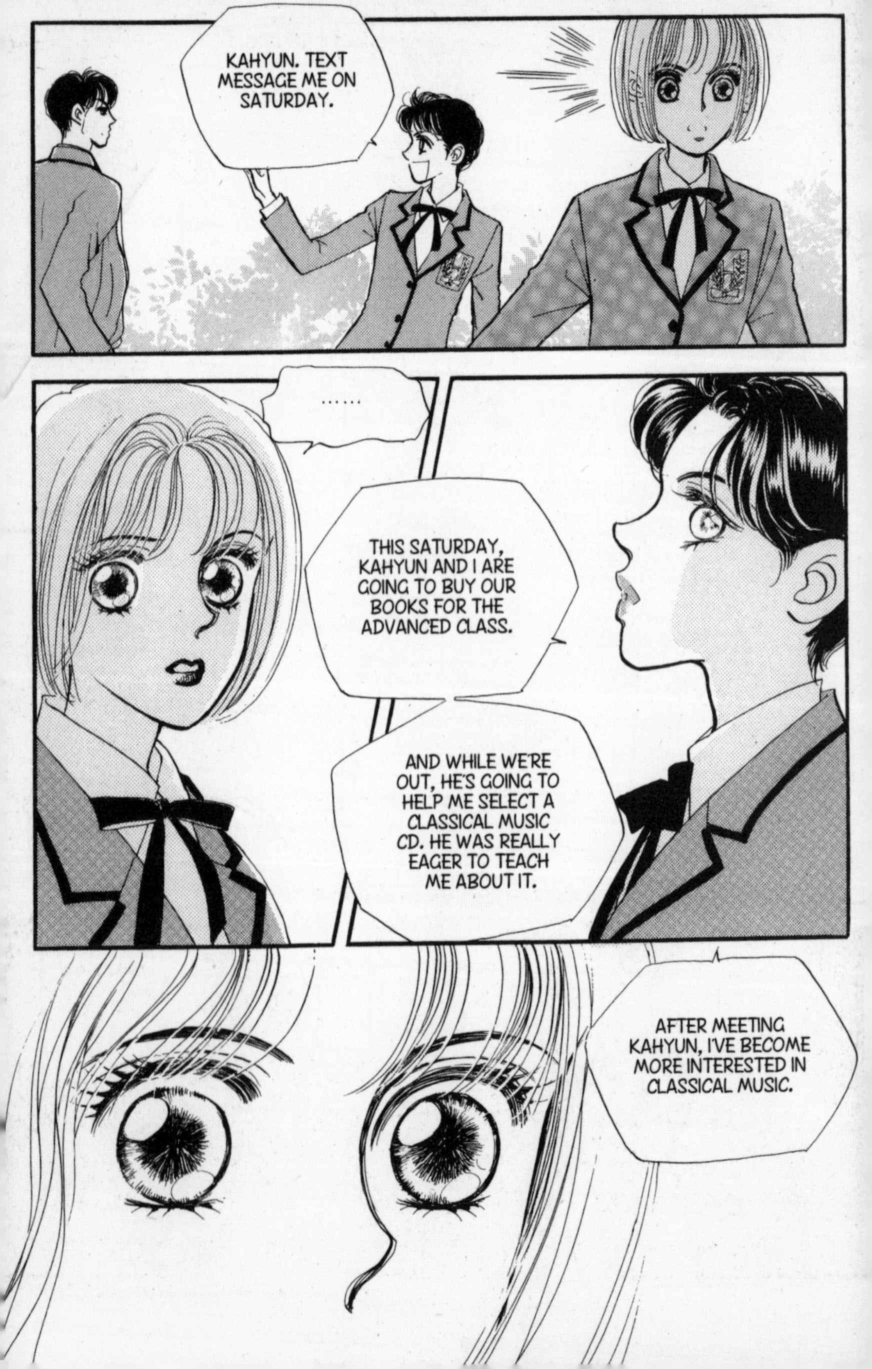
KAHYUN. TEXT MESSAGE ME ON SATURDAY.
......
THIS SATURDAY, KAHYUN AND I ARE GOING TO BUY OUR BOOKS FOR THE ADVANCED CLASS.
AND WHILE WE'RE OUT, HE'S GOING TO HELP ME SELECT A CLASSICAL MUSIC CD. HE WAS REALLY EAGER TO TEACH ME ABOUT IT.
AFTER MEETING KAHYUN, I'VE BECOME MORE INTERESTED IN CLASSICAL MUSIC.

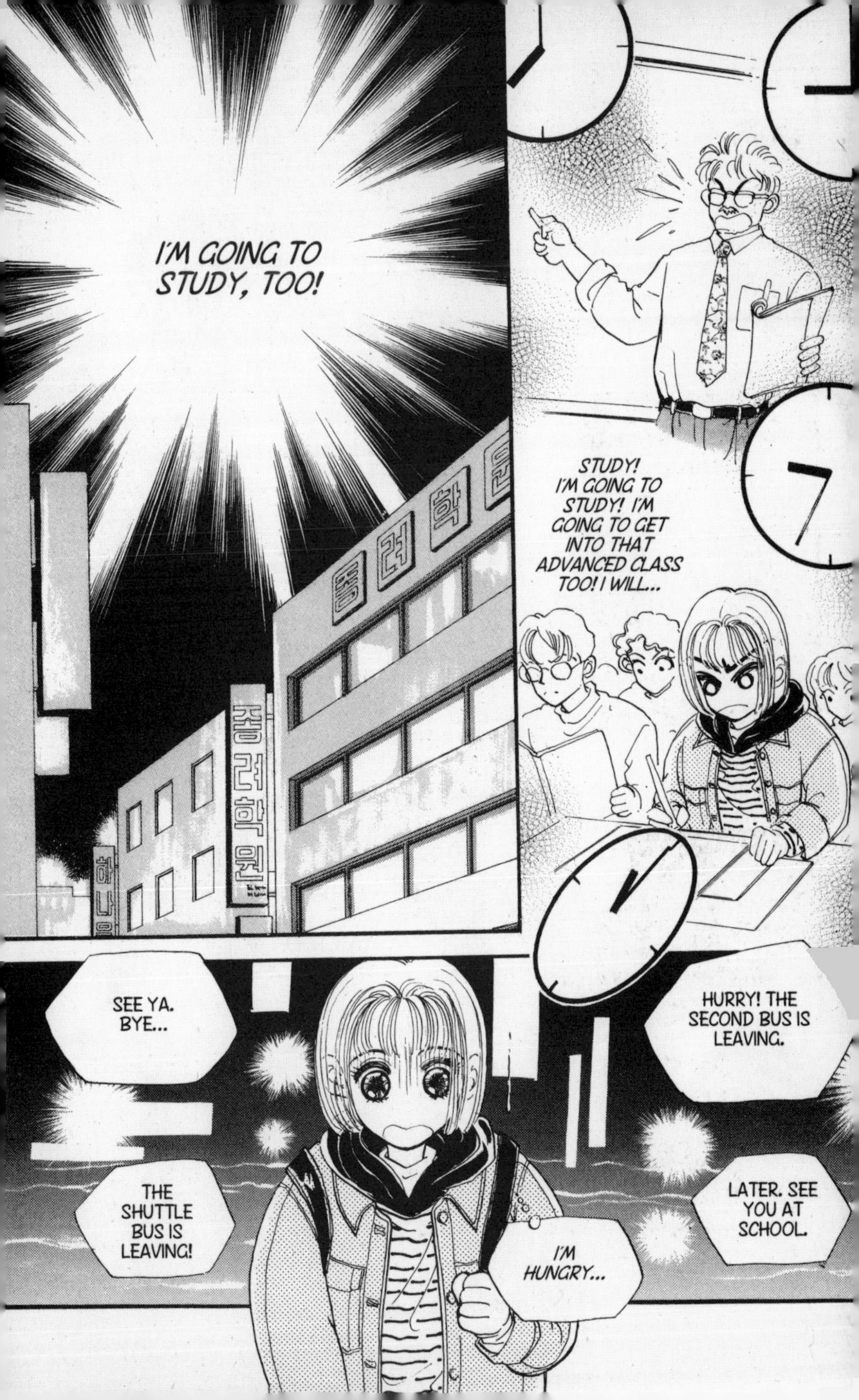
I'M GOING TO STUDY, TOO!
STUDY! I'M GOING TO STUDY! I'M GOING TO GET INTO THAT ADVANCED CLASS TOO! I WILL...
SEE YA. BYE...
HURRY! THE SECOND BUS IS LEAVING.
LATER. SEE YOU AT SCHOOL.
THE SHUTTLE BUS IS LEAVING!
I'M HUNGRY...

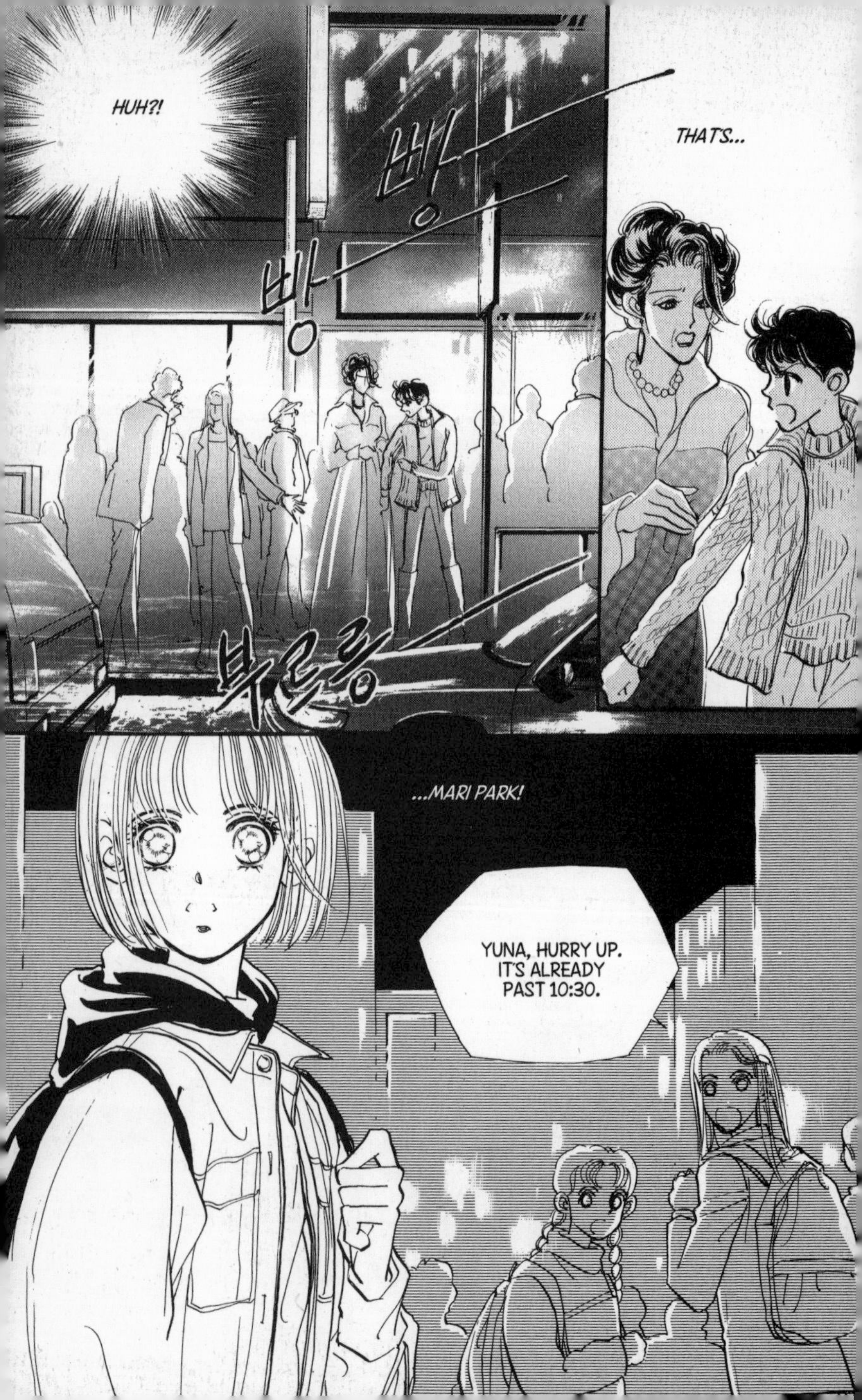
HUH?!
빵
빵
부르릉
THATS...
...MARI PARK!
YUNA, HURRY UP. IT'S ALREADY PAST 10:30.

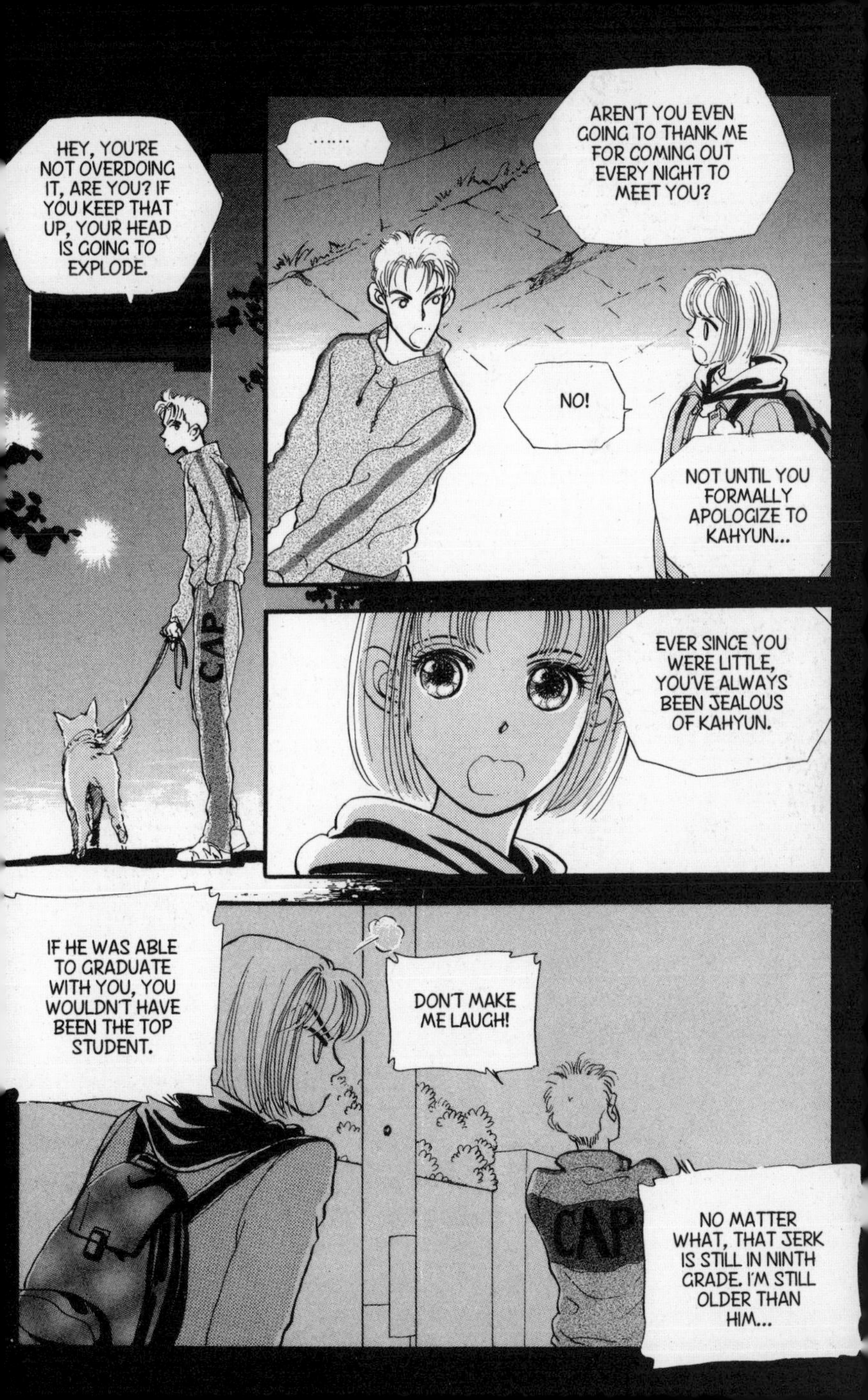
HEY, YOU'RE NOT OVERDOING IT, ARE YOU? IF YOU KEEP THAT UP, YOUR HEAD IS GOING TO EXPLODE.
......
AREN'T YOU EVEN GOING TO THANK ME FOR COMING OUT EVERY NIGHT TO MEET YOU?
NO!
NOT UNTIL YOU FORMALLY APOLOGIZE TO KAHYUN...
EVER SINCE YOU WERE LITTLE, YOU'VE ALWAYS BEEN JEALOUS OF KAHYUN.
IF HE WAS ABLE TO GRADUATE WITH YOU, YOU WOULDN'T HAVE BEEN THE TOP STUDENT.
DON'T MAKE ME LAUGH!
NO MATTER WHAT, THAT JERK IS STILL IN NINTH GRADE. I'M STILL OLDER THAN HIM...

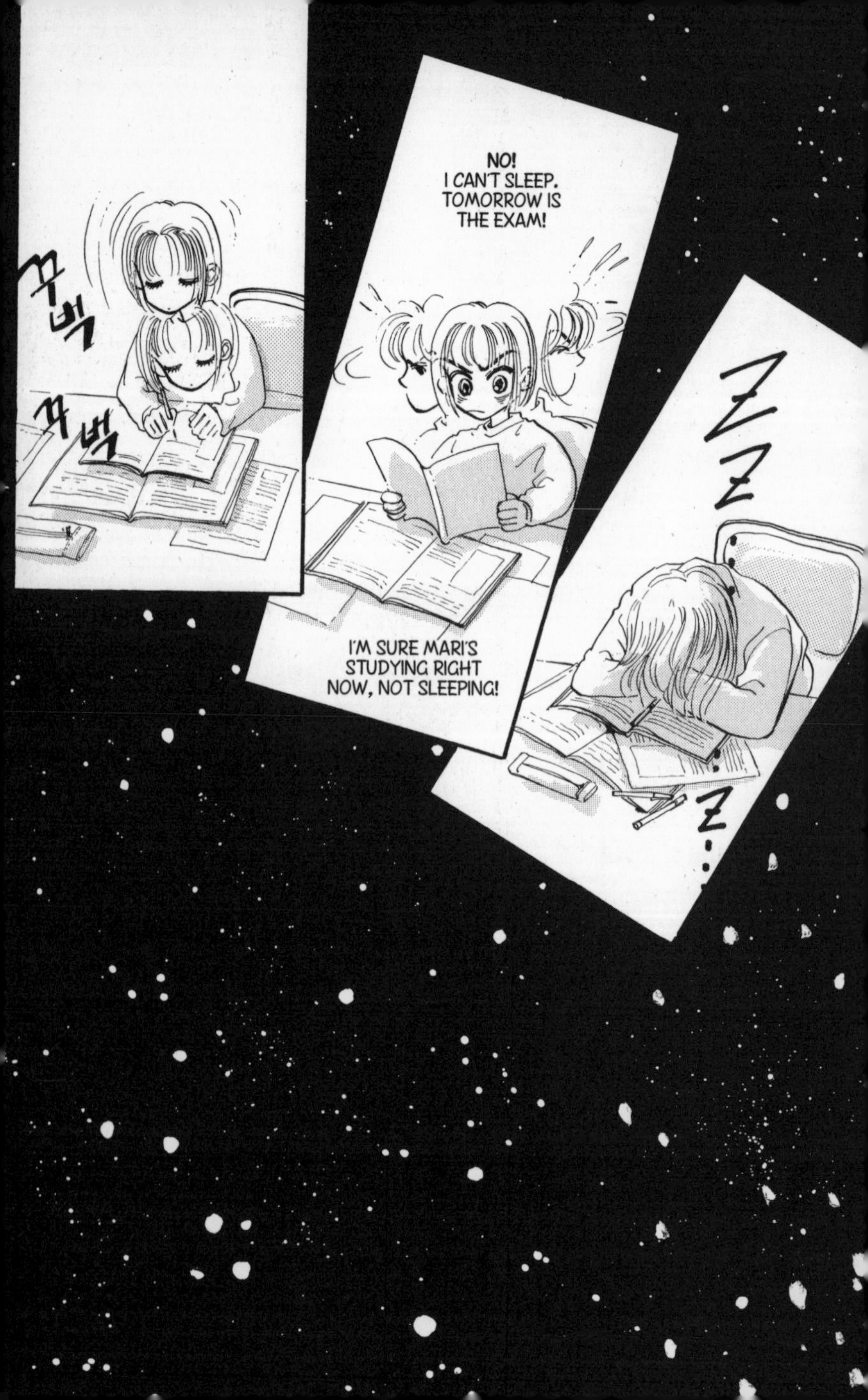
꾸벅
꾸벅
NO! I CAN'T SLEEP. TOMORROW IS THE EXAM!
I'M SURE MARI'S STUDYING RIGHT NOW, NOT SLEEPING!
ZZZ
Z...

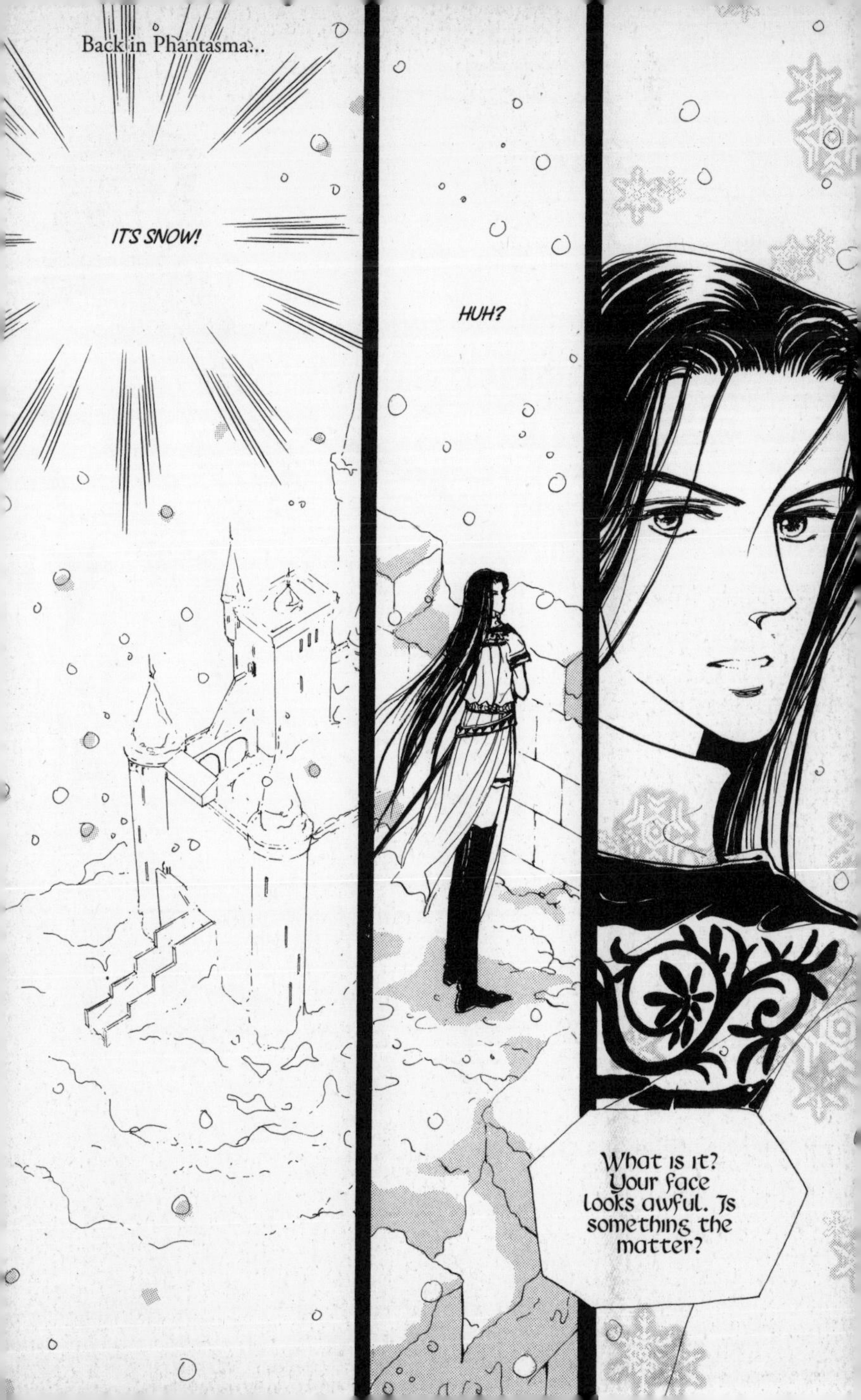
Back in Phantasma...
IT'S SNOW!
HUH?
What is it? Your face looks awful. Is something the matter?

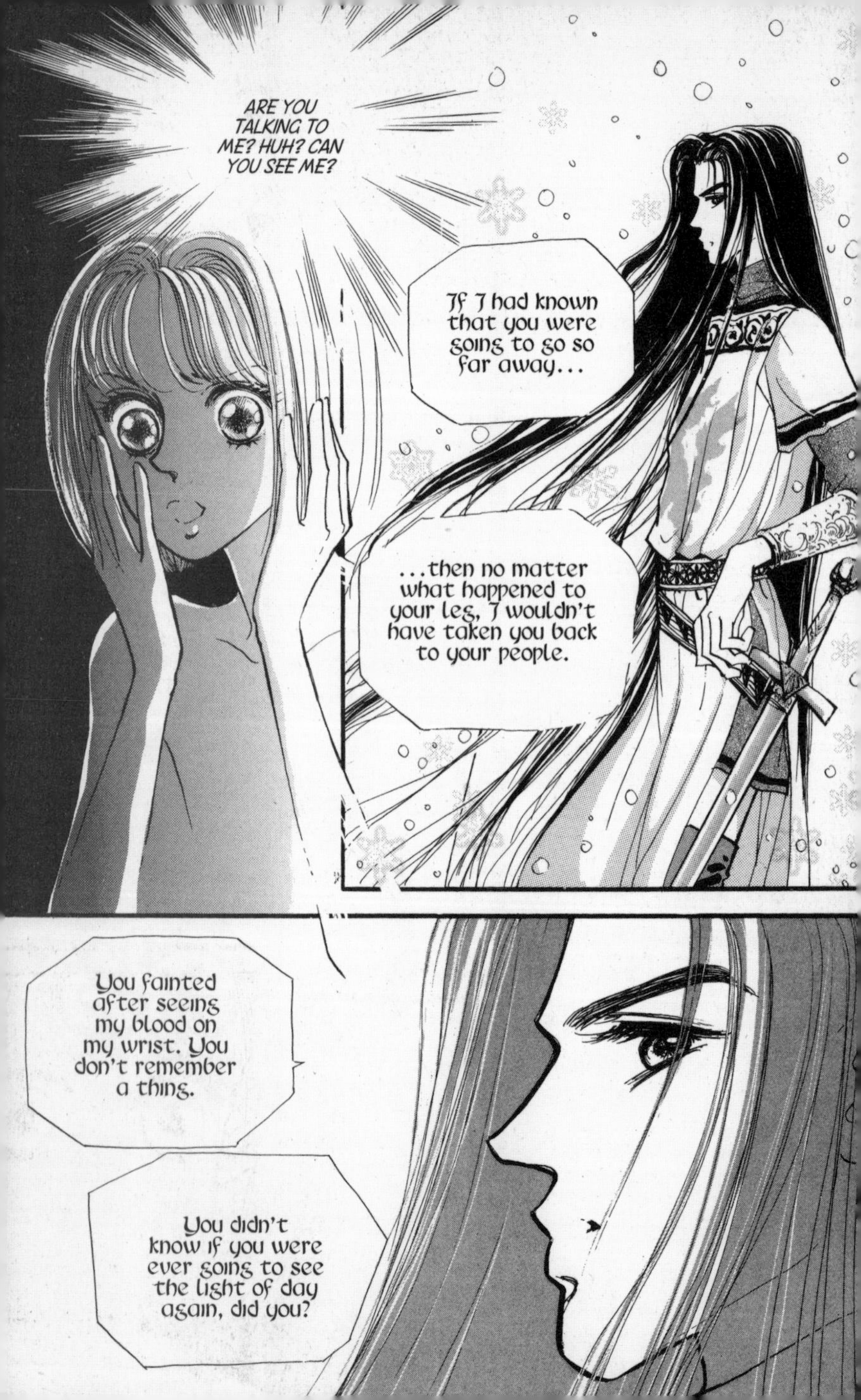

ARE YOU TALKING TO ME? HUH? CAN YOU SEE ME?
If I had known that you were going to go so far away...
...then no matter what happened to your leg, I wouldn't have taken you back to your people.
You fainted after seeing my blood on my wrist. You don't remember a thing.
You didn't know if you were ever going to see the light of day again, did you?

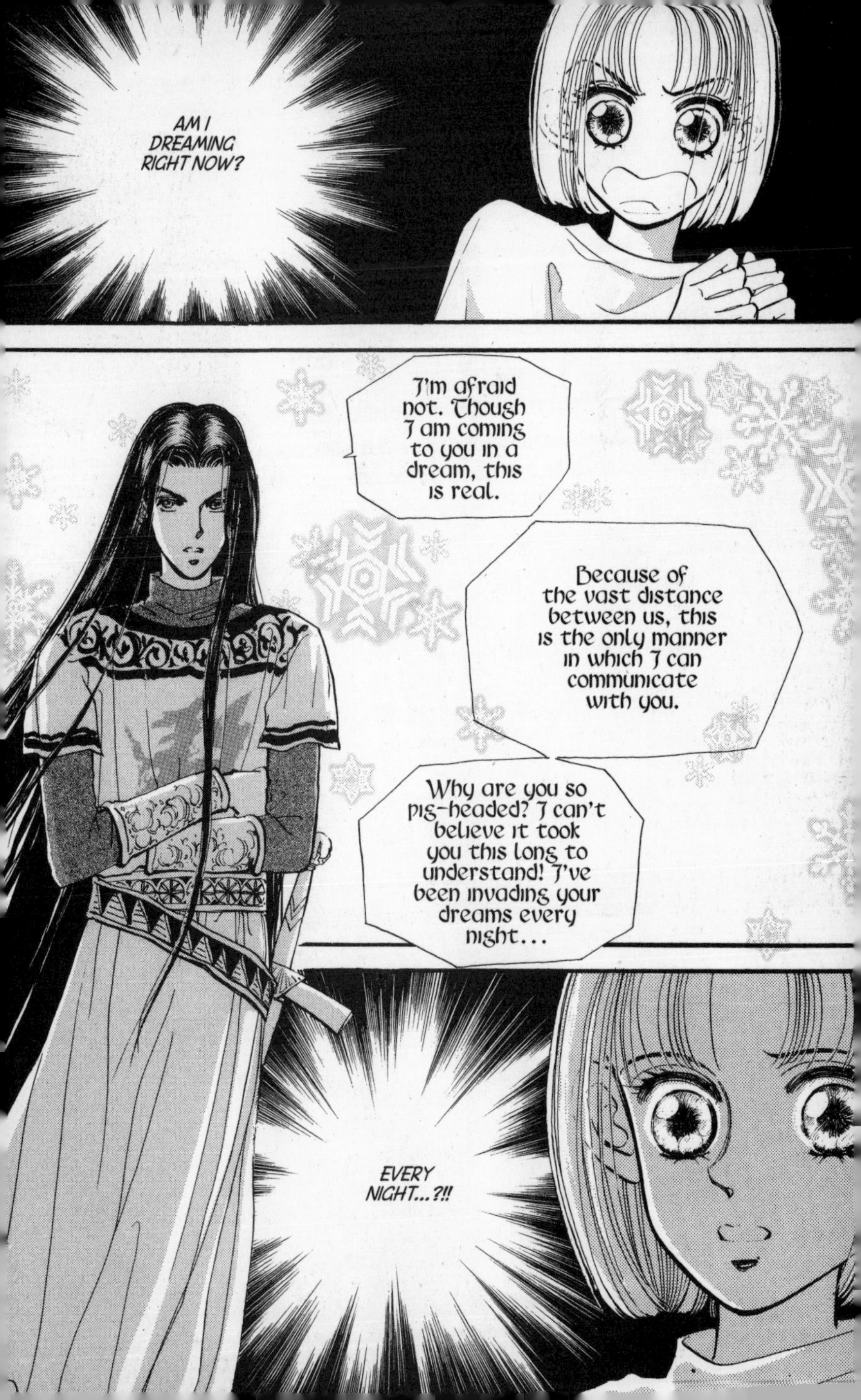
AM I DREAMING RIGHT NOW?
I'm afraid not. Though I am coming to you in a dream, this is real.
Because of the vast distance between us, this is the only manner in which I can communicate with you.
Why are you so pig-headed? I can't believe it took you this long to understand! I've been invading your dreams every night...
EVERY NIGHT...?!!

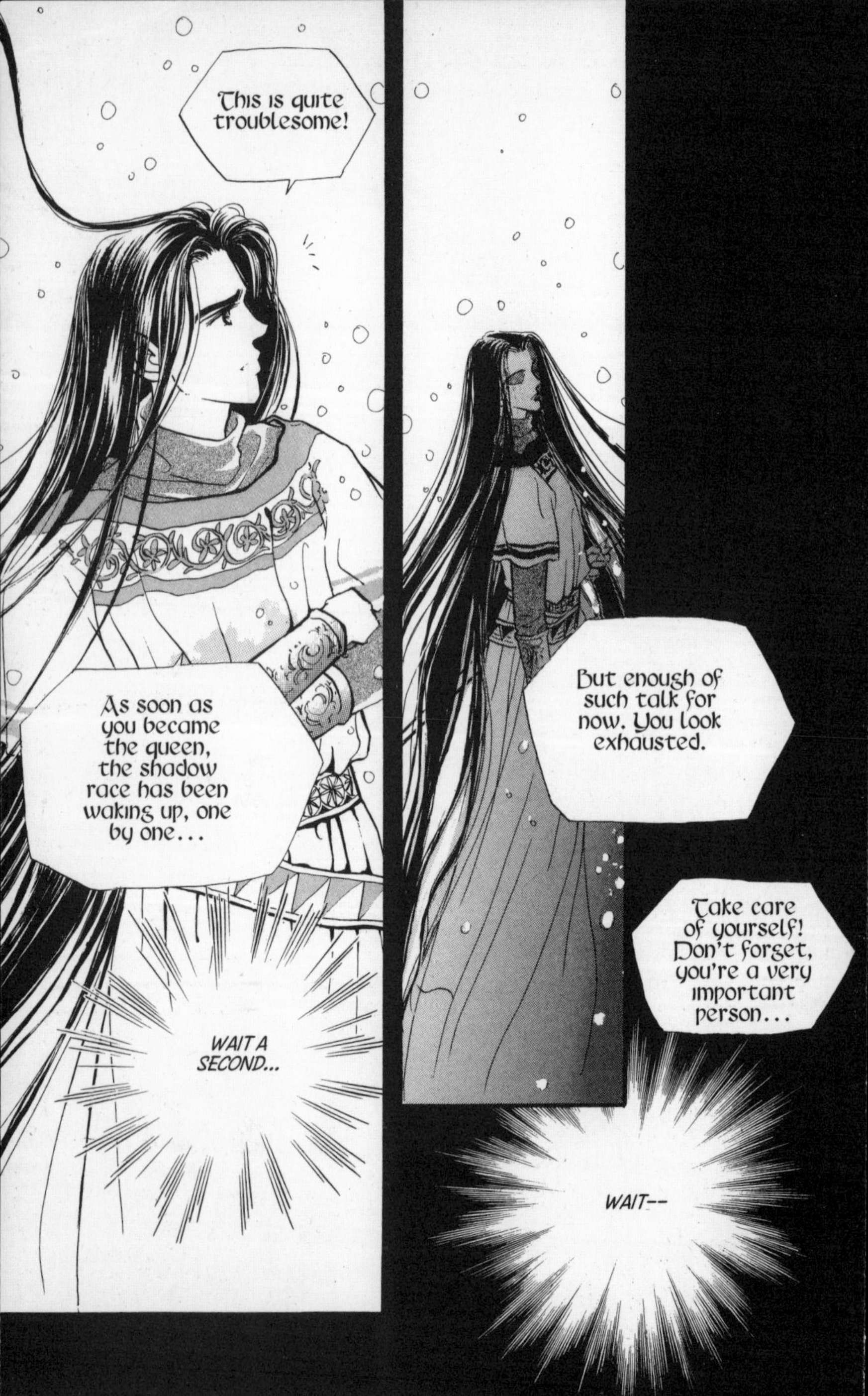
This is quite troublesome!
As soon as you became the queen, the shadow race has been waking up, one by one...
WAIT A SECOND...
But enough of such talk for now. You look exhausted.
Take care of yourself! Don't forget, you're a very important person...
WAIT--

The next day...

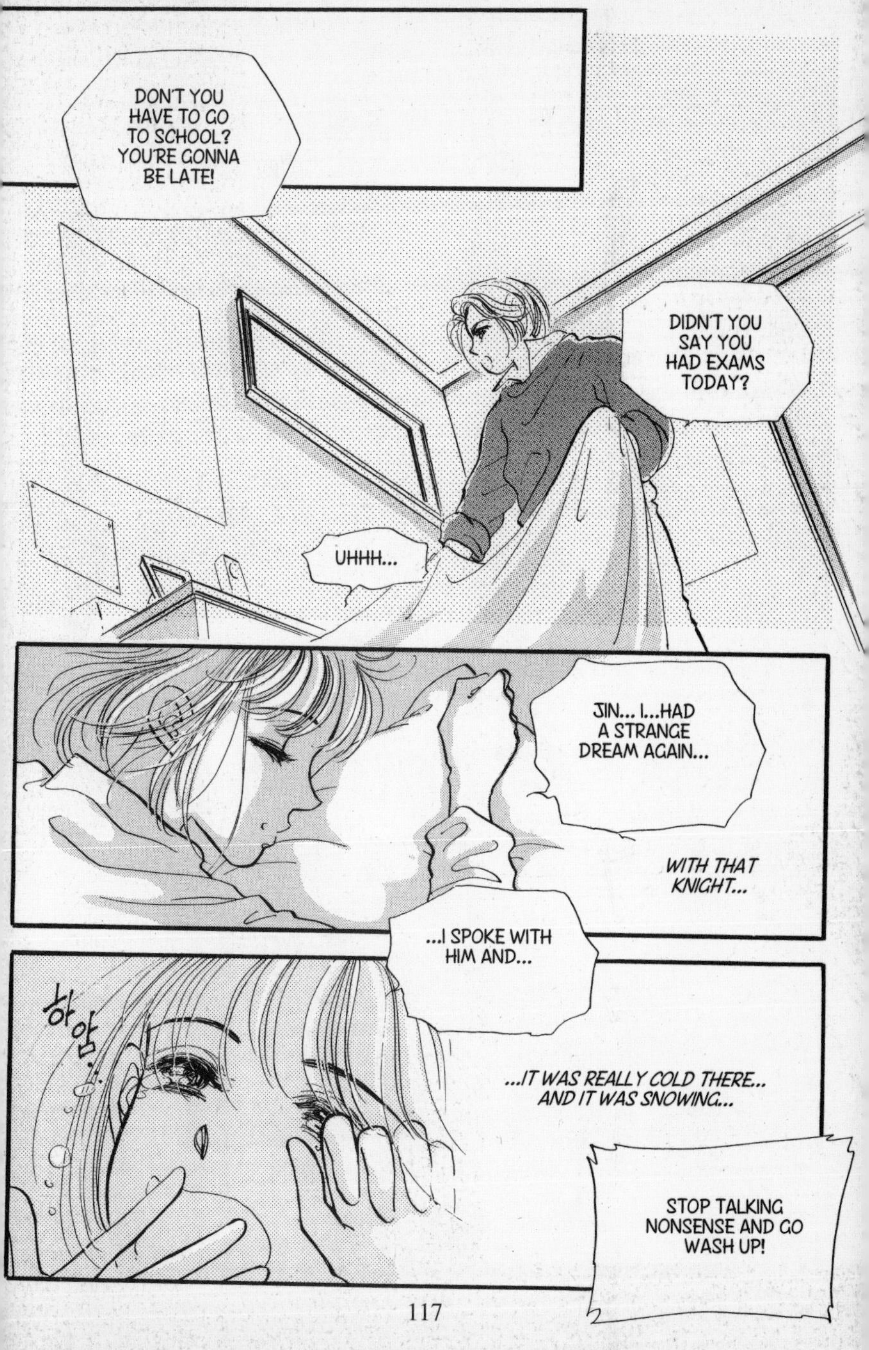
DON'T YOU HAVE TO GO TO SCHOOL? YOU'RE GONNA BE LATE!
DIDN'T YOU SAY YOU HAD EXAMS TODAY?
UHHH...
JIN... I...HAD A STRANGE DREAM AGAIN...
WITH THAT KNIGHT...
...I SPOKE WITH HIM AND...
하암
...IT WAS REALLY COLD THERE... AND IT WAS SNOWING...
STOP TALKING NONSENSE AND GO WASH UP!

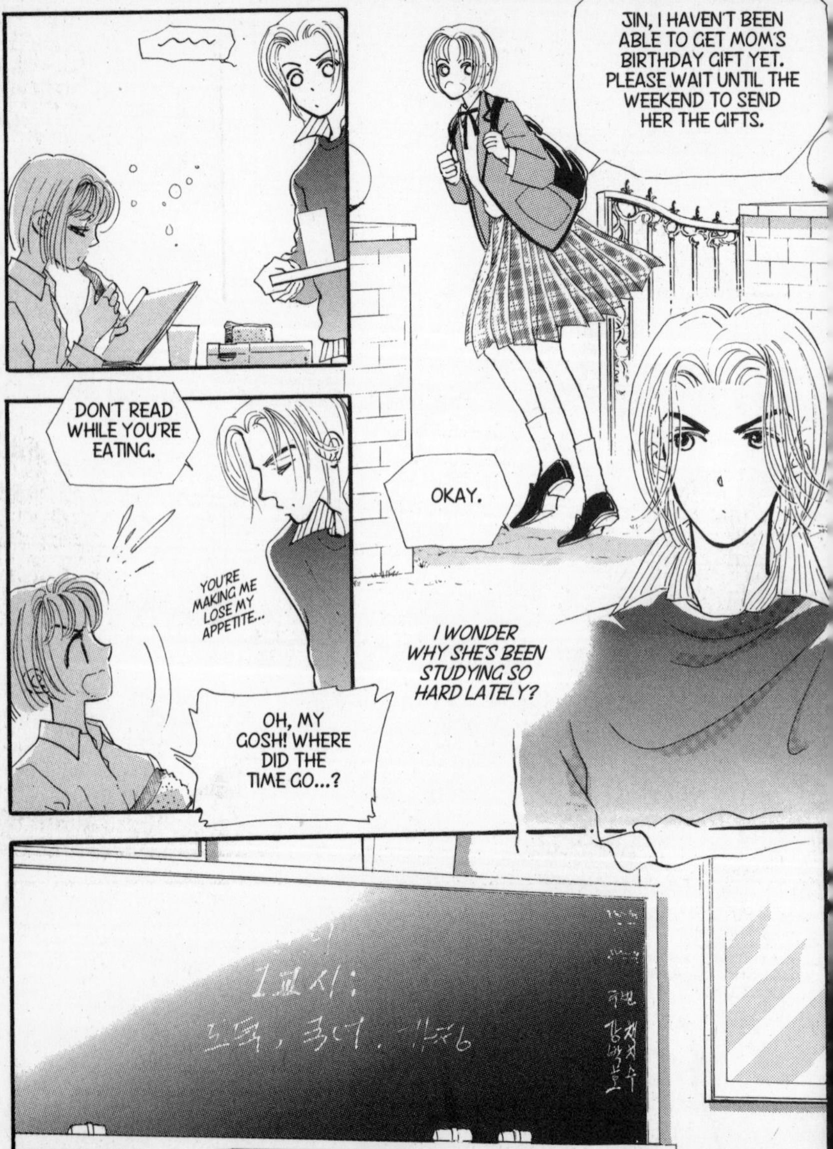
DON'T READ WHILE YOU'RE EATING.
YOU'RE MAKING ME LOSE MY APPETITE...
OH, MY GOSH! WHERE DID THE TIME GO...?
JIN, I HAVEN'T BEEN ABLE TO GET MOM'S BIRTHDAY GIFT YET. PLEASE WAIT UNTIL THE WEEKEND TO SEND HER THE GIFTS.
OKAY.
I WONDER WHY SHE'S BEEN STUDYING SO HARD LATELY?

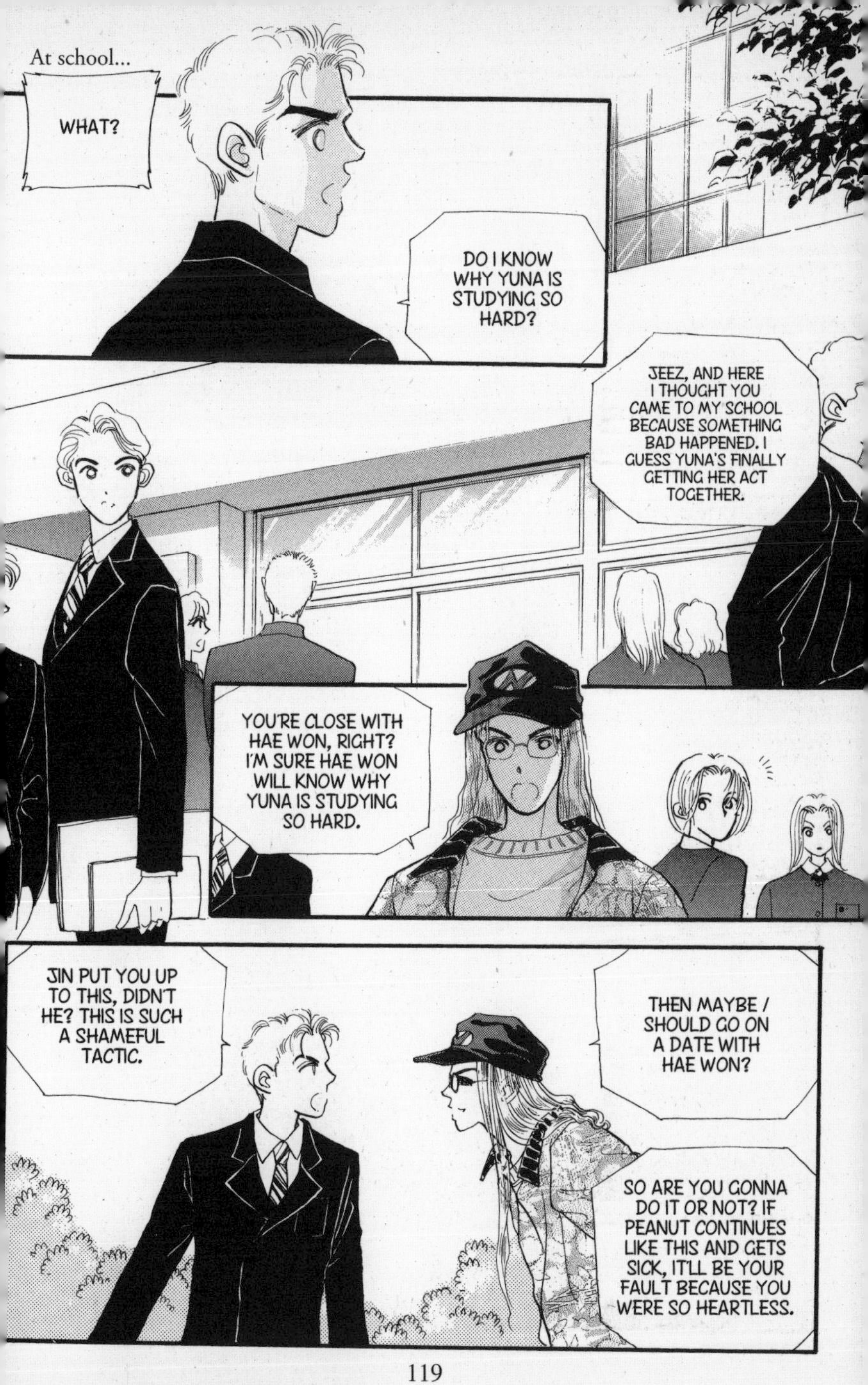
At school...
WHAT?
DO I KNOW WHY YUNA IS STUDYING SO HARD?
JEEZ, AND HERE I THOUGHT YOU CAME TO MY SCHOOL BECAUSE SOMETHING BAD HAPPENED. I GUESS YUNA'S FINALLY GETTING HER ACT TOGETHER.
YOU'RE CLOSE WITH HAE WON, RIGHT? I'M SURE HAE WON WILL KNOW WHY YUNA IS STUDYING SO HARD.
JIN PUT YOU UP TO THIS, DIDN'T HE? THIS IS SUCH A SHAMEFUL TACTIC.
THEN MAYBE I SHOULD GO ON A DATE WITH HAE WON?
SO ARE YOU GONNA DO IT OR NOT? IF PEANUT CONTINUES LIKE THIS AND GETS SICK, IT'LL BE YOUR FAULT BECAUSE YOU WERE SO HEARTLESS.

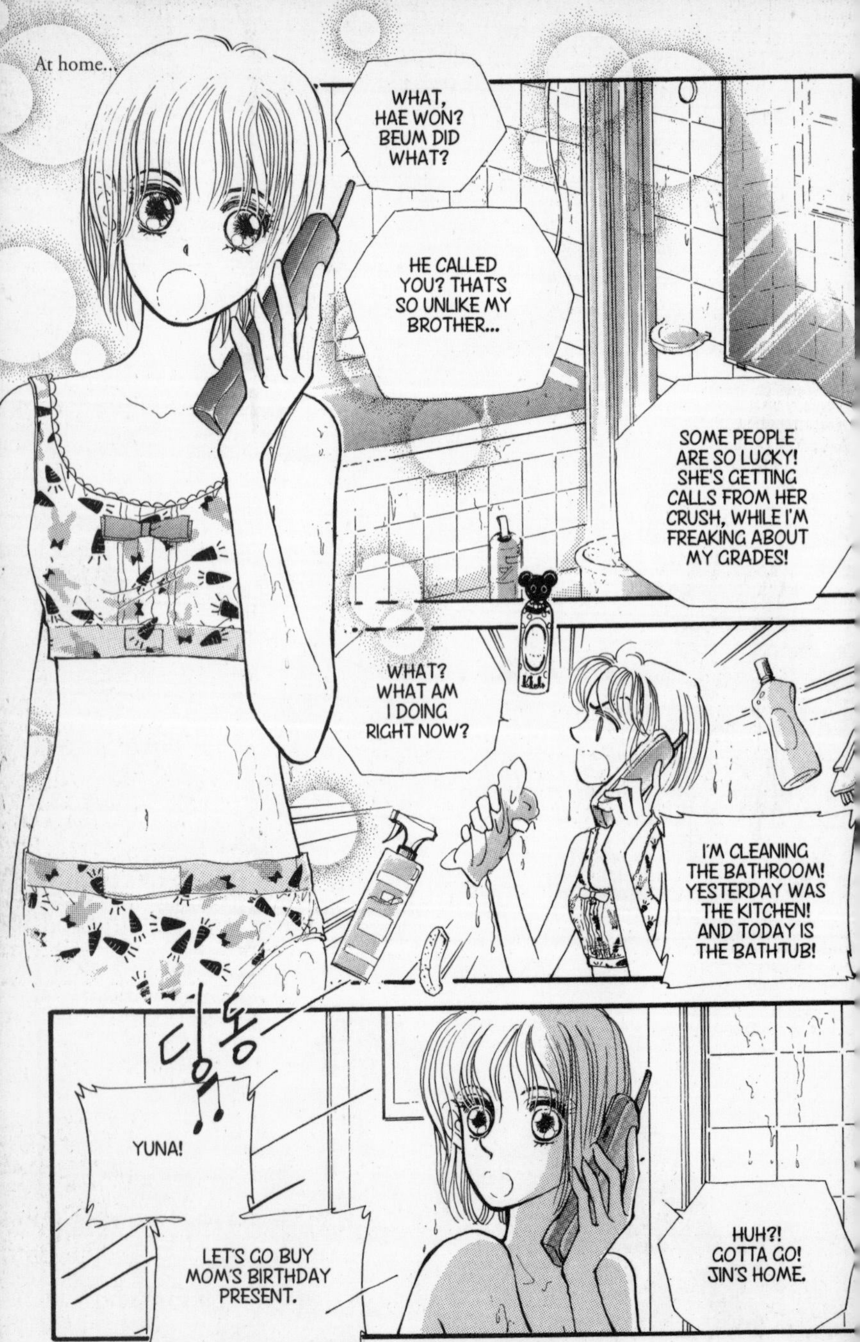
At home...
WHAT, HAE WON? BEUM DID WHAT?
HE CALLED YOU? THAT'S SO UNLIKE MY BROTHER...
SOME PEOPLE ARE SO LUCKY! SHE'S GETTING CALLS FROM HER CRUSH, WHILE I'M FREAKING ABOUT MY GRADES!
WHAT? WHAT AM I DOING RIGHT NOW?
I'M CLEANING THE BATHROOM! YESTERDAY WAS THE KITCHEN! AND TODAY IS THE BATHTUB!
딩동
YUNA!
LET'S GO BUY MOM'S BIRTHDAY PRESENT.
HUH?! GOTTA GO! JIN'S HOME.

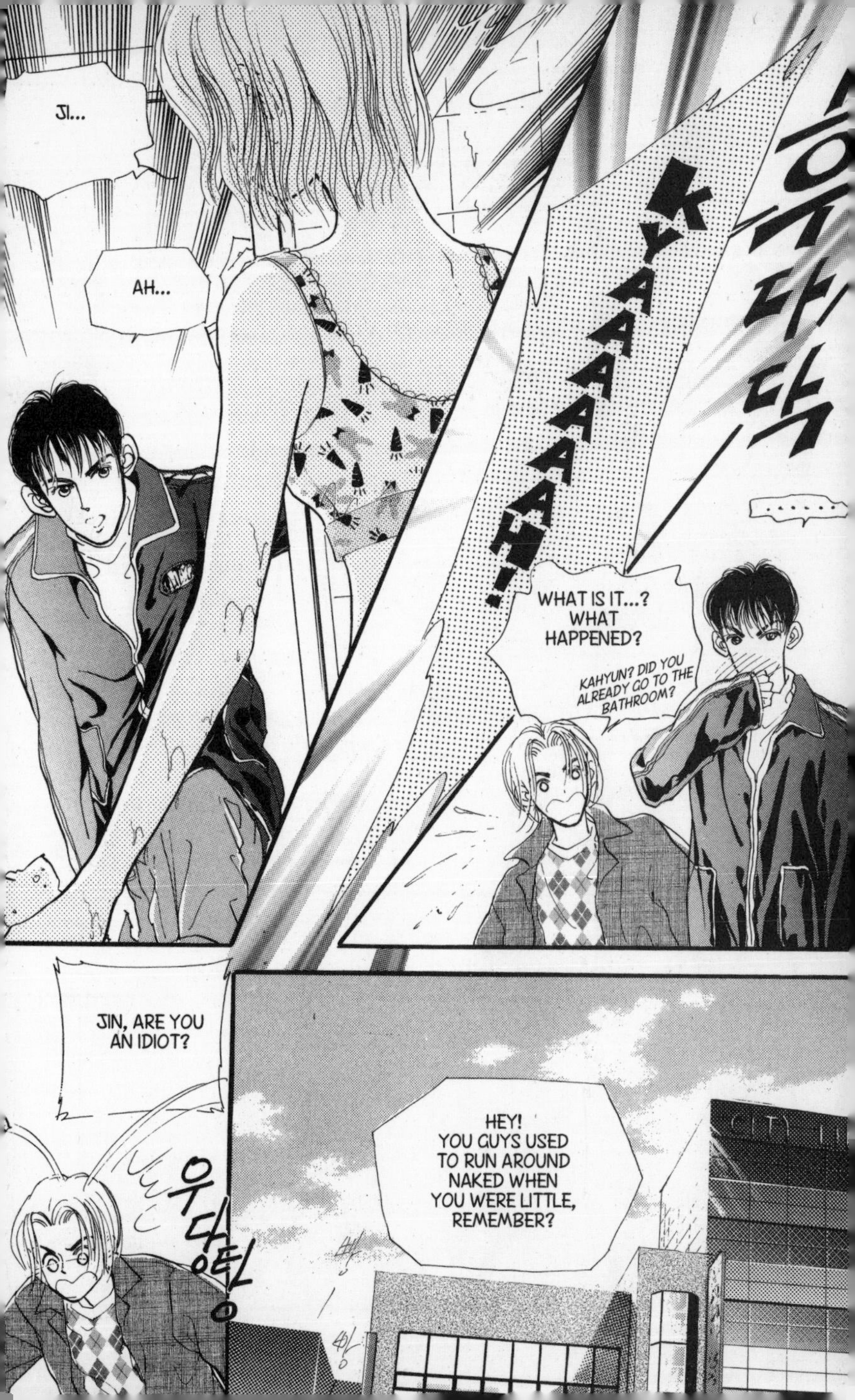
JI...
AH...
KYAAAAAAAH!!
......
WHAT IS IT...? WHAT HAPPENED?
KAHYUN? DID YOU ALREADY GO TO THE BATHROOM?
JIN, ARE YOU AN IDIOT?
HEY! YOU GUYS USED TO RUN AROUND NAKED WHEN YOU WERE LITTLE, REMEMBER?

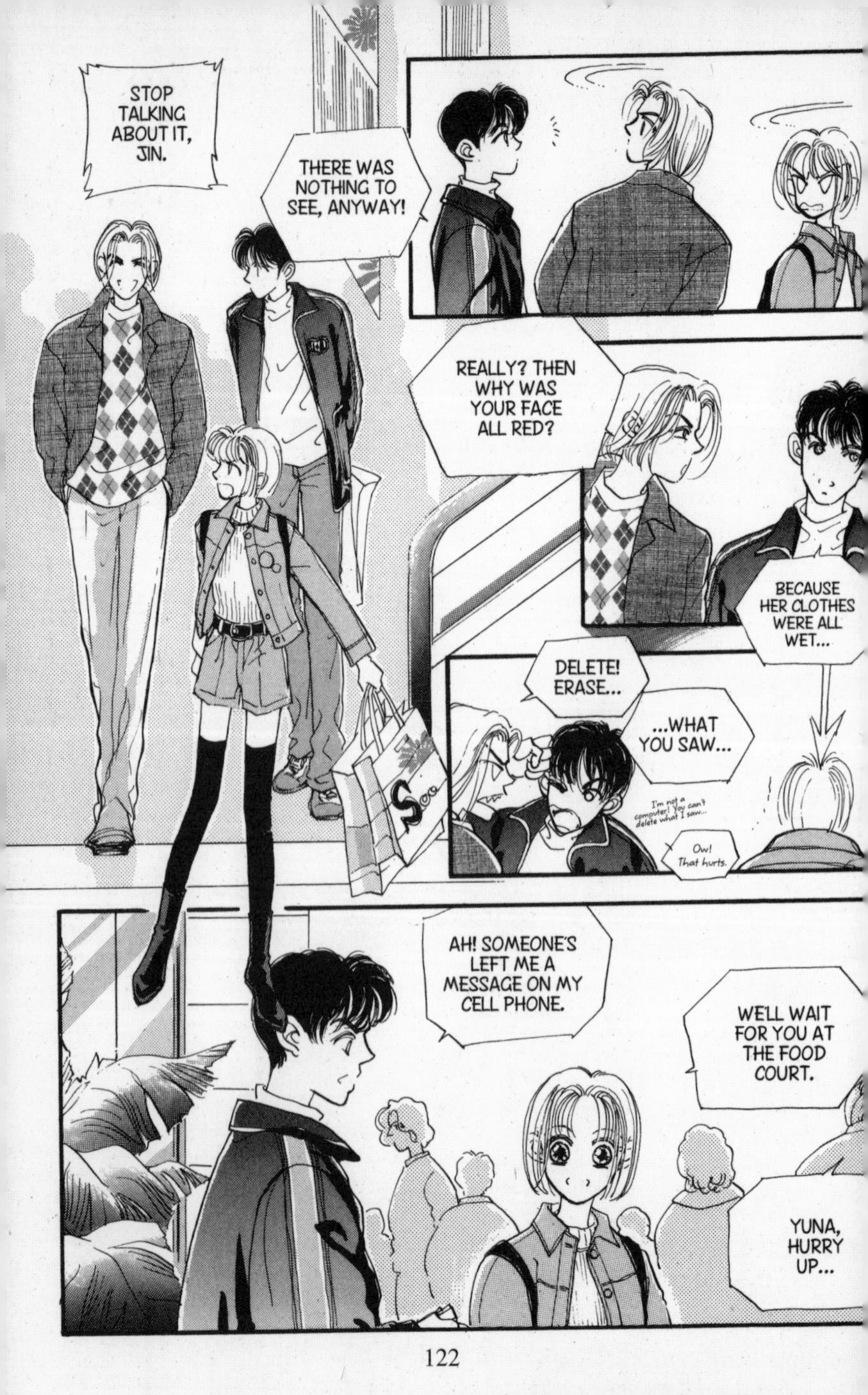

STOP TALKING ABOUT IT, JIN.
THERE WAS NOTHING TO SEE, ANYWAY!
REALLY? THEN WHY WAS YOUR FACE ALL RED?
BECAUSE HER CLOTHES WERE ALL WET...
DELETE! ERASE...
...WHAT YOU SAW...
I'm not a computer! You can't delete what I saw...
Ow! That hurts.
AH! SOMEONE'S LEFT ME A MESSAGE ON MY CELL PHONE.
WE'LL WAIT FOR YOU AT THE FOOD COURT.
YUNA, HURRY UP...

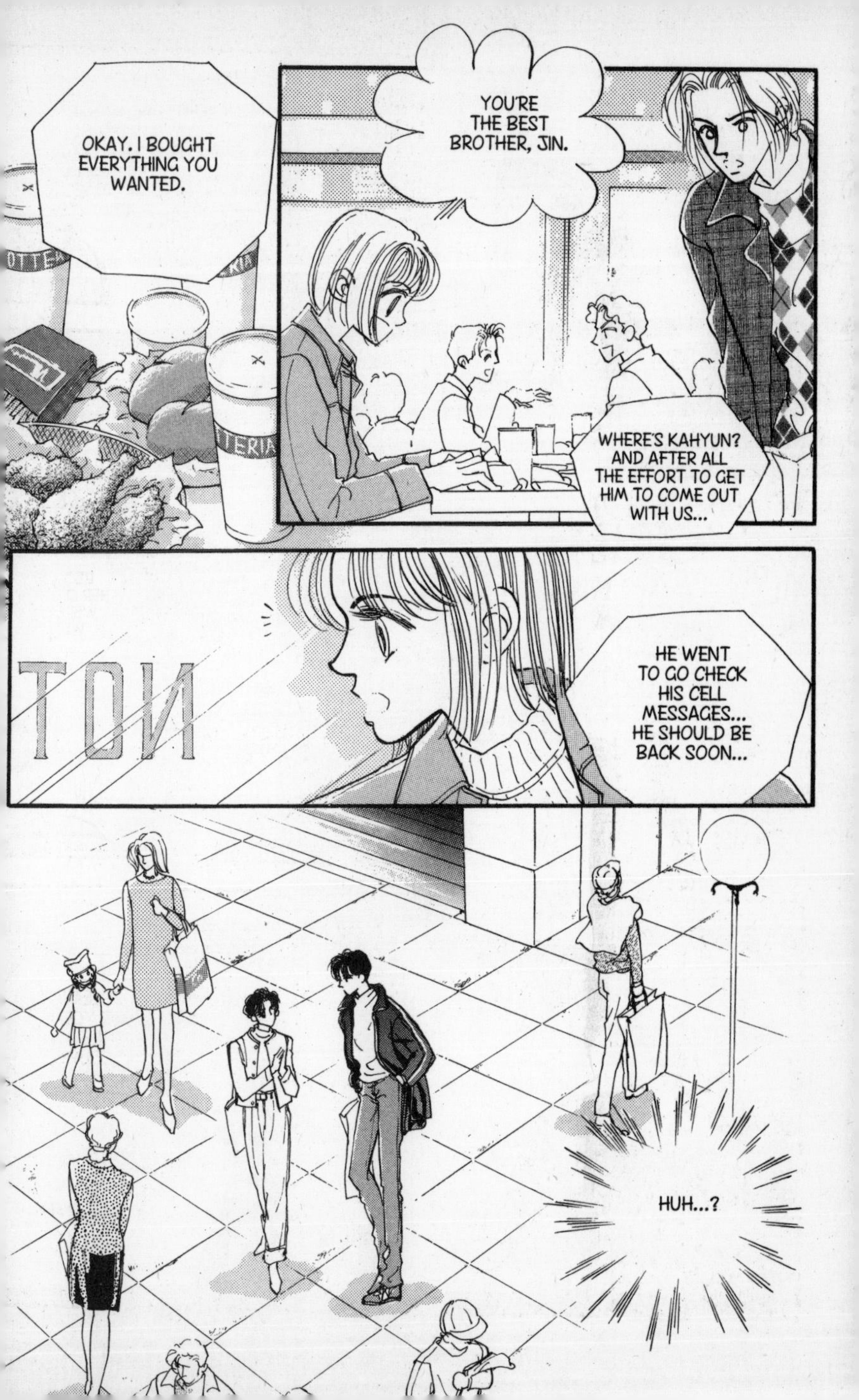
OKAY. I BOUGHT EVERYTHING YOU WANTED.
YOU'RE THE BEST BROTHER, JIN.
WHERE'S KAHYUN? AND AFTER ALL THE EFFORT TO GET HIM TO COME OUT WITH US...
HE WENT TO GO CHECK HIS CELL MESSAGES... HE SHOULD BE BACK SOON...
HUH...?

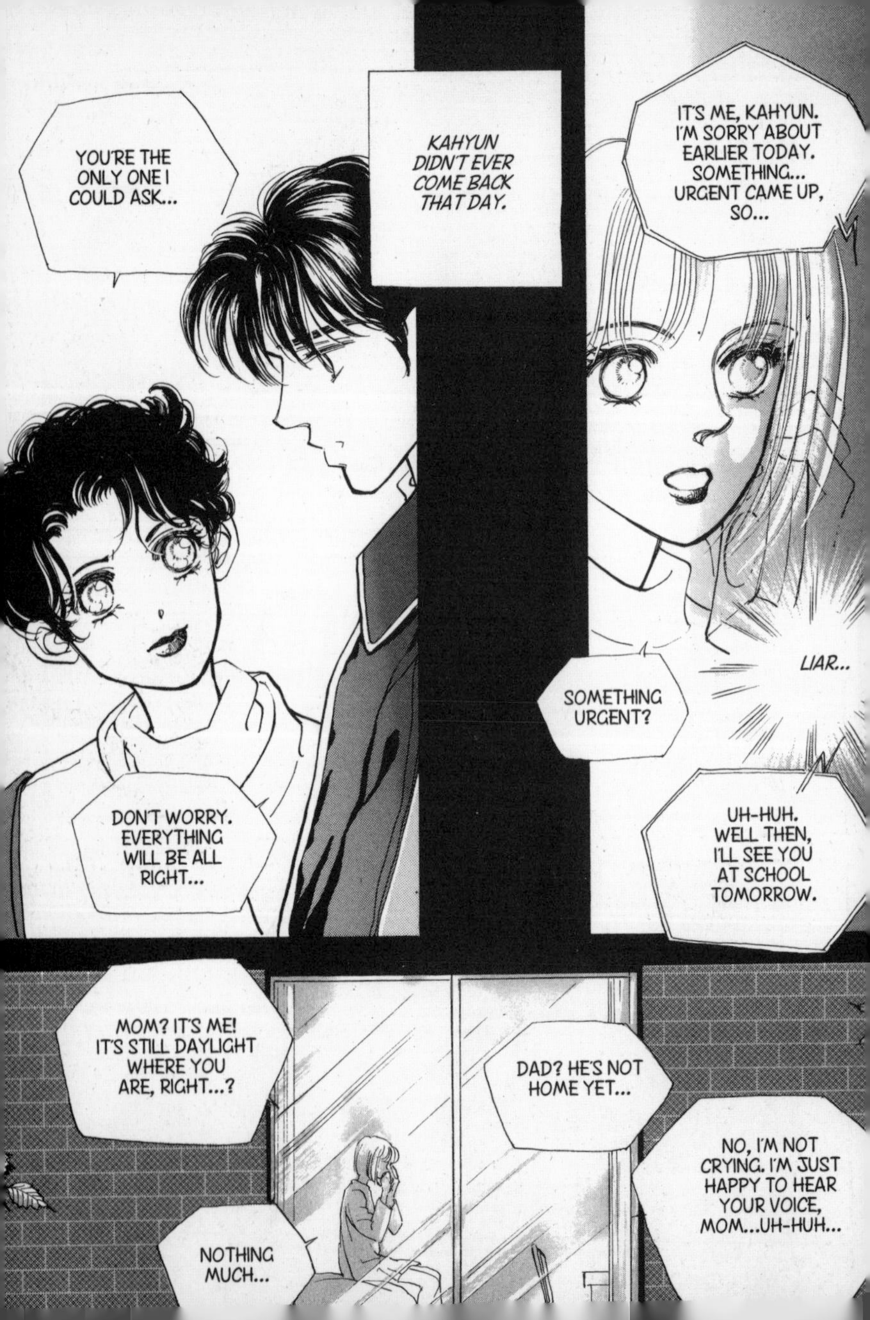
YOU'RE THE ONLY ONE I COULD ASK...
DON'T WORRY. EVERYTHING WILL BE ALL RIGHT...
KAHYUN DIDN'T EVER COME BACK THAT DAY.
IT'S ME, KAHYUN. I'M SORRY ABOUT EARLIER TODAY. SOMETHING... URGENT CAME UP, SO...
SOMETHING URGENT?
LIAR...
UH-HUH. WELL THEN, I'LL SEE YOU AT SCHOOL TOMORROW.
MOM? IT'S ME! IT'S STILL DAYLIGHT WHERE YOU ARE, RIGHT...?
NOTHING MUCH...
DAD? HE'S NOT HOME YET...
NO, I'M NOT CRYING. I'M JUST HAPPY TO HEAR YOUR VOICE, MOM...UH-HUH...

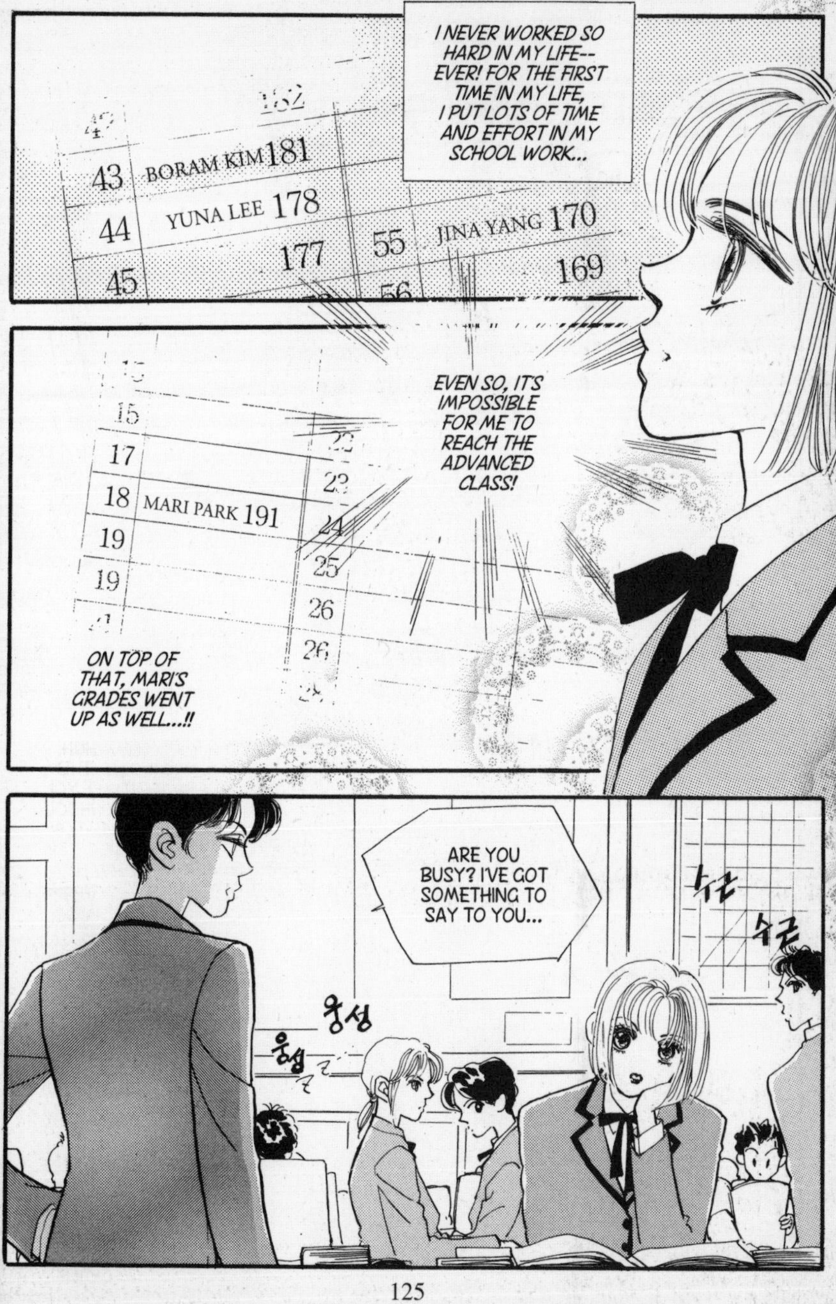
I NEVER WORKED SO HARD IN MY LIFE-- EVER! FOR THE FIRST TIME IN MY LIFE, I PUT LOTS OF TIME AND EFFORT IN MY SCHOOL WORK...
43 BORAM KIM 181
44 YUNA LEE 178
45 177
55 JINA YANG 170
169
18 MARI PARK 191
EVEN SO, IT'S IMPOSSIBLE FOR ME TO REACH THE ADVANCED CLASS!
ON TOP OF THAT, MARI'S GRADES WENT UP AS WELL...!!
ARE YOU BUSY? I'VE GOT SOMETHING TO SAY TO YOU...
수근
수근
웅성
웅성

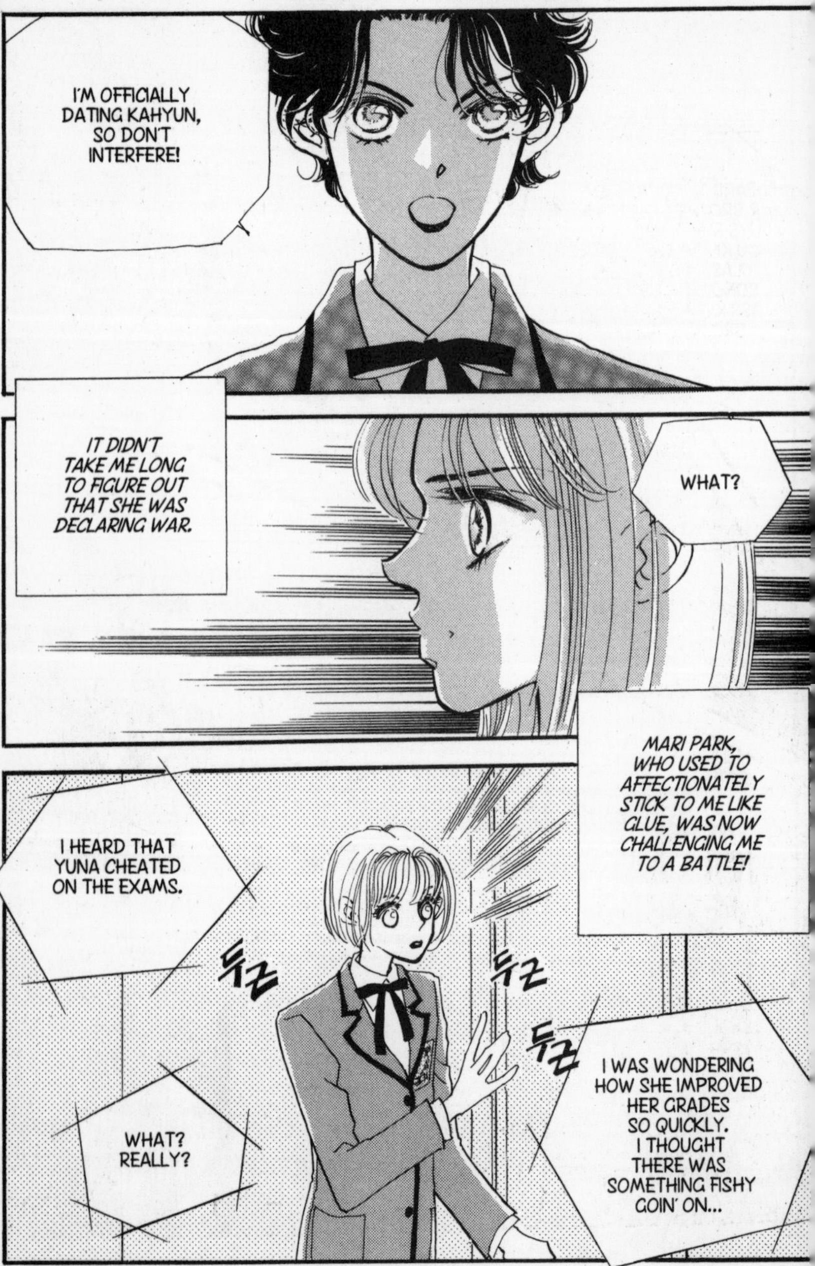
I'M OFFICIALLY DATING KAHYUN, SO DON'T INTERFERE!
IT DIDN'T TAKE ME LONG TO FIGURE OUT THAT SHE WAS DECLARING WAR.
WHAT?
MARI PARK, WHO USED TO AFFECTIONATELY STICK TO ME LIKE GLUE, WAS NOW CHALLENGING ME TO A BATTLE!
I HEARD THAT YUNA CHEATED ON THE EXAMS.
두근
두근
두근
WHAT? REALLY?
I WAS WONDERING HOW SHE IMPROVED HER GRADES SO QUICKLY. I THOUGHT THERE WAS SOMETHING FISHY GOIN' ON...

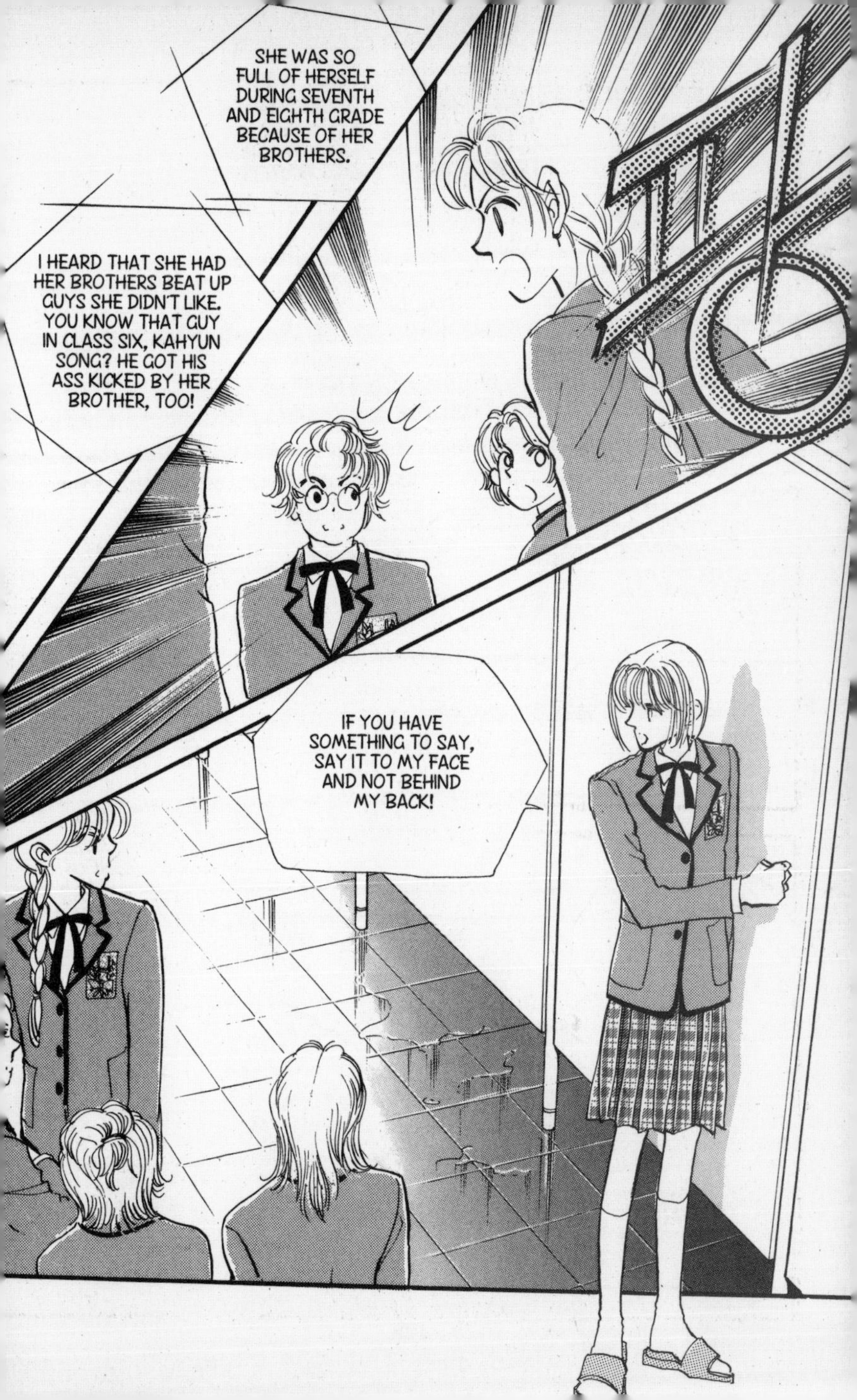
SHE WAS SO FULL OF HERSELF DURING SEVENTH AND EIGHTH GRADE BECAUSE OF HER BROTHERS.
I HEARD THAT SHE HAD HER BROTHERS BEAT UP GUYS SHE DIDN'T LIKE. YOU KNOW THAT GUY IN CLASS SIX, KAHYUN SONG? HE GOT HIS ASS KICKED BY HER BROTHER, TOO!
IF YOU HAVE SOMETHING TO SAY, SAY IT TO MY FACE AND NOT BEHIND MY BACK!

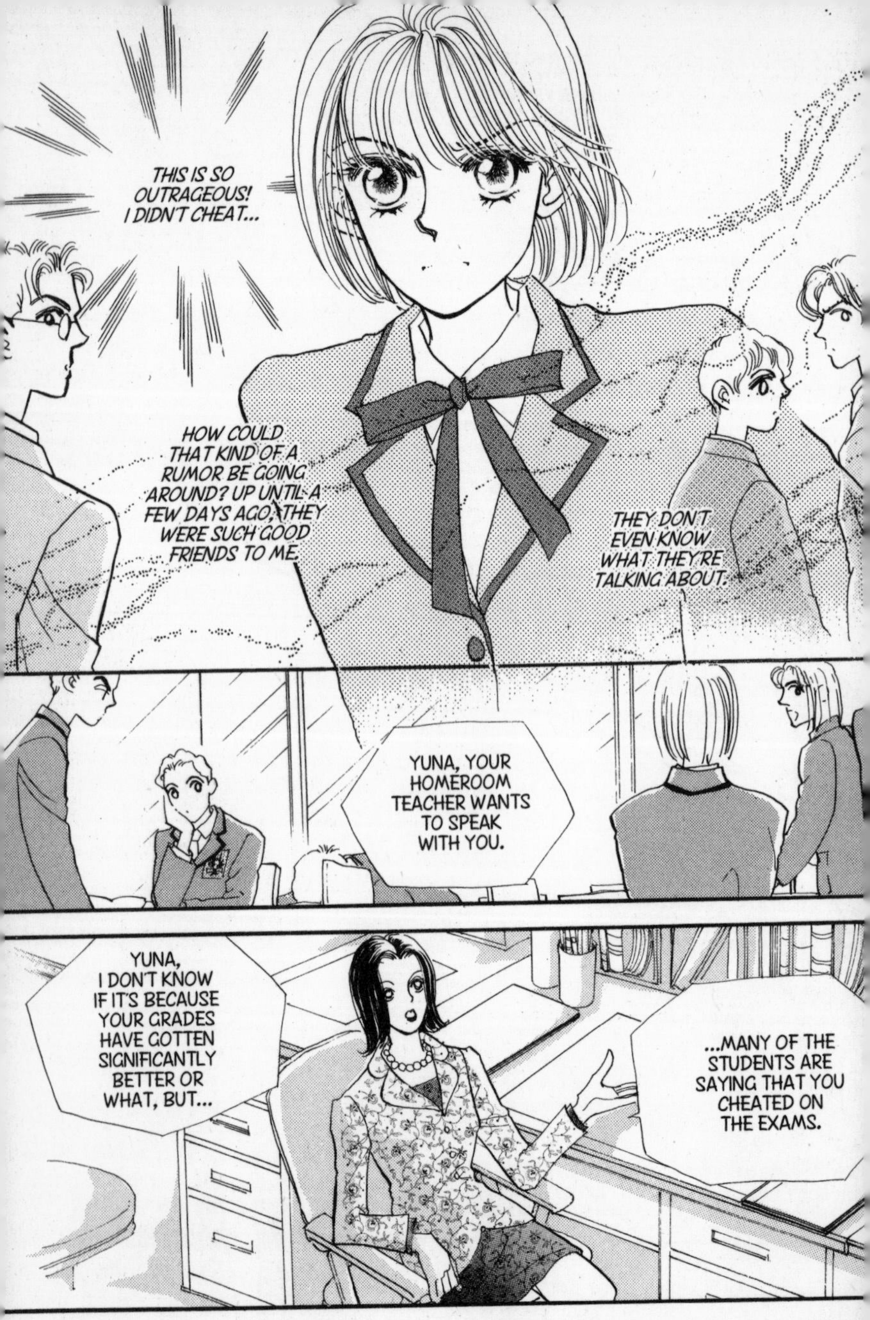
THIS IS SO OUTRAGEOUS! I DIDN'T CHEAT...
HOW COULD THAT KIND OF A RUMOR BE GOING AROUND? UP UNTIL A FEW DAYS AGO, THEY WERE SUCH GOOD FRIENDS TO ME.
THEY DON'T EVEN KNOW WHAT THEY'RE TALKING ABOUT.
YUNA, YOUR HOMEROOM TEACHER WANTS TO SPEAK WITH YOU.
YUNA, I DON'T KNOW IF IT'S BECAUSE YOUR GRADES HAVE GOTTEN SIGNIFICANTLY BETTER OR WHAT, BUT...
...MANY OF THE STUDENTS ARE SAYING THAT YOU CHEATED ON THE EXAMS.

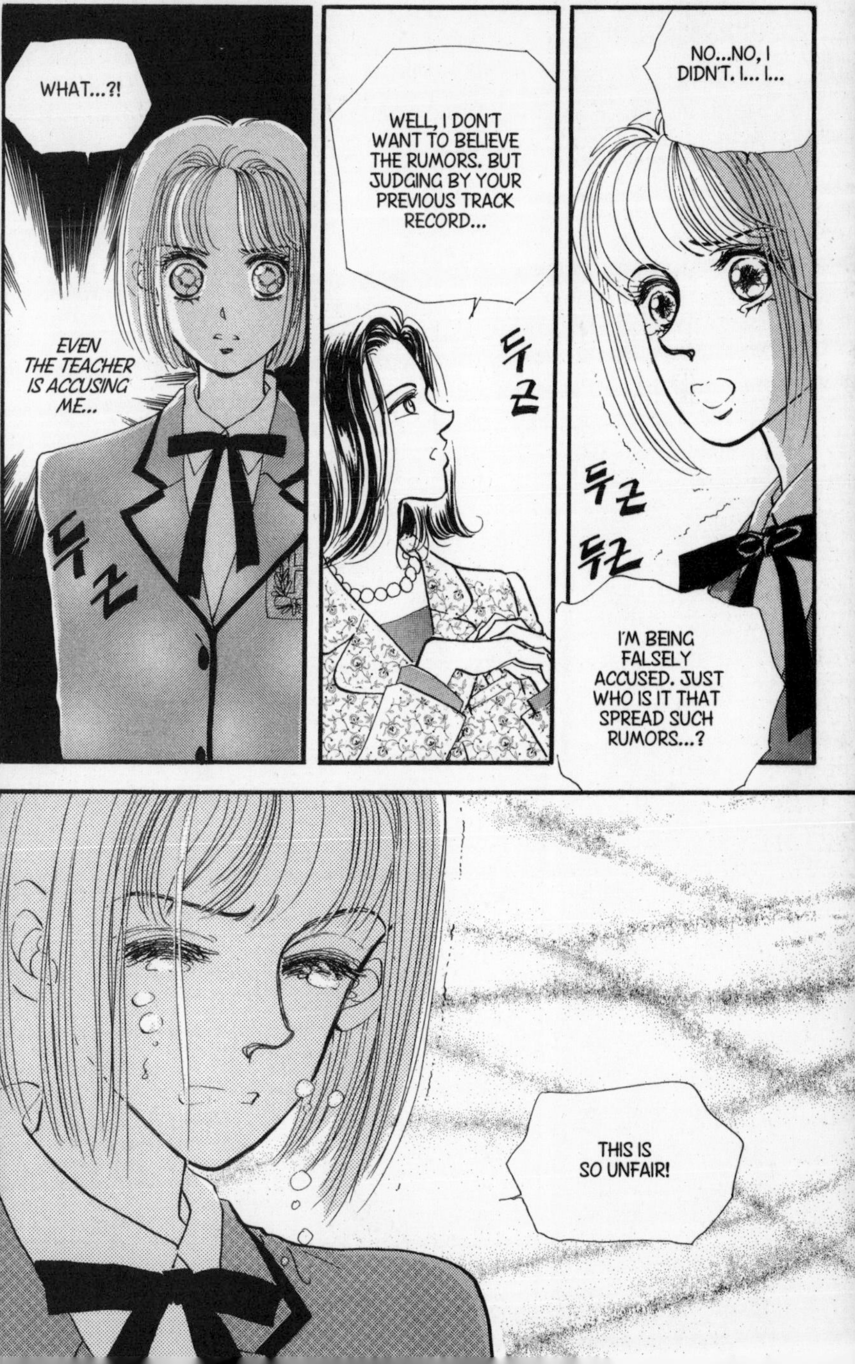
WHAT...?!
EVEN THE TEACHER IS ACCUSING ME...
두근
WELL, I DON'T WANT TO BELIEVE THE RUMORS. BUT JUDGING BY YOUR PREVIOUS TRACK RECORD...
두근
NO...NO, I DIDN'T. I... I...
두근
두근
I'M BEING FALSELY ACCUSED. JUST WHO IS IT THAT SPREAD SUCH RUMORS...?
THIS IS SO UNFAIR!

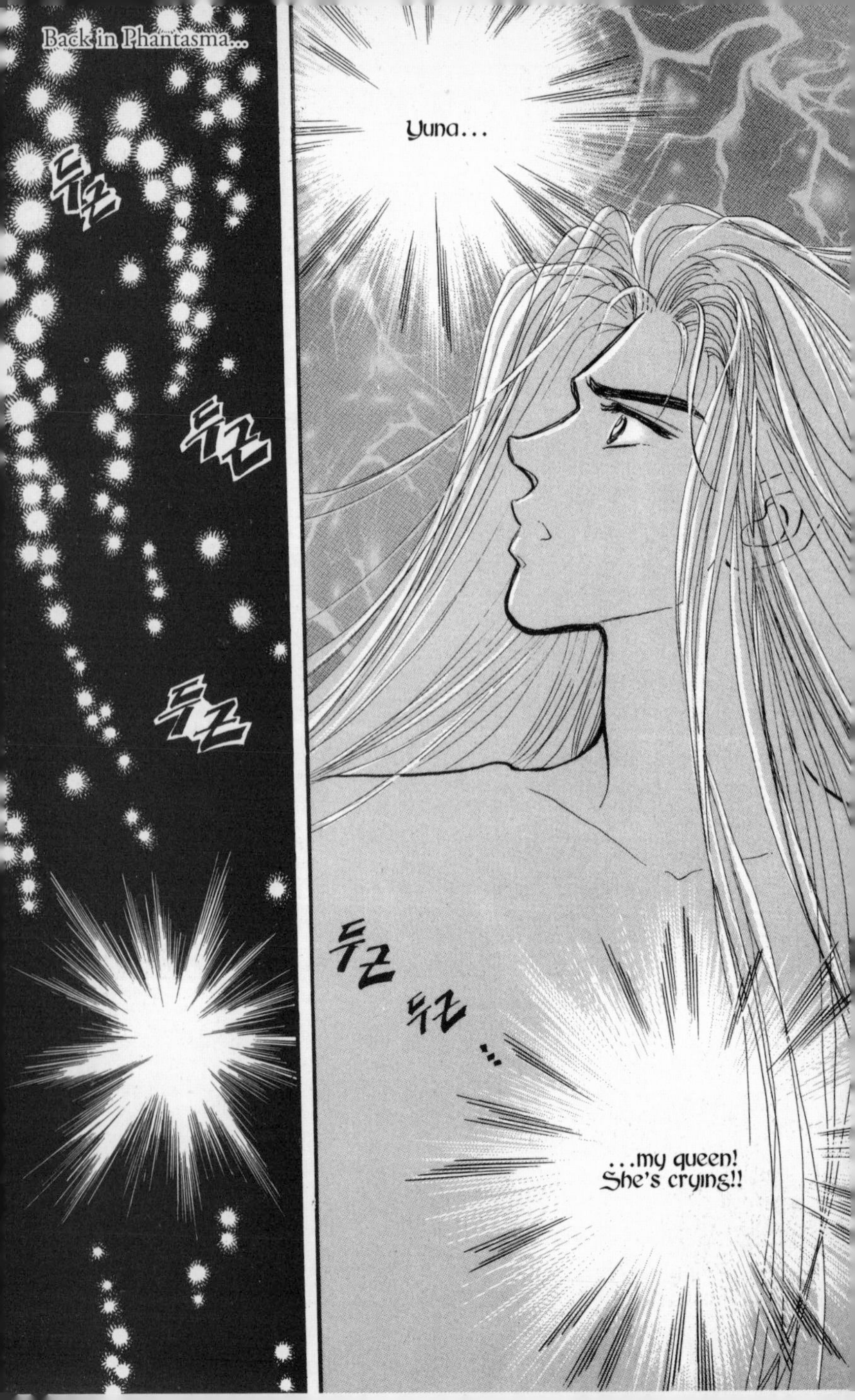
Back in Phantasma...
두근
두근
두근
Yuna...
두근 두근 ...
...my queen! She's crying!!

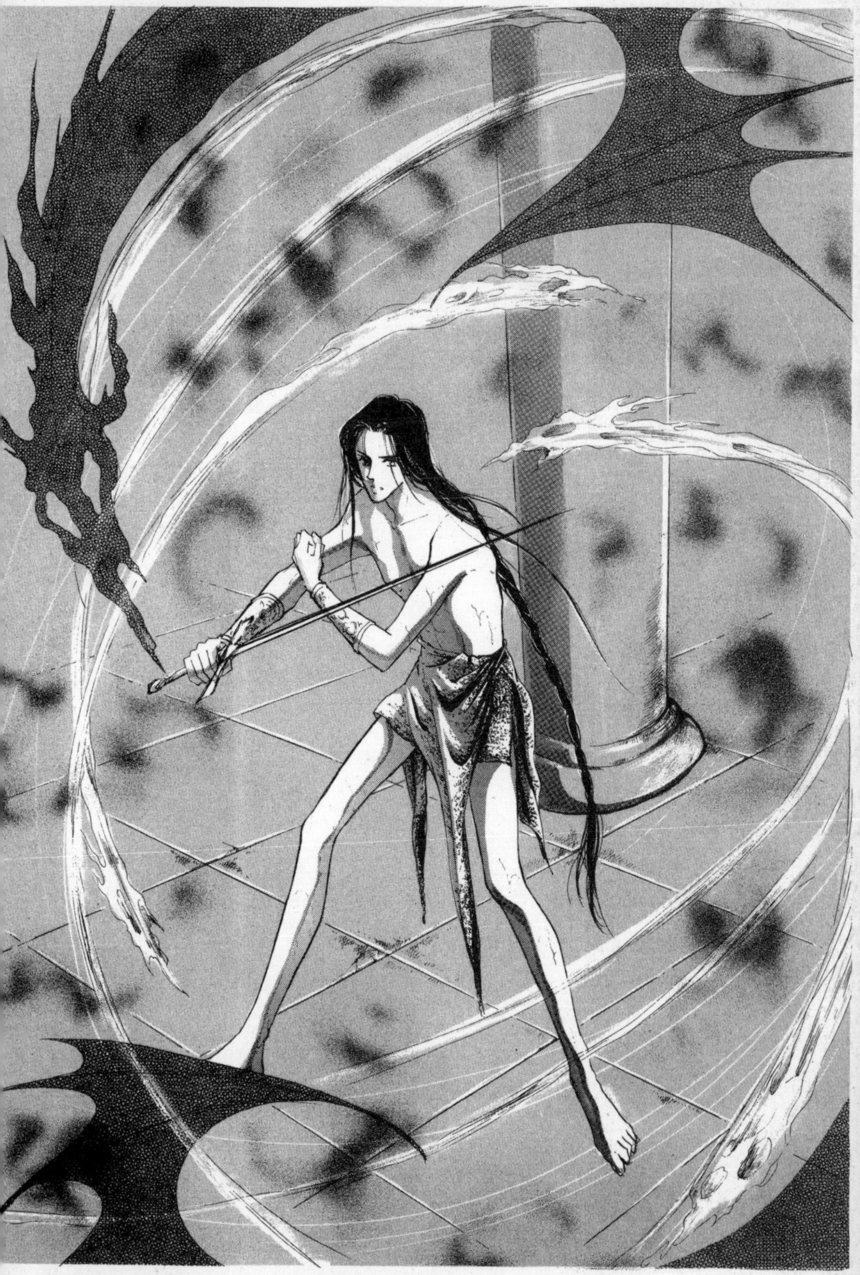

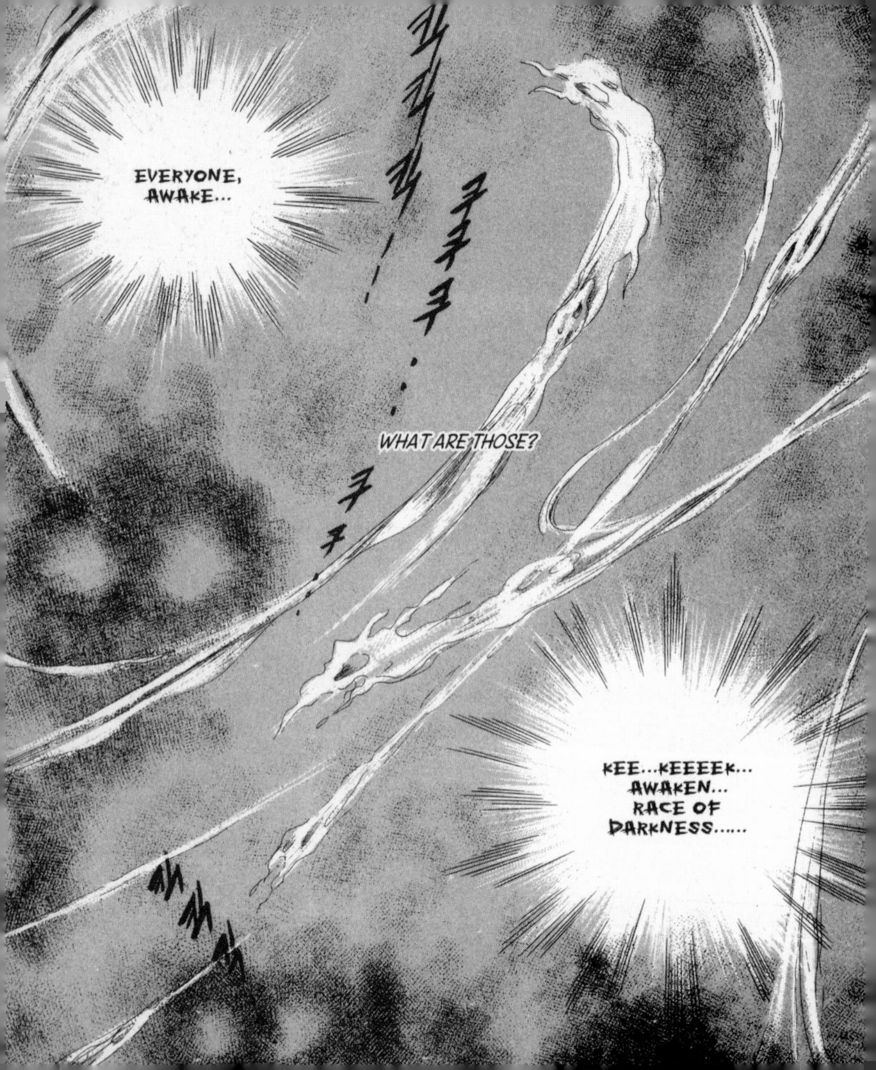
EVERYONE, AWAKE...
WHAT ARE THOSE?
KEE...KEEEEK... AWAKEN... RACE OF DARKNESS......

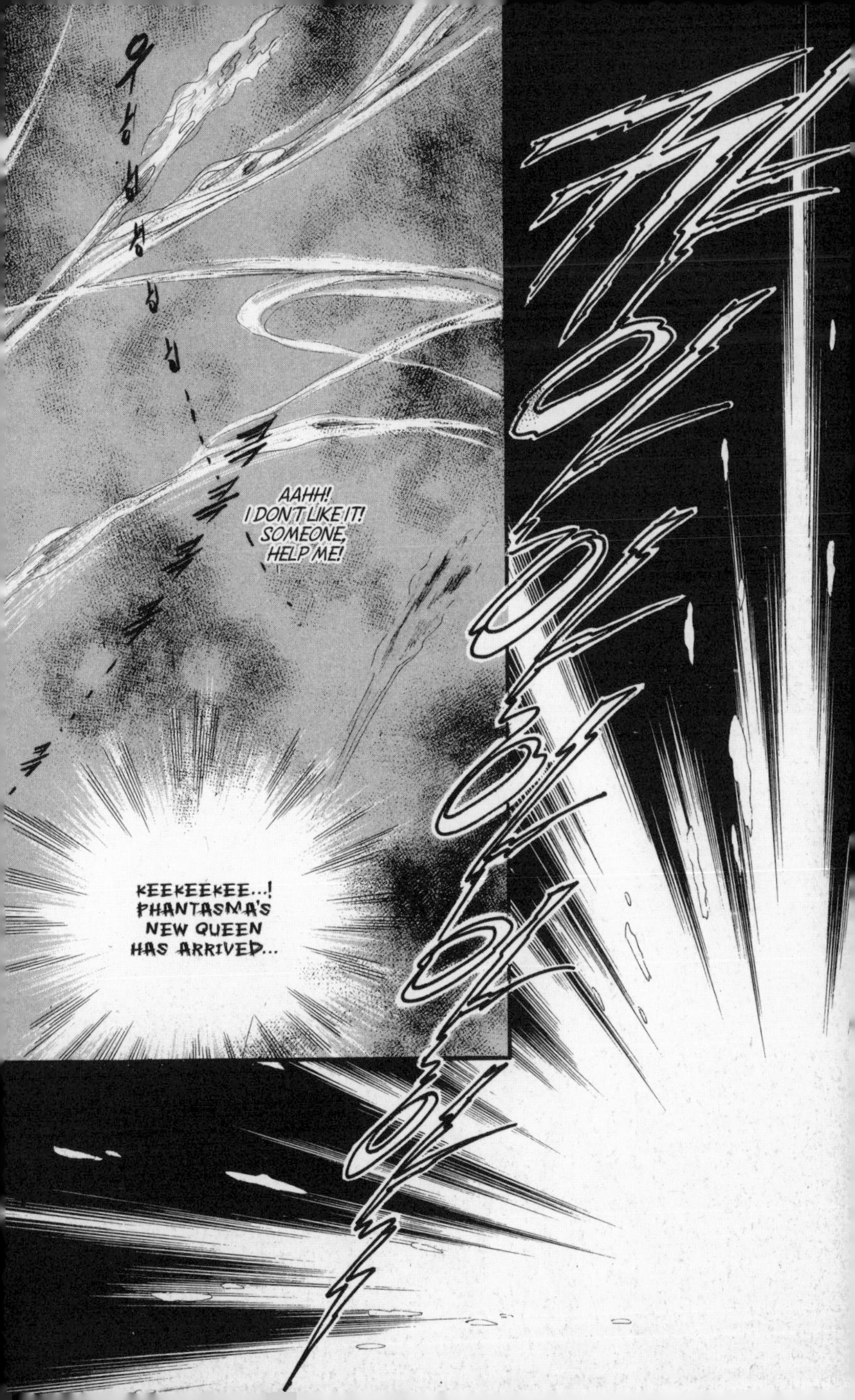
AAHH! I DON'T LIKE IT! SOMEONE, HELP ME!
KEEKEEKEE...! PHANTASMA'S NEW QUEEN HAS ARRIVED...

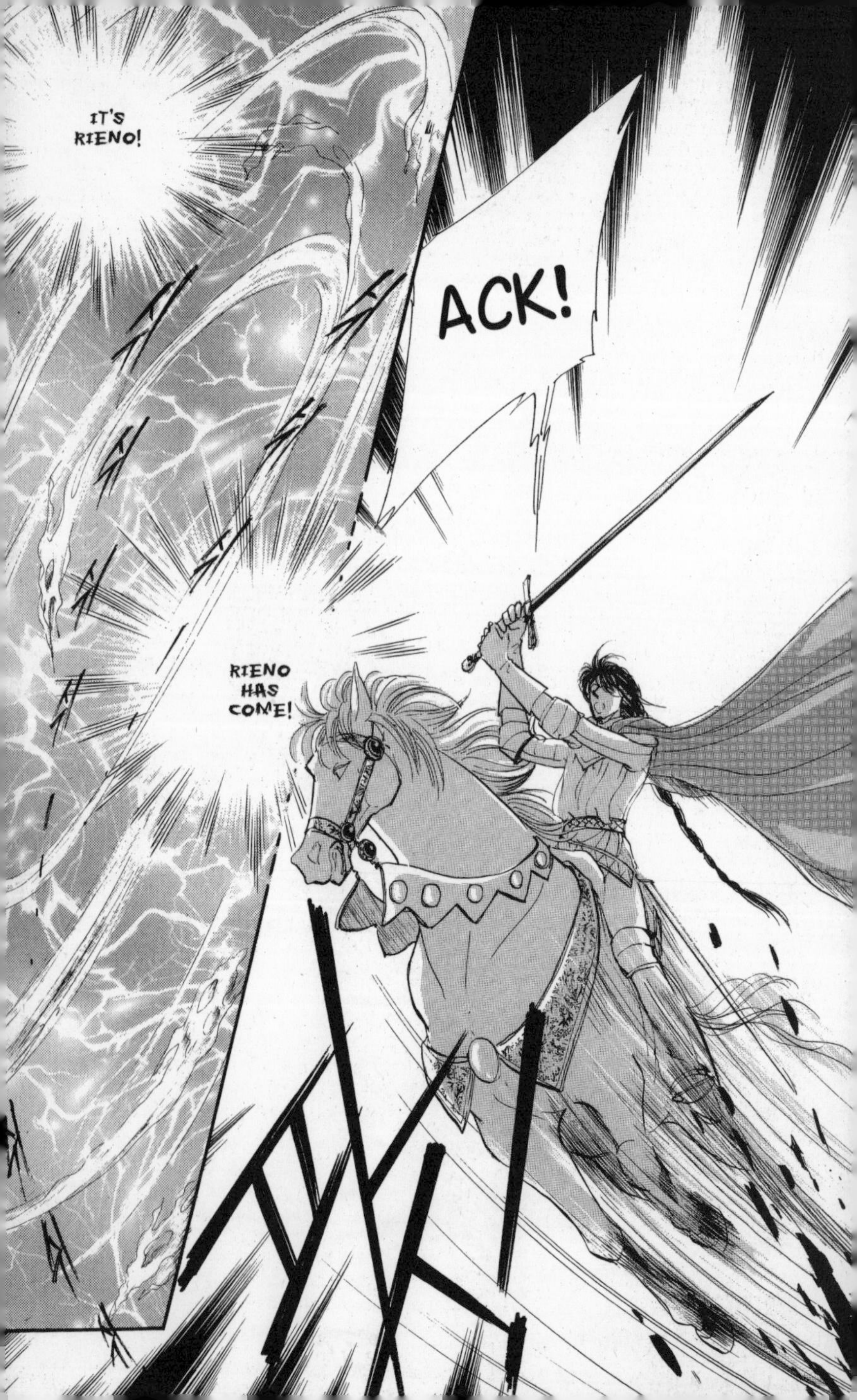
IT'S RIENO!
ACK!
RIENO HAS COME!

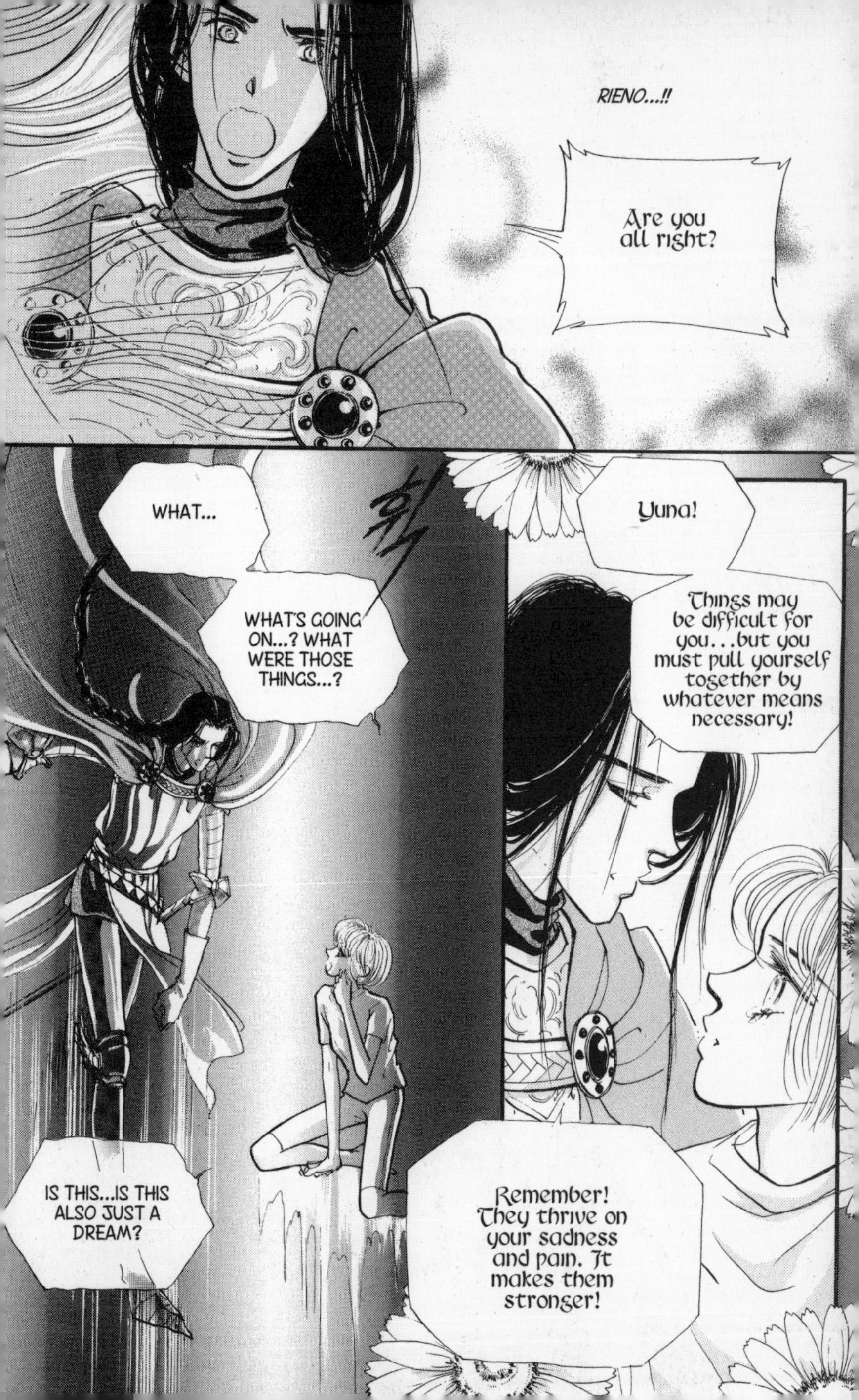
RIENO...!!
Are you all right?
WHAT...
WHAT'S GOING ON...? WHAT WERE THOSE THINGS...?
IS THIS...IS THIS ALSO JUST A DREAM?
Yuna!
Things may be difficult for you...but you must pull yourself together by whatever means necessary!
Remember! They thrive on your sadness and pain. It makes them stronger!

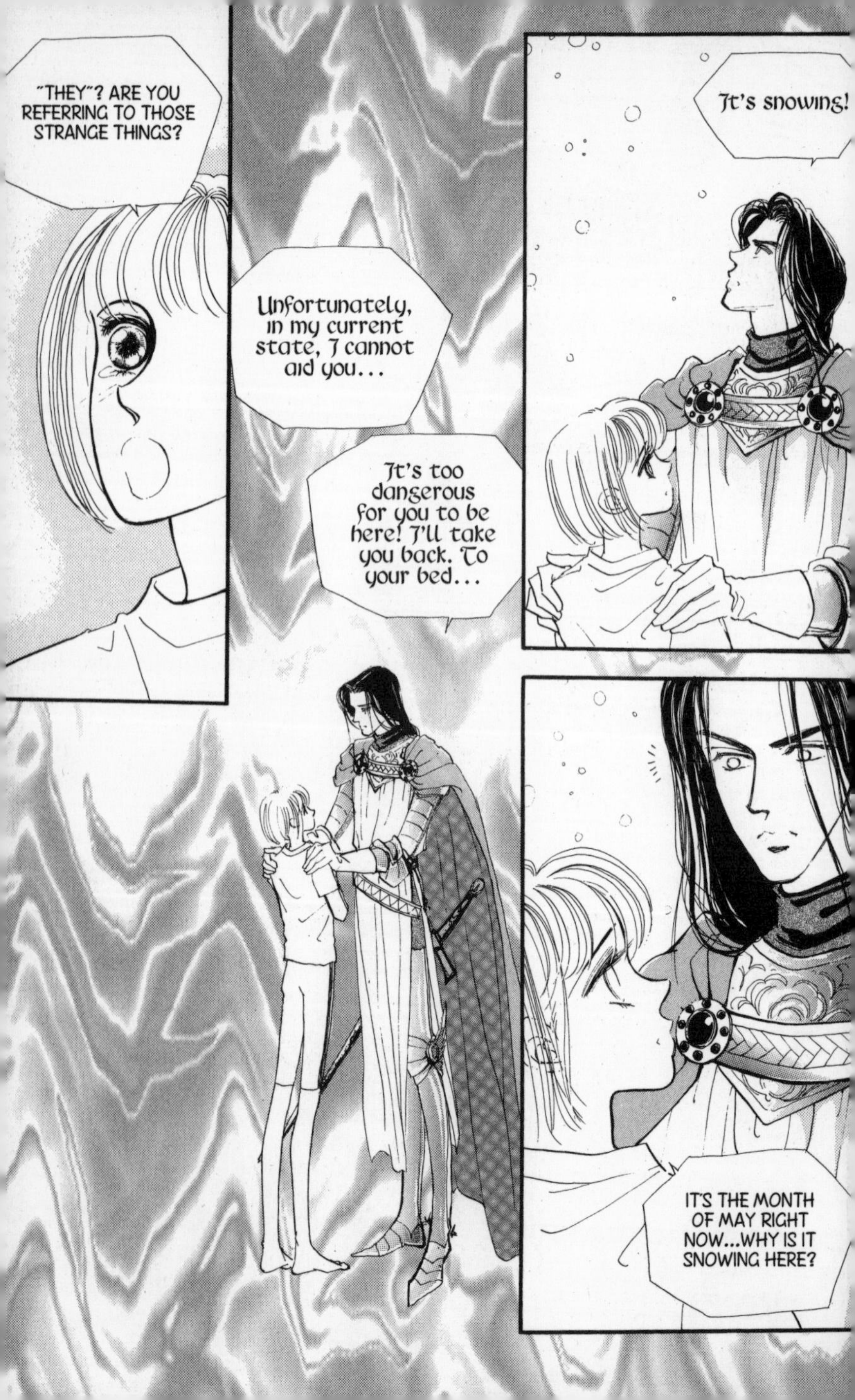
"THEY"? ARE YOU REFERRING TO THOSE STRANGE THINGS?
Unfortunately, in my current state, I cannot aid you...
It's too dangerous for you to be here! I'll take you back. To your bed...
It's snowing!
IT'S THE MONTH OF MAY RIGHT NOW...WHY IS IT SNOWING HERE?

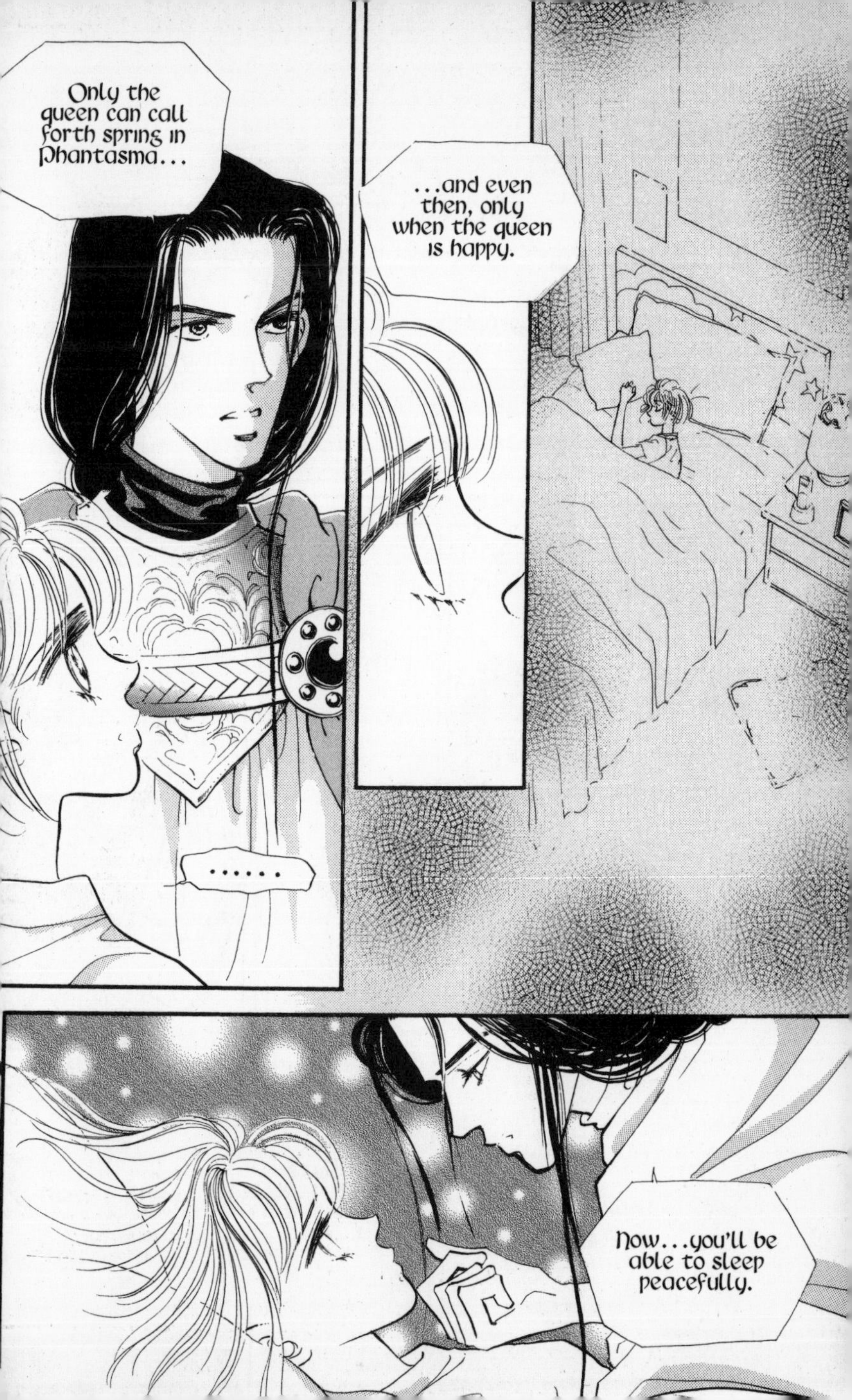
Only the queen can call forth spring in Phantasma...
...and even then, only when the queen is happy.
......
Now...you'll be able to sleep peacefully.

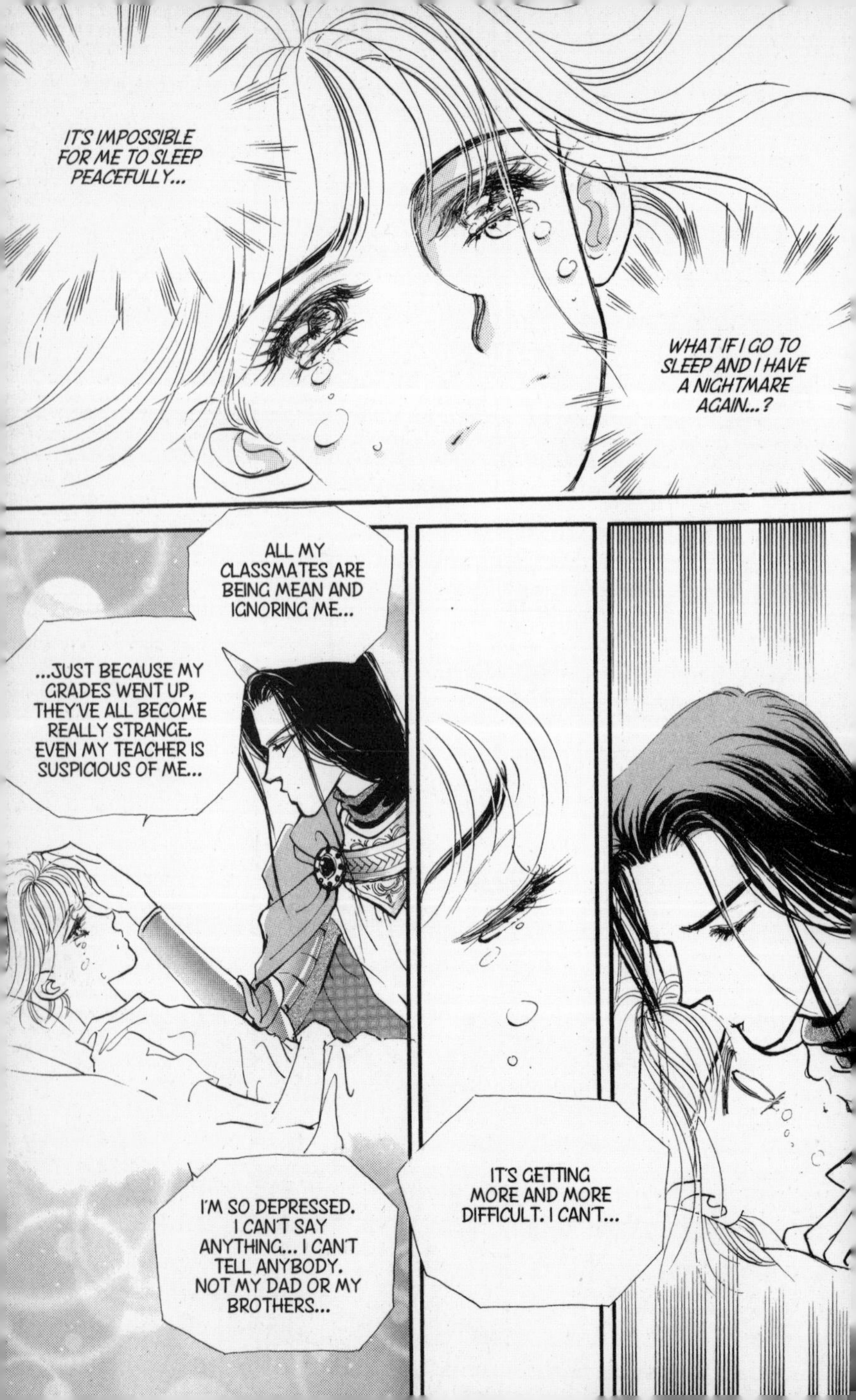
IT'S IMPOSSIBLE FOR ME TO SLEEP PEACEFULLY...
WHAT IF I GO TO SLEEP AND I HAVE A NIGHTMARE AGAIN...?
ALL MY CLASSMATES ARE BEING MEAN AND IGNORING ME...
...JUST BECAUSE MY GRADES WENT UP, THEY'VE ALL BECOME REALLY STRANGE. EVEN MY TEACHER IS SUSPICIOUS OF ME...
I'M SO DEPRESSED. I CAN'T SAY ANYTHING... I CAN'T TELL ANYBODY. NOT MY DAD OR MY BROTHERS...
IT'S GETTING MORE AND MORE DIFFICULT. I CAN'T...

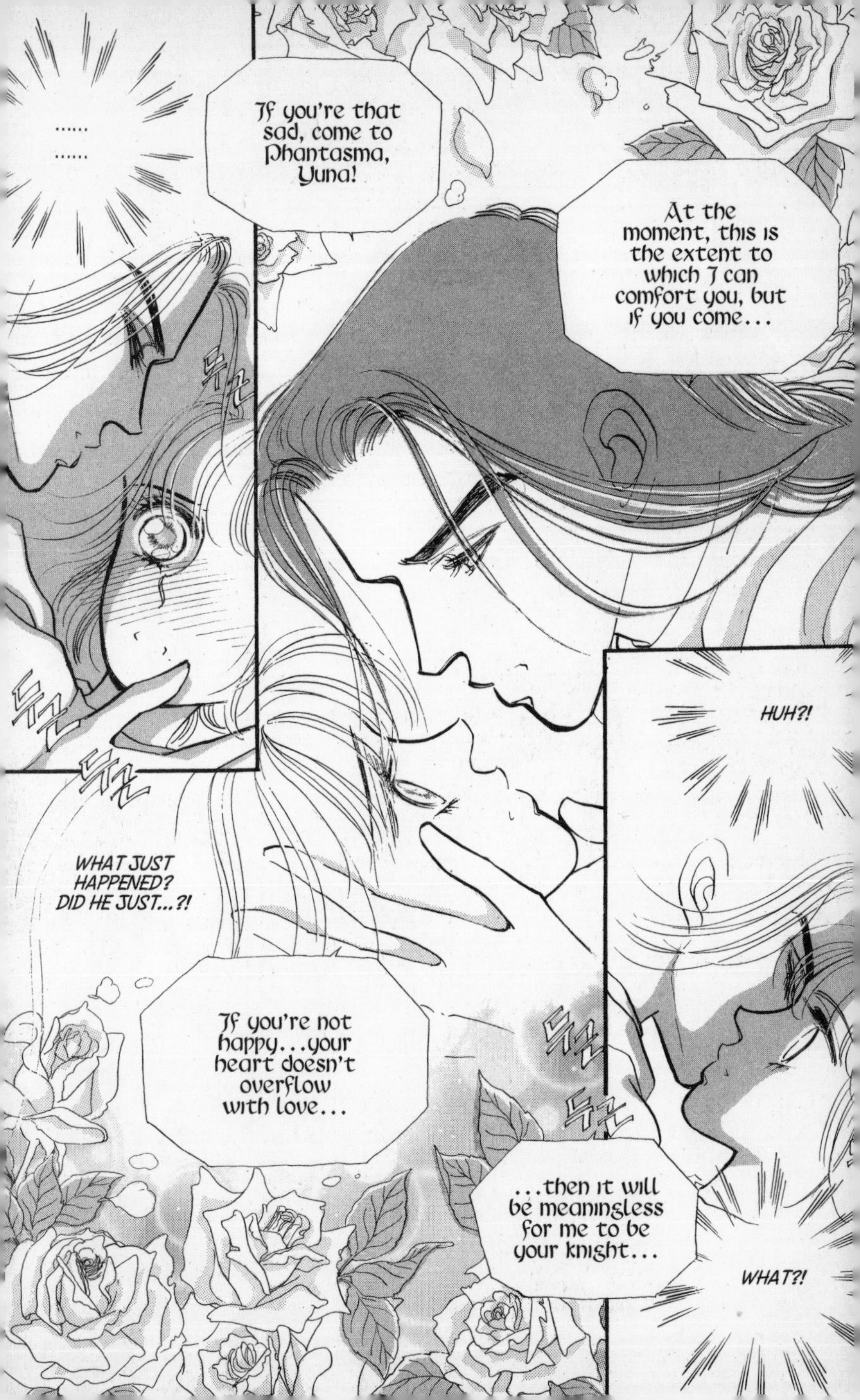

......
......
두근
두근
두근
If you're that sad, come to Phantasma, Yuna!
At the moment, this is the extent to which I can comfort you, but if you come...
WHAT JUST HAPPENED? DID HE JUST...?!
If you're not happy...your heart doesn't overflow with love...
두근
두근
...then it will be meaningless for me to be your knight...
HUH?!
WHAT?!

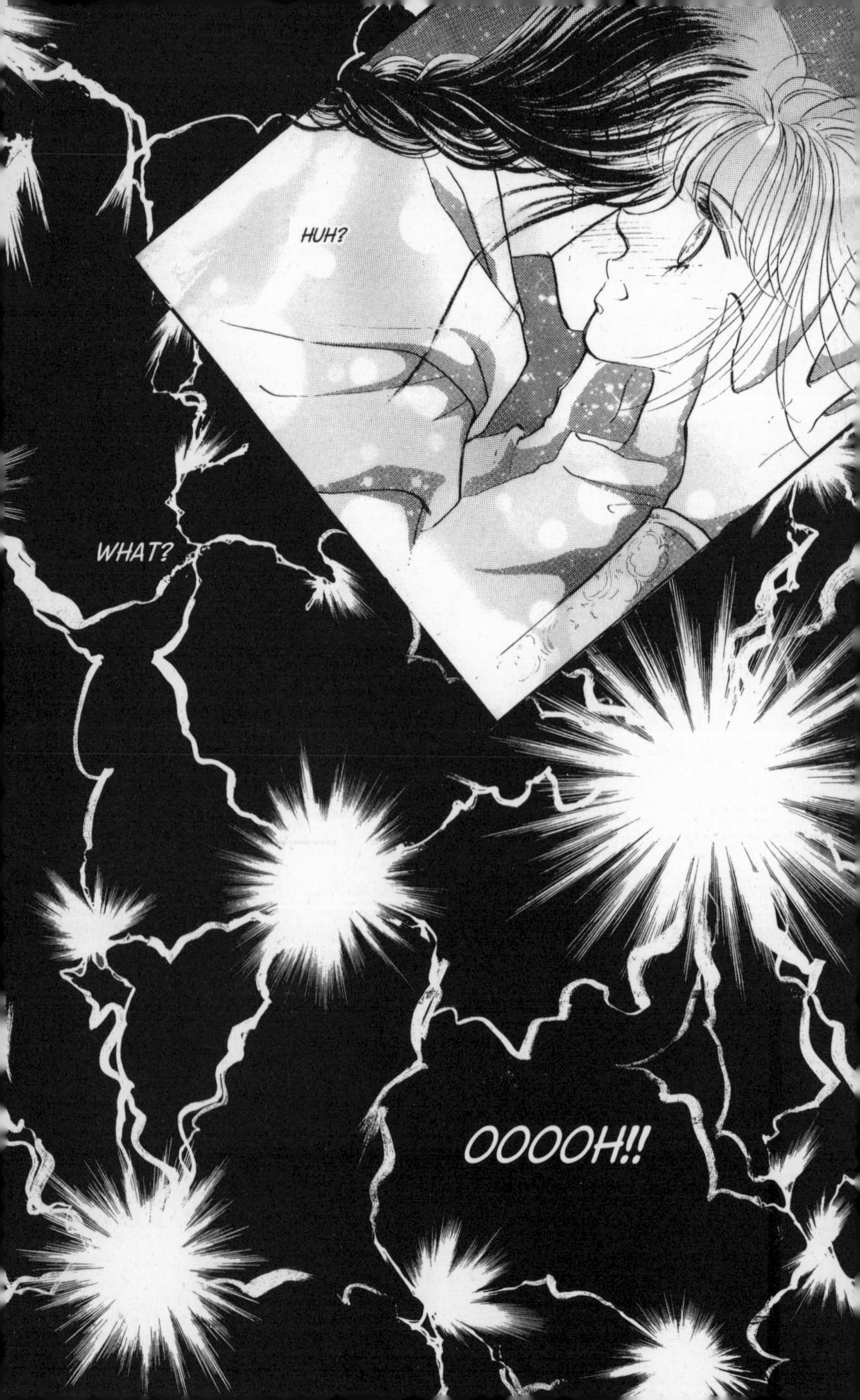
HUH?
WHAT?
OOOOH!!

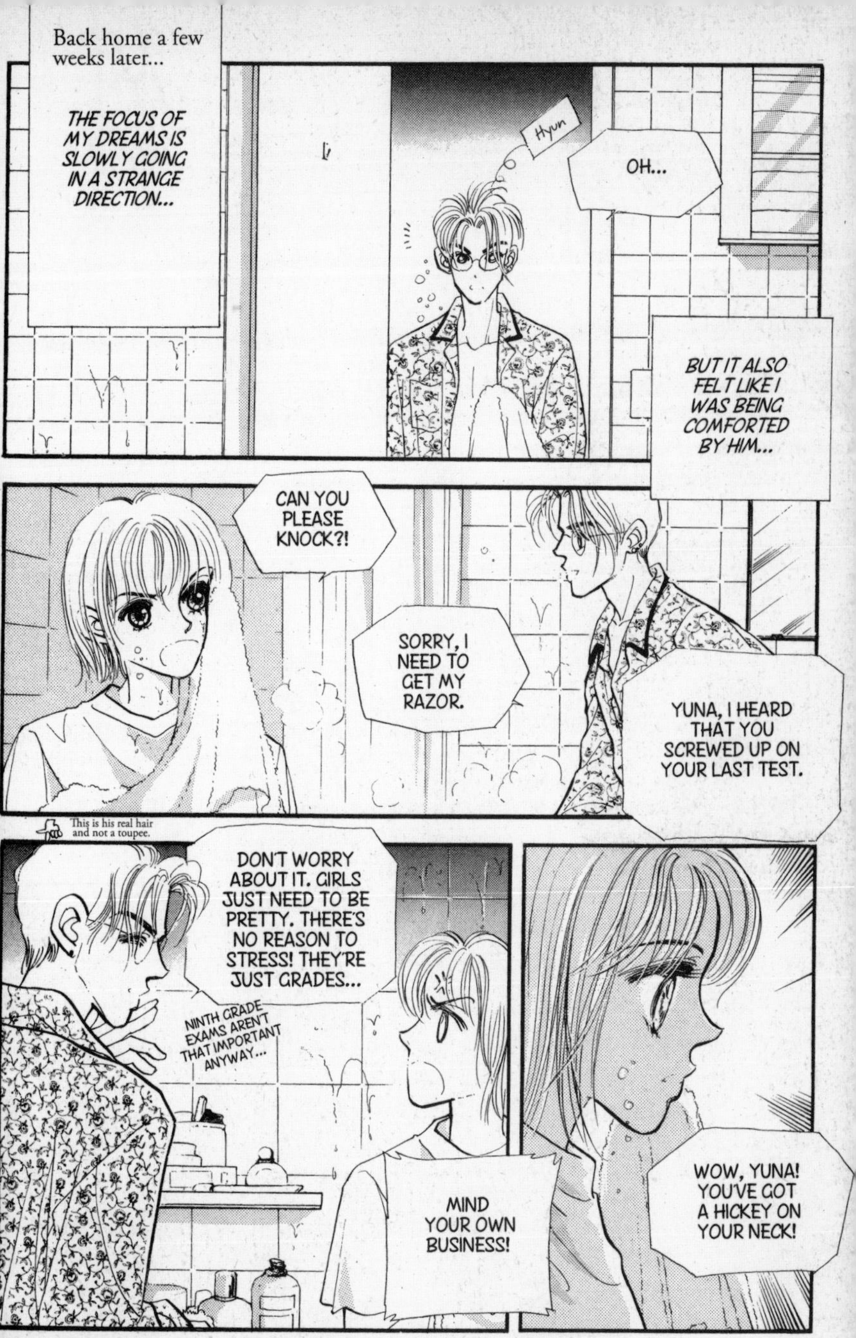

Back home a few weeks later...
THE FOCUS OF MY DREAMS IS SLOWLY GOING IN A STRANGE DIRECTION...
Hyun
OH...
BUT IT ALSO FELT LIKE I WAS BEING COMFORTED BY HIM...
CAN YOU PLEASE KNOCK?!
SORRY, I NEED TO GET MY RAZOR.
YUNA, I HEARD THAT YOU SCREWED UP ON YOUR LAST TEST.
This is his real hair and not a toupee.
DON'T WORRY ABOUT IT. GIRLS JUST NEED TO BE PRETTY. THERE'S NO REASON TO STRESS! THEY'RE JUST GRADES...
NINTH GRADE EXAMS AREN'T THAT IMPORTANT ANYWAY...
MIND YOUR OWN BUSINESS!
WOW, YUNA! YOU'VE GOT A HICKEY ON YOUR NECK!

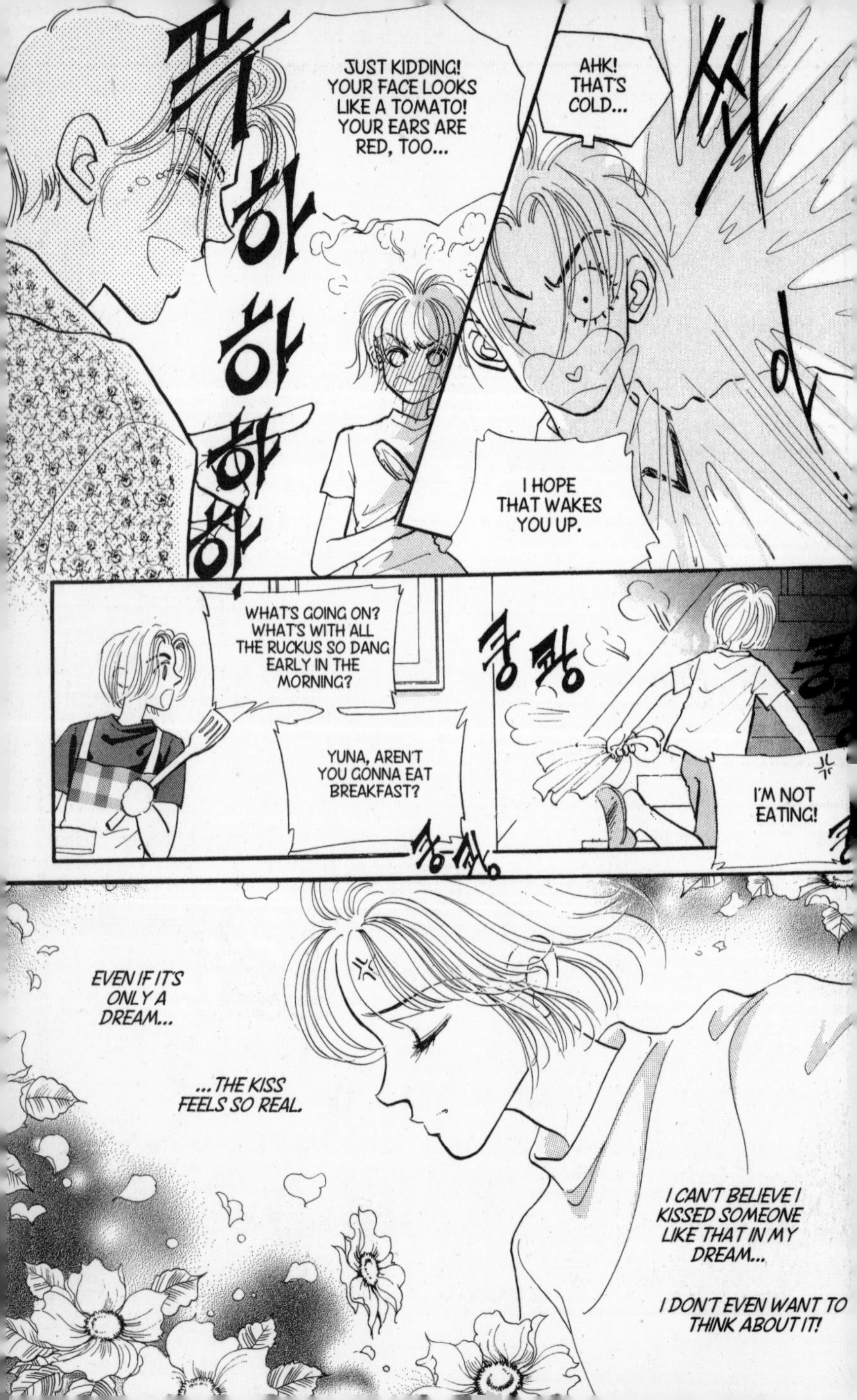
JUST KIDDING! YOUR FACE LOOKS LIKE A TOMATO! YOUR EARS ARE RED, TOO...
AHK! THAT'S COLD...
I HOPE THAT WAKES YOU UP.
WHAT'S GOING ON? WHAT'S WITH ALL THE RUCKUS SO DANG EARLY IN THE MORNING?
YUNA, AREN'T YOU GONNA EAT BREAKFAST?
쿵쾅
I'M NOT EATING!
EVEN IF IT'S ONLY A DREAM...
...THE KISS FEELS SO REAL.
I CAN'T BELIEVE I KISSED SOMEONE LIKE THAT IN MY DREAM...
I DON'T EVEN WANT TO THINK ABOUT IT!

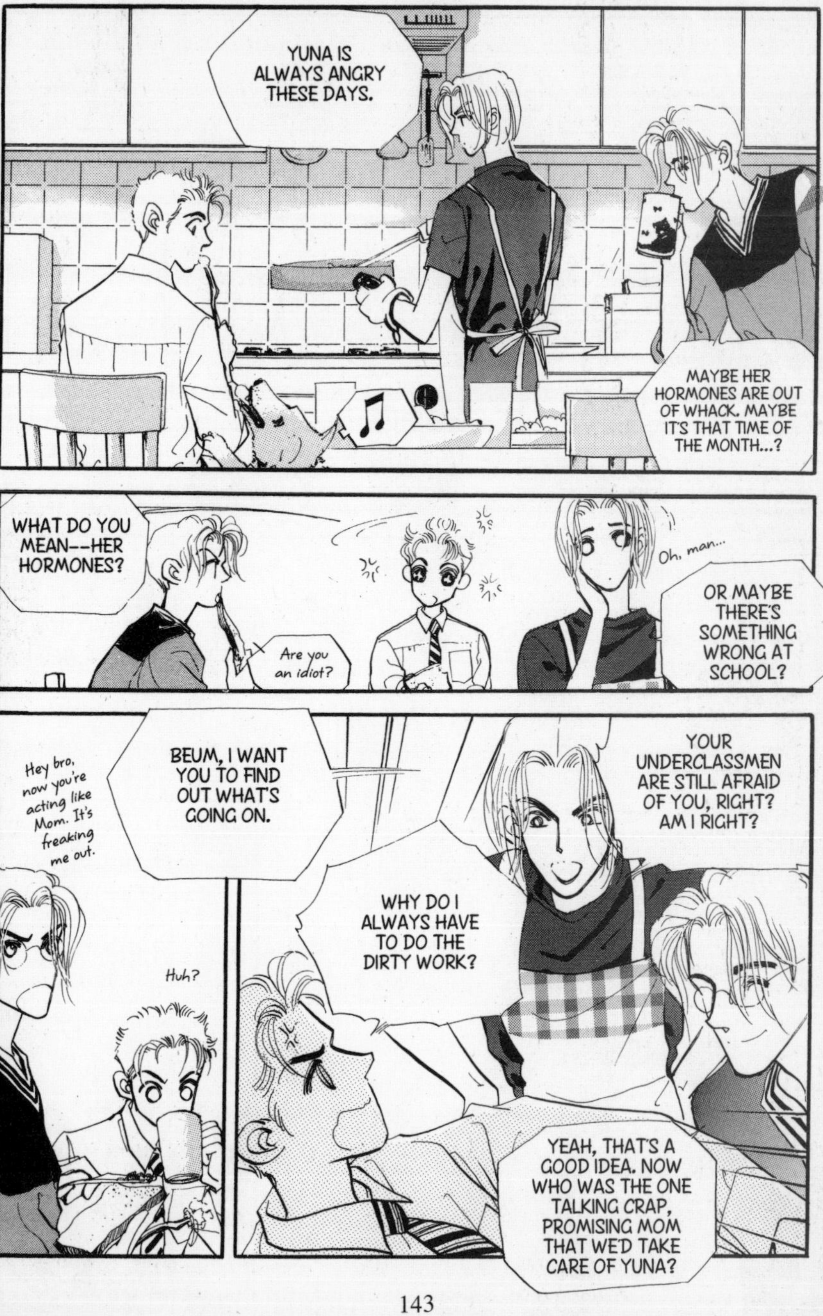
YUNA IS ALWAYS ANGRY THESE DAYS.
♫
MAYBE HER HORMONES ARE OUT OF WHACK. MAYBE IT'S THAT TIME OF THE MONTH...?
WHAT DO YOU MEAN--HER HORMONES?
Are you an idiot?
Oh, man...
OR MAYBE THERE'S SOMETHING WRONG AT SCHOOL?
Hey bro, now you're acting like Mom. It's freaking me out.
BEUM, I WANT YOU TO FIND OUT WHAT'S GOING ON.
YOUR UNDERCLASSMEN ARE STILL AFRAID OF YOU, RIGHT? AM I RIGHT?
Huh?
WHY DO I ALWAYS HAVE TO DO THE DIRTY WORK?
YEAH, THAT'S A GOOD IDEA. NOW WHO WAS THE ONE TALKING CRAP, PROMISING MOM THAT WE'D TAKE CARE OF YUNA?

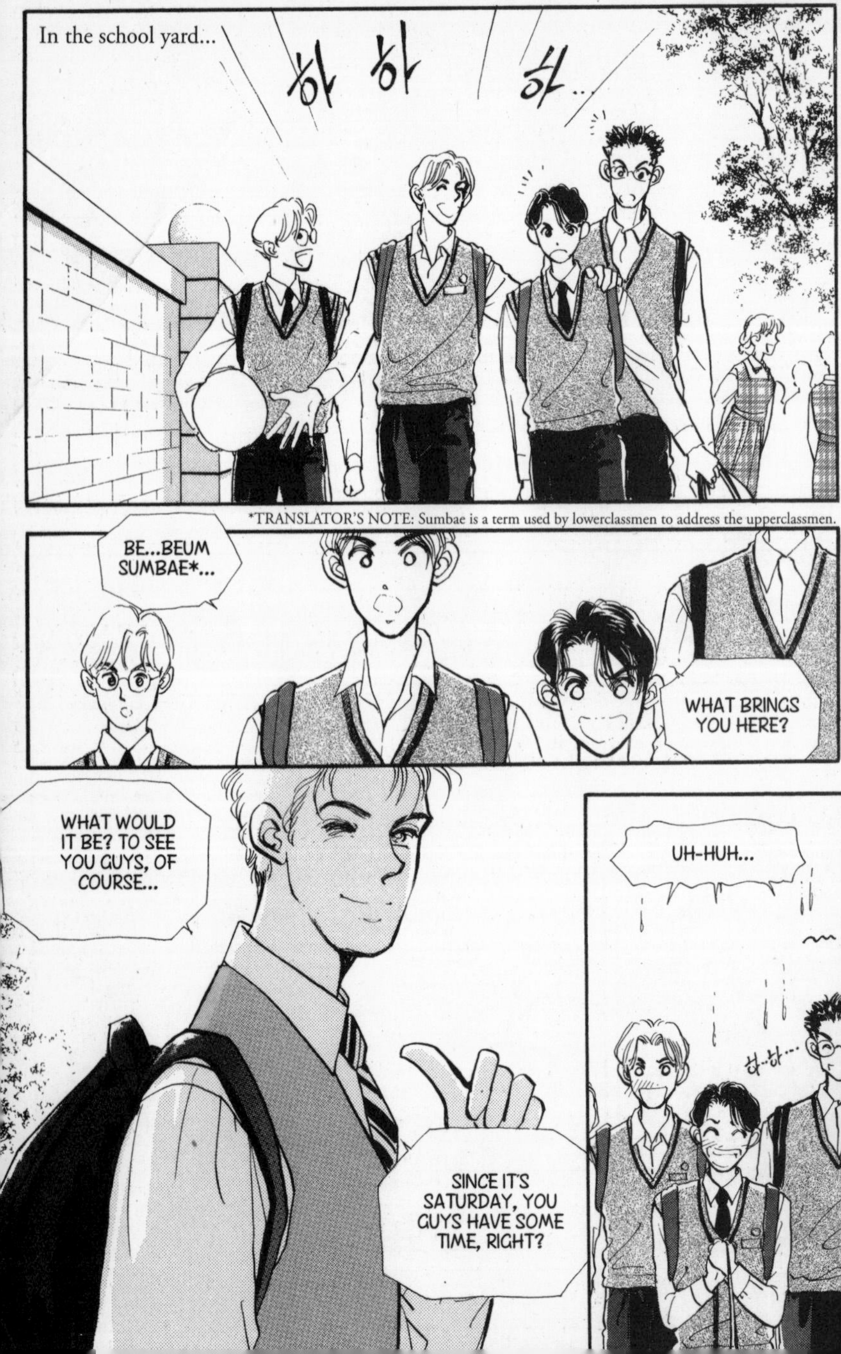

In the school yard...
하 하 하...
BE...BEUM SUMBAE*...
WHAT BRINGS YOU HERE?
WHAT WOULD IT BE? TO SEE YOU GUYS, OF COURSE...
SINCE IT'S SATURDAY, YOU GUYS HAVE SOME TIME, RIGHT?
UH-HUH...
하..하...

*TRANSLATOR'S NOTE: Sumbae is a term used by lowerclassmen to address the upperclassmen.

Back in the classroom...

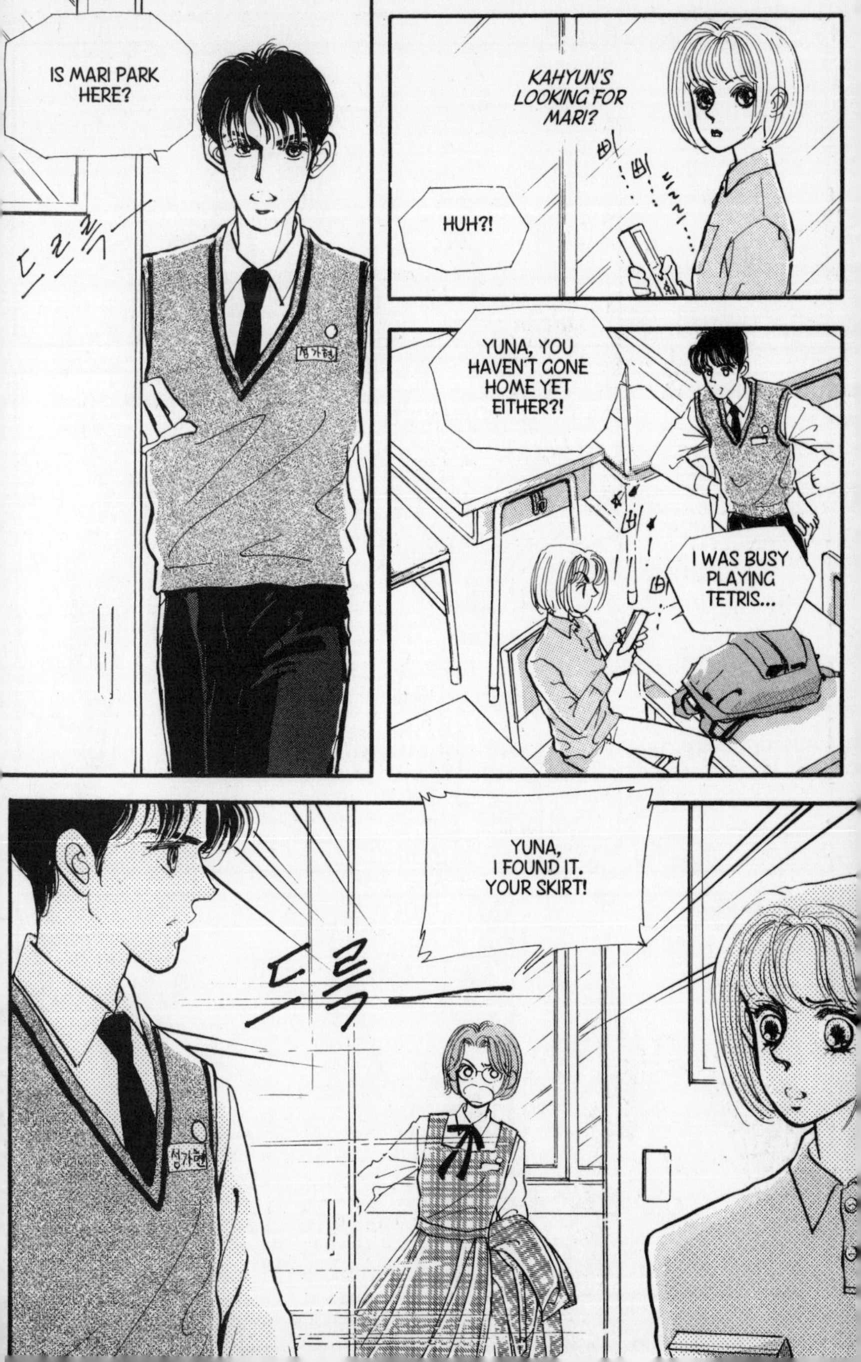
IS MARI PARK HERE?
KAHYUN'S LOOKING FOR MARI?
HUH?!
YUNA, YOU HAVEN'T GONE HOME YET EITHER?!
I WAS BUSY PLAYING TETRIS...
YUNA, I FOUND IT. YOUR SKIRT!

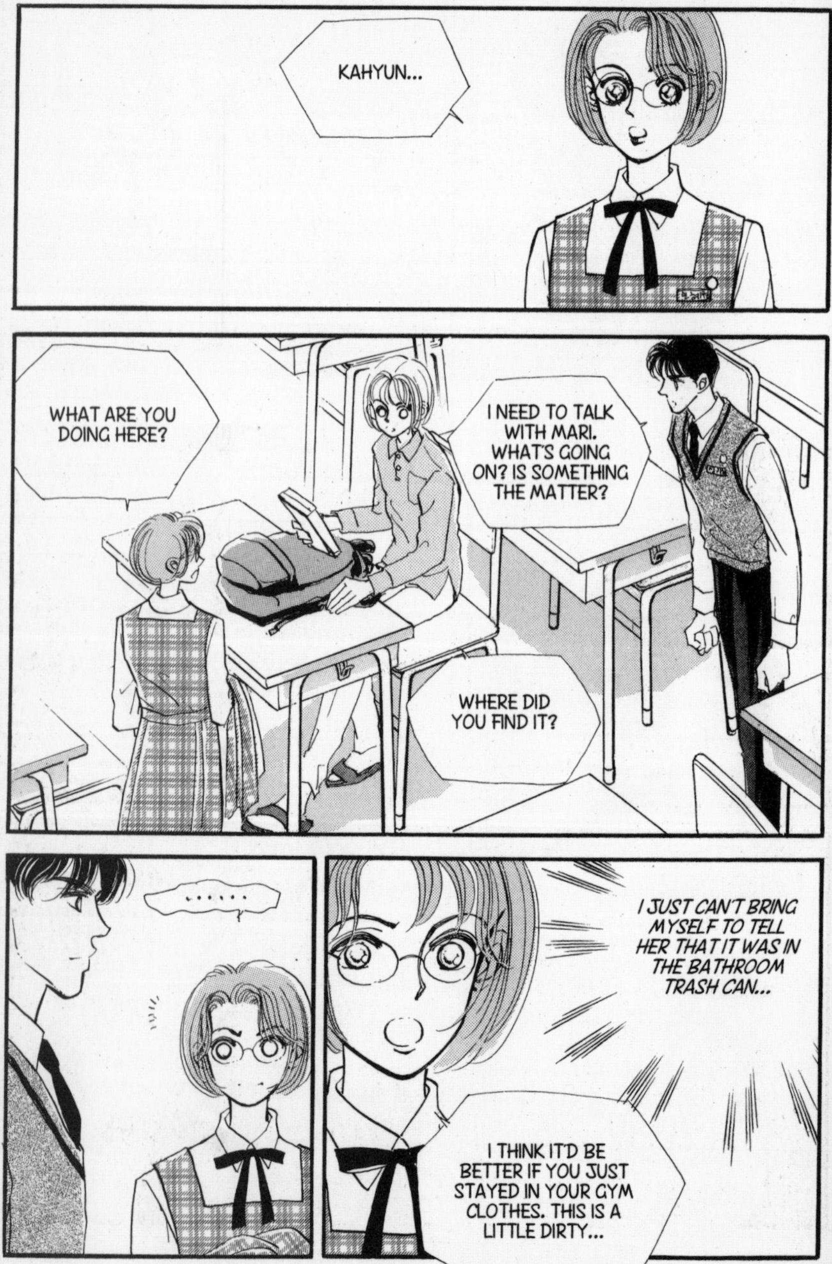
KAHYUN...
WHAT ARE YOU DOING HERE?
I NEED TO TALK WITH MARI. WHAT'S GOING ON? IS SOMETHING THE MATTER?
WHERE DID YOU FIND IT?
......
I JUST CAN'T BRING MYSELF TO TELL HER THAT IT WAS IN THE BATHROOM TRASH CAN...
I THINK IT'D BE BETTER IF YOU JUST STAYED IN YOUR GYM CLOTHES. THIS IS A LITTLE DIRTY...

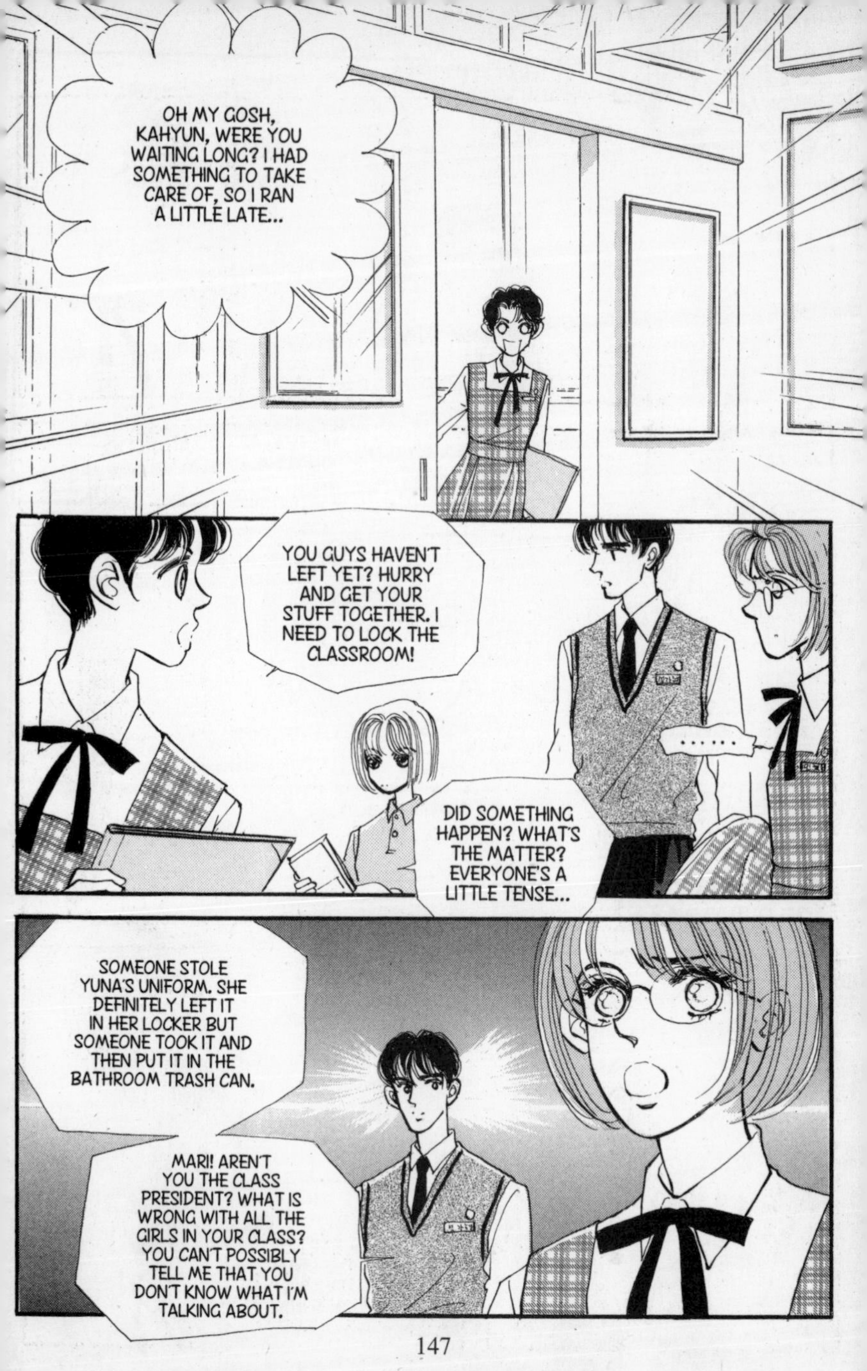
OH MY GOSH, KAHYUN, WERE YOU WAITING LONG? I HAD SOMETHING TO TAKE CARE OF, SO I RAN A LITTLE LATE...
YOU GUYS HAVEN'T LEFT YET? HURRY AND GET YOUR STUFF TOGETHER. I NEED TO LOCK THE CLASSROOM!
......
DID SOMETHING HAPPEN? WHAT'S THE MATTER? EVERYONE'S A LITTLE TENSE...
SOMEONE STOLE YUNA'S UNIFORM. SHE DEFINITELY LEFT IT IN HER LOCKER BUT SOMEONE TOOK IT AND THEN PUT IT IN THE BATHROOM TRASH CAN.
MARI! AREN'T YOU THE CLASS PRESIDENT? WHAT IS WRONG WITH ALL THE GIRLS IN YOUR CLASS? YOU CAN'T POSSIBLY TELL ME THAT YOU DON'T KNOW WHAT I'M TALKING ABOUT.

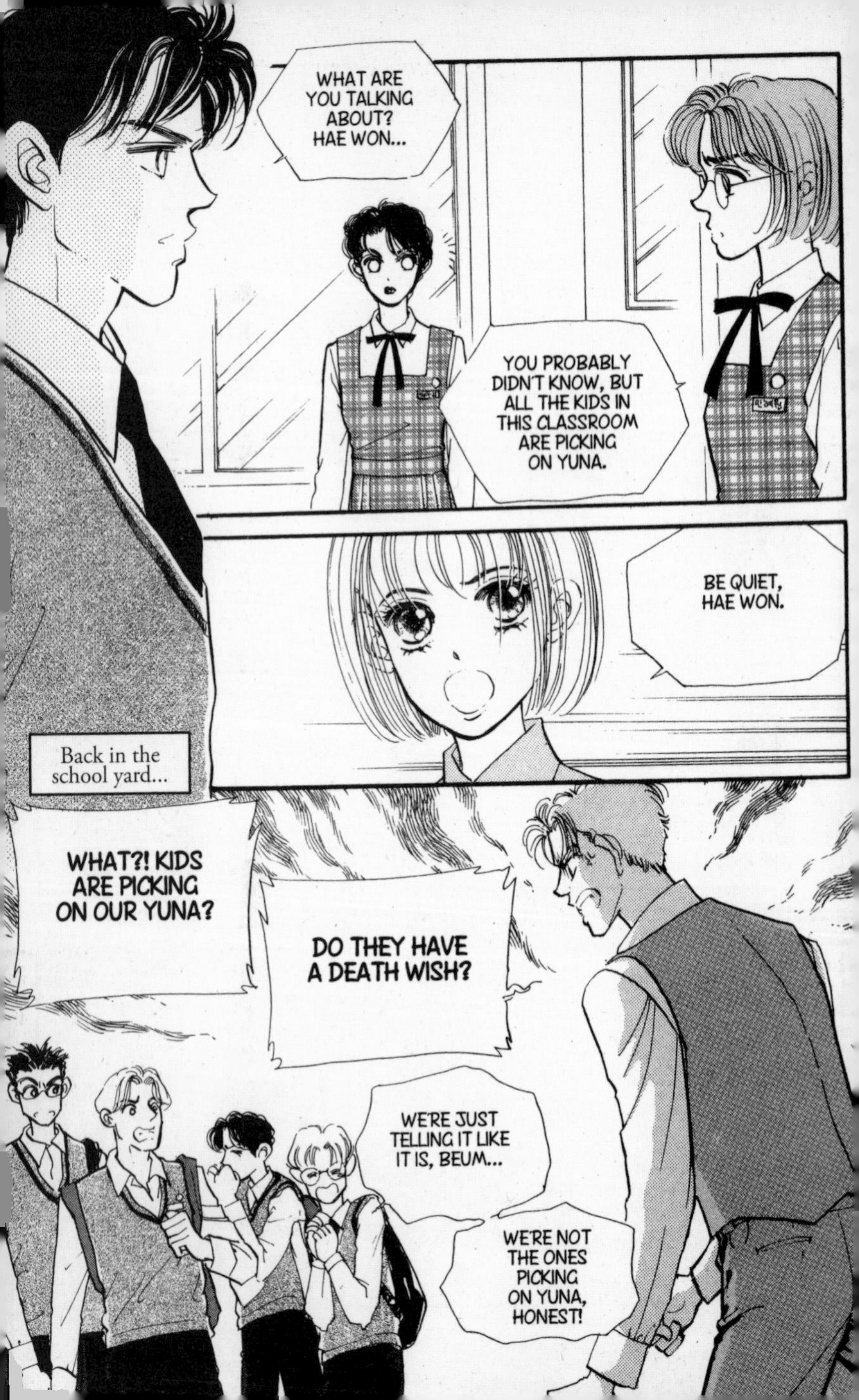
WHAT ARE YOU TALKING ABOUT? HAE WON...
YOU PROBABLY DIDN'T KNOW, BUT ALL THE KIDS IN THIS CLASSROOM ARE PICKING ON YUNA.
BE QUIET, HAE WON.
Back in the school yard...
WHAT?! KIDS ARE PICKING ON OUR YUNA?
DO THEY HAVE A DEATH WISH?
WE'RE JUST TELLING IT LIKE IT IS, BEUM...
WE'RE NOT THE ONES PICKING ON YUNA, HONEST!

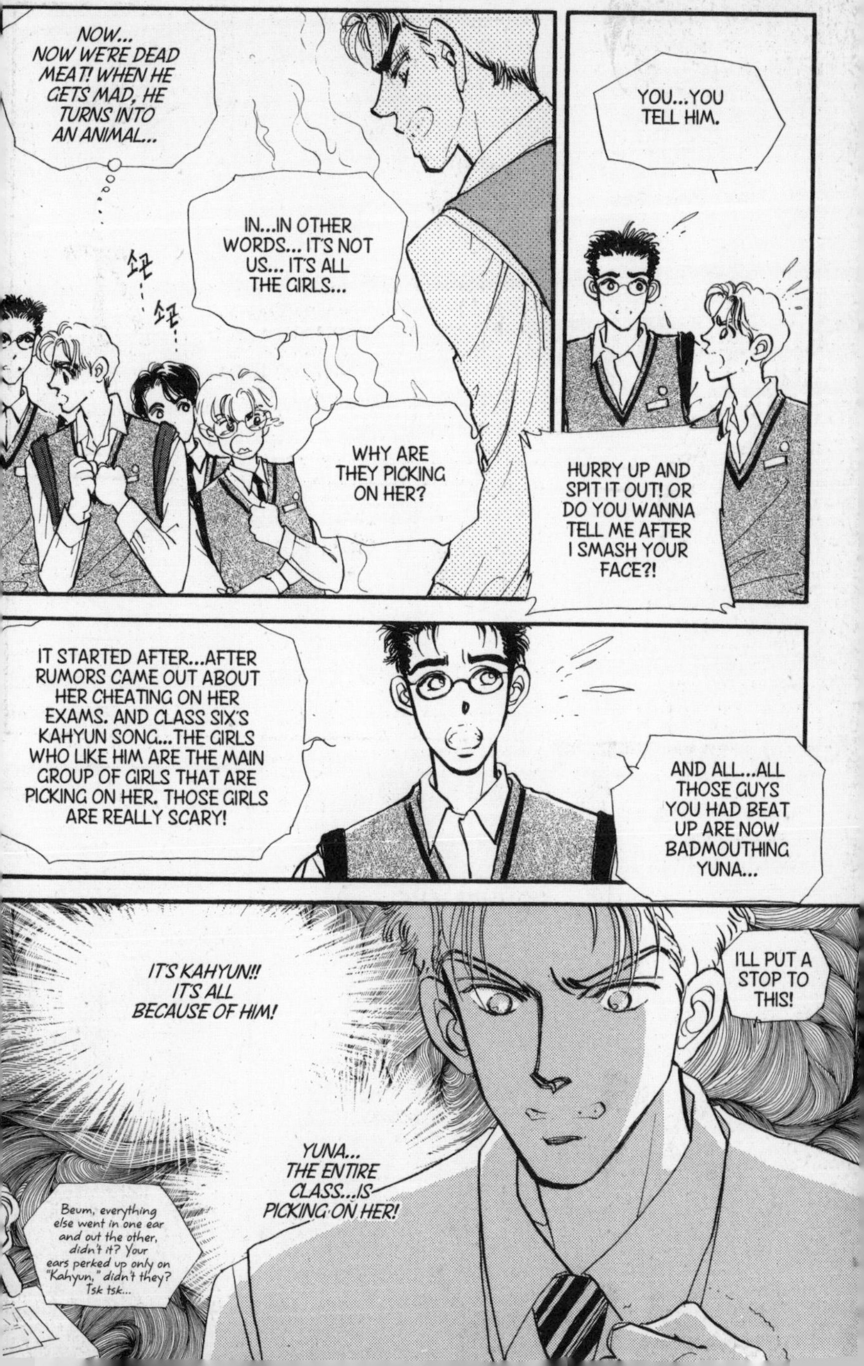
NOW... NOW WE'RE DEAD MEAT! WHEN HE GETS MAD, HE TURNS INTO AN ANIMAL...
IN...IN OTHER WORDS... IT'S NOT US... IT'S ALL THE GIRLS...
WHY ARE THEY PICKING ON HER?
YOU...YOU TELL HIM.
HURRY UP AND SPIT IT OUT! OR DO YOU WANNA TELL ME AFTER I SMASH YOUR FACE?!
IT STARTED AFTER...AFTER RUMORS CAME OUT ABOUT HER CHEATING ON HER EXAMS. AND CLASS SIX'S KAHYUN SONG...THE GIRLS WHO LIKE HIM ARE THE MAIN GROUP OF GIRLS THAT ARE PICKING ON HER. THOSE GIRLS ARE REALLY SCARY!
AND ALL...ALL THOSE GUYS YOU HAD BEAT UP ARE NOW BADMOUTHING YUNA...
IT'S KAHYUN!! IT'S ALL BECAUSE OF HIM!
I'LL PUT A STOP TO THIS!
YUNA... THE ENTIRE CLASS...IS PICKING ON HER!
Beum, everything else went in one ear and out the other, didn't it? Your ears perked up only on "Kahyun," didn't they? Tsk tsk...

Back in the classroom...

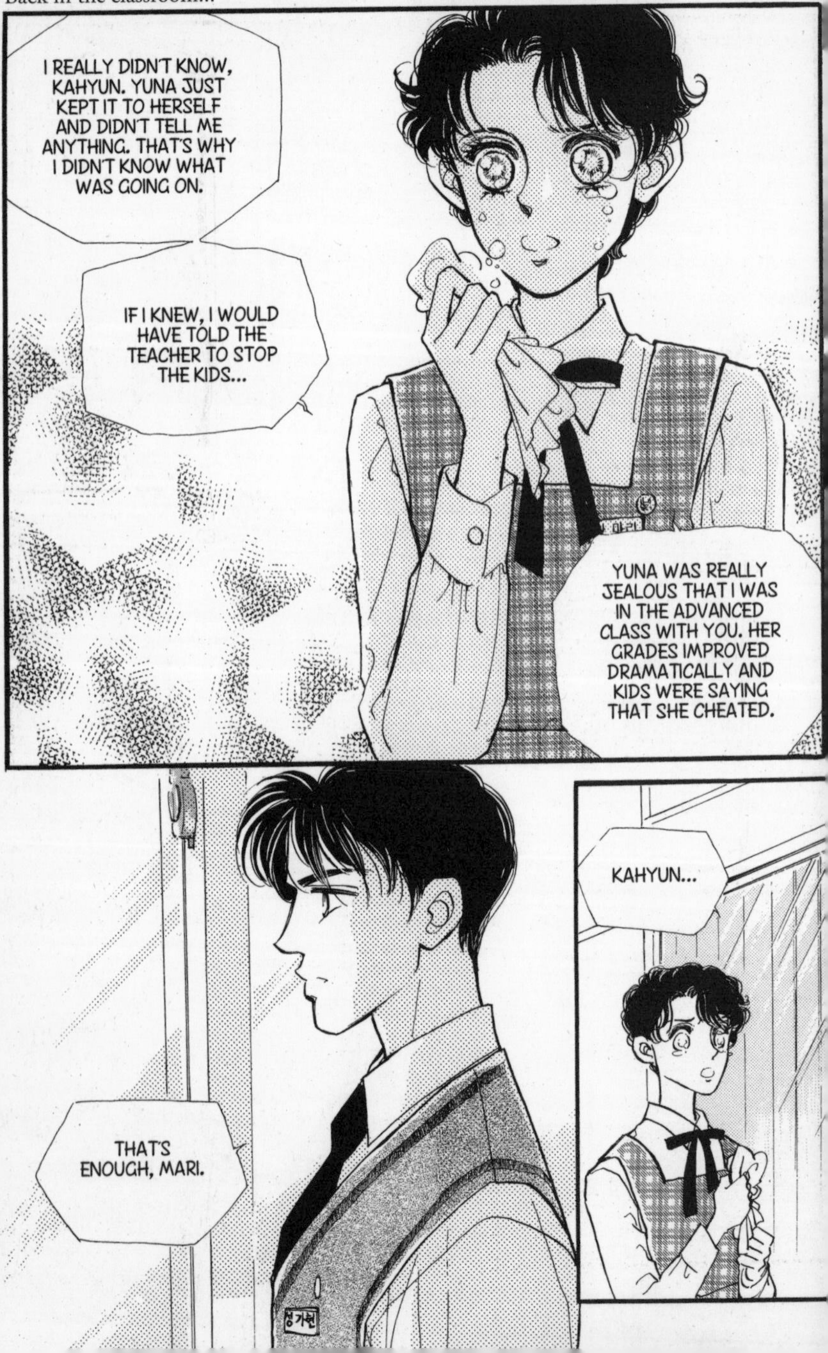
I REALLY DIDN'T KNOW, KAHYUN. YUNA JUST KEPT IT TO HERSELF AND DIDN'T TELL ME ANYTHING. THAT'S WHY I DIDN'T KNOW WHAT WAS GOING ON.
IF I KNEW, I WOULD HAVE TOLD THE TEACHER TO STOP THE KIDS...
YUNA WAS REALLY JEALOUS THAT I WAS IN THE ADVANCED CLASS WITH YOU. HER GRADES IMPROVED DRAMATICALLY AND KIDS WERE SAYING THAT SHE CHEATED.
THAT'S ENOUGH, MARI.
KAHYUN...

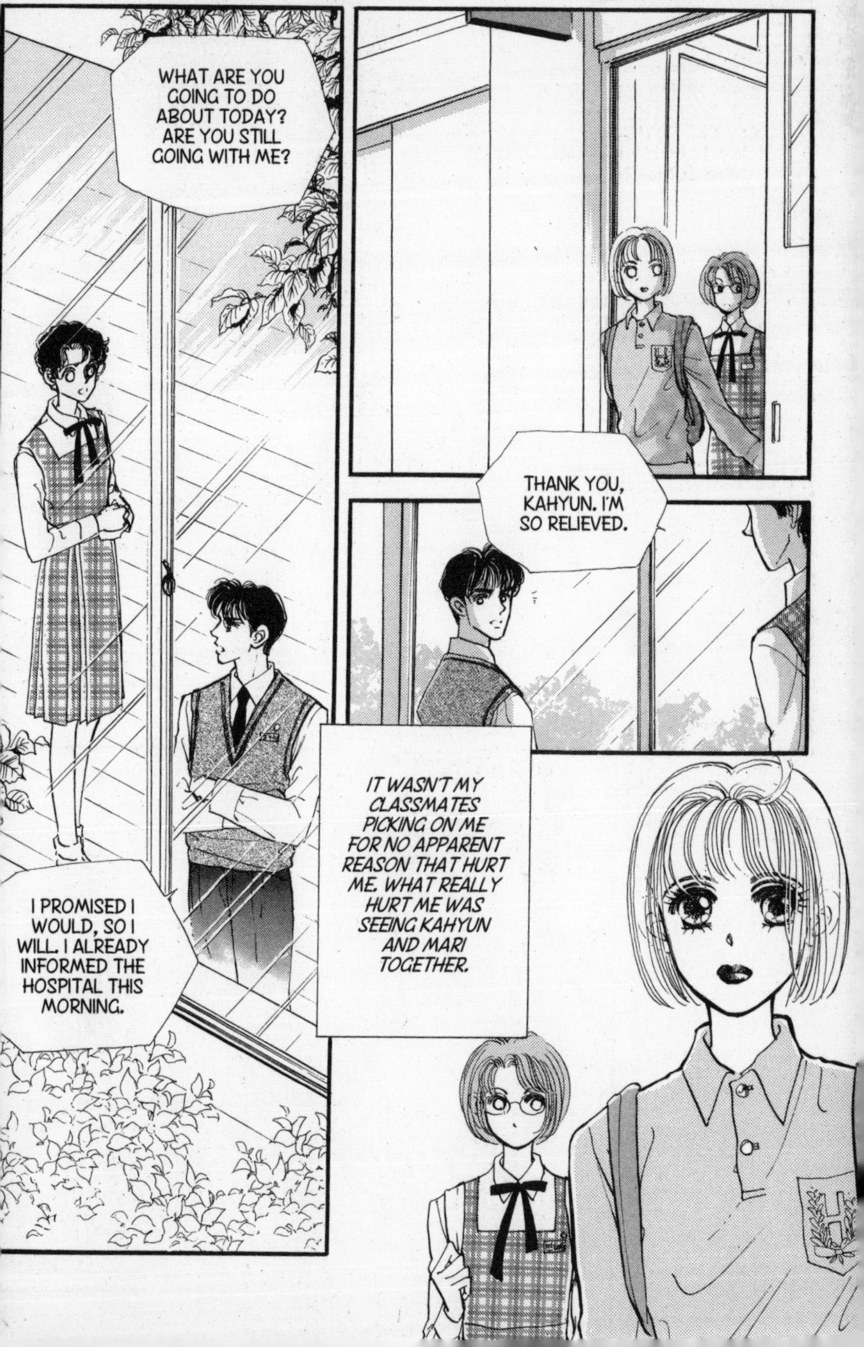
WHAT ARE YOU GOING TO DO ABOUT TODAY? ARE YOU STILL GOING WITH ME?
I PROMISED I WOULD, SO I WILL. I ALREADY INFORMED THE HOSPITAL THIS MORNING.
THANK YOU, KAHYUN. I'M SO RELIEVED.
IT WASN'T MY CLASSMATES PICKING ON ME FOR NO APPARENT REASON THAT HURT ME. WHAT REALLY HURT ME WAS SEEING KAHYUN AND MARI TOGETHER.

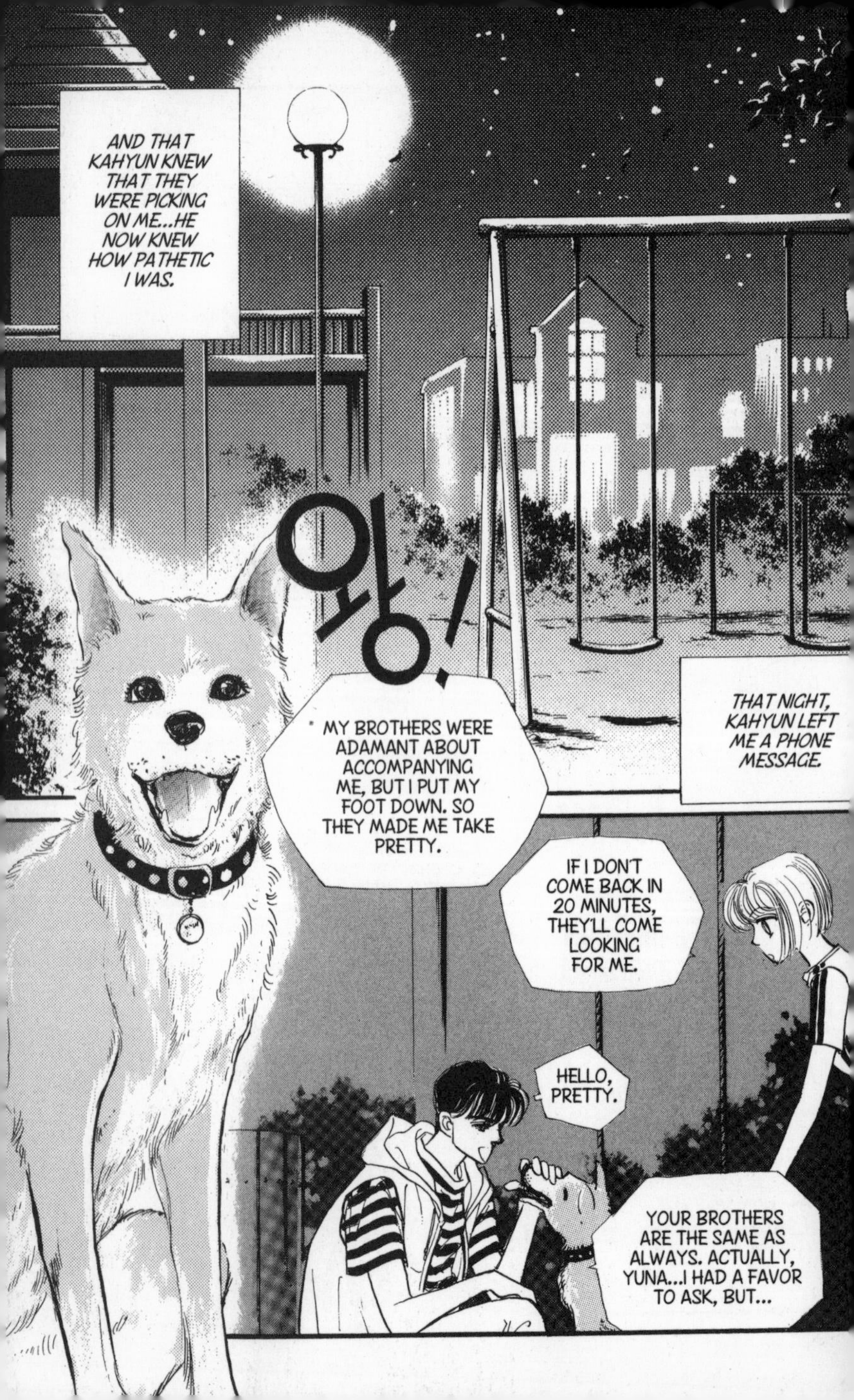
AND THAT KAHYUN KNEW THAT THEY WERE PICKING ON ME...HE NOW KNEW HOW PATHETIC I WAS.
THAT NIGHT, KAHYUN LEFT ME A PHONE MESSAGE.
앙!
MY BROTHERS WERE ADAMANT ABOUT ACCOMPANYING ME, BUT I PUT MY FOOT DOWN. SO THEY MADE ME TAKE PRETTY.
IF I DON'T COME BACK IN 20 MINUTES, THEY'LL COME LOOKING FOR ME.
HELLO, PRETTY.
YOUR BROTHERS ARE THE SAME AS ALWAYS. ACTUALLY, YUNA...I HAD A FAVOR TO ASK, BUT...

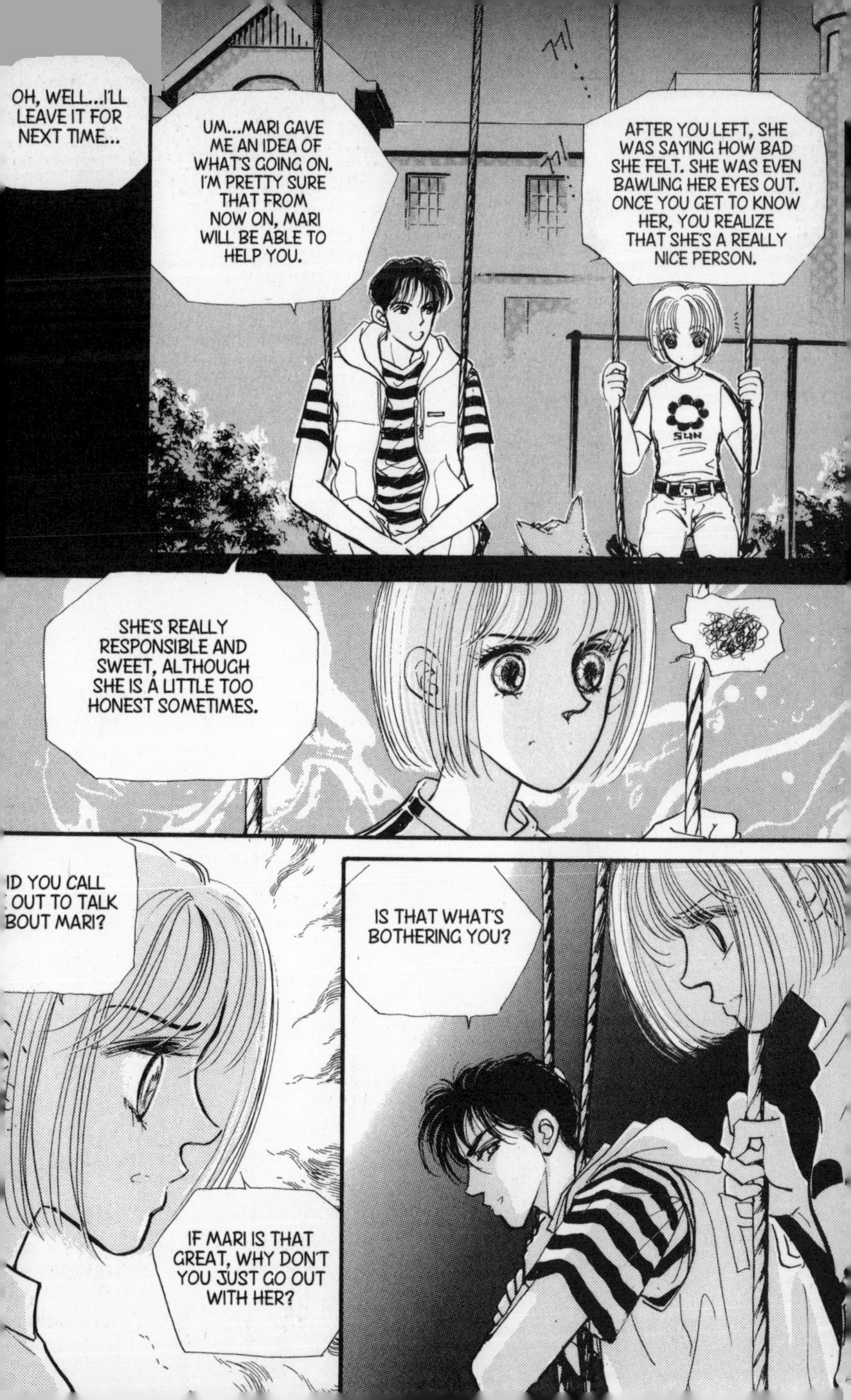
OH, WELL...I'LL LEAVE IT FOR NEXT TIME...
UM...MARI GAVE ME AN IDEA OF WHAT'S GOING ON. I'M PRETTY SURE THAT FROM NOW ON, MARI WILL BE ABLE TO HELP YOU.
AFTER YOU LEFT, SHE WAS SAYING HOW BAD SHE FELT. SHE WAS EVEN BAWLING HER EYES OUT. ONCE YOU GET TO KNOW HER, YOU REALIZE THAT SHE'S A REALLY NICE PERSON.
SHE'S REALLY RESPONSIBLE AND SWEET, ALTHOUGH SHE IS A LITTLE TOO HONEST SOMETIMES.
ID YOU CALL
OUT TO TALK
BOUT MARI?
IF MARI IS THAT GREAT, WHY DON'T YOU JUST GO OUT WITH HER?
IS THAT WHAT'S BOTHERING YOU?

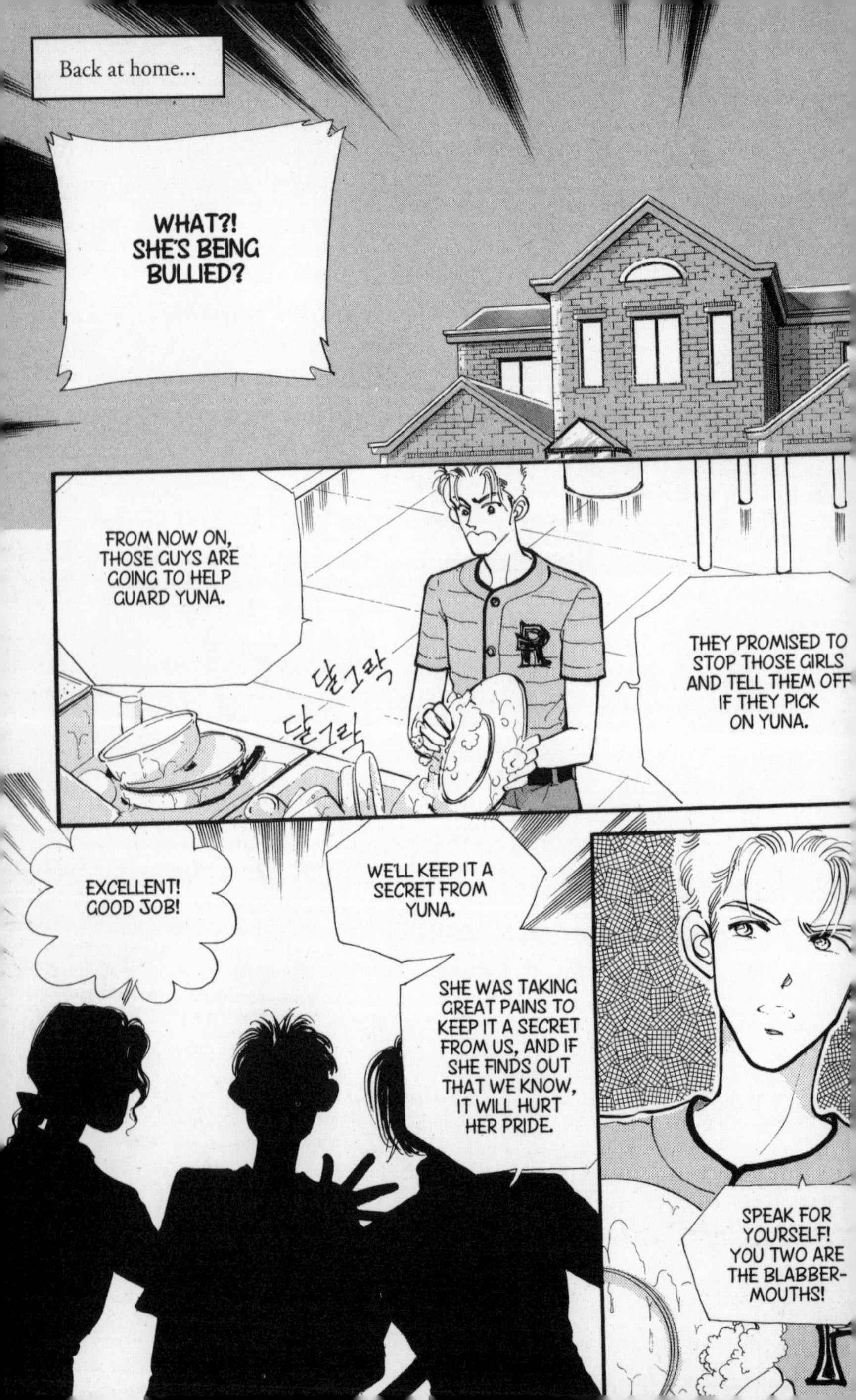
Back at home...
WHAT?! SHE'S BEING BULLIED?
FROM NOW ON, THOSE GUYS ARE GOING TO HELP GUARD YUNA.
달그락
달그락
THEY PROMISED TO STOP THOSE GIRLS AND TELL THEM OFF IF THEY PICK ON YUNA.
EXCELLENT! GOOD JOB!
WE'LL KEEP IT A SECRET FROM YUNA.
SHE WAS TAKING GREAT PAINS TO KEEP IT A SECRET FROM US, AND IF SHE FINDS OUT THAT WE KNOW, IT WILL HURT HER PRIDE.
SPEAK FOR YOURSELF! YOU TWO ARE THE BLABBER-MOUTHS!

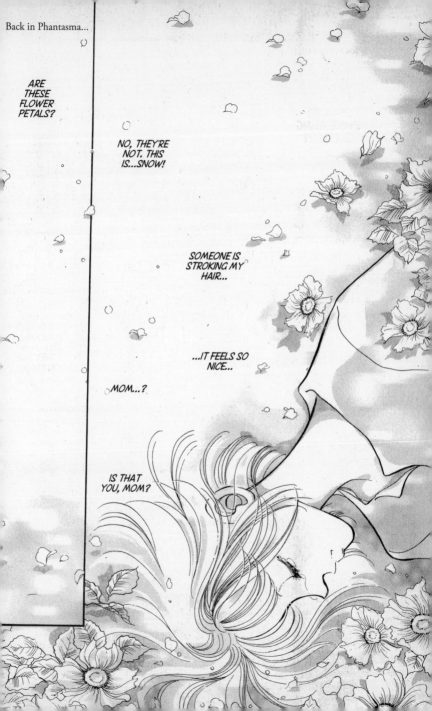

ARE THESE FLOWER PETALS?

NO, THEY'RE NOT. THIS IS...SNOW!

SOMEONE IS STROKING MY HAIR...

...IT FEELS SO NICE...

MOM...?

IS THAT YOU, MOM?

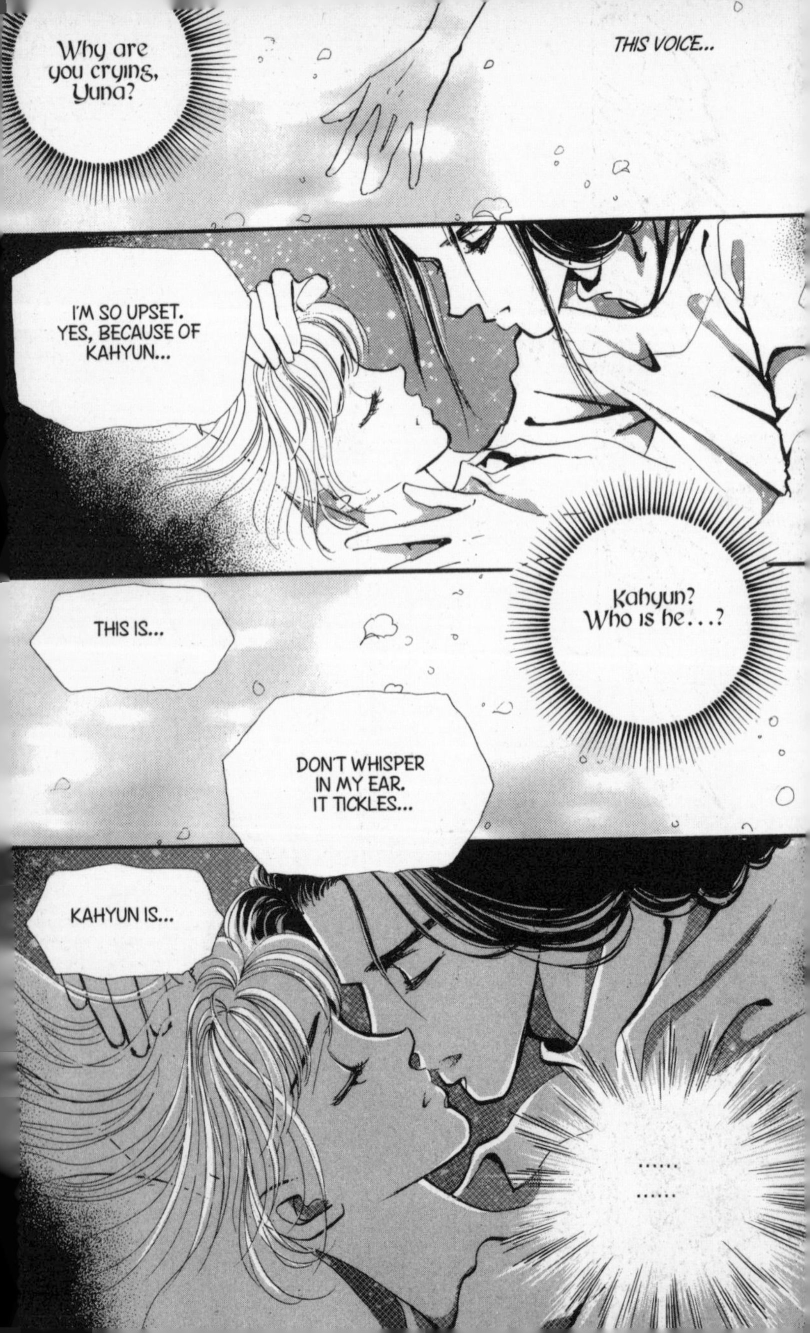
Why are you crying, Yuna?
THIS VOICE...
I'M SO UPSET. YES, BECAUSE OF KAHYUN...
THIS IS...
Kahyun? Who is he...?
DON'T WHISPER IN MY EAR. IT TICKLES...
KAHYUN IS...
......
......

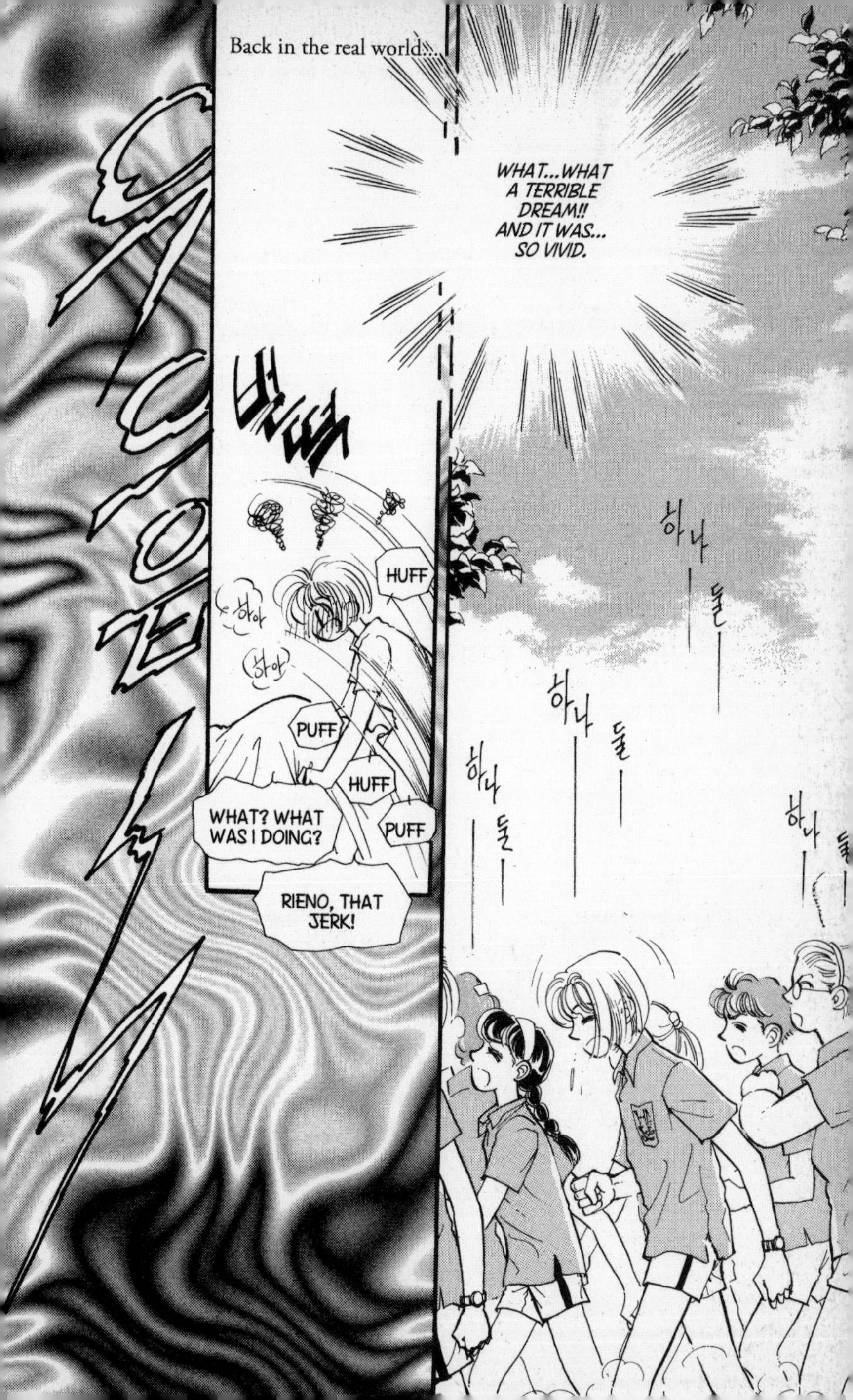
Back in the real world...
벌떡
HUFF
하아
하아
PUFF
HUFF
WHAT? WHAT WAS I DOING?
PUFF
RIENO, THAT JERK!
WHAT...WHAT A TERRIBLE DREAM!! AND IT WAS... SO VIVID.
하나 둘
하나 둘
하나 둘
하나 둘

I CAN'T STAND P.E.!

I FEEL LIKE THROWING UP!

TEACHER, SHE FAINTED!

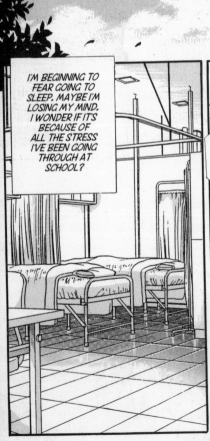

I'M BEGINNING TO FEAR GOING TO SLEEP. MAYBE I'M LOSING MY MIND. I WONDER IF IT'S BECAUSE OF ALL THE STRESS I'VE BEEN GOING THROUGH AT SCHOOL?

ARE YOU OKAY NOW? YOU'RE IN THE NURSE'S OFFICE!

THE NURSE SAID YOU HAD SUNSTROKE AND YOU'RE ALSO ANEMIC.

MARI PARK...

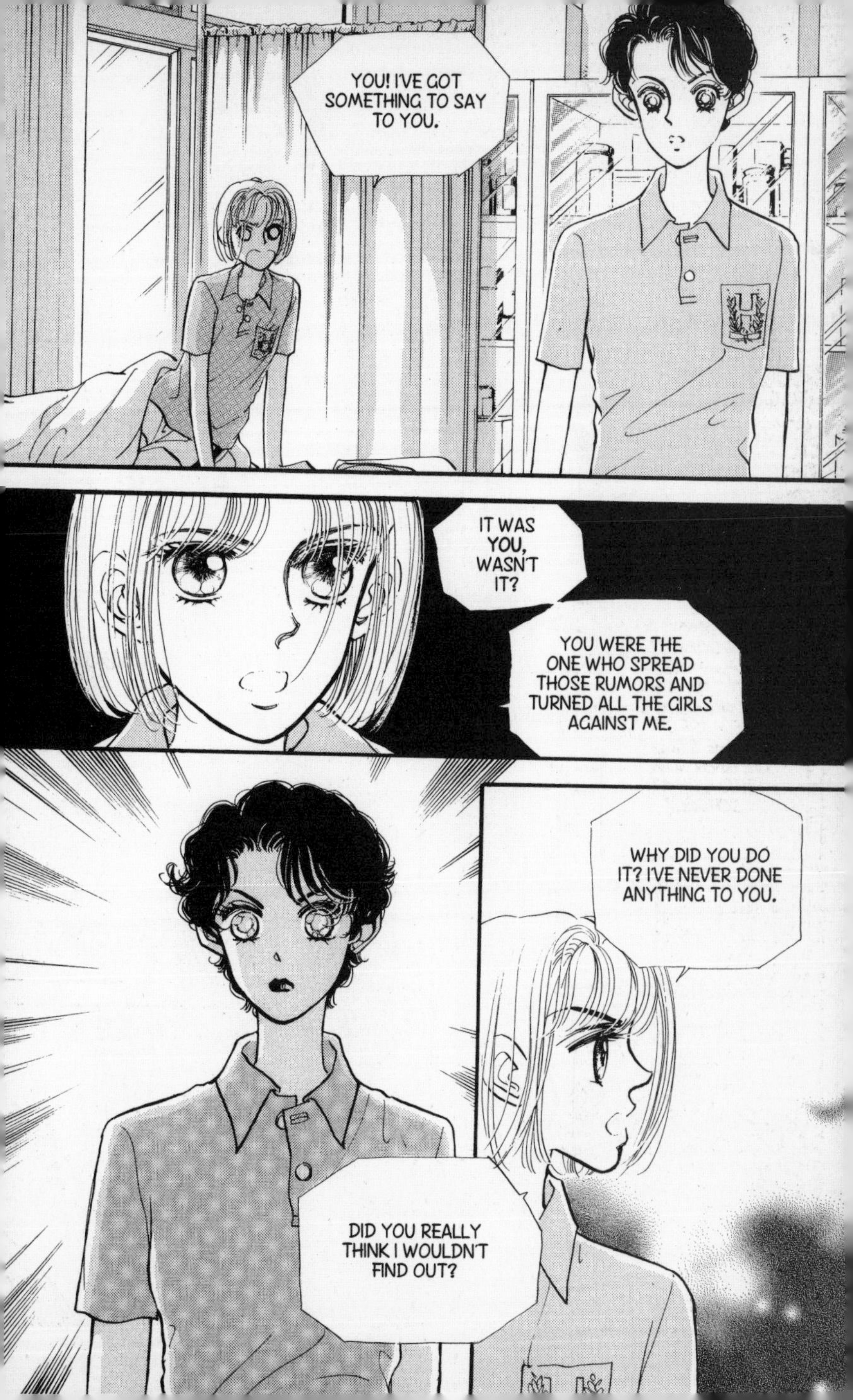
YOU! I'VE GOT SOMETHING TO SAY TO YOU.
IT WAS YOU, WASN'T IT?
YOU WERE THE ONE WHO SPREAD THOSE RUMORS AND TURNED ALL THE GIRLS AGAINST ME.
DID YOU REALLY THINK I WOULDN'T FIND OUT?
WHY DID YOU DO IT? I'VE NEVER DONE ANYTHING TO YOU.

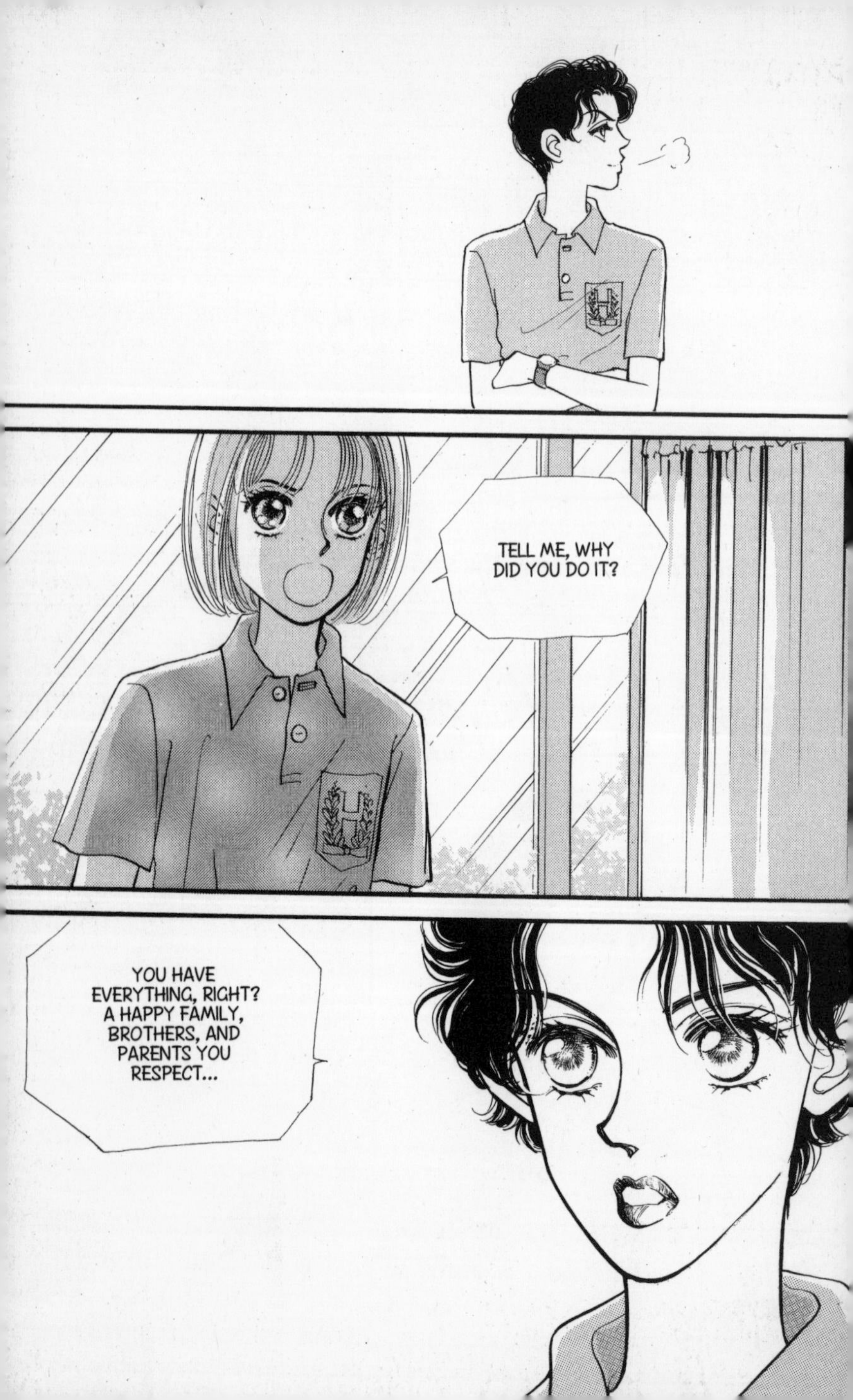
TELL ME, WHY DID YOU DO IT?
YOU HAVE EVERYTHING, RIGHT? A HAPPY FAMILY, BROTHERS, AND PARENTS YOU RESPECT...

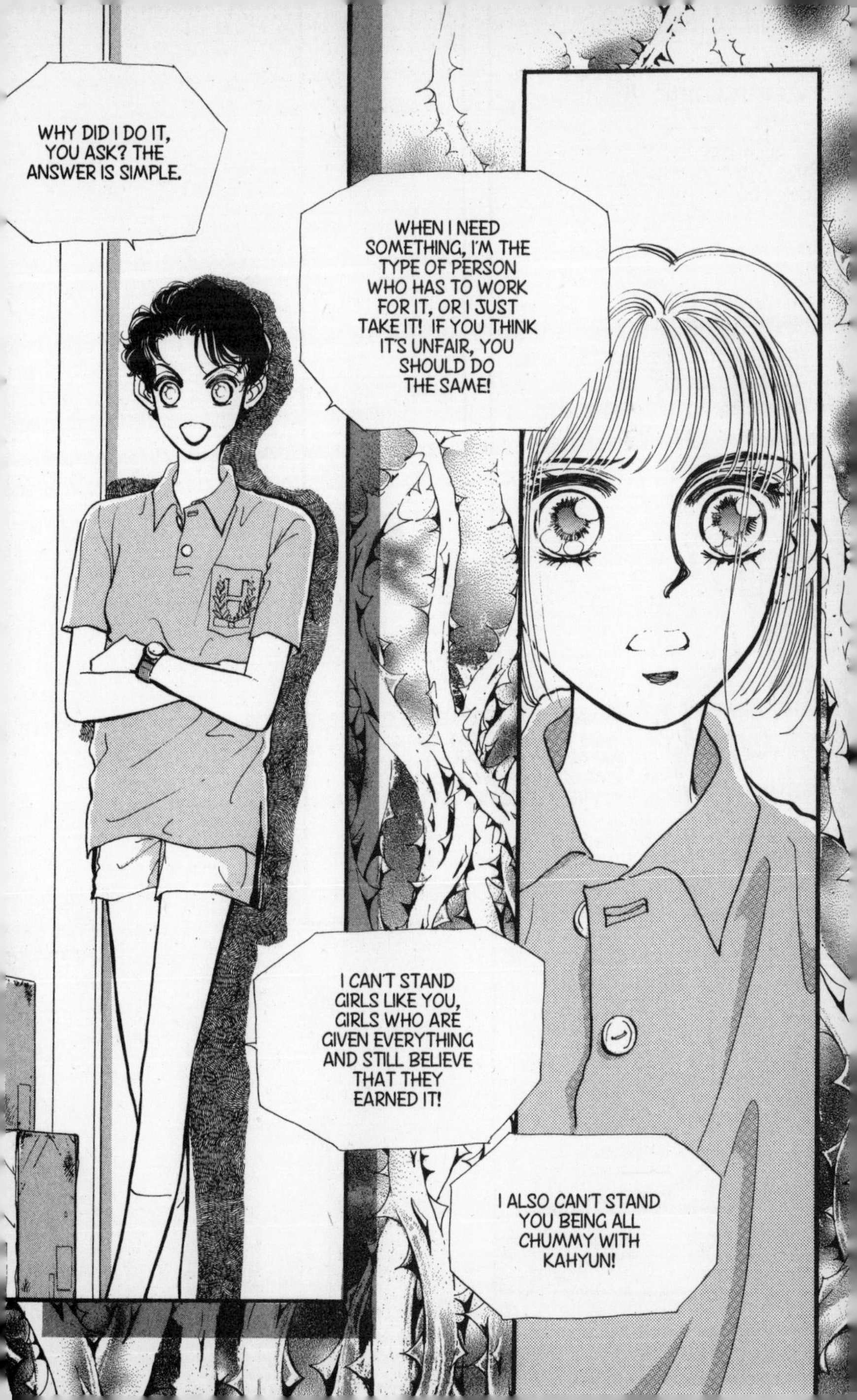
WHY DID I DO IT, YOU ASK? THE ANSWER IS SIMPLE.
WHEN I NEED SOMETHING, I'M THE TYPE OF PERSON WHO HAS TO WORK FOR IT, OR I JUST TAKE IT! IF YOU THINK IT'S UNFAIR, YOU SHOULD DO THE SAME!
I CAN'T STAND GIRLS LIKE YOU, GIRLS WHO ARE GIVEN EVERYTHING AND STILL BELIEVE THAT THEY EARNED IT!
I ALSO CAN'T STAND YOU BEING ALL CHUMMY WITH KAHYUN!

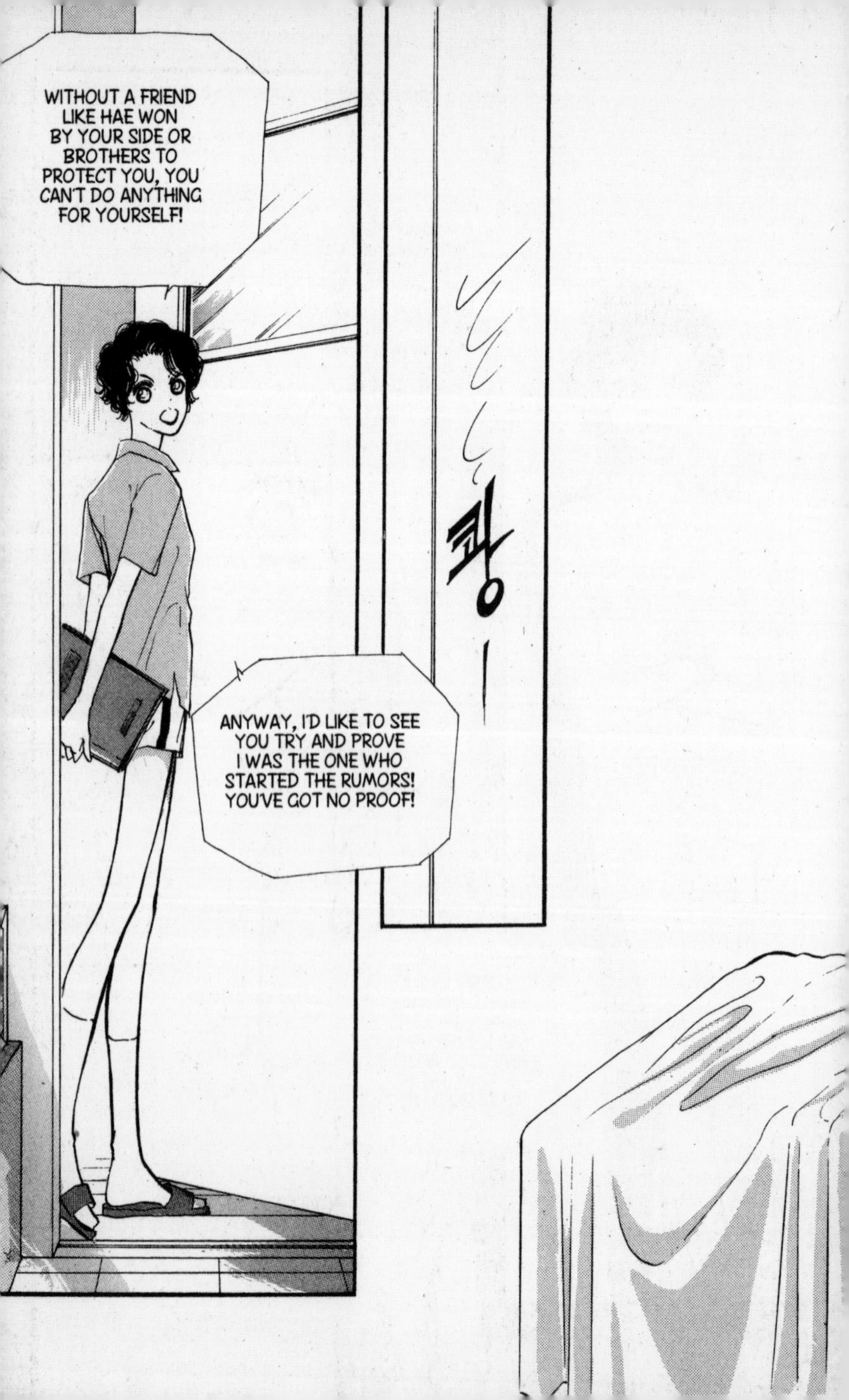
WITHOUT A FRIEND LIKE HAE WON BY YOUR SIDE OR BROTHERS TO PROTECT YOU, YOU CAN'T DO ANYTHING FOR YOURSELF!
ANYWAY, I'D LIKE TO SEE YOU TRY AND PROVE I WAS THE ONE WHO STARTED THE RUMORS! YOU'VE GOT NO PROOF!
쾅-

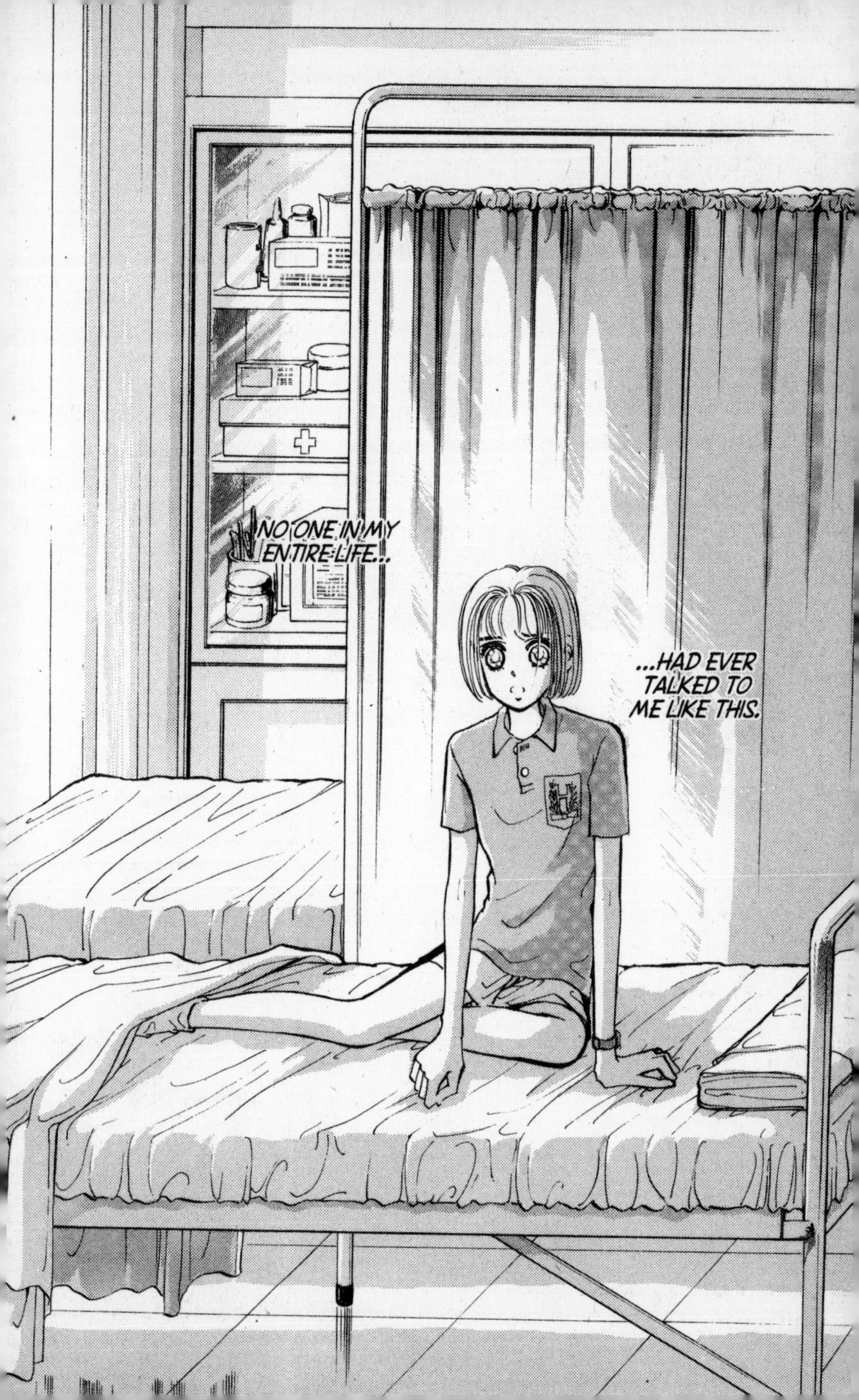
NO ONE IN MY ENTIRE LIFE...
...HAD EVER TALKED TO ME LIKE THIS.

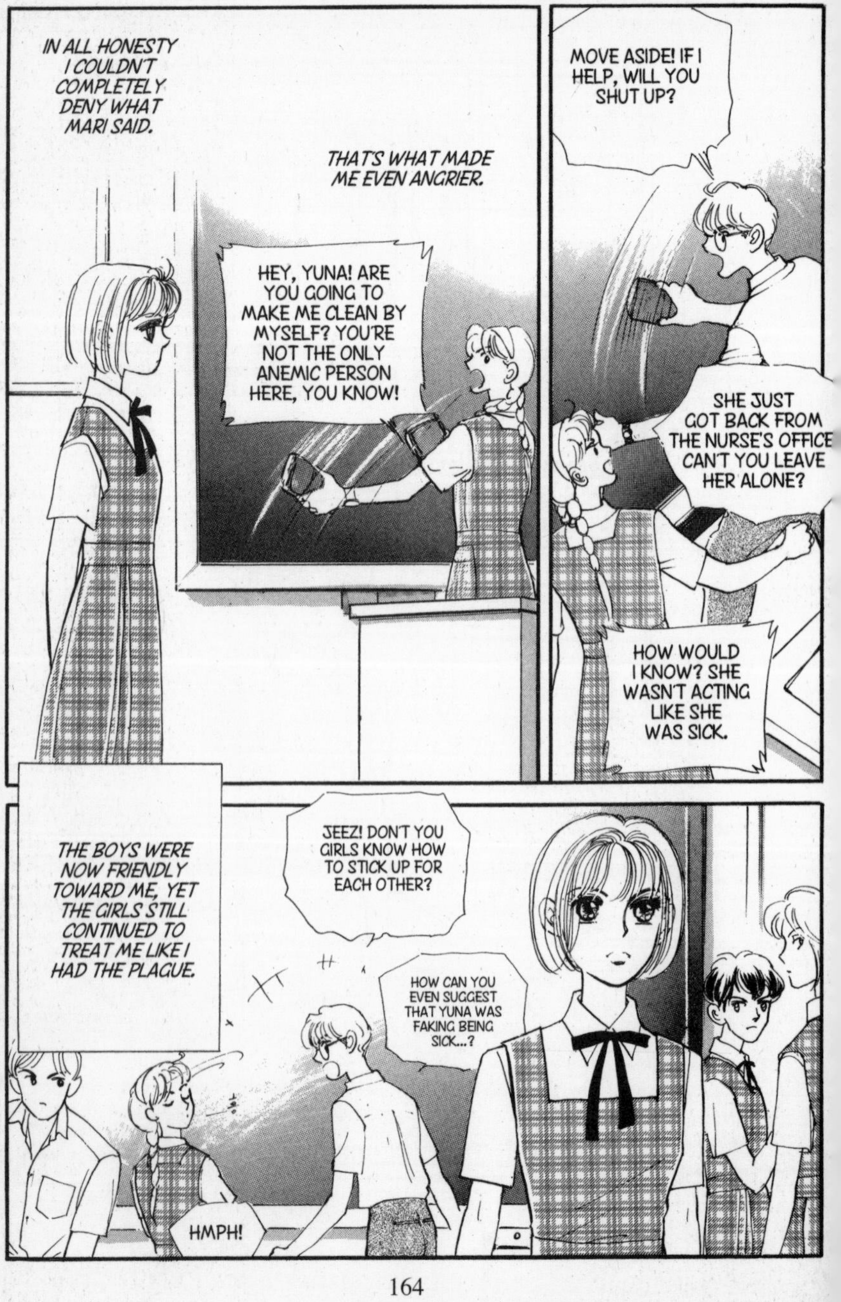
IN ALL HONESTY I COULDN'T COMPLETELY DENY WHAT MARI SAID.
THAT'S WHAT MADE ME EVEN ANGRIER.
HEY, YUNA! ARE YOU GOING TO MAKE ME CLEAN BY MYSELF? YOU'RE NOT THE ONLY ANEMIC PERSON HERE, YOU KNOW!
MOVE ASIDE! IF I HELP, WILL YOU SHUT UP?
SHE JUST GOT BACK FROM THE NURSE'S OFFICE CAN'T YOU LEAVE HER ALONE?
HOW WOULD I KNOW? SHE WASN'T ACTING LIKE SHE WAS SICK.
THE BOYS WERE NOW FRIENDLY TOWARD ME, YET THE GIRLS STILL CONTINUED TO TREAT ME LIKE I HAD THE PLAGUE.
JEEZ! DON'T YOU GIRLS KNOW HOW TO STICK UP FOR EACH OTHER?
HOW CAN YOU EVEN SUGGEST THAT YUNA WAS FAKING BEING SICK...?
HMPH!

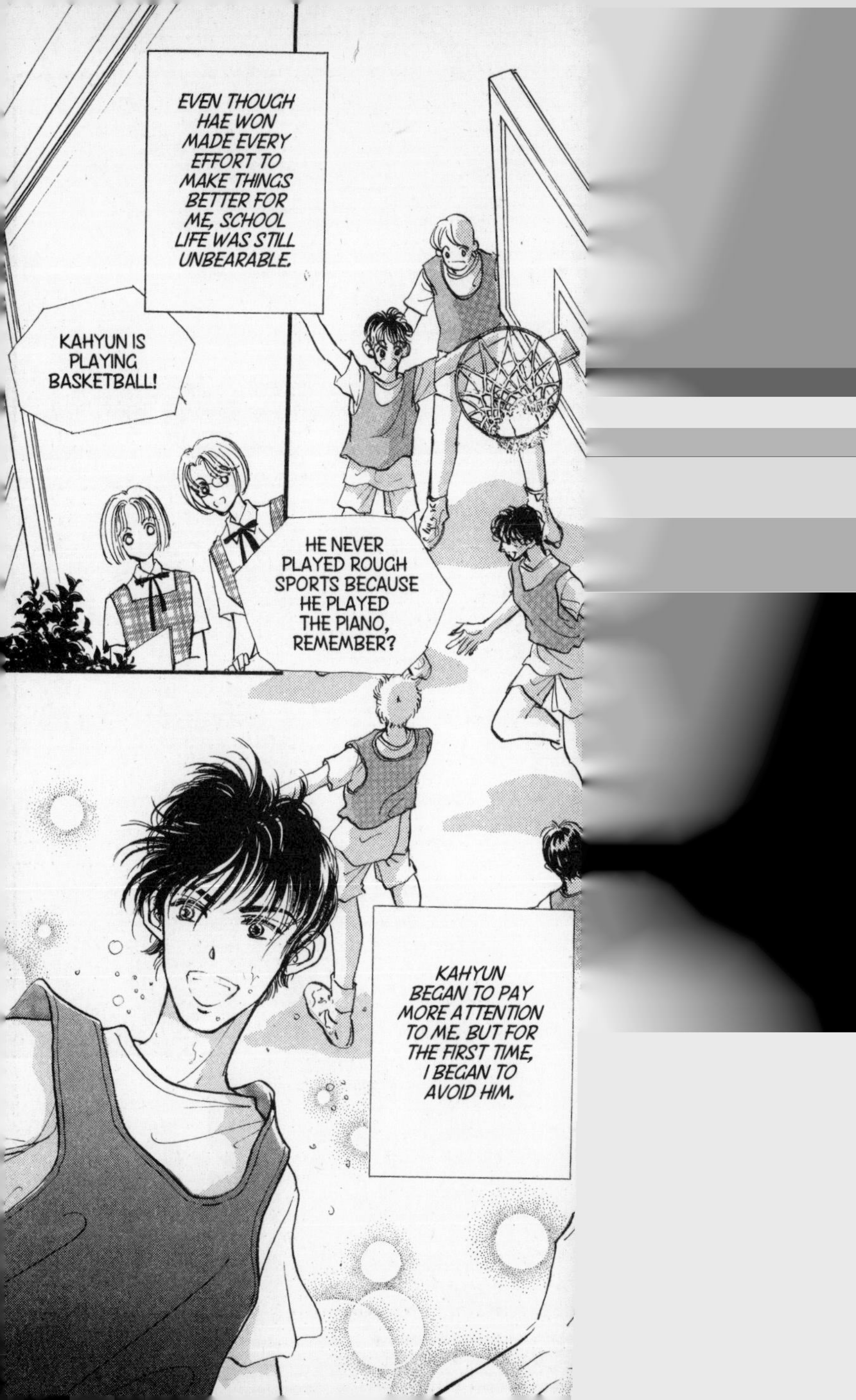

EVEN THOUGH HAE WON MADE EVERY EFFORT TO MAKE THINGS BETTER FOR ME, SCHOOL LIFE WAS STILL UNBEARABLE.
KAHYUN IS PLAYING BASKETBALL!
HE NEVER PLAYED ROUGH SPORTS BECAUSE HE PLAYED THE PIANO, REMEMBER?
KAHYUN BEGAN TO PAY MORE ATTENTION TO ME. BUT FOR THE FIRST TIME, I BEGAN TO AVOID HIM.

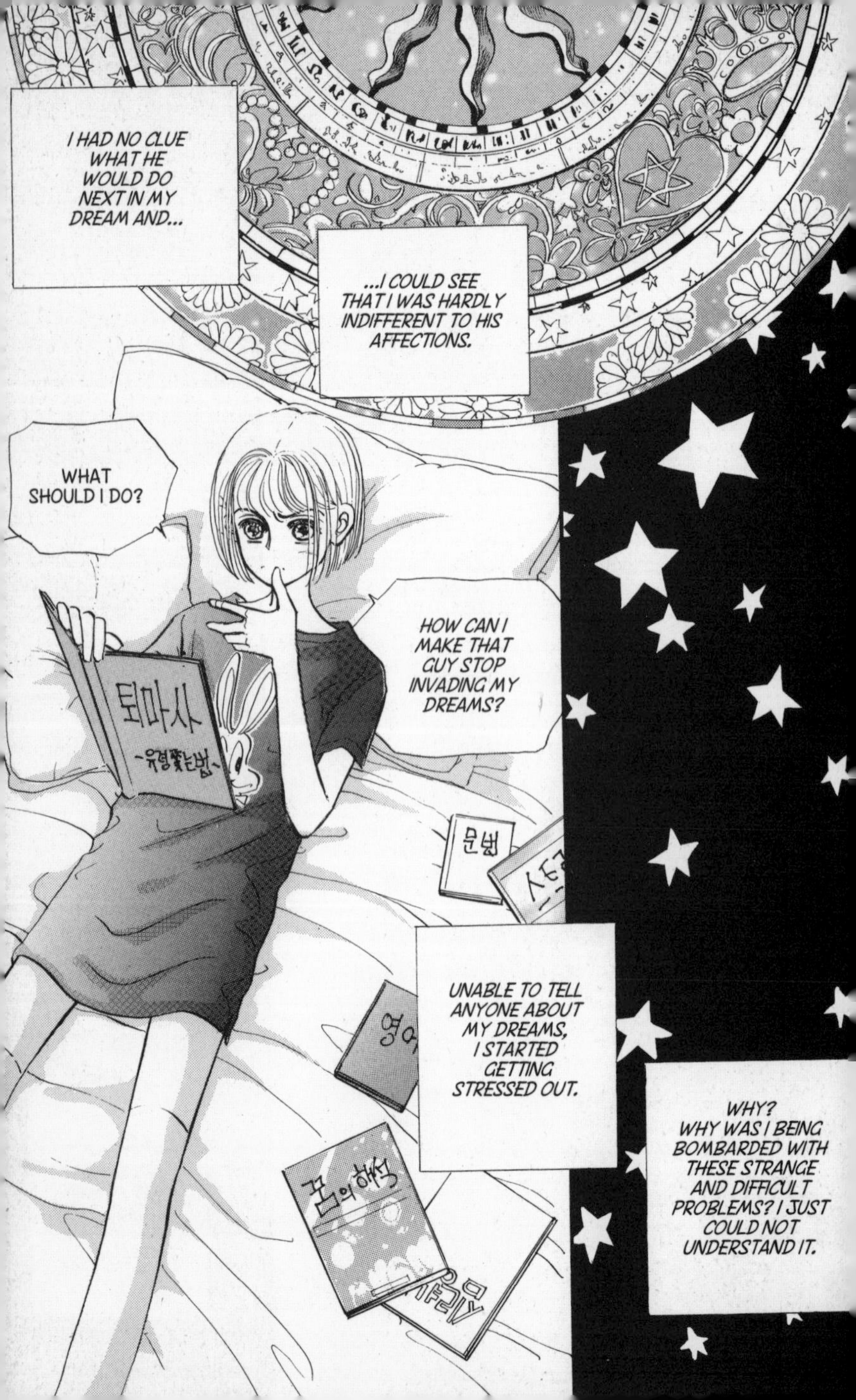
I HAD NO CLUE WHAT HE WOULD DO NEXT IN MY DREAM AND...
...I COULD SEE THAT I WAS HARDLY INDIFFERENT TO HIS AFFECTIONS.
WHAT SHOULD I DO?
퇴마사
~유령쫓는법~
HOW CAN I MAKE THAT GUY STOP INVADING MY DREAMS?
문법
UNABLE TO TELL ANYONE ABOUT MY DREAMS, I STARTED GETTING STRESSED OUT.
꿈의 해석
WHY? WHY WAS I BEING BOMBARDED WITH THESE STRANGE AND DIFFICULT PROBLEMS? I JUST COULD NOT UNDERSTAND IT.

Back in Phantasma...again!

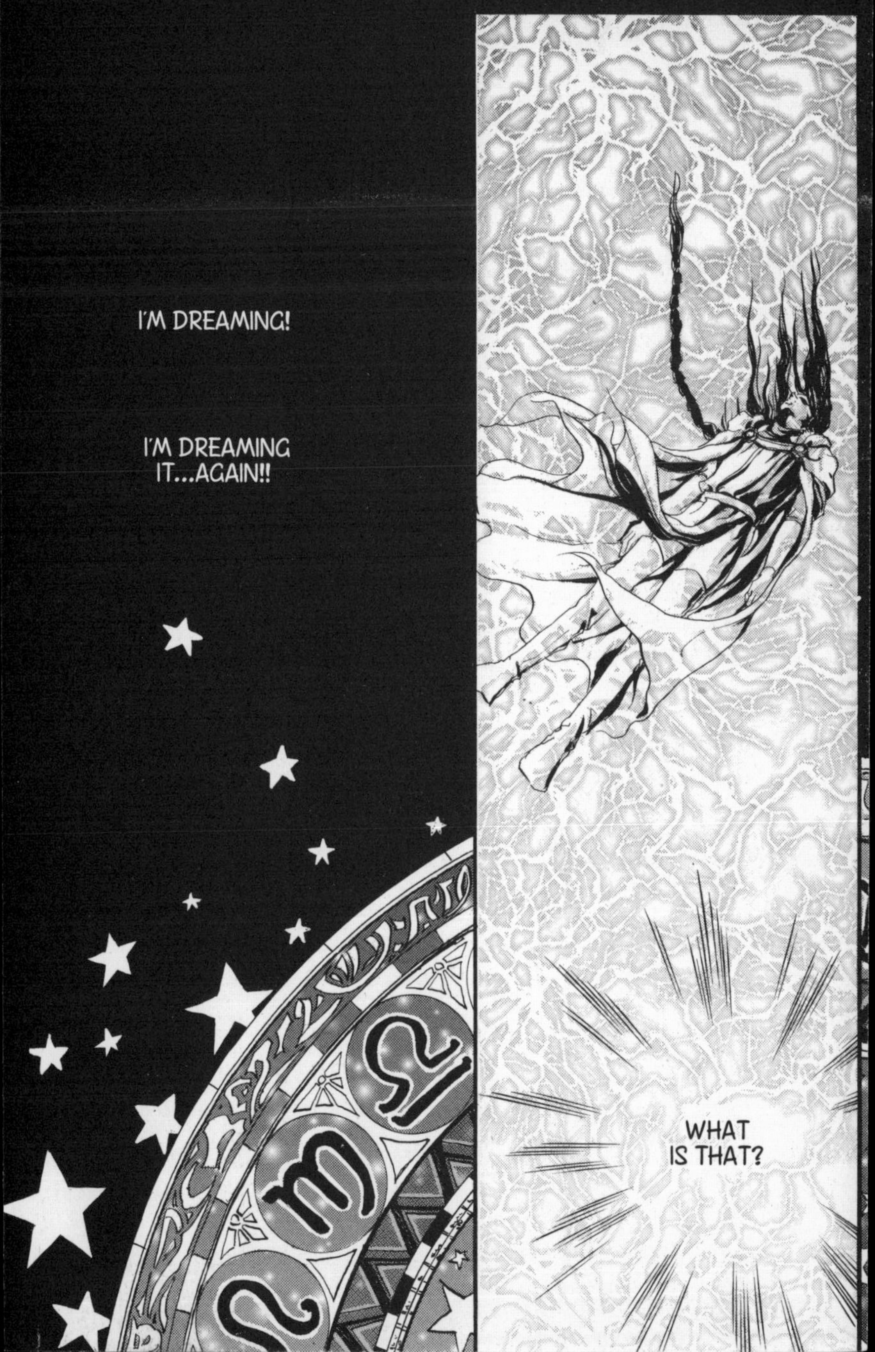
I'M DREAMING!
I'M DREAMING IT...AGAIN!!
WHAT IS THAT?

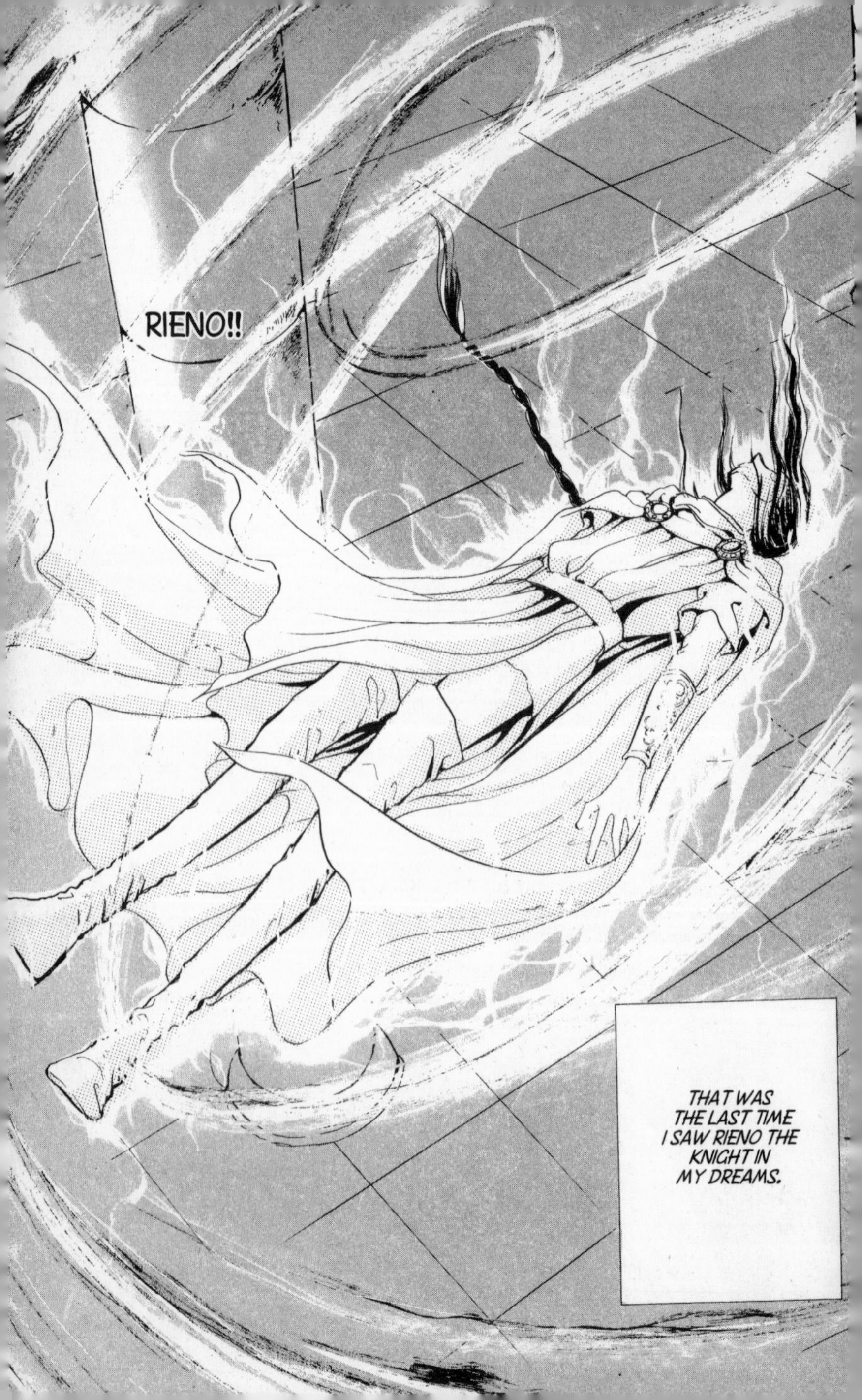
RIENO!!
THAT WAS THE LAST TIME I SAW RIENO THE KNIGHT IN MY DREAMS.

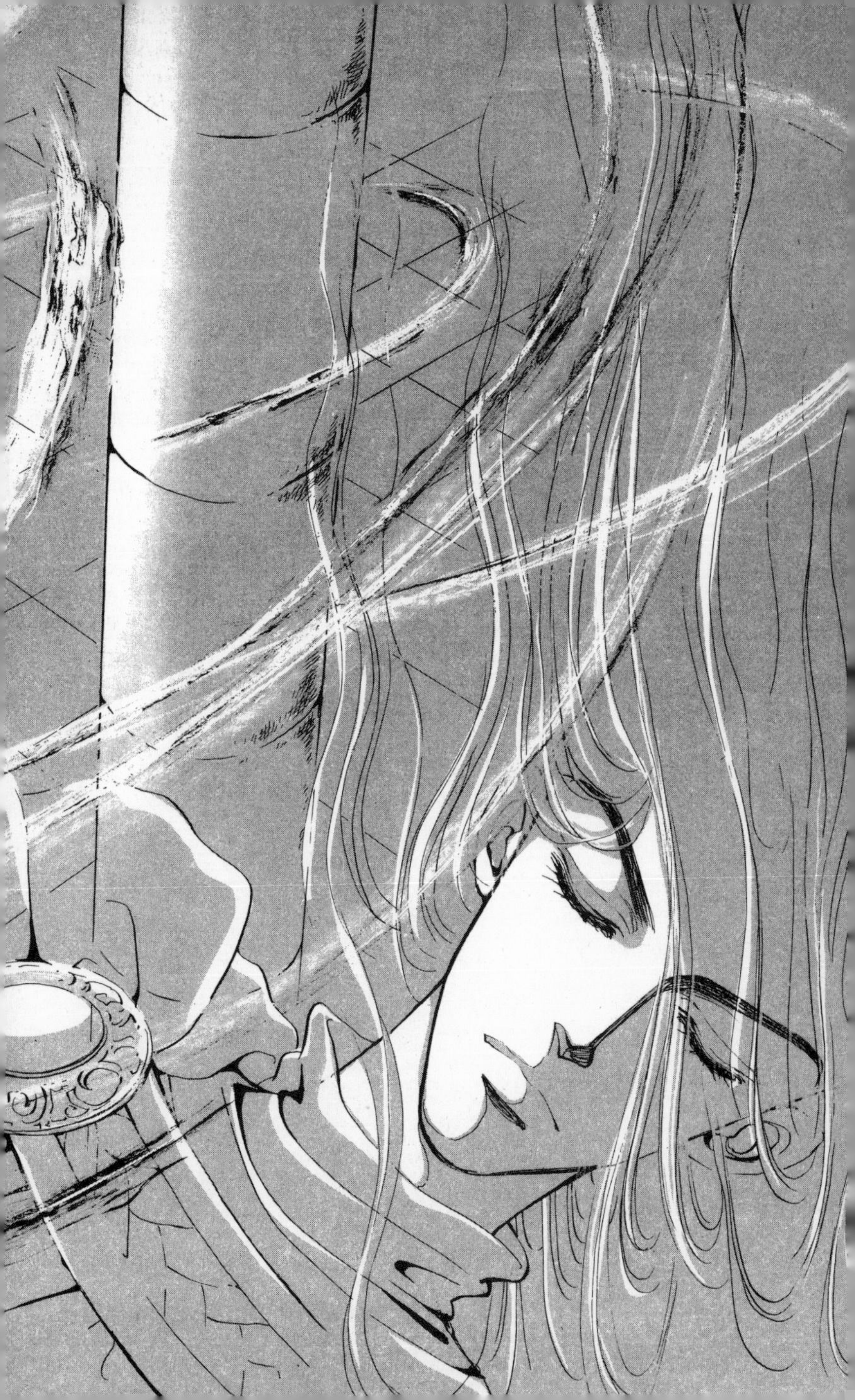

Back home...

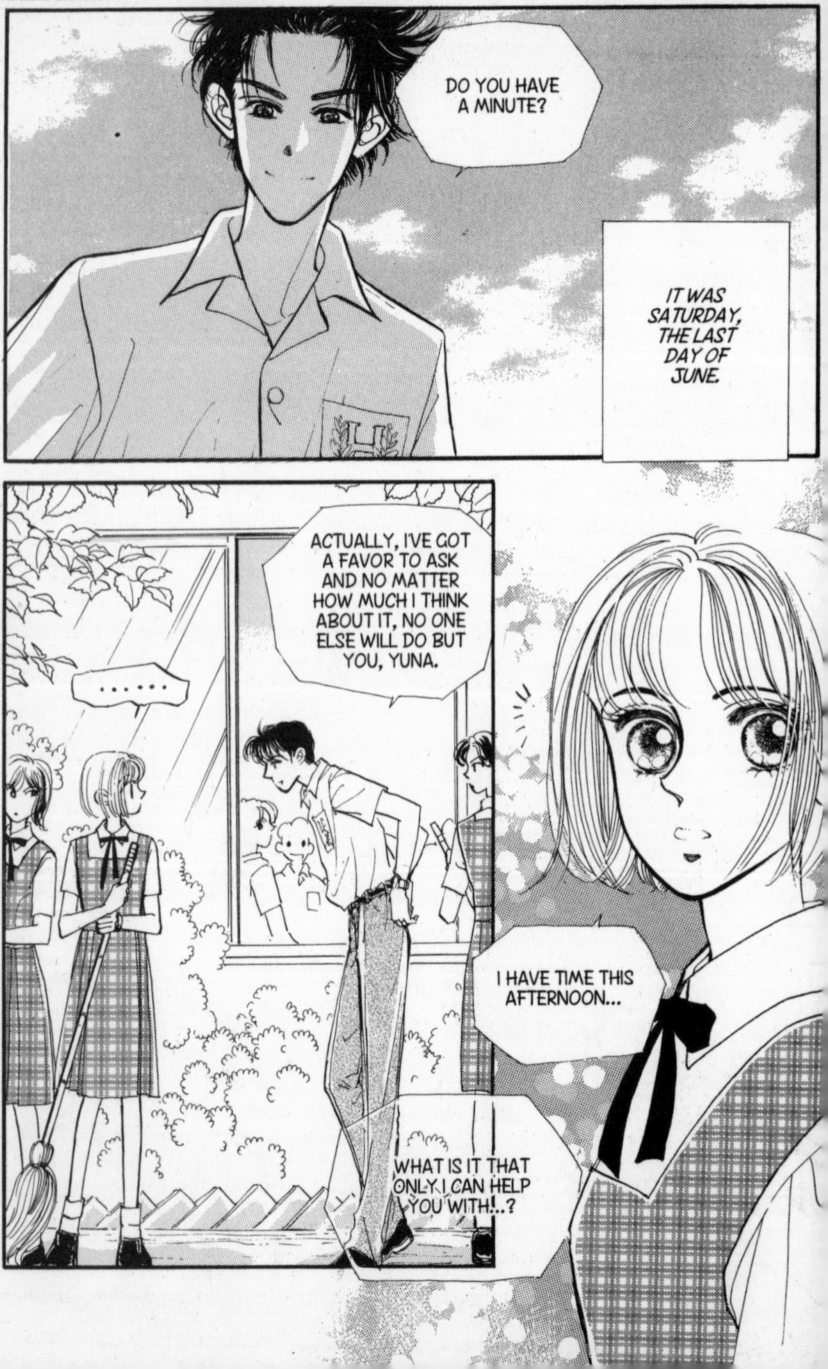
DO YOU HAVE A MINUTE?
IT WAS SATURDAY, THE LAST DAY OF JUNE.
ACTUALLY, I'VE GOT A FAVOR TO ASK AND NO MATTER HOW MUCH I THINK ABOUT IT, NO ONE ELSE WILL DO BUT YOU, YUNA.
......
I HAVE TIME THIS AFTERNOON...
WHAT IS IT THAT ONLY I CAN HELP YOU WITH!..?

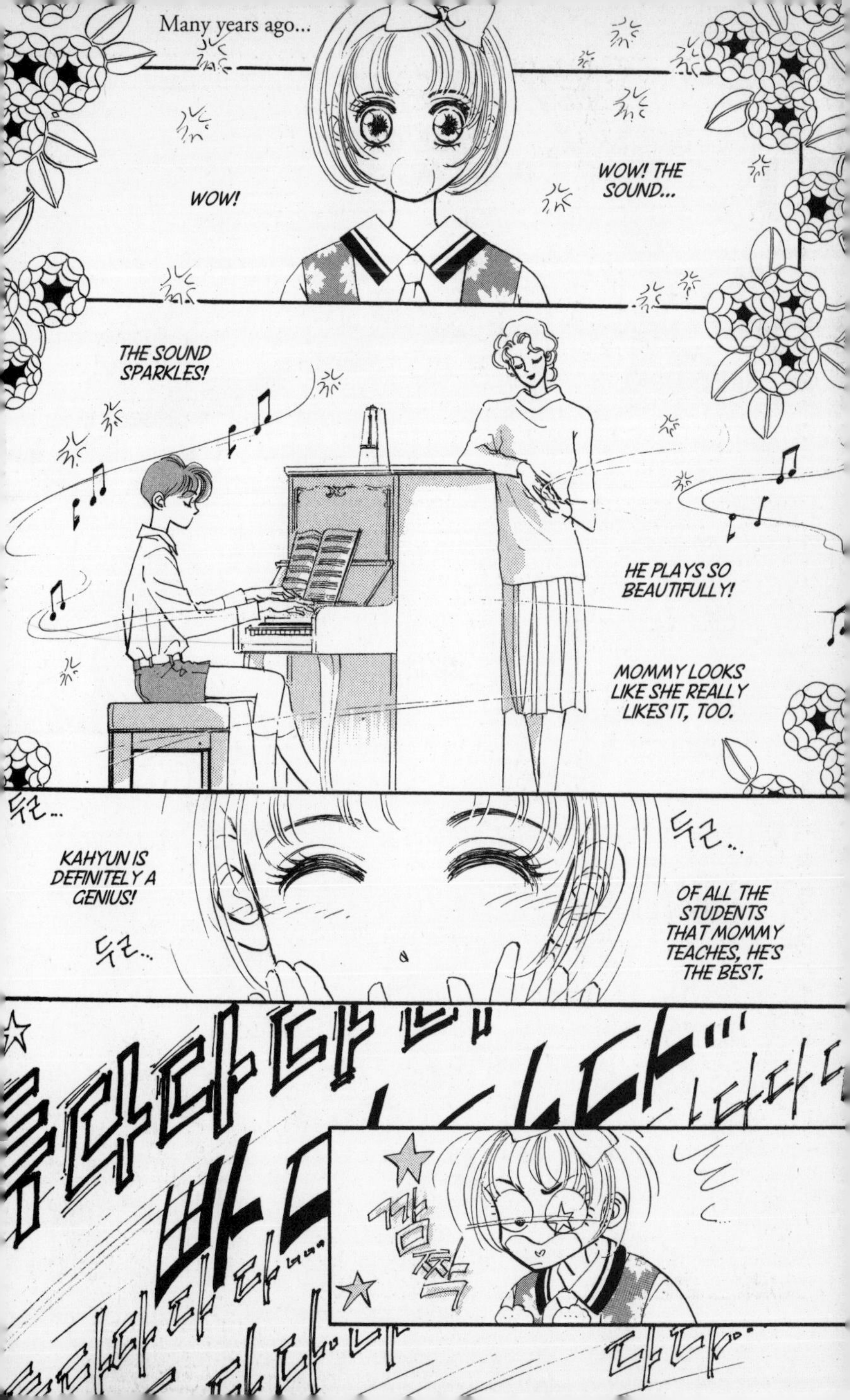
Many years ago...
WOW!
WOW! THE SOUND...
THE SOUND SPARKLES!
HE PLAYS SO BEAUTIFULLY!
MOMMY LOOKS LIKE SHE REALLY LIKES IT, TOO.
두근...
KAHYUN IS DEFINITELY A GENIUS!
두근...
두근...
OF ALL THE STUDENTS THAT MOMMY TEACHES, HE'S THE BEST.
깜짝

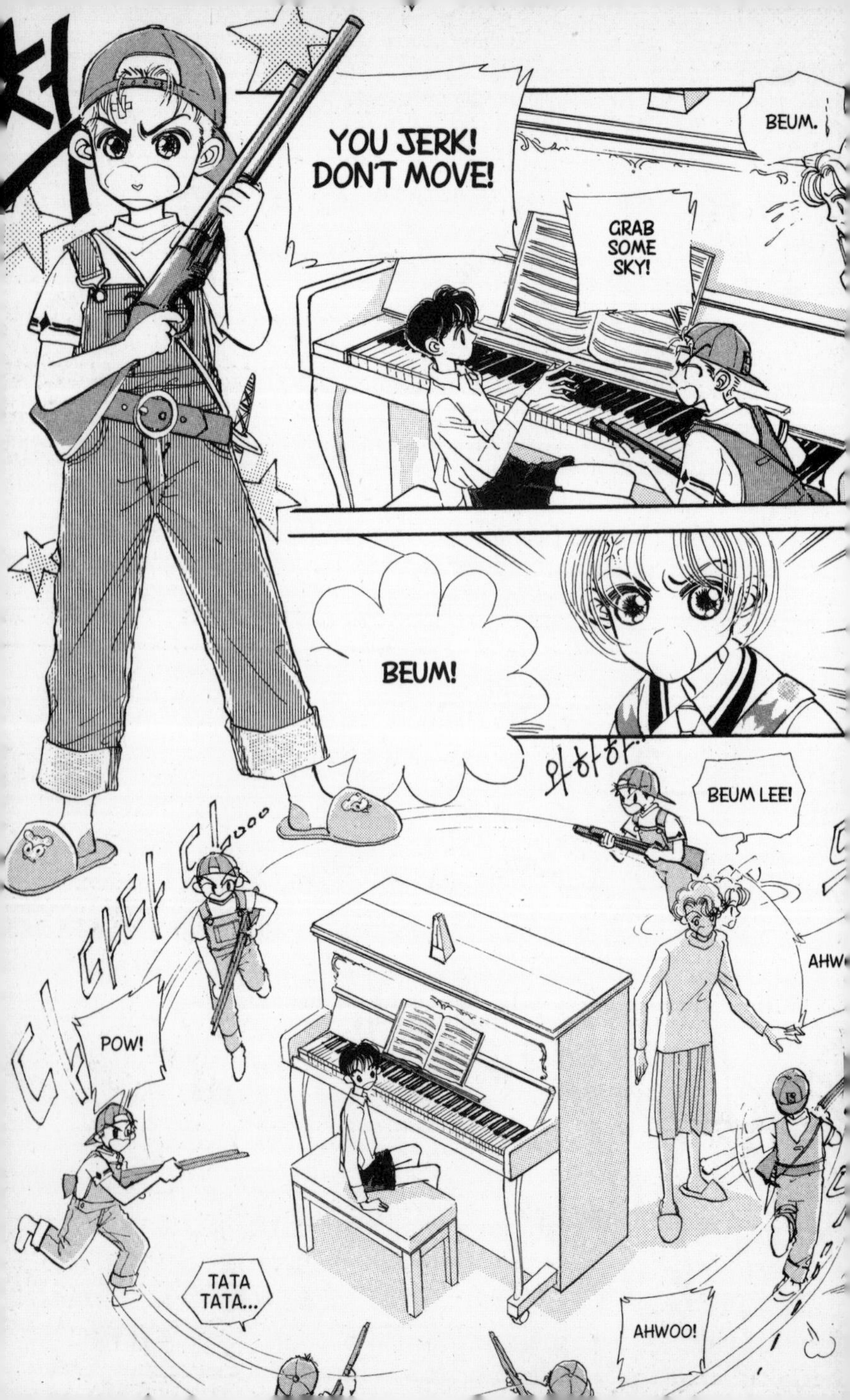
YOU JERK! DON'T MOVE!
BEUM.
GRAB SOME SKY!
BEUM!
와하하
BEUM LEE!
POW!
AHW
TATA TATA...
AHWOO!

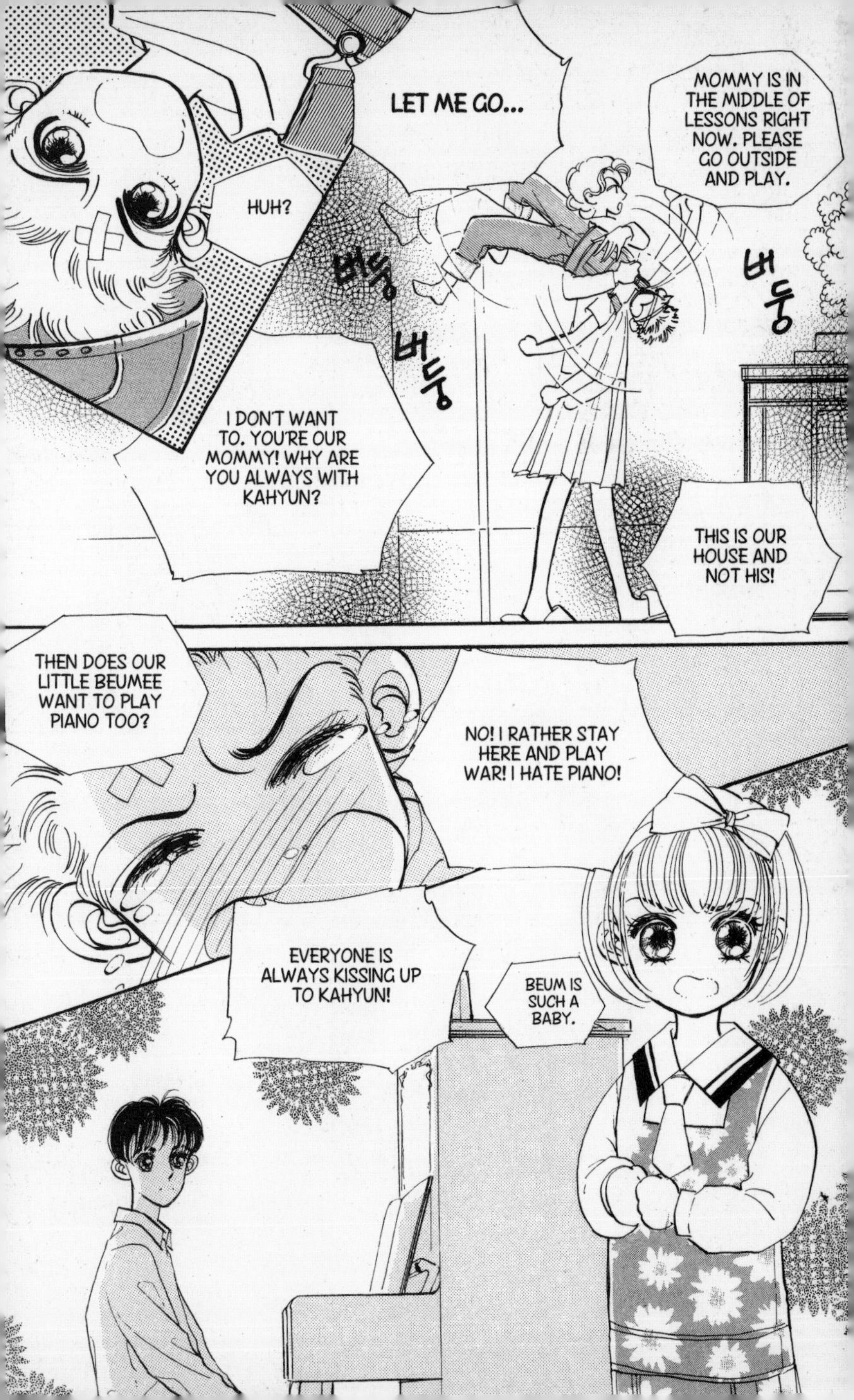
HUH?
LET ME GO...
MOMMY IS IN THE MIDDLE OF LESSONS RIGHT NOW. PLEASE GO OUTSIDE AND PLAY.
버둥
버둥
버둥
I DON'T WANT TO. YOU'RE OUR MOMMY! WHY ARE YOU ALWAYS WITH KAHYUN?
THIS IS OUR HOUSE AND NOT HIS!
THEN DOES OUR LITTLE BEUMEE WANT TO PLAY PIANO TOO?
NO! I RATHER STAY HERE AND PLAY WAR! I HATE PIANO!
EVERYONE IS ALWAYS KISSING UP TO KAHYUN!
BEUM IS SUCH A BABY.

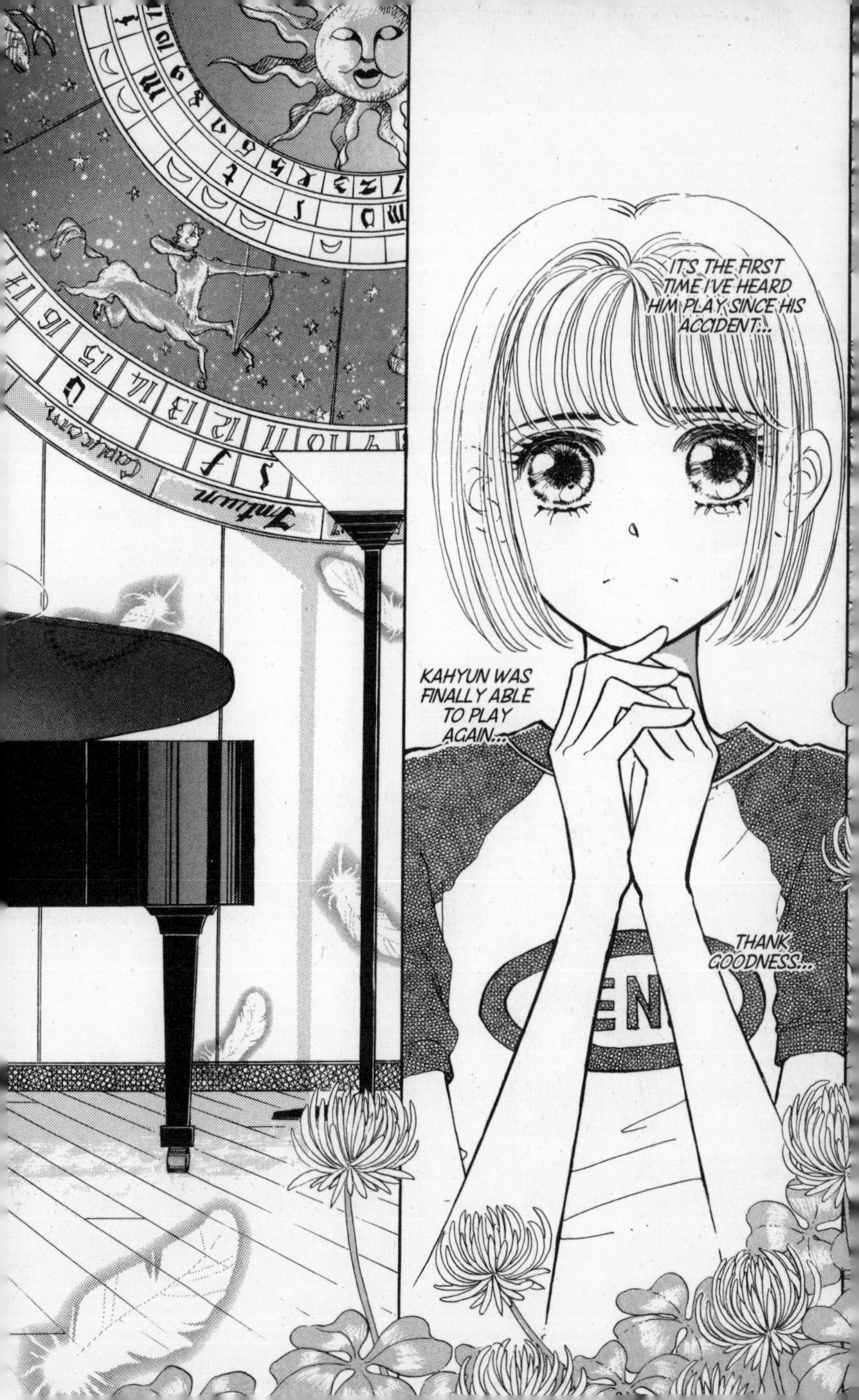
IT'S THE FIRST TIME I'VE HEARD HIM PLAY SINCE HIS ACCIDENT...
KAHYUN WAS FINALLY ABLE TO PLAY AGAIN...
THANK GOODNESS...

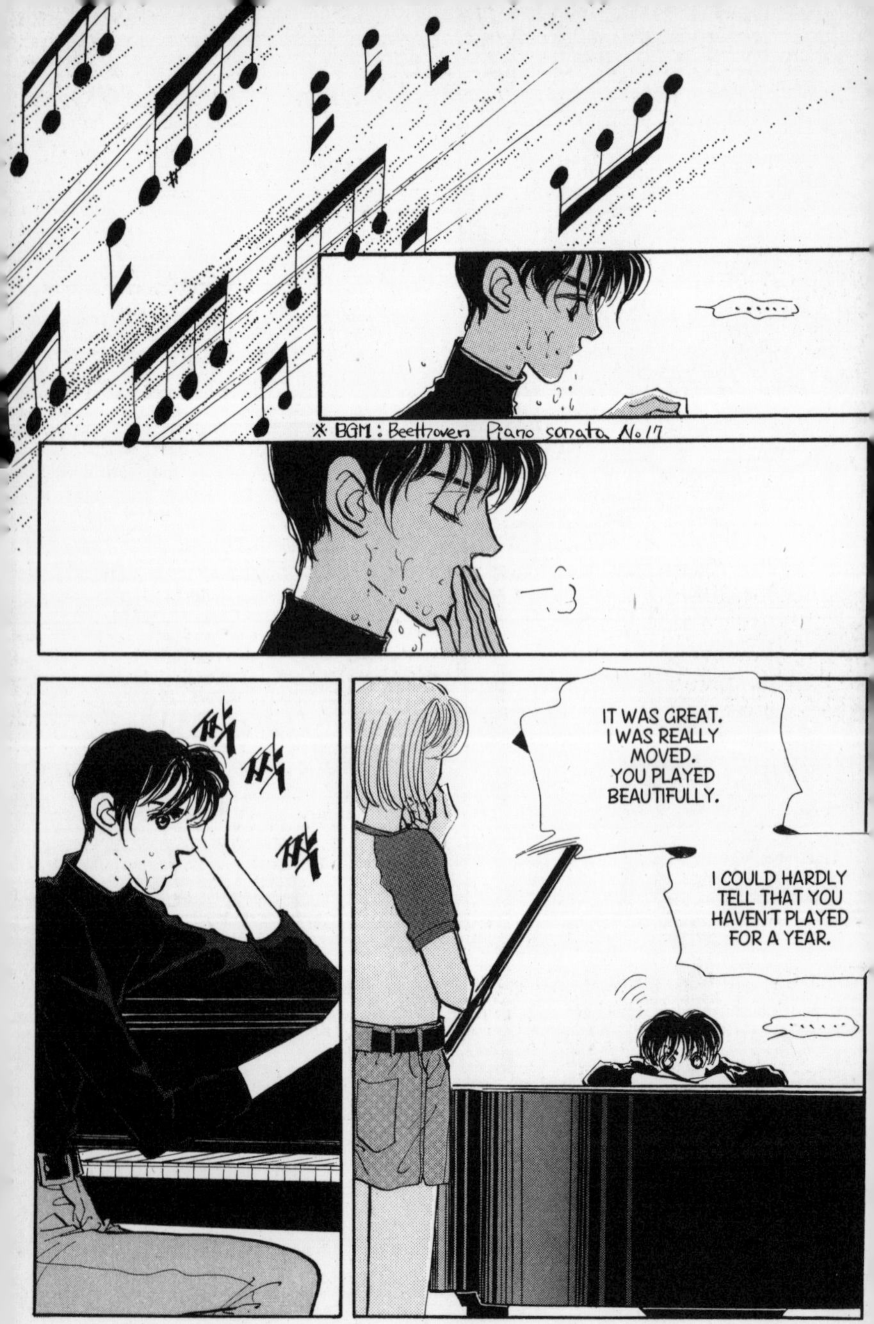
......
※BGM: Beethoven Piano sonata No.17
IT WAS GREAT. I WAS REALLY MOVED. YOU PLAYED BEAUTIFULLY.
I COULD HARDLY TELL THAT YOU HAVEN'T PLAYED FOR A YEAR.
......

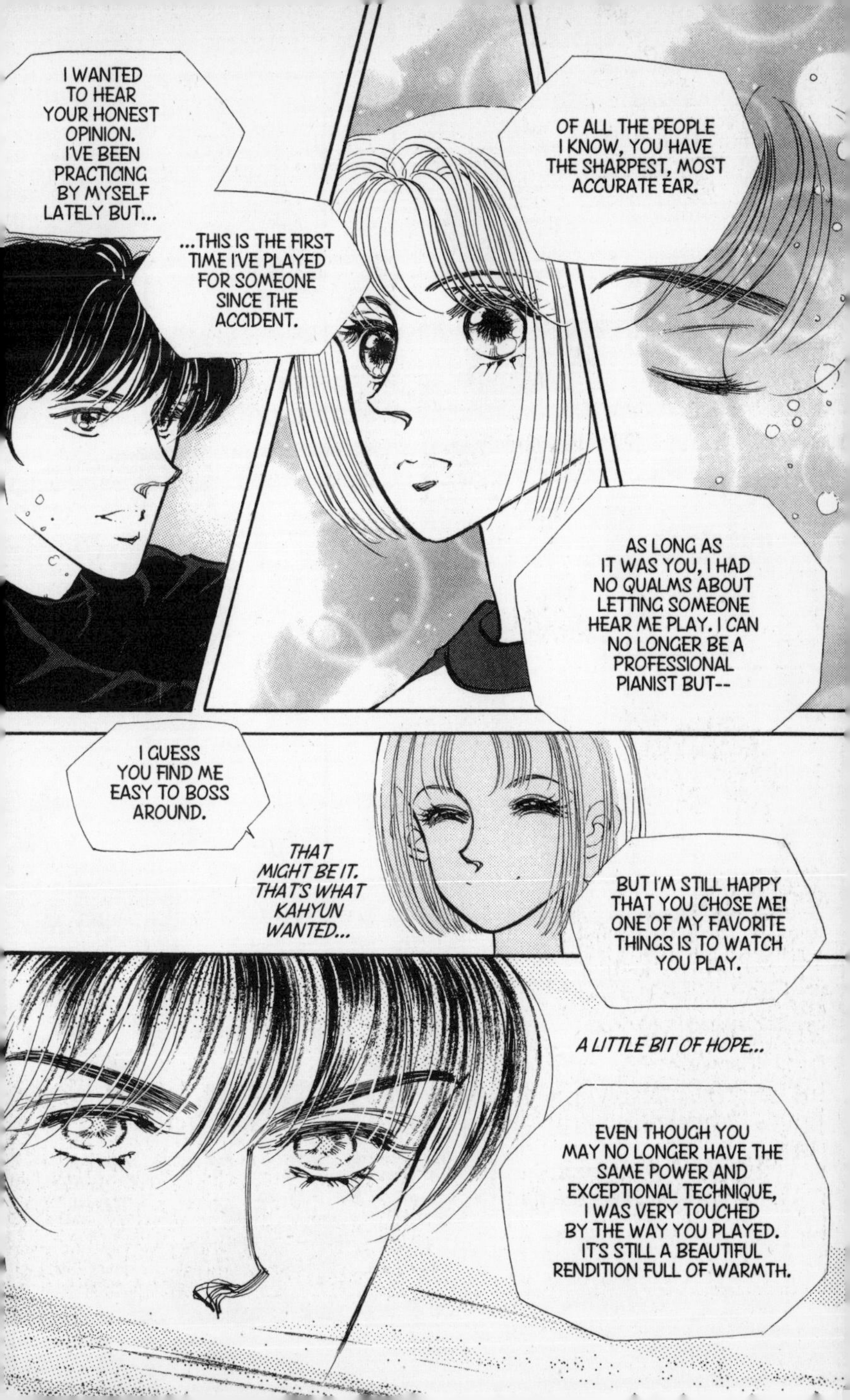
I WANTED TO HEAR YOUR HONEST OPINION. I'VE BEEN PRACTICING BY MYSELF LATELY BUT...
...THIS IS THE FIRST TIME I'VE PLAYED FOR SOMEONE SINCE THE ACCIDENT.
OF ALL THE PEOPLE I KNOW, YOU HAVE THE SHARPEST, MOST ACCURATE EAR.
AS LONG AS IT WAS YOU, I HAD NO QUALMS ABOUT LETTING SOMEONE HEAR ME PLAY. I CAN NO LONGER BE A PROFESSIONAL PIANIST BUT--
I GUESS YOU FIND ME EASY TO BOSS AROUND.
THAT MIGHT BE IT. THAT'S WHAT KAHYUN WANTED...
BUT I'M STILL HAPPY THAT YOU CHOSE ME! ONE OF MY FAVORITE THINGS IS TO WATCH YOU PLAY.
A LITTLE BIT OF HOPE...
EVEN THOUGH YOU MAY NO LONGER HAVE THE SAME POWER AND EXCEPTIONAL TECHNIQUE, I WAS VERY TOUCHED BY THE WAY YOU PLAYED. IT'S STILL A BEAUTIFUL RENDITION FULL OF WARMTH.

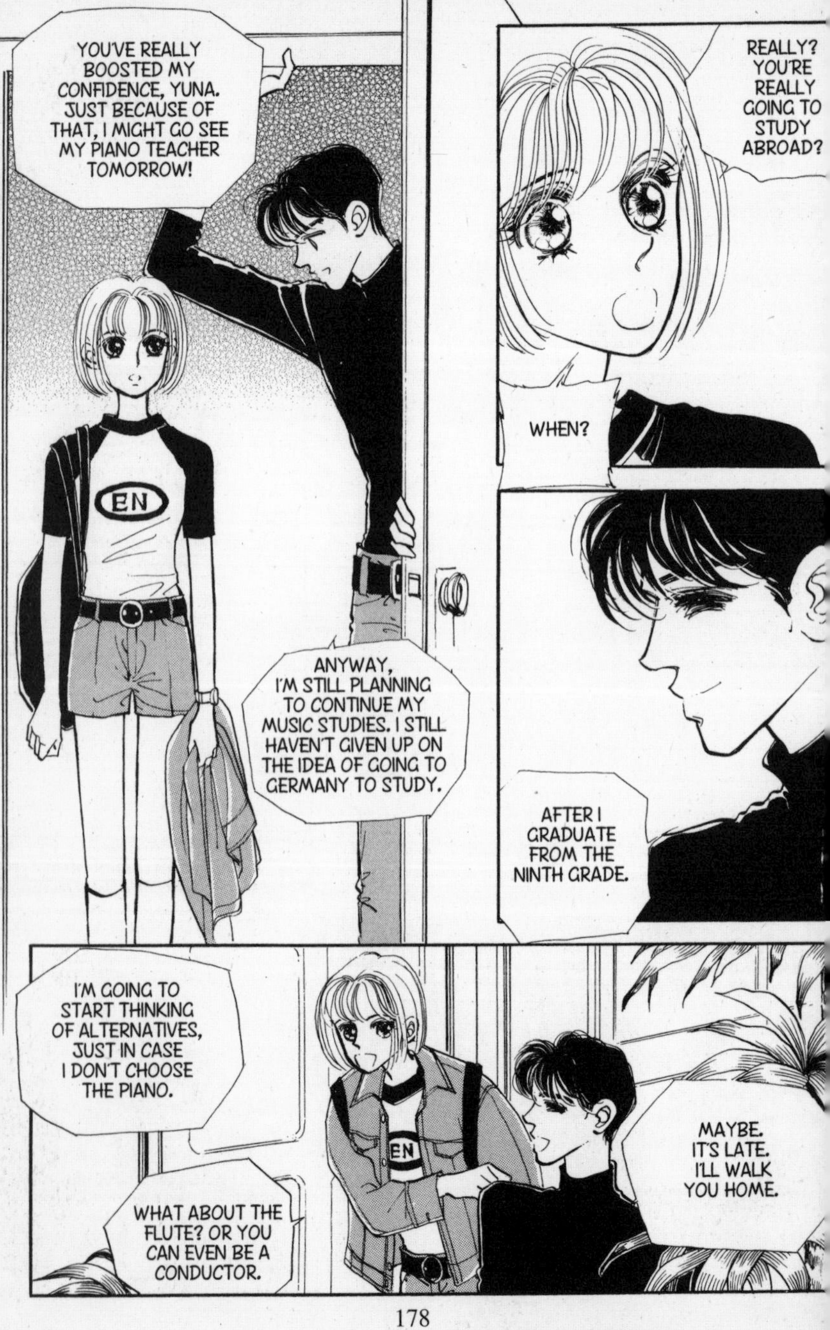
YOU'VE REALLY BOOSTED MY CONFIDENCE, YUNA. JUST BECAUSE OF THAT, I MIGHT GO SEE MY PIANO TEACHER TOMORROW!
ANYWAY, I'M STILL PLANNING TO CONTINUE MY MUSIC STUDIES. I STILL HAVEN'T GIVEN UP ON THE IDEA OF GOING TO GERMANY TO STUDY.
REALLY? YOU'RE REALLY GOING TO STUDY ABROAD?
WHEN?
AFTER I GRADUATE FROM THE NINTH GRADE.
I'M GOING TO START THINKING OF ALTERNATIVES, JUST IN CASE I DON'T CHOOSE THE PIANO.
WHAT ABOUT THE FLUTE? OR YOU CAN EVEN BE A CONDUCTOR.
MAYBE. IT'S LATE. I'LL WALK YOU HOME.

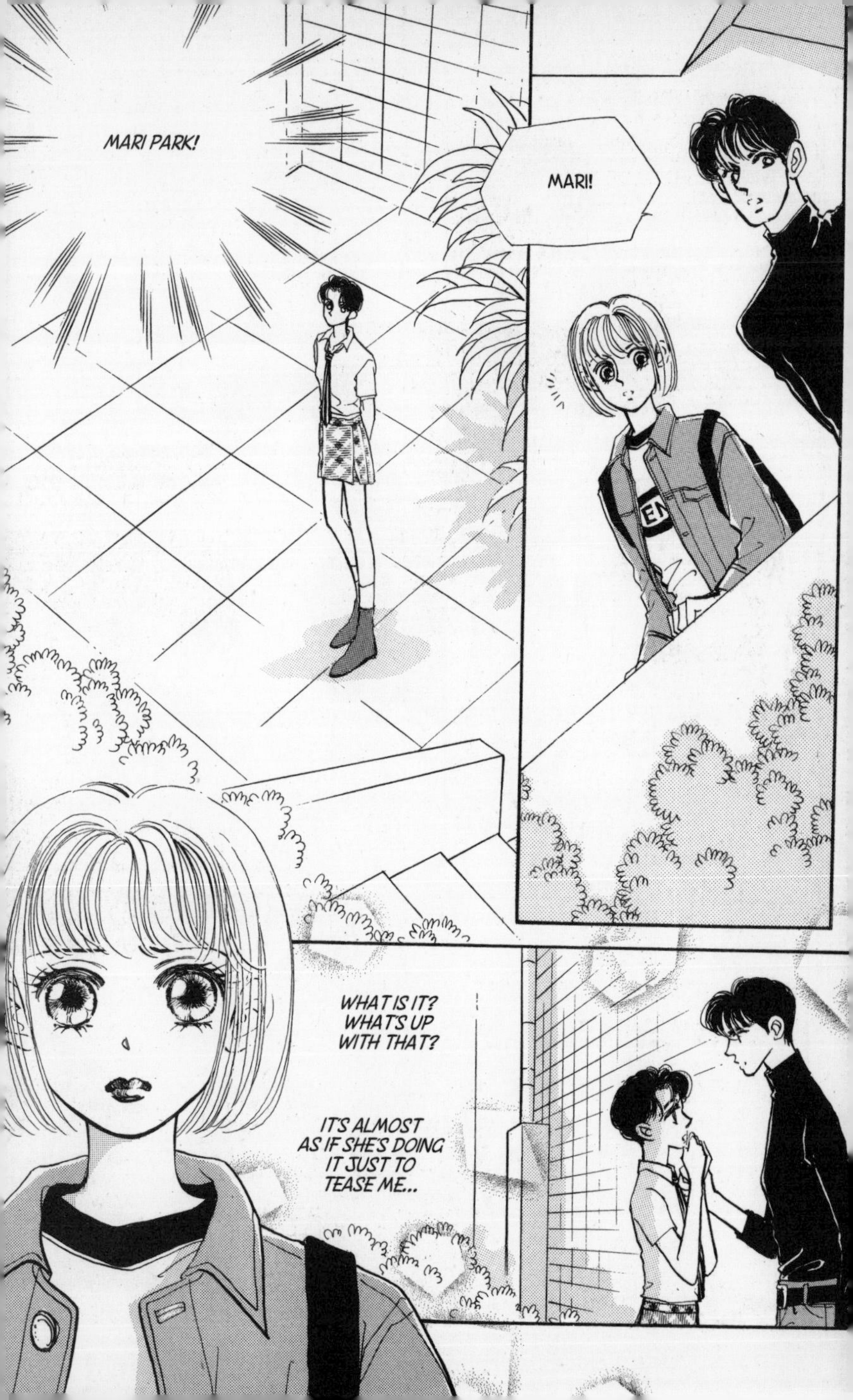
MARI PARK!
MARI!
WHAT IS IT? WHAT'S UP WITH THAT?
IT'S ALMOST AS IF SHE'S DOING IT JUST TO TEASE ME...

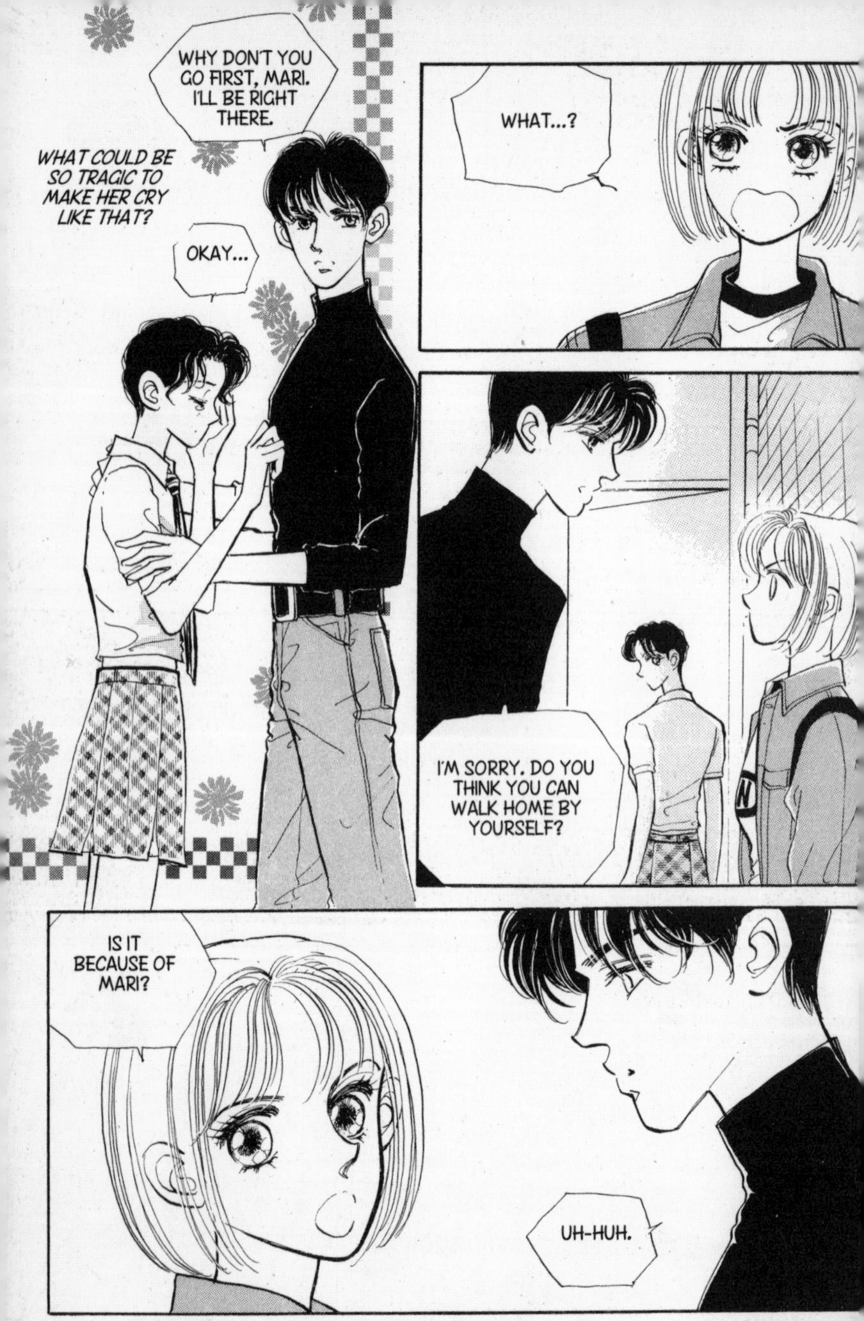
WHY DON'T YOU GO FIRST, MARI. I'LL BE RIGHT THERE.
WHAT COULD BE SO TRAGIC TO MAKE HER CRY LIKE THAT?
OKAY...
WHAT...?
I'M SORRY. DO YOU THINK YOU CAN WALK HOME BY YOURSELF?
IS IT BECAUSE OF MARI?
UH-HUH.

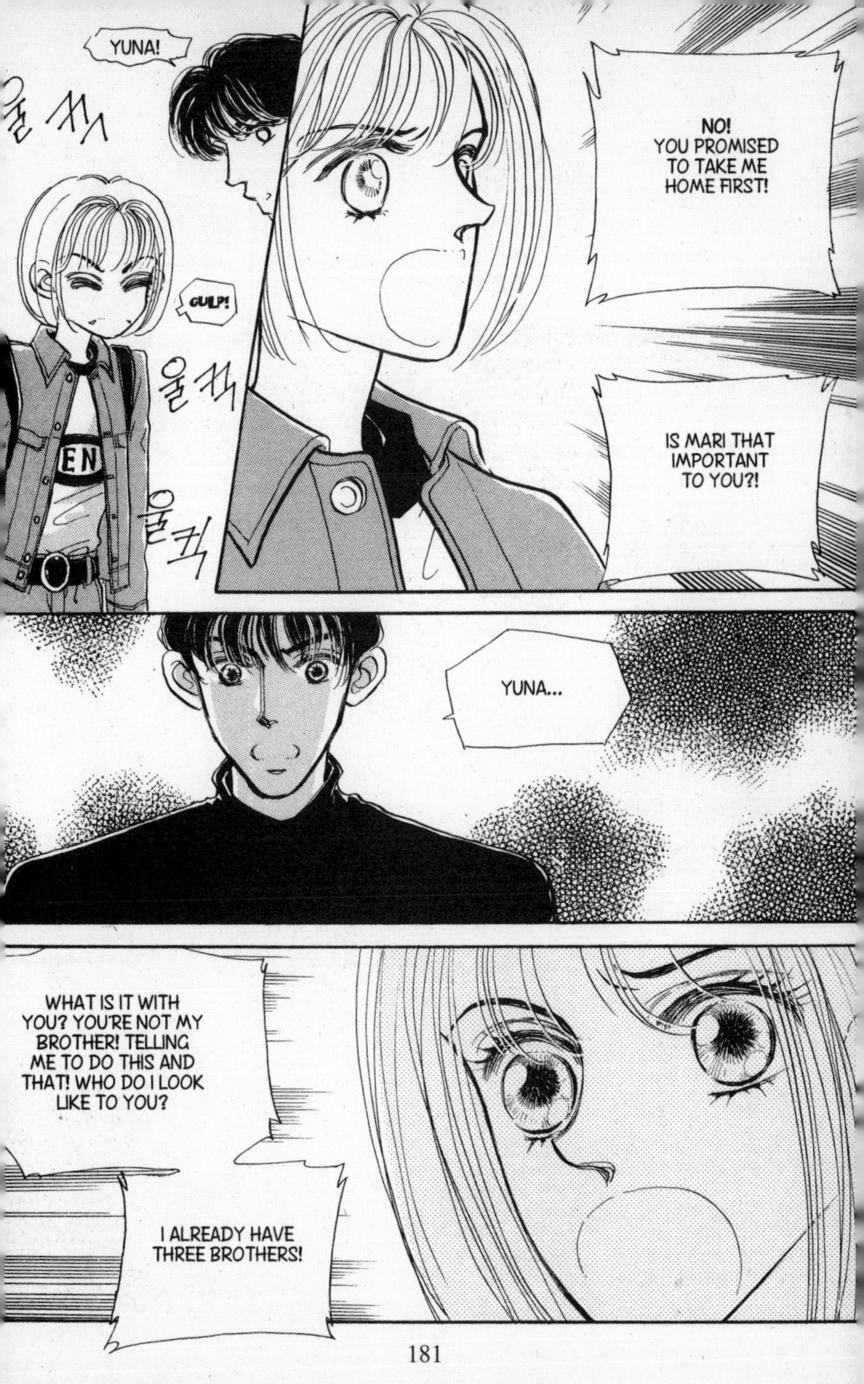
YUNA!
GULP!
NO! YOU PROMISED TO TAKE ME HOME FIRST!
IS MARI THAT IMPORTANT TO YOU?!
YUNA...
WHAT IS IT WITH YOU? YOU'RE NOT MY BROTHER! TELLING ME TO DO THIS AND THAT! WHO DO I LOOK LIKE TO YOU?
I ALREADY HAVE THREE BROTHERS!

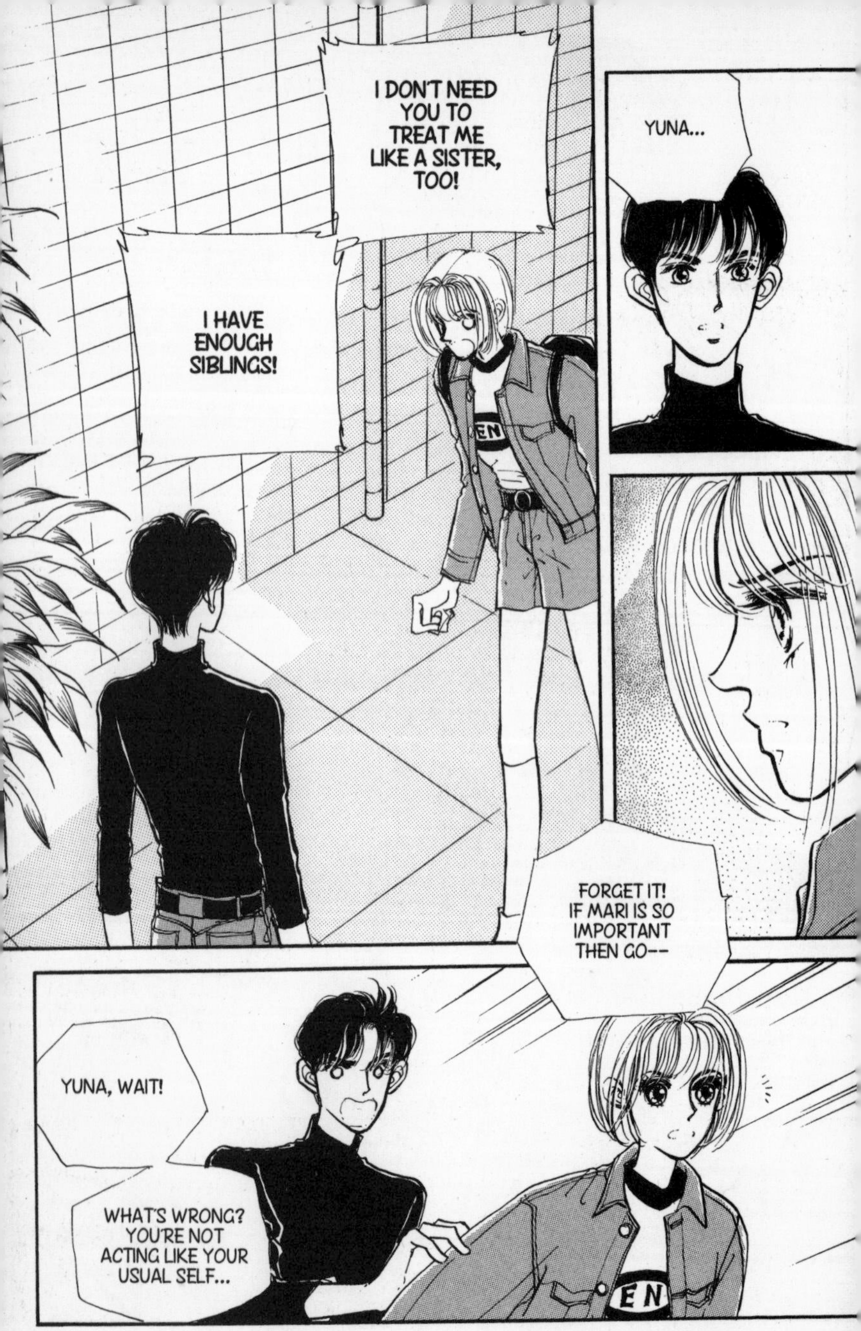
I DON'T NEED YOU TO TREAT ME LIKE A SISTER, TOO!
I HAVE ENOUGH SIBLINGS!
YUNA...
FORGET IT! IF MARI IS SO IMPORTANT THEN GO--
YUNA, WAIT!
WHAT'S WRONG? YOU'RE NOT ACTING LIKE YOUR USUAL SELF...

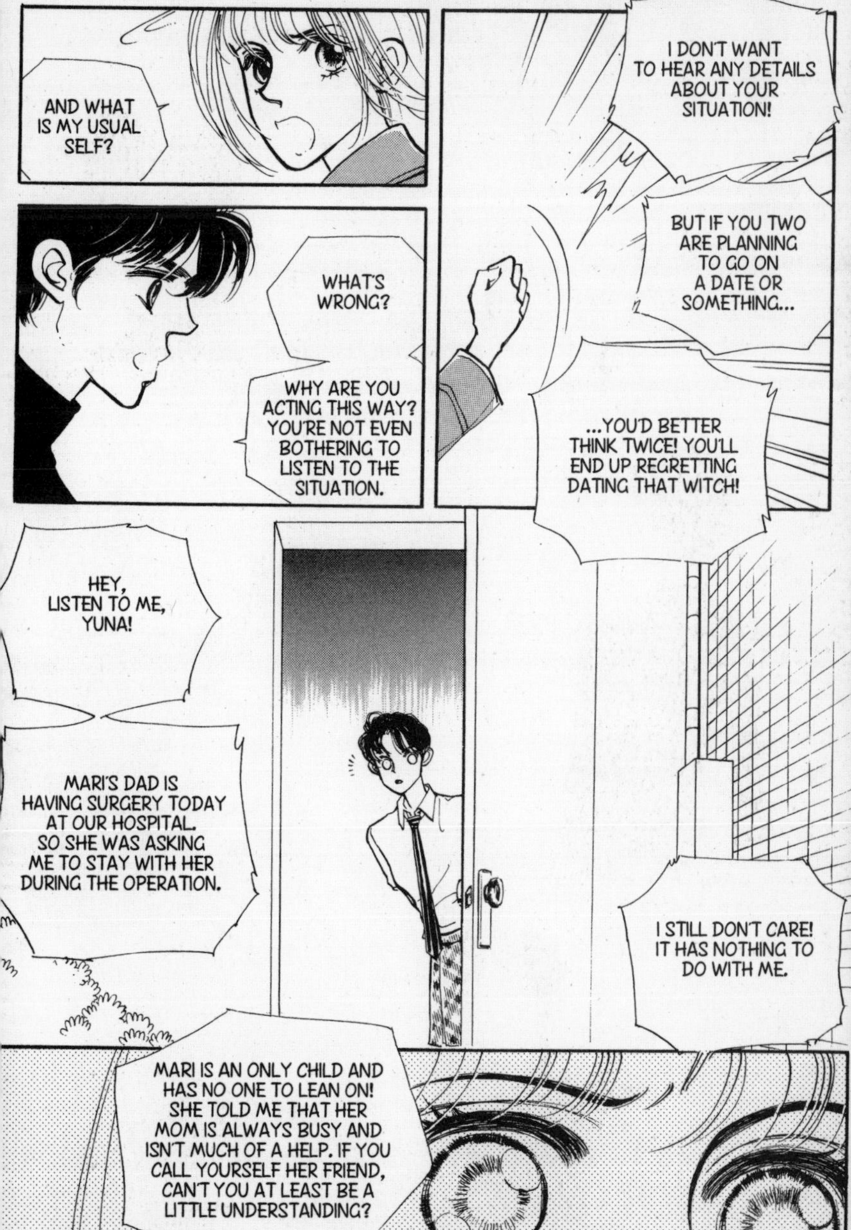
AND WHAT IS MY USUAL SELF?
WHAT'S WRONG?
WHY ARE YOU ACTING THIS WAY? YOU'RE NOT EVEN BOTHERING TO LISTEN TO THE SITUATION.
I DON'T WANT TO HEAR ANY DETAILS ABOUT YOUR SITUATION!
BUT IF YOU TWO ARE PLANNING TO GO ON A DATE OR SOMETHING...
...YOU'D BETTER THINK TWICE! YOU'LL END UP REGRETTING DATING THAT WITCH!
HEY, LISTEN TO ME, YUNA!
MARI'S DAD IS HAVING SURGERY TODAY AT OUR HOSPITAL. SO SHE WAS ASKING ME TO STAY WITH HER DURING THE OPERATION.
I STILL DON'T CARE! IT HAS NOTHING TO DO WITH ME.
MARI IS AN ONLY CHILD AND HAS NO ONE TO LEAN ON! SHE TOLD ME THAT HER MOM IS ALWAYS BUSY AND ISN'T MUCH OF A HELP. IF YOU CALL YOURSELF HER FRIEND, CAN'T YOU AT LEAST BE A LITTLE UNDERSTANDING?

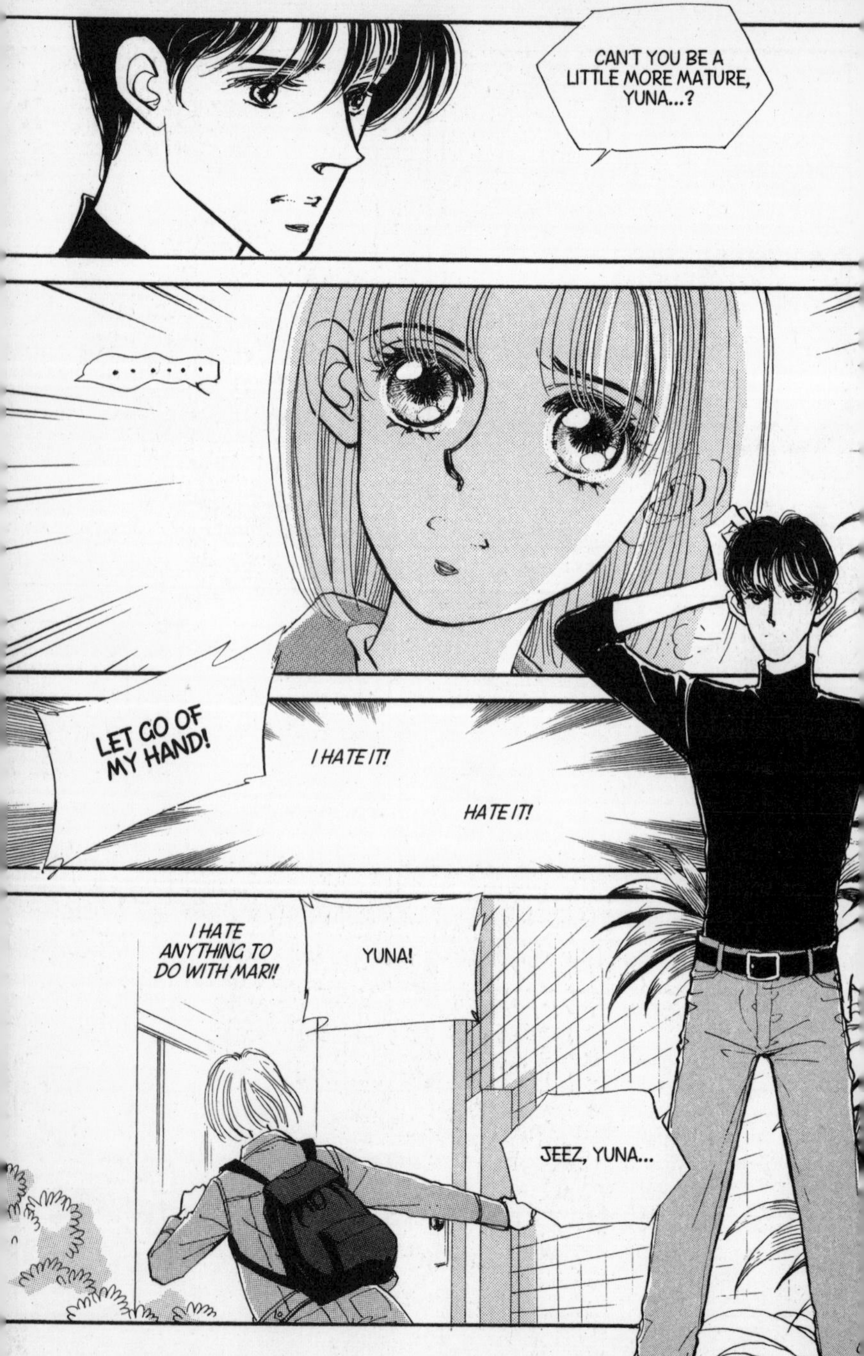
CAN'T YOU BE A LITTLE MORE MATURE, YUNA...?
......
LET GO OF MY HAND!
I HATE IT!
HATE IT!
I HATE ANYTHING TO DO WITH MARI!
YUNA!
JEEZ, YUNA...

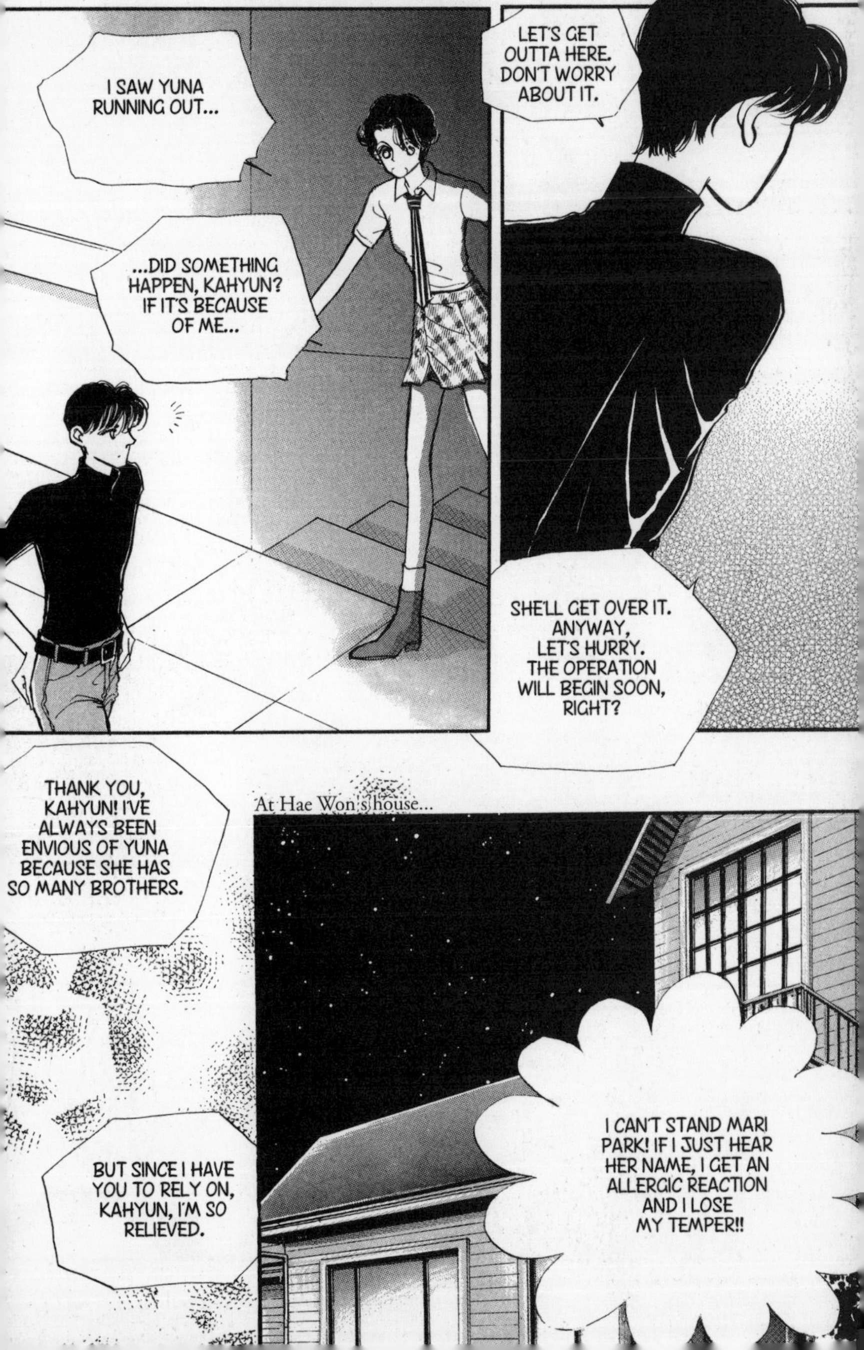
I SAW YUNA RUNNING OUT...
...DID SOMETHING HAPPEN, KAHYUN? IF IT'S BECAUSE OF ME...
LET'S GET OUTTA HERE. DON'T WORRY ABOUT IT.
SHE'LL GET OVER IT. ANYWAY, LET'S HURRY. THE OPERATION WILL BEGIN SOON, RIGHT?
THANK YOU, KAHYUN! I'VE ALWAYS BEEN ENVIOUS OF YUNA BECAUSE SHE HAS SO MANY BROTHERS.
BUT SINCE I HAVE YOU TO RELY ON, KAHYUN, I'M SO RELIEVED.
At Hae Won's house...
I CAN'T STAND MARI PARK! IF I JUST HEAR HER NAME, I GET AN ALLERGIC REACTION AND I LOSE MY TEMPER!!

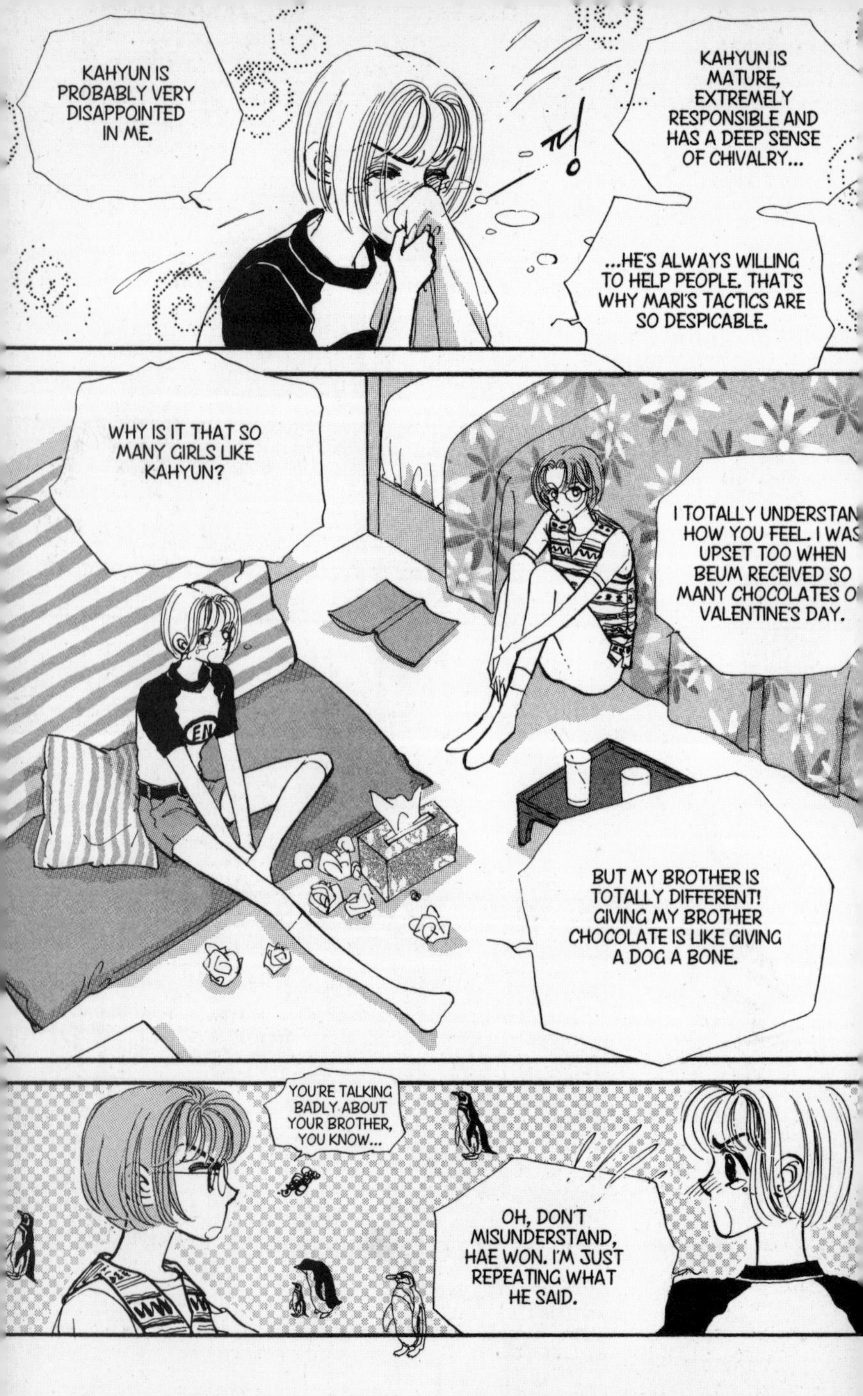
KAHYUN IS PROBABLY VERY DISAPPOINTED IN ME.
ㅠㅠ
KAHYUN IS MATURE, EXTREMELY RESPONSIBLE AND HAS A DEEP SENSE OF CHIVALRY...
...HE'S ALWAYS WILLING TO HELP PEOPLE. THAT'S WHY MARI'S TACTICS ARE SO DESPICABLE.
WHY IS IT THAT SO MANY GIRLS LIKE KAHYUN?
I TOTALLY UNDERSTAN HOW YOU FEEL. I WAS UPSET TOO WHEN BEUM RECEIVED SO MANY CHOCOLATES O VALENTINE'S DAY.
BUT MY BROTHER IS TOTALLY DIFFERENT! GIVING MY BROTHER CHOCOLATE IS LIKE GIVING A DOG A BONE.
YOU'RE TALKING BADLY ABOUT YOUR BROTHER, YOU KNOW...
OH, DON'T MISUNDERSTAND, HAE WON. I'M JUST REPEATING WHAT HE SAID.

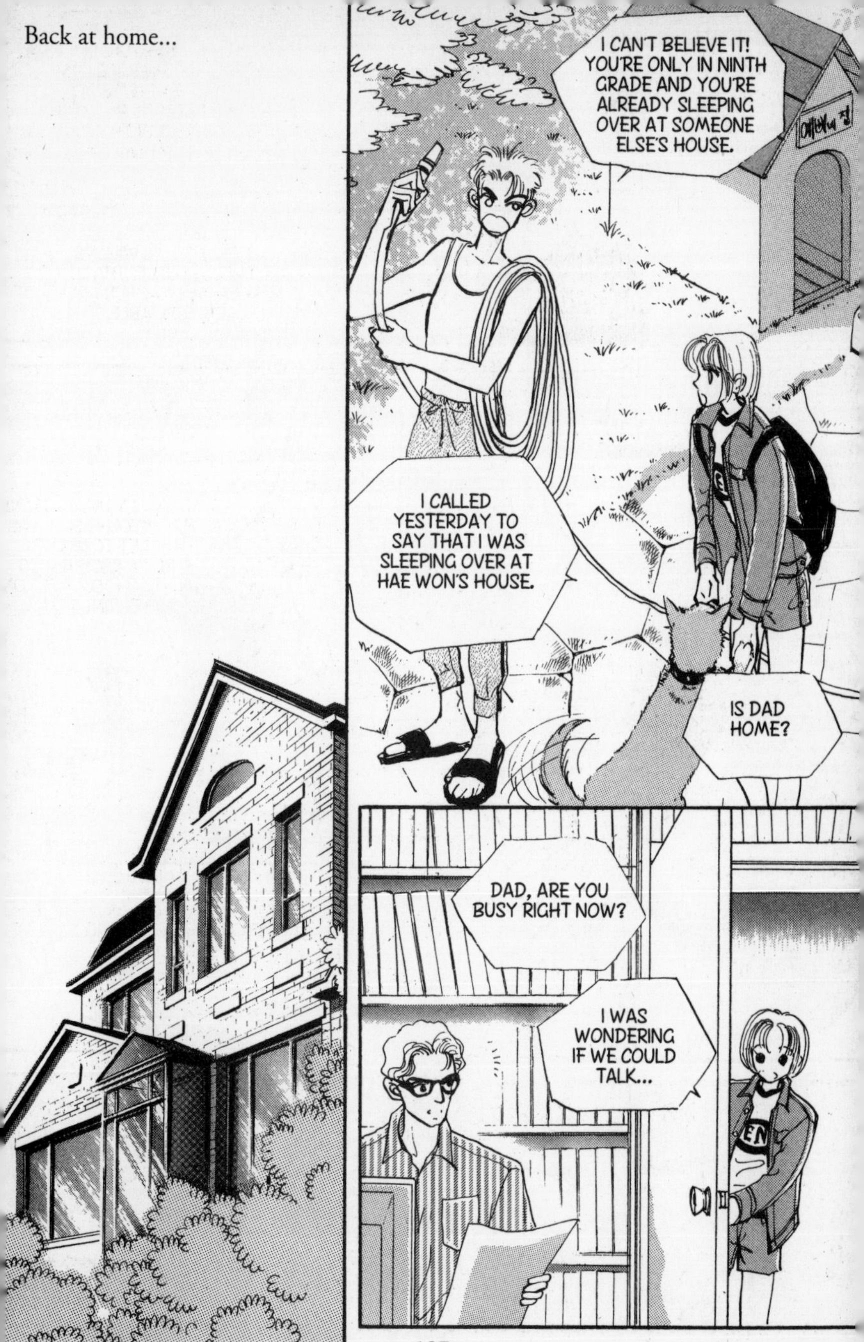

Back at home...
I CAN'T BELIEVE IT! YOU'RE ONLY IN NINTH GRADE AND YOU'RE ALREADY SLEEPING OVER AT SOMEONE ELSE'S HOUSE.
I CALLED YESTERDAY TO SAY THAT I WAS SLEEPING OVER AT HAE WON'S HOUSE.
IS DAD HOME?
DAD, ARE YOU BUSY RIGHT NOW?
I WAS WONDERING IF WE COULD TALK...

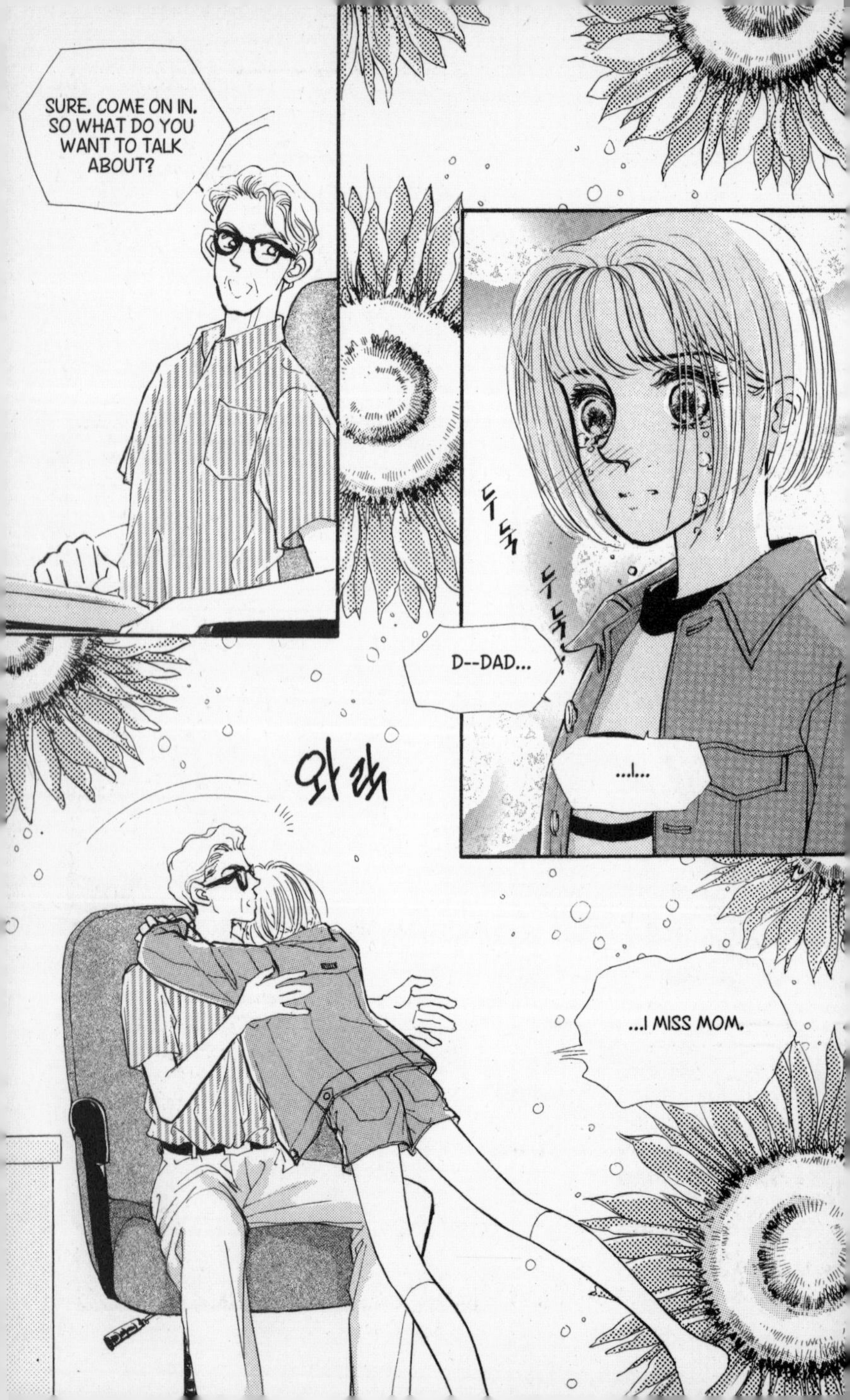
SURE. COME ON IN. SO WHAT DO YOU WANT TO TALK ABOUT?
두둑
두둑
D--DAD...
...I...
와락
...I MISS MOM.

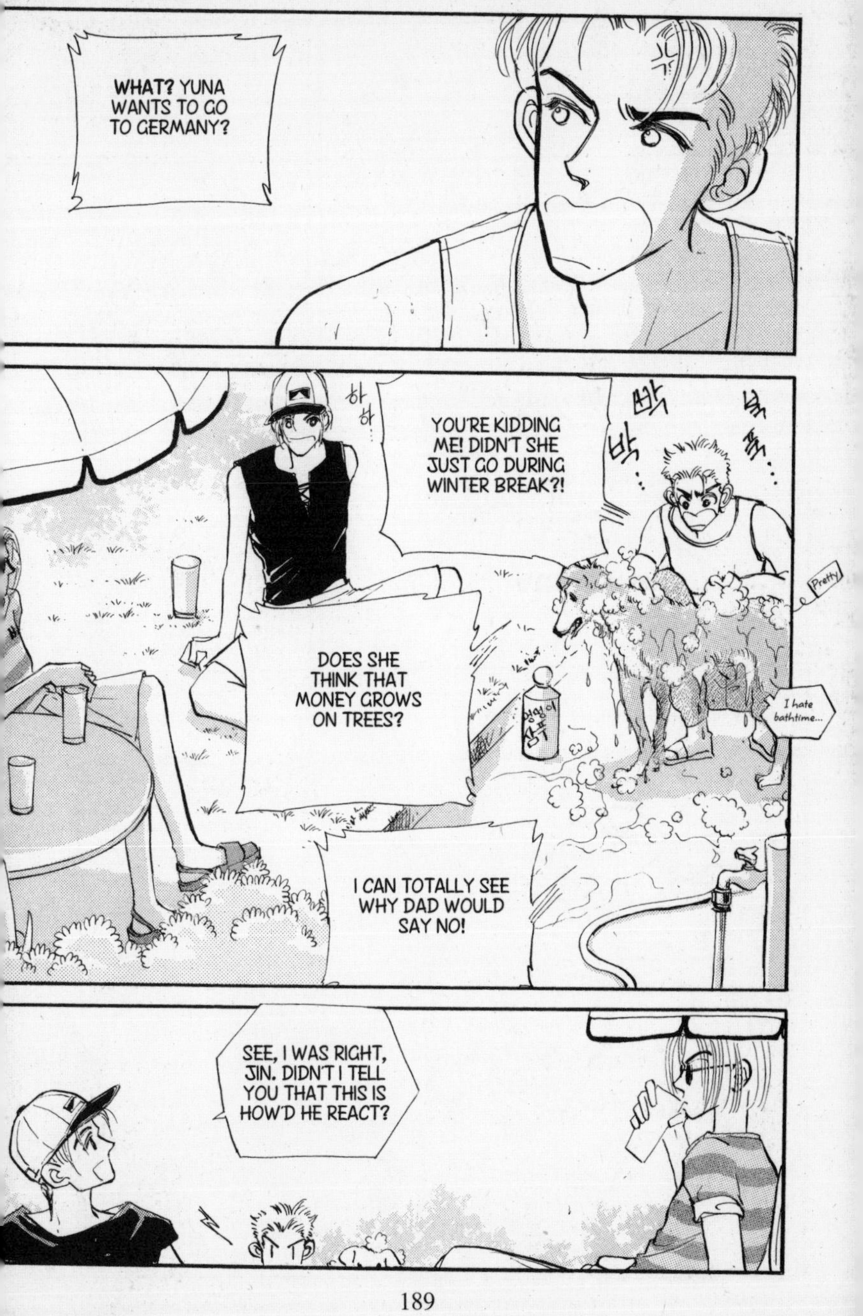
WHAT? YUNA WANTS TO GO TO GERMANY?
하하...
YOU'RE KIDDING ME! DIDN'T SHE JUST GO DURING WINTER BREAK?!
빡박...
북북...
Pretty
DOES SHE THINK THAT MONEY GROWS ON TREES?
I hate bathtime...
I CAN TOTALLY SEE WHY DAD WOULD SAY NO!
SEE, I WAS RIGHT, JIN. DIDN'T I TELL YOU THAT THIS IS HOW'D HE REACT?

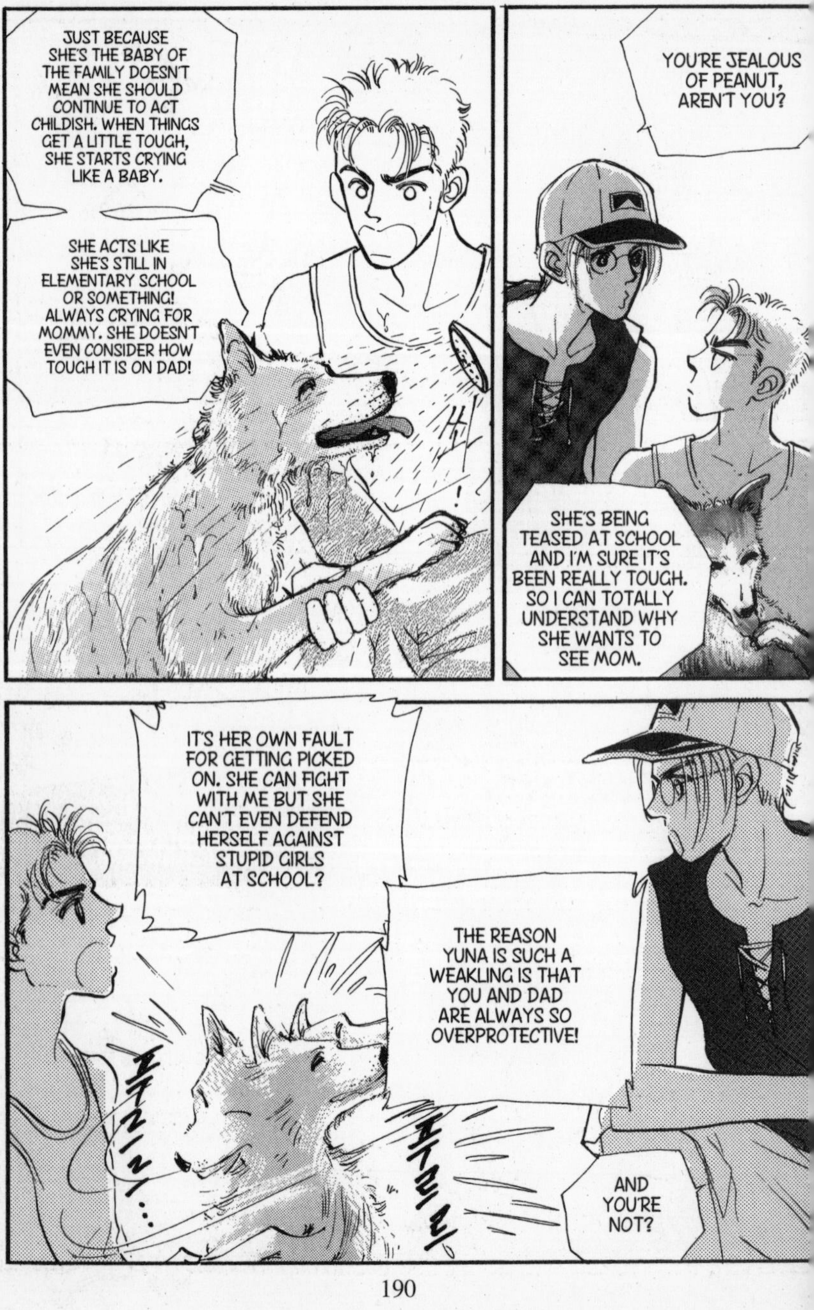
JUST BECAUSE SHE'S THE BABY OF THE FAMILY DOESN'T MEAN SHE SHOULD CONTINUE TO ACT CHILDISH. WHEN THINGS GET A LITTLE TOUGH, SHE STARTS CRYING LIKE A BABY.
SHE ACTS LIKE SHE'S STILL IN ELEMENTARY SCHOOL OR SOMETHING! ALWAYS CRYING FOR MOMMY. SHE DOESN'T EVEN CONSIDER HOW TOUGH IT IS ON DAD!
!
YOU'RE JEALOUS OF PEANUT, AREN'T YOU?
SHE'S BEING TEASED AT SCHOOL AND I'M SURE IT'S BEEN REALLY TOUGH. SO I CAN TOTALLY UNDERSTAND WHY SHE WANTS TO SEE MOM.
IT'S HER OWN FAULT FOR GETTING PICKED ON. SHE CAN FIGHT WITH ME BUT SHE CAN'T EVEN DEFEND HERSELF AGAINST STUPID GIRLS AT SCHOOL?
THE REASON YUNA IS SUCH A WEAKLING IS THAT YOU AND DAD ARE ALWAYS SO OVERPROTECTIVE!
AND YOU'RE NOT?

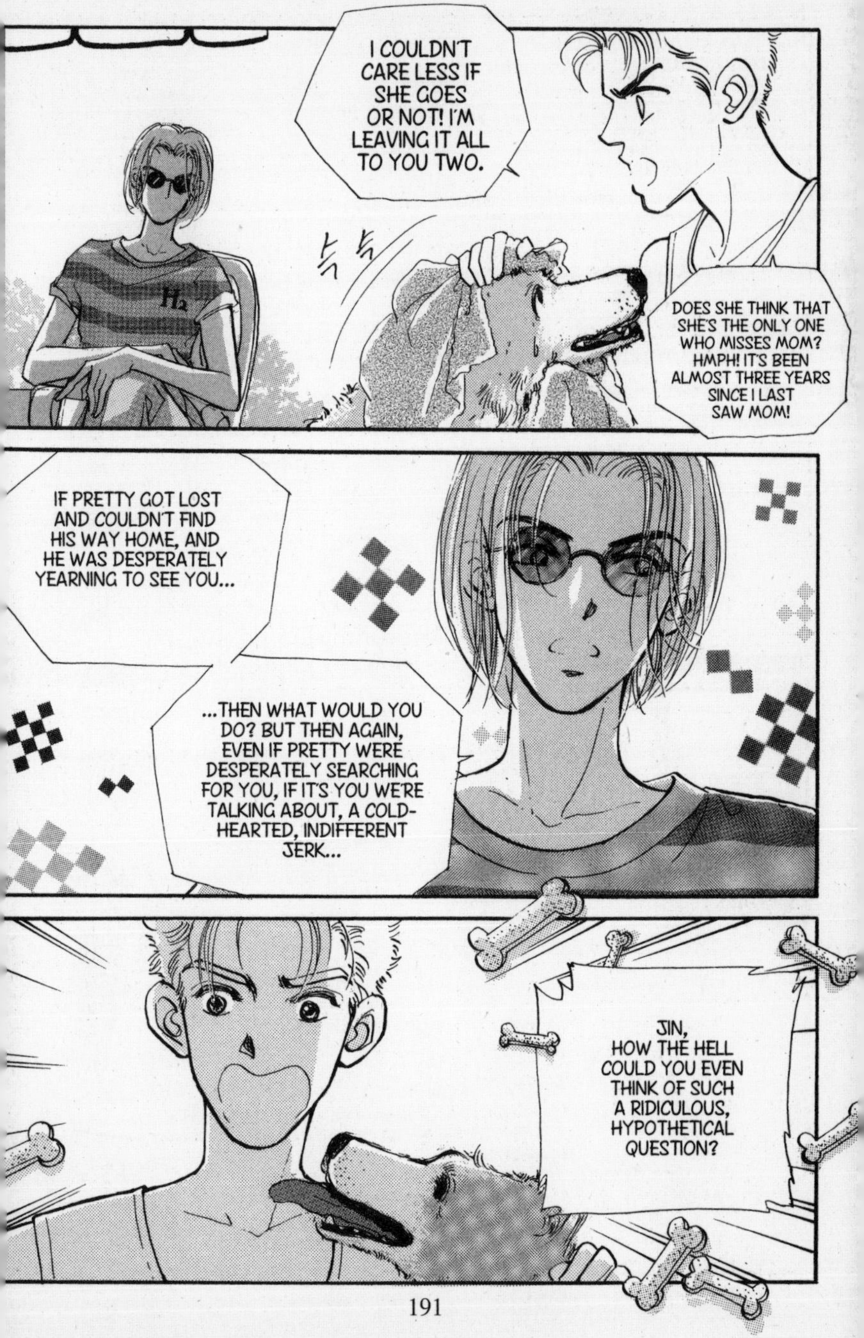
I COULDN'T CARE LESS IF SHE GOES OR NOT! I'M LEAVING IT ALL TO YOU TWO.
DOES SHE THINK THAT SHE'S THE ONLY ONE WHO MISSES MOM? HMPH! IT'S BEEN ALMOST THREE YEARS SINCE I LAST SAW MOM!
IF PRETTY GOT LOST AND COULDN'T FIND HIS WAY HOME, AND HE WAS DESPERATELY YEARNING TO SEE YOU...
...THEN WHAT WOULD YOU DO? BUT THEN AGAIN, EVEN IF PRETTY WERE DESPERATELY SEARCHING FOR YOU, IF IT'S YOU WE'RE TALKING ABOUT, A COLD-HEARTED, INDIFFERENT JERK...
JIN, HOW THE HELL COULD YOU EVEN THINK OF SUCH A RIDICULOUS, HYPOTHETICAL QUESTION?

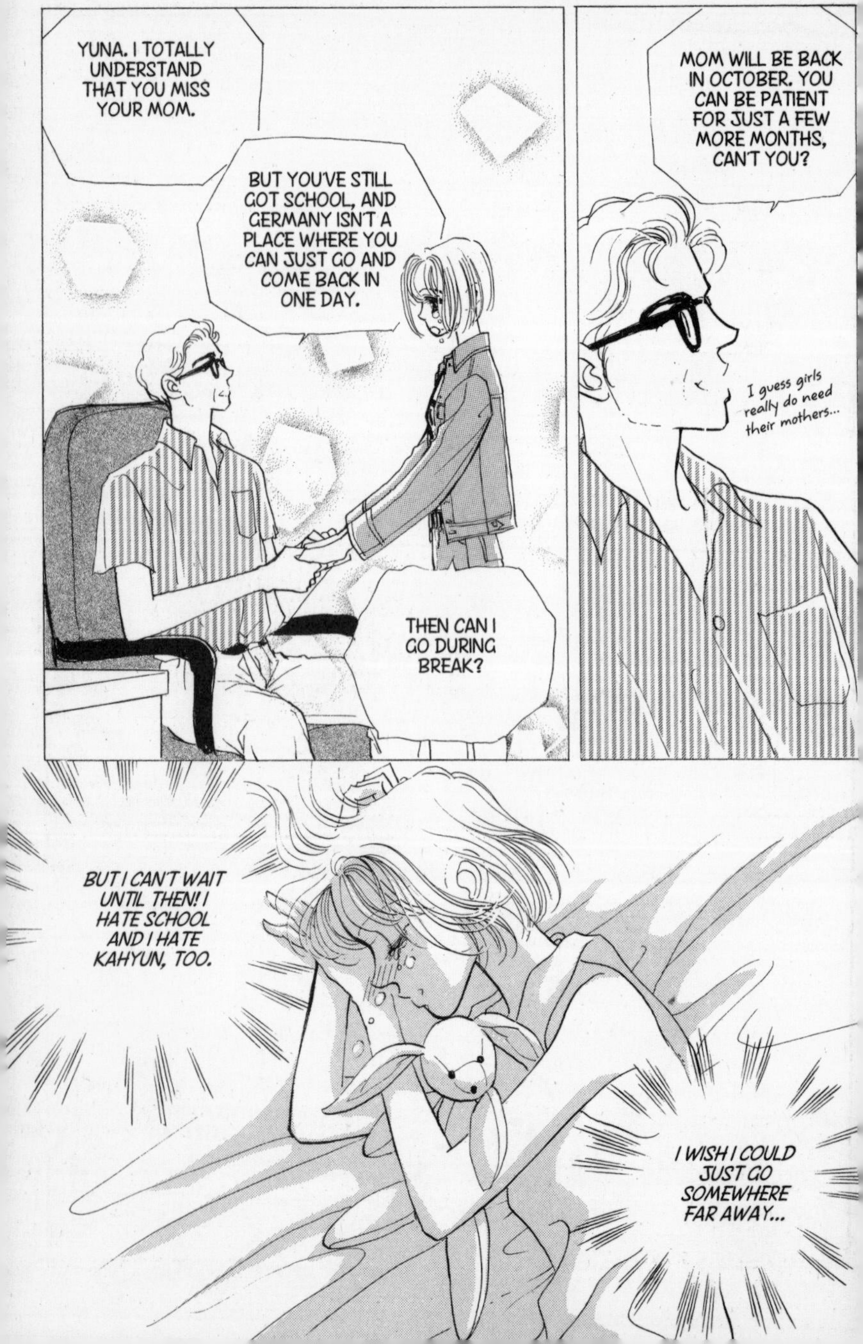
YUNA. I TOTALLY UNDERSTAND THAT YOU MISS YOUR MOM.
BUT YOU'VE STILL GOT SCHOOL, AND GERMANY ISN'T A PLACE WHERE YOU CAN JUST GO AND COME BACK IN ONE DAY.
THEN CAN I GO DURING BREAK?
MOM WILL BE BACK IN OCTOBER. YOU CAN BE PATIENT FOR JUST A FEW MORE MONTHS, CAN'T YOU?
I guess girls really do need their mothers...
BUT I CAN'T WAIT UNTIL THEN! I HATE SCHOOL AND I HATE KAHYUN, TOO.
I WISH I COULD JUST GO SOMEWHERE FAR AWAY...

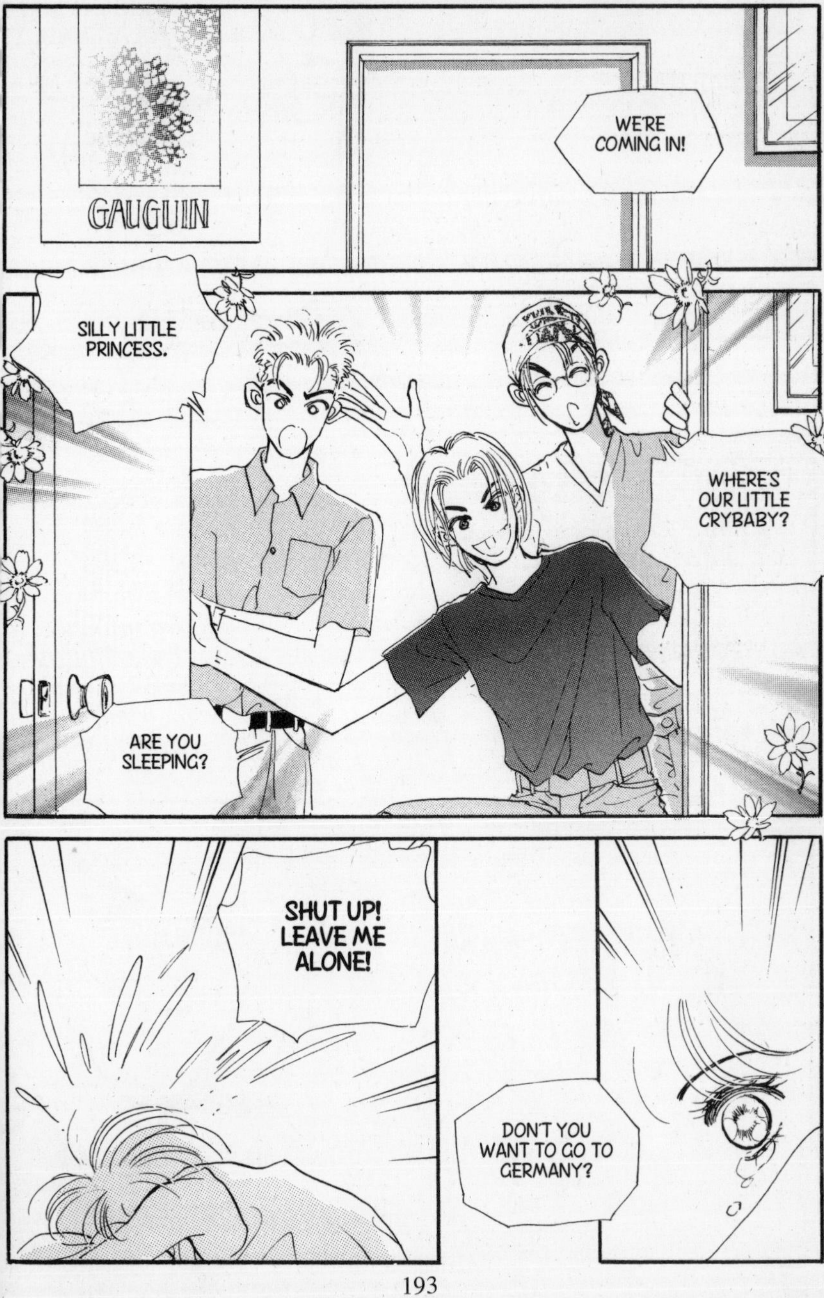
GAUGUIN
WE'RE COMING IN!
SILLY LITTLE PRINCESS.
WHERE'S OUR LITTLE CRYBABY?
ARE YOU SLEEPING?
SHUT UP! LEAVE ME ALONE!
DON'T YOU WANT TO GO TO GERMANY?

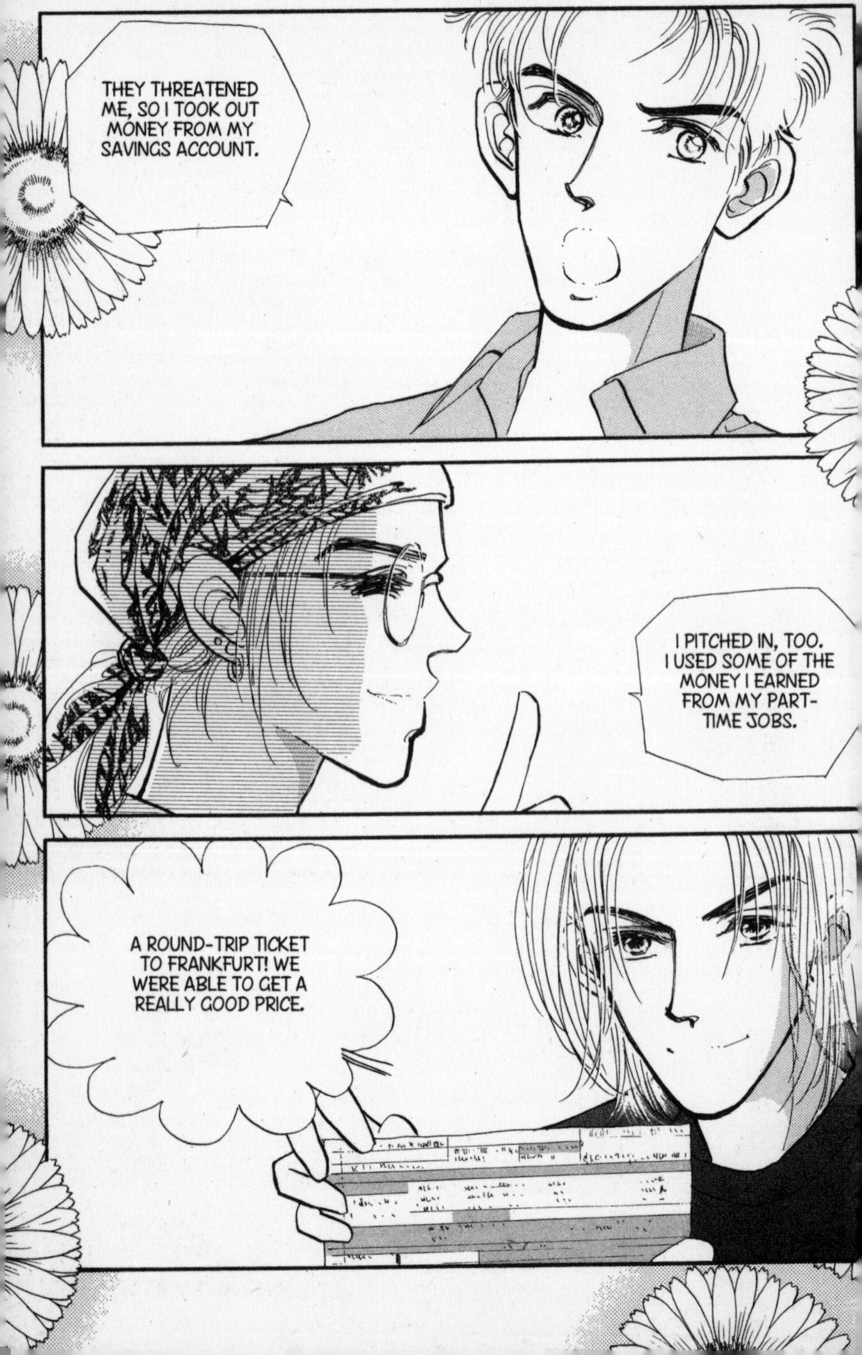
THEY THREATENED ME, SO I TOOK OUT MONEY FROM MY SAVINGS ACCOUNT.
I PITCHED IN, TOO. I USED SOME OF THE MONEY I EARNED FROM MY PART-TIME JOBS.
A ROUND-TRIP TICKET TO FRANKFURT! WE WERE ABLE TO GET A REALLY GOOD PRICE.

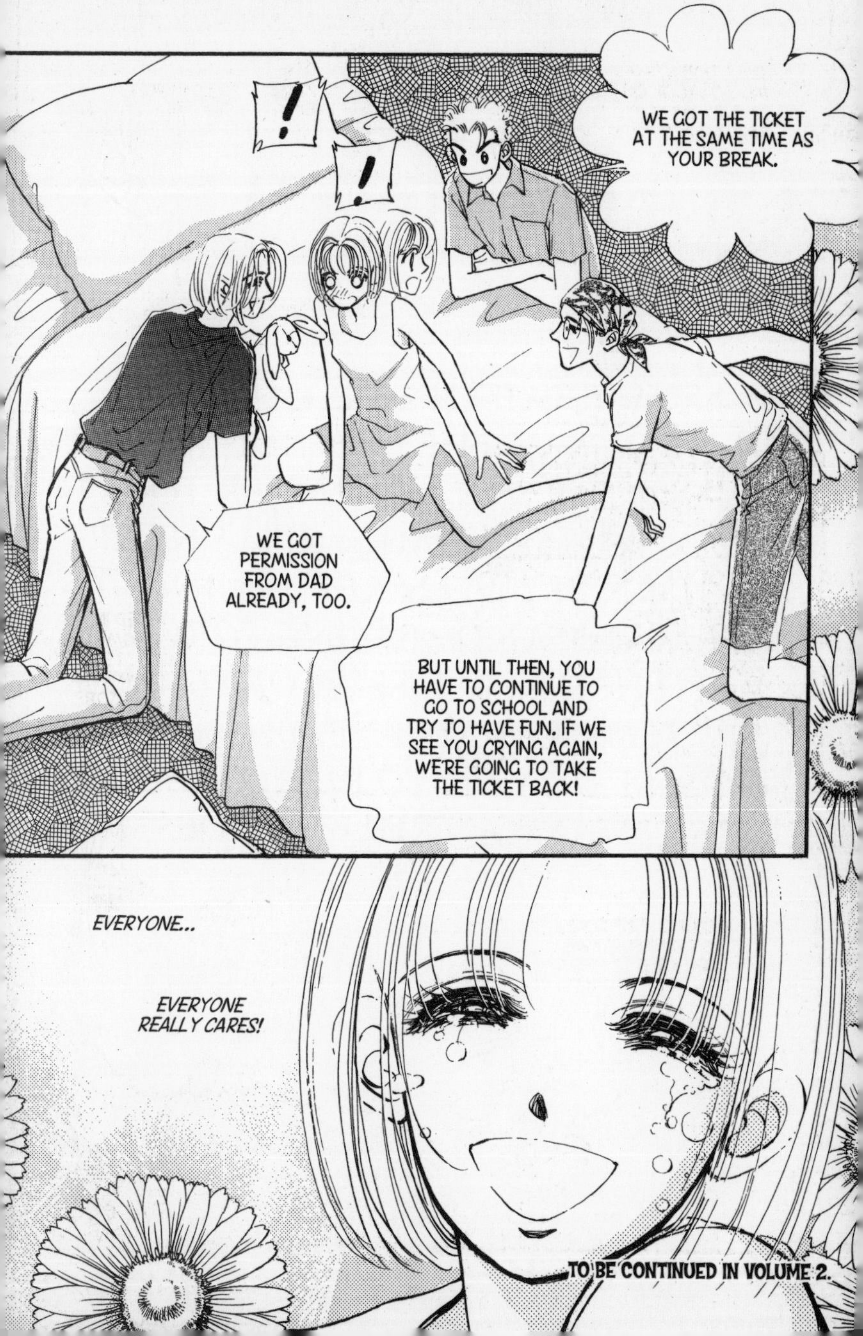
!
!
WE GOT THE TICKET AT THE SAME TIME AS YOUR BREAK.
WE GOT PERMISSION FROM DAD ALREADY, TOO.
BUT UNTIL THEN, YOU HAVE TO CONTINUE TO GO TO SCHOOL AND TRY TO HAVE FUN. IF WE SEE YOU CRYING AGAIN, WE'RE GOING TO TAKE THE TICKET BACK!
EVERYONE...
EVERYONE REALLY CARES!
TO BE CONTINUED IN VOLUME 2.

IN THE NEXT VOLUME OF...

THE QUEEN'S KNIGHT

NOW THAT YUNA IS QUEEN OF PHANTASMA, THE DASHING KNIGHT RIENO DOESN'T WANT HER TO GO BACK TO HER HOME. YUNA'S HEART IS TORN BETWEEN RETURNING TO GERMANY AND MOVING FORWARD WITH HER NEW LIFE AS QUEEN. SHE ATTEMPTS TO LEAVE...BUT FINDS HERSELF DRAWN TO RIENO'S CASTLE. IS PHANTASMA TRULY HER DESTINY?

AVAILABLE JANUARY 2005

LEGAL DRUG ™

When no ordinary prescription will do...

FROM CLAMP
CREATORS OF
CHOBITS
& TOKYO
BABYLON

OT
OLDER TEEN
AGE 16+

ALSO AVAILABLE FROM  TOKYOPOP®

MANGA

.HACK//LEGEND OF THE TWILIGHT
@LARGE
ABENOBASHI: MAGICAL SHOPPING ARCADE
A.I. LOVE YOU
AI YORI AOSHI
ALICHINO
ANGELIC LAYER
ARM OF KANNON
BABY BIRTH
BATTLE ROYALE
BATTLE VIXENS
BOYS BE...
BRAIN POWERED
BRIGADOON
B'TX
CANDIDATE FOR GODDESS, THE
CARDCAPTOR SAKURA
CARDCAPTOR SAKURA - MASTER OF THE CLOW
CHOBITS
CHRONICLES OF THE CURSED SWORD
CLAMP SCHOOL DETECTIVES
CLOVER
COMIC PARTY
CONFIDENTIAL CONFESSIONS
CORRECTOR YUI
COWBOY BEBOP
COWBOY BEBOP: SHOOTING STAR
CRAZY LOVE STORY
CRESCENT MOON
CROSS
CULDCEPT
CYBORG 009
D•N•ANGEL
DEARS
DEMON DIARY
DEMON OROORON, THE
DEUS VITAE
DIGIMON
DIGIMON TAMERS
DIGIMON ZERO TWO
DOLL
DRAGON HUNTER
DRAGON KNIGHTS
DRAGON VOICE
DREAM SAGA
DUKLYON: CLAMP SCHOOL DEFENDERS
EERIE QUEERIE!
ERICA SAKURAZAWA: COLLECTED WORKS
ET CETERA
ETERNITY
EVIL'S RETURN
FAERIES' LANDING
FAKE
FLCL
FLOWER OF THE DEEP SLEEP, THE
FORBIDDEN DANCE
FRUITS BASKET

G GUNDAM
GATEKEEPERS
GETBACKERS
GIRL GOT GAME
GRAVITATION
GTO
GUNDAM SEED ASTRAY
GUNDAM WING
GUNDAM WING: BATTLEFIELD OF PACIFISTS
GUNDAM WING: ENDLESS WALTZ
GUNDAM WING: THE LAST OUTPOST (G-UNIT)
HANDS OFF!
HAPPY MANIA
HARLEM BEAT
HYPER RUNE
I.N.V.U.
IMMORTAL RAIN
INITIAL D
INSTANT TEEN: JUST ADD NUTS
ISLAND
JING: KING OF BANDITS
JING: KING OF BANDITS - TWILIGHT TALES
JULINE
KARE KANO
KILL ME, KISS ME
KINDAICHI CASE FILES, THE
KING OF HELL
KODOCHA: SANA'S STAGE
LAMENT OF THE LAMB
LEGAL DRUG
LEGEND OF CHUN HYANG, THE
LES BIJOUX
LOVE HINA
LOVE OR MONEY
LUPIN III
LUPIN III: WORLD'S MOST WANTED
MAGIC KNIGHT RAYEARTH I
MAGIC KNIGHT RAYEARTH II
MAHOROMATIC: AUTOMATIC MAIDEN
MAN OF MANY FACES
MARMALADE BOY
MARS
MARS: HORSE WITH NO NAME
MINK
MIRACLE GIRLS
MIYUKI-CHAN IN WONDERLAND
MODEL
MOURYOU KIDEN: LEGEND OF THE NYMPHS
NECK AND NECK
ONE
ONE I LOVE, THE
PARADISE KISS
PARASYTE
PASSION FRUIT
PEACH GIRL
PEACH GIRL: CHANGE OF HEART
PET SHOP OF HORRORS
PITA-TEN
PLANET LADDER

ALSO AVAILABLE FROM TOKYOPOP®

LOVE (TRIANGLES) CAN DRIVE A GIRL TO THE EDG

TOKYOPOP®

Crazy Love Story

www.TOKYOPOP.c